Protestant war

MANCHESTER
1824

Manchester University Press

To Dorothy

Protestant war

The 'British' of Ireland and the wars of the three kingdoms

ROBERT ARMSTRONG

Manchester University Press

Manchester and New York

distributed exclusively in the USA by Palgrave

Published by Manchester University Press
Oxford Road, Manchester M13 9NR, UK
and Room 400, 175 Fifth Avenue, New York, NY 10010, USA
www.manchesteruniversitypress.co.uk

Distributed exclusively in the USA by
Palgrave, 175 Fifth Avenue, New York,
NY 10010, USA

Distributed exclusively in Canada by
UBC Press, University of British Columbia, 2029 West Mall,
Vancouver, BC, Canada V6T 1Z2

British Library Cataloguing-in-Publication Data
A catalogue record for this book is available from the British Library

Library of Congress Cataloging-in-Publication Data applied for

ISBN 0 7190 6983 1 *hardback*
EAN 978 0 7190 6983 3

First published 2005

14 13 12 11 10 09 08 07 06 05   10 9 8 7 6 5 4 3 2 1

Typeset in India
by Mudra Typesetters, Pondicherry
Printed in Great Britain
by Biddles Limited, King's Lynn

Contents

Acknowledgements

This book has been a long time in the making. That it would emerge in the end was unlikely at times, and there are many people without whom it could never have been completed. The PhD dissertation around which this book has been constructed was supported by a scholarship from the Department of Education for Northern Ireland. From Professor Aidan Clarke, my research supervisor, I gained the benefits of his wide yet exact scholarship and his fund of historical wisdom, and am indebted for his guidance, advocacy and advice over many years. I have benefited from the professionalism and courtesy of the staff of the several libraries and archives where I have worked, notably the Bodleian Library, Oxford, the British Library, London, the National Library of Ireland, Dublin, the Public Record Office, London, the Public Record Office of Northern Ireland, Belfast, the libraries of the Queen's University, Belfast, the University of London and University College, Dublin, and most especially, and for many years, the library of Trinity College, Dublin, who have toiled to deliver multiple, obscure and often weighty volumes and answer many queries, with customary diligence and patience.

It has been a privilege to work in a succession of posts which expanded my historical horizons and enabled me to soak up the variety and richness of historical research, and I wish to record my thanks to those who made this possible: Mr James McGuire at the *Dictionary of Irish Biography* and, at the *Oxford Dictionary of National Biography*, the late Professor Colin Matthew and Professor John Morrill, a valued source of counsel since his time as external examiner of my PhD dissertation. Successive heads of the department of Modern History at Trinity College, Professors Aidan Clarke, John Horne and Jane Ohlmeyer have presided over a department in which it has been a privilege to teach. Colleagues and friends provided discerning questions, sage advice, a sense of the bigger picture and welcome distraction. It has been a privilege, too, to participate in the scholarly world of early modern Irish and British history. Among the many from whom I have received much, I would particularly like to thank Ciaran Brady, John Cooper, Patrick Geoghegan, Vivienne Larminie, Br'd McGrath, Jane Ohlmeyer, Micheál Ó

Siochrú, David Scott, Tim Wales and especially Tadhg Ó hAnnracháin for all they have contributed to my thinking and writing on the seventeenth century, and not least, in some cases, for having endured the reading of draft chapters, to my gain. Patrick Little deserves a special word of thanks. For years we have worked on related questions, and the fact that the result was not rivalry but an exchange of ideas and information which proved greatly beneficial to me at least is no small tribute to Patrick's generosity and integrity. The staff of Manchester University Press deserve considerable thanks, in particular Jonathan Bevan and Alison Welsby for all their courtesy and patience.

My family have been my greatest support at all times, even while suffering a husband, father, son or brother partially resident in another century. My parents, Henry and Elizabeth Armstrong, have been loyal and generous as only they can be, through many ups and downs, always encouraging me to press forward and providing a haven just when it was needed. Stephen and Elaine Armstrong, Ruth and Joseph Aiken and Philip Armstrong have helped out in all sorts of practical ways and listened sympathetically to various tales of woe. My sons, Alan and Tom, have constantly reminded me of the richness of life lived in the present, and provided the joys of escape into a world of jokes, games and more important books on space-rockets and trains. Dorothy, my wife, has lived with this book, in various forms, as long as she has known me. Just to put up with us both would have been more than enough to ask, but instead she has made it all possible, and made it all worthwhile, and all the while still the model of graciousness we all know her to be. The dedication is a small reward.

Abbreviations

BL	British Library, London
Carte MSS	Bodleian Library, Oxford, Carte MSS
CJ	*Journals of the House of Commons* (London, 1742–)
CJI	*Journals of the House of Commons of the Kingdom of Ireland* (19 vols in 21, Dublin, 1796–1800)
CSPD	*Calendar of state papers, domestic series, of the reign of Charles I*, ed. John Bruce, W. D. Hamilton and S. C. Lomas (23 vols, London, 1858–97)
CSPI	*Calendar of state papers relating to Ireland of the reign of Charles I*, ed. R. P. Mahaffy (4 vols, London, 1900–3)
CSP Venice	*Calendar of state papers and manuscripts relating to English affairs, existing in the archives and collections of Venice*, ed. Rawdon Brown et al. (38 vols in 40, London, 1864–1940)
HMC	Historical Manuscripts Commission
IMC	Irish Manuscripts Commission
Letter-book	John Lowe (ed.), *Letter-book of the earl of Clanricarde 1643–1647* (IMC, Dublin, 1983)
LJ	*Journals of the House of Lords* (London, 1767–)
LJI	*Journals of the House of Lords of the Kingdom of Ireland* (8 vols, Dublin, 1779–1800)
Private journals	W. H. Coates, Anne Steele Young and V. F. Snow (eds) *The private journals of the Long Parliament* (3 vols, New Haven, 1982–92)
PRO	Public Record Office, London
PRONI	Public Record Office of Northern Ireland, Belfast

NOTE: For convenience, throughout this book when the term 'Parliament' is used, and a particular national parliament not specified, then the reference will be to the Parliament of England. The Parliaments of Ireland and of Scotland are always specified as such. The year is taken to begin on 1 January, and years are given in the text accordingly.

In the case of pamphlets and newsbooks, I have cited the call numbers from the British Library Thomason tracts collection, where available. These are usually in the form 'E354 (6)'.

Introduction:
politics in a virtual kingdom

Sir John Clotworthy was a discontented man. His world was not as it should be, and he was disposed to do something, indeed many things, to set it right. He certainly came of proactive stock. His father, Sir Hugh Clotworthy, veteran of years of service in arms, on land and at sea, had accumulated office and property as one of the pillars of Jacobean Ulster. In 1630 Sir John inherited not only the lush properties which his father had gathered up in Co. Antrim, but his right and duty to command the king's boats of war on Lough Neagh, and the attached 15s per day. Ulster was not far removed from a land of war, from the blistering devastation of the 1590s, the years of Elizabeth I's struggle with Hugh O'Neill, earl of Tyrone, and his allies. Clotworthy prospered. He dominated Antrim town, a parliamentary borough; held the right to licence alehouses and the sale of wine and spirits in east Ulster; and spread his interests into neighbouring Co. Londonderry, one of the plantation counties, where he became tenant to the Drapers' Company of London.[1] Like his father he was deemed 'hospitable' to puritan-inclined ministers of the Church of Ireland who were, by the 1620s, caught up in a movement of religious revival. His was a 'godly' household, where his mother, Mary Langford, and his wife, Margaret Jones, were 'both of them very virtuous and religious women'.[2]

Yet things were still not right, and as the years passed, they simply got worse. It was not just that Clotworthy was located in an island where Catholicism, for him a corrupt and dangerous faith, predominated. For all he could see the Protestant state, far from following through on its prohibition of 'popery', was allowing it to flourish, as it even encroached on his 'own town' of Antrim. The findings of recent research on the remarkable ability

---

[1] Raymond Gillespie, *Colonial Ulster: the settlement of east Ulster, 1600–1641* (Cork, 1985), pp. 42, 106, 121, 131; Samuel M'Skimin, *The history and antiquities of the county of the town of Carrickfergus* (new edition, Belfast, 1909), pp. 483–4; Nicholas Canny, *Making Ireland British 1580–1650* (Oxford, 2001), pp. 236–7.

[2] Patrick Adair, *A true narrative of the rise and progress of the Presbyterian church in Ireland*, ed. W. D. Killen (Belfast, 1866), p. 17.

of the Irish Catholic church not merely to cling on, but to rebuild itself is testimony to his recognition of a present, and for him worrying, reality.[3] Not that the Protestant established church was much better. As it puffed itself up in outward pomp, he lamented, it sagged in true spiritual faith. In civil matters, too, things were going downhill once Charles I had entrenched his powerful viceroy Thomas Wentworth, latterly earl of Strafford, atop the Irish political system. The 'New English', post-Reformation Protestant settlers, servitors and landowners (let alone their fellows from Scotland) were being sidelined under the new dispensation. Clotworthy lost some of his offices and perquisites and failed to garner others he believed his due, while Wentworth oversaw the confiscation of the Londonderry properties granted by James I to the city of London, and with it Sir John's leases.[4]

By the 1630s things had come to such a pass that Clotworthy contemplated the attractions of re-planting himself to New England. He donated some money to publish 'seasonable treatises' to shore up 'destitute . . . reformed churches' in the New World, in association with discontented and disillusioned men in England.[5] In the meantime he battled away on all fronts. By the summer of 1638 he had taken up the cause of the Scottish Covenanters, in revolt against the religious and civil policies of Charles I, to the extent that he had established personal contact with leading figures in Scotland, and was acting as a conduit between them and prominent sympathizers in England.[6] He was set on the course which would take him into the English Long Parliament in 1640, whence he would link the English and Irish assaults on the beleaguered Strafford from the very onset of the session.[7] Clotworthy was no more typical of his community, the Protestants of Ireland, than any other individual. In some respects he was more atypical than most. He was more obviously of a 'puritan' disposition than others of the Protestant elite, barely any of whom would countenance such support of the Covenanting cause – far more of the great and mighty of Protestant Ireland took commissions in the army raised by Strafford to quash the cause of the Covenant.[8] Clotworthy proved much more representative of his fellows in a shared discomfort with, even alienation from, a regime which had once

---

[3] Tadhg Ó hAnnracháin, *Catholic Reformation in Ireland: the mission of Rinuccini 1645–1649* (Oxford, 2002), chapter 2.

[4] Gillespie, *Colonial Ulster*, pp. 106, 146; Jane H. Ohlmeyer, 'Strafford, the "Londonderry business" and the "New British history" ', in J. F. Merritt (ed.), *The political world of Thomas Wentworth, earl of Strafford, 1621–1641* (Cambridge, 1996), pp. 216–29.

[5] Jason Peacey, 'Seasonable treatises: a godly project of the 1630s', *English Historical Review* 113 (1998), 671–2, 677, 679.

[6] P. H. Donald, *An uncounselled king: Charles I and the Scottish troubles 1637–1641* (Cambridge, 1990), pp. 191–6.

[7] Aidan Clarke, *The Old English in Ireland, 1625–1642* (London, 1966), pp. 133–4.

[8] Carte MS 1, fos 181–5.

seemed inseparably bound to the fortunes of the established 'Protestant interest' in Ireland – at once props to and beneficiaries of the Protestant state – and in the shared necessity of addressing their concerns in a 'British' or at least an Anglo–Irish context.

Both questions were inextricably entwined with the nature of that peculiar polity, the kingdom of Ireland. The kingdom was, strictly speaking, not yet a century old, with a statute in 1541 enacting that Henry VIII and his successors, 'kings of England', 'have the name, style, title, and honour of king of this land of Ireland, and all manner honours, pre-eminences, dignities, and other things whatsoever they be, to the estate and majesty of a king imperial appertaining or belonging'.[9] Ciaran Brady has described the sixteenth-century kingdom as 'a constitutional fiction', an 'aspiration rather than an achievement', 'a kingdom in an inchoate sense only, a polity that was in the process of becoming a kingdom'.[10] One hundred years on, the kingdom of Ireland was still not the solid political outcrop of a stable and ordered society which was the shared aspiration of the rulers, and many of the ruled, of seventeenth-century Europe. The 'state' in Ireland, and the term was one readily resorted to, was a physical presence across the island now, of chief governors and privy councillors issuing orders from Dublin, of cash in state coffers, soldiers in garrisons, justices at work in the central law courts or on circuit. Like other early modern states, it was 'embodied in political offices' and 'might, potentially, be used to do almost anything'.[11] If a 'modern conception of the state' is one which distinguishes 'its authority from that of the whole society or community over which its powers are exercised',[12] in Ireland that distinction was not merely 'over' but 'over against'. The state in Ireland was predicated upon the need to do certain things, overseeing the social, religious and political transformation of the kingdom over which it presided. Indeed, it has been argued, 'the state in Ireland . . . stood aloof from the society it supposedly served', even 'enjoyed an independence that would have been impossible for any other state in Europe during peacetime' because propped up with financial subsidies from England and freed from the restraints imposed by relying upon the co-operation of indigenous landed

[9] Edmund Curtis and R. B. McDowell (eds), *Irish historical documents 1172–1922* (London, 1943), p. 77.

[10] Ciaran Brady, 'The decline of the Irish kingdom', in Mark Greengrass (ed.), *Conquest and coalescence: the shaping of the state in early modern Europe* (London, 1990), p. 94; Brady, 'England's defence and Ireland's reform: the dilemma of the Irish viceroys, 1541–1641', in Brendan Bradshaw and John Morrill (eds), *The British problem c.1534–1707* (Houndmills, Basingstoke, 1996), p. 92.

[11] Michael J. Braddick, *State formation in early modern England c.1550–1700* (Cambridge, 2000), pp. 20–1, 48.

[12] Quentin Skinner, 'The state', in Terence Ball, James Farr and Russell L. Hanson (eds), *Political innovation and conceptual change* (Cambridge, 1989), p. 112.

society.[13] And what that state was engaged in, by force and fraud as well
as occasional legal benevolence and constitutional construction, was
making the kingdom what it deigned to be, at once 'settled' and 'civil', and
'English'.

The kingdom of Ireland was an 'English' kingdom. It was not just 'united
and knit to the imperial crown of the realm of England'[14] but was a kingdom
designedly modelled upon English norms structurally, socially and above
all legally. Whether that was best brought about by squeezing the raw material
of Irish society into English moulds or infusing successive doses of English
(or, with the accession of James VI and I, English and Scots) in the mix was
another matter. 'Anglicization', for all its being a historians' word, aptly
enough pulls together the various mooted aspirations and schemes. If any
concept can challenge for a position as the dominant discourse of early
seventeenth-century Irish politics, this is it, for while it can hardly be imagined
that it held sway over the majority of the island's population, it was, eagerly
or reluctantly, bought into by the power elites, and those who aspired to
such a position. 'Anglicization', in a sense a code for a 'settled' kingdom,
spans the 'kingdom' or 'colony' depictions of Ireland as it spans the alternative
paths of the law, the sword or the plantation in fulfilment of its goals,[15] and
even spans the professed aspirations of the old (and still largely Catholic)
'colony' and the new.[16] All could speak the language of creating a civil and
settled kingdom, even when presiding over social upheaval or bloody war.
The position of the 'Old English' in the early seventeenth century serves to
shed light on their Protestant fellows whose political attitudes and ideas
have attracted less attention.[17] Nicholas Canny has depicted them as
engaged in an 'old Anglicization' of Ireland,[18] engaging with a rapidly changing
order of commercial acceleration in landholding and trade, and the advance

---

[13] Canny, *Making Ireland British*, p. 302.

[14] Curtis and McDowell (eds), *Irish historical documents*, p. 77.

[15] Nicholas Canny, 'The attempted Anglicisation of Ireland in the seventeenth century: an
exemplar of "British History" ', in Merritt (ed.), *Thomas Wentworth*, pp. 159–67; Brady,
'Decline', pp. 111–12.

[16] It has become conventional to distinguish between the 'Old Irish' (of Gaelic stock), the
'Old English', used for the descendants – literal or figurative – of the 'colony' of the twelfth
and succeeding centuries and retaining a Catholic confession, and the 'New English' Protestants, who arrived in the sixteenth and seventeenth centuries, accompanied, after 1603, by an
influx of Protestant Scots, principally to Ulster, though of course all manner of individual
variants and exceptions arose.

[17] Much, though, can be gained from Canny, *Making Ireland British* and Michael Perceval-
Maxwell, *The outbreak of the Irish rebellion of 1641* (Dublin, 1994).

[18] Nicholas Canny, 'Irish, Scottish and Welsh responses to centralisation, c.1530–1640: a
comparative perspective', in Alexander Grant and Keith Stringer (eds), *Uniting the kingdom?
The making of British history* (London, 1995), pp. 153–4.

of both common law and Counter-Reformation Catholicism.[19] An increasingly self-conscious community 'generated by the collective need of the Catholic colonists' to address the incompatibility which their monarch saw between their loyalty and their faith, they had as their frame of reference the now-established order of an Ireland 'entirely subdued' only in 1603.[20] To fulfil the kingdom might, for some clerics, entail regaining the sanctity of being a truly Catholic kingdom.[21] For many Catholic nobles and gentlemen it meant not only gaining a place within the established order, but re-connecting state and society, allowing 'the nobility and other prime gentlemen' to displace 'persons of mean worth or value' (as often as not new arrivals to Ireland) and to re-take their rightful place in a land deemed to have enjoyed a 'settled government many hundred years'.[22] For others it meant reducing the jagged edges of the Irish state with its garrisons and provost-marshals, however tamed from earlier days.[23] Either way was the path to a truly settled kingdom and, in Irish conditions, one 'knit' to England and regulated by common law.

From the perspective of the 'state', of course, such visions were rarely the path to their proclaimed goals, though the realities of the late 1620s and 1630s in fact allowed such a sub-Anglicization to proceed untrammelled. The more dynamic vision of the state blended stop-start plantation enthusiasms with an awareness of the need to secure control of old-established legal and constitutional mechanisms as a means to 'the second phase of the conquest', the conquest of the old, Catholic, colony. It also involved 'an assumption of the necessary identity of interests between the government and the incoming settlers which events were to show was ill-founded'.[24]

---

[19] Tadhg Ó hAnnracháin notes that Counter-Reformation Catholicism 'may also have provided the psychological ballast which allowed modernising elements of the Gaelic elite . . . to embrace other aspects of Anglicisation with greater speed', while counselling that this does not mean that the movement in Gaelic Ireland was merely a 'diffusion of old English culture', but that 'a parallel if connected development' was in train: Ó hAnnracháin, 'A typical anomaly? The success of the Irish Counter-Reformation', in Judith Devlin and Howard B. Clarke (eds), *European encounters: essays in memory of Albert Lovett* (Dublin, 2003), p. 89.

[20] Aidan Clarke, 'Colonial identity in early seventeenth-century Ireland', in T. W. Moody (ed.), *Nationality and the pursuit of national independence* (Belfast, 1978), pp. 58–60.

[21] Bernadette Cunningham, 'Representations of king, parliament and the Irish people in Geoffrey Keating's *Foras Feasa ar Éirinn* and John Lynch's *Cambrensis Eversus* (1662)', in Jane H. Ohlmeyer (ed.), *Political thought in seventeenth-century Ireland: kingdom or colony* (Cambridge, 2000), pp. 131–54.

[22] Phrases from the 1641 petition of lords Gormanston and Kilmallock, on behalf of 'divers others of the nobility of Ireland', quoted in Perceval-Maxwell, *Outbreak*, p. 139.

[23] Sir John Temple, *The Irish rebellion* (6th edition, Dublin, 1724), pp. 70–1; HMC *Egmont MSS* (London, 1905), i, p. 143.

[24] Aidan Clarke, 'The genesis of the Ulster rising of 1641', in Peter Roebuck (ed.), *Plantation to partition* (Belfast, 1981), pp. 42–3.

Government and New English spokesmen articulated notions which blurred into, as well as challenged, those of the Old English elite, notably the commitment to an Ireland which, like England, would be a constitutional kingdom, a kingdom 'as well political as regal'.[25] Protestant writers could be found to proclaim the notion that 'the divisions and conflicts of Ireland's past were accidental and ephemeral' now, and indeed a whole 'spate of officially inspired publications' enunciating just such a theme were produced during the lord deputyship of Thomas Wentworth from 1633.[26] Much was made of the purging of old laws erecting distinctions between '*Irish* enemies', '*English* rebels' and loyal subjects, or laws of hostile intent against the Scots.[27] This was despite that fact that all were not now equal, even in 'national' terms, with the 'natives' excepted from plantation schemes, and the reality that this new dispensation was one founded, after all, on English norms. Jacobean Protestant writers from Sir John Davies, attorney-general, to archbishop James Ussher undertook the necessary task of making Irish history safe for Protestants. Davies condemned the weaknesses of the old colony but his applied concept of conquest carefully preserved 'imperial' and legal continuity where it could further government goals while ensuring 'all laws and customs repugnant to the laws of the conquering power . . . were either destroyed or subject to modification'.[28] Even so hardened a proponent of plantation as Sir William Parsons, future lord justice, decked out his arguments with claims to be fulfilling 'an English civilizing mission which dated back to the twelfth century'.[29]

The crucial distinction, of course, was the belief that Ireland, in being an 'English' kingdom, must necessarily be a Protestant kingdom too. Ussher famously advocated the doctrinal identity of the 'ancient' religion of Ireland with that professed by the established church in his day. Protestant claims also reached back through the darkened ages to establish a necessary connection between an 'imperial' kingship and a repudiation of Rome, calling for a resumption of usurped jurisdiction as a necessary component of any 'English' kingdom.[30] 'The assumption of papal power within the realm of England', after all, 'was necessarily treasonable by its very definition'.[31]

The novelty and danger of Wentworth's political thinking, at least for his

---

[25] The Fortescuean phrase is from the 1644 'Declaration how . . . the laws and statutes of England . . . came to be in force in Ireland', in Walter Harris (ed.), *Hibernica* (2 vols, Dublin, 1747–50), i, 31.

[26] Brady, 'England's defence and Ireland's reform', p. 113.

[27] See Richard Bolton, *The statutes of Ireland* (Dublin, 1621), especially the 'Epistle'.

[28] Hans S. Pawlisch, *Sir John Davies and the conquest of Ireland* (Cambridge, 1985), pp. 9–11, 113–21.

[29] Canny, *Making Ireland British*, p. 249.

[30] Pawlisch, *Sir John Davies*, pp. 118–19.

[31] D. Alan Orr, *Treason and the state: law, politics and ideology in the English civil war* (Cambridge, 2002), p. 108.

many critics, lay in his capacity to deploy accepted concepts and institutions only to subvert and manipulate them to produce a distinctive vision of the Irish kingdom.[32] Wentworth spoke the language of laws and parliaments, while making of them suitable vehicles for royal power.[33] He operated established constitutional mechanisms for regulating internal arrangements and relations with England, and gave enhanced emphasis to Ireland as 'a separate and legislatively autonomous kingdom' but as a means for enhancing the power of monarch and executive within Ireland.[34] His plans for plantation were notably extensive but left little scope for benefiting existing 'British' inhabitants.[35] Wentworth, notoriously, managed to pull together Catholic and Protestant opponents to bring about his downfall. The great showpiece of his 1641 trial was at once an event in Irish, in English and in three-kingdom history. It is true that the coalition of interests, even within Ireland, was a fragile one. Protestant rivals could hope to seize directly the levers of power from the tottering Wentworth as Catholics could not. But a consideration of the 'constitutionalist' movement of 1640–41 as a whole, even of the distinctively Old English agenda within it, can give an indication of the political resources which the Protestants of Ireland could share in, and would deploy in the years after the great divide of the 1641 rising. Aidan Clarke has drawn attention to the longstanding old English concern to combine 'their dependence upon the crown for protection against their enemies' in Ireland and 'their parliamentary tradition'. There was a desperate need for 'reopening the constitutional lines of communication with the king of Ireland' and a determination to balance a defence of the legislative autonomy of the Irish Parliament with a claim to 'share England's legal and constitutional inheritance'. The 'leading Catholic spokesman', Patrick Darcy, 'argued that entitlement to the full benefit of the common law included the right of access to all the remedies available' including appeal from Ireland to the court of king's bench or the House of Lords in England. The 'Queries' generated by the Irish Commons to test the nature of the government there were sent to the English Commons to give an opinion on 'points of law', a move which expressed 'a sense not of inferiority, but of partnership'.[36] Hope lay in the

[32] Brady, 'England's defence and Ireland's reform', pp. 113–16.

[33] Anthony Milton, 'Thomas Wentworth and the political thought of the personal rule', in Merritt (ed.), *Thomas Wentworth*, pp. 140–1, 145–8.

[34] Aidan Clarke, 'Colonial constitutional attitudes in Ireland, 1640–60', *Proceedings of the Royal Irish Academy* 90C (1990), 367; Michael Perceval-Maxwell, 'Ireland and the monarchy in the early Stuart multiple kingdom', *Historical Journal* 34 (1991) 288–9.

[35] Canny, 'Attempted Anglicisation of Ireland', pp. 170–84.

[36] Aidan Clarke, 'Patrick Darcy and the constitutional relationship between Ireland and Britain', in Ohlmeyer (ed.), *Political thought*, pp. 39, 43; Clarke, 'Colonial constitutional attitudes', p. 368; T. W. Moody et al. (eds), *A new history of Ireland*, iii, *Early modern Ireland* (Oxford, 1976), p. 286.

multiplicity of pathways to power or redress. Along the way the Parliament of England was sidled in as another guarantor of laws and liberties within Ireland, without in any sense admitting some dependent relationship.

What Darcy and the 'constitutionalist' movement as a whole were doing was exploiting the fruitful ambiguities in the Anglo–Irish political nexus. The individuals concerned were not 'constitutional absolutists' but those who were working out a national salvation by available and appropriate means. When, in the desperate circumstances of the 1640s, the Protestants of Ireland looked to their king, to the Parliament of England or to the Parliament of Ireland to defend their interests, this was hardly a novel response to their wartime plight, but fitted snugly enough into the fluid pre-war political arrangements. Irish institutions could be, and were now, used to block unpleasant and unwelcome directives from Westminster, but Westminster in turn could be appealed to in order to preserve at least the essence of the Protestant Irish kingdom from enemies within and without when it could no longer preserve itself within the English 'empire'. Back in November 1640 the Remonstrance of the Parliament of Ireland had declaimed the 'happy subjection of this kingdom to the imperial crown of England' and linked this to the intention that the 'loyal and dutiful people of this land of Ireland . . . should be governed according to the municipal and fundamental laws of England . . .'.[37] Rather than pitching a 'constitutionalist' stance, adamant in defence of the institutional autonomy and equality of the Irish kingdom, against an 'imperialist' strand within Protestant thinking, with a greater purchase on the notion of Ireland as a dependent component of an English 'empire', it is perhaps more fruitful to remember that such ideas could be held together, and deployed for different purposes.[38] Perhaps the terminology of 'empire' is condemned to mislead. English 'empire' did not imply English parliamentary sovereignty,[39] but a regulating and protective function. It was the setting for the common law framework which, in Alan Orr's words, 'gave form and composition to the corporate polity of king and kingdom' and meant that Ireland was 'rendered a body politic by the same policy of law as England, the English common law', at least notionally.[40] Much as English naval vessels, at least intermittently, patrolled the coasts of Ireland, so 'empire' patrolled the ideological parameters, fending off the intrusions of international 'popery'.

Of course, from the perspective of England, security was always the top priority where Ireland was concerned. The defence of 'England' (as monarchy,

---

[37] Curtis and McDowell (eds), *Irish historical documents*, p. 142.

[38] Cf. Perceval-Maxwell, 'Ireland and the monarchy', pp. 285, 290.

[39] Patrick Little, 'The English Parliament and the Irish constitution, 1641–9', in Micheál Ó Siochrú (ed.), *Kingdoms in crisis: Ireland in the 1640s* (Dublin, 2001), p. 117.

[40] Orr, *Treason and the state*, pp. 47–8.

or polity) and of the English must needs be undertaken in, and not just against intrusions from or through, Ireland. Ireland was at one and the same time one of the ancient domains of the crown of England, and hence in some sort a 'national' concern of Englishmen, and a site for the struggle with international Catholicism. It was at once more foreign and more familiar than even lowland or Protestant or English-reading parts of Scotland, for while it boasted a Gaelic 'barbarity' and trenchant Catholicism long feared or scorned in England, Ireland was also peopled by those who were, quite literally, 'brethren by blood' as well as 'by religion' to the politically prominent in England. In the 1620s English Parliaments could concern themselves with Ireland without stepping into the dangerous waters of legislative authority by choosing to present themselves as a surrogate voice for the grievances of Ireland, a stance enhanced by the 'virtual representation' within the Houses of those with interests, of land, office or kin, in Ireland.[41] There, too, fruitful ambiguity could burgeon.

The legacy of the Wentworth years was the sense of threat to English liberties from internally generated Irish dangers, from Wentworth's ability to tap the Irish Parliament, Irish purses and Irish manpower to create his 'popish army'. If Patrick Darcy was more concerned to define the internal workings of the Irish constitution than to address the niceties of Anglo–Irish constitutional interchange, so, in 1641, the 'primary concern of the English parliament . . . was not to establish control over Ireland, but to limit the power of the monarchy in England'.[42] Yet in securing to itself implicit powers to police the 'English crown' both against international popery and the subversion of the common law[43] it was working to an agenda which could at once draw the co-operation of the Irish Parliament and scatter fear and anger abroad in Ireland. From being considered a friendly sister-parliament, Westminster moved to becoming the target of Irish Catholic fears that its encroachment on the royal prerogative, blended with its anti-Catholic zeal, would wreak their ruin. It is not hard to find evidence of 'contradiction' in pronouncements on Ireland–England relations in the fraught circumstances of 1641.[44] Yet the extension of Westminster's involvement in matters Irish and the pronouncements of legislative

[41] Victor Treadwell, *Buckingham and Ireland 1616–1628: a study in Anglo–Irish politics* (Dublin, 1998), pp. 156, 299–300. Treadwell points up the 'sheer novelty' of the 1621 Westminster debates, 'a new chapter in the history of Anglo–Irish relations' (p. 157).

[42] Perceval-Maxwell, 'Ireland and the monarchy', p. 291.

[43] Note the claim made by the managers of Wentworth's trial that he could indeed be tried according to the laws of Ireland, but that the Parliament of England, as supreme interpreter of English common law, could interpret that law as it was modified and applied in Ireland: Orr, *Treason and the state*, p. 87, note 134.

[44] Perceval-Maxwell, 'Ireland and the monarchy', pp. 289–91.

competence over Ireland indicated an emergent danger, and a breach with
the conventions followed in the 1620s.[45] Westminster was engaged in a process
of clarification which paralleled a broader urge to definition within the
domestic sphere of prerogative and law to counter the exploitation of
perceived grey areas by an unduly intrusive monarchy.[46] Yet closing down
those complexities, at inter-kingdom level, was a route to confrontation,
not resolution.

If the Parliament of England worried about security from Irish threats,
and the Parliament of Ireland looked to Westminster to help guarantee its
escape from tyranny, the Covenanter regime in Scotland partook of both
developments. The Wentworth regime, with its new-raised army poised
across the narrow sea-crossing in Ulster, had more obviously threatened the
northern kingdom that it had England, and with the approval of many
prominent Old and New English.[47] It had also more emphatically set its face
against the Scots resident in Ireland. The plantation of Ulster was the firstborn
of the Jacobean union of England and Scotland. James VI and I had intended
'that Scots and English should function as equal partners in a civilizing and
reforming endeavour', 'the establishment in Ulster . . . of a settler society
where Scottish and English Protestants became joint participants in a
common enterprise which was described as "British" '. Such aspirations soon
soured. The Scots were 'forced to accept their role in the plantation as
supplementary to that of the English', instead developing Scottish
microcosms, 'enclaves' or 'sub-communities' within an English framework.[48]
Matters only deteriorated with the arrival of Wentworth, for whom 'the
evidence of general anti-Scottish sentiments' even before the outbreak of the
Scottish troubles in 1637 'is strong'.[49] The language of 'British' slipped into
abeyance before the stolid language of English and Scots; only the common
peril of 1641 would revive its common usage for the Protestants of Ireland.

By 1640 Edinburgh had felt the need to call upon the Parliament of England
as a guarantor against threats from Ireland, though also demanding the
participation of the recently reprobate Irish Parliament, at once furthering
the intrusion of Westminster into the neighbouring island and double-locking
against danger by seeking to operate through Dublin. With the 1641 rising
in Ireland the Scottish regime felt driven to act, to safeguard not merely its

[45] Clarke, 'Darcy', pp. 40–1, 44–5.

[46] Glenn Burgess, *The politics of the ancient constitution* (University Park, Pennsylvania,
1992), pp. 179–80, 220–1 and chapters 7 and 8 in general.

[47] Canny, *Making Ireland British*, pp. 291–2.

[48] Nicholas Canny, 'The origins of empire: an introduction', in Nicholas Canny (ed.), *The
Oxford history of the British Empire*, i, *The origins of empire* (Oxford, 1998), pp. 2, 12–14.

[49] David Stevenson, *Scottish Covenanters and Irish confederates: Scottish–Irish relations in
the mid-seventeenth century* (Belfast, 1981), p. 14.

shores but its fellow-Scots in Ireland, through the despatch of an army to Ulster. Scotland is a necessary component in the narrative which follows,[50] yet English–Irish relations took priority within Ireland. The 'Scottish revolution' was something which could be exported to Ireland as a model for action or seep in via Ireland's Scottish community, but it could conceivably be blocked, as Wentworth tried to do, or submerged, even diluted, within a 'British' project, though in the event its radical, religious, potential escaped with profound consequences for the Irish future. The English civil wars, on the other hand, were something in which Ireland, and perhaps especially Protestant Ireland, could not avoid being caught up, for the determination of the nature of the English polity necessarily impinged upon the form and content of the 'kingdom of Ireland'. For the English political nation, too, there was always a tendency towards keeping Scotland at arm's-length; even co-operation was in the form of alliance, for mutual benefit. Ireland could not so easily be shunted aside.

This brief survey of the calm before the storm of 1641 suggests two sets of questions to be pursued. Firstly, there is the question of where this study slots into the still-evolving world of 'three kingdom' studies or 'British history'. All manner of means of formulating and perceiving such studies have been advanced, but what can be said, surely, is that the 1640s is one of those particularly contested moments in the history of the 'Atlantic archipelago' where some form of external perspective on any one kingdom can be valuable, if not essential.[51] This study quite consciously prioritizes the Anglo–Irish interface, and adopts the position that royal, royalist and parliamentarian concerns in England can be more fully understood through looking at them from an Irish viewpoint, using such an angle of vision to determine more clearly the contours of the rival movements. By moving out from the Protestants of Ireland, though, this study cannot simply adopt the approach of comparative 'national' histories. If there can be 'no stably "British" archimedian point'[52] from which to view the events of the 1640s, so there is no sole or simple 'English' or 'Irish' location either. Working out from Protestants of Ireland, and working across the increasing integration of that community into the webs of power centred on Westminster, means engaging with some of the challenges faced by those developing a 'multi-centred' approach to a national history, as that of England, concerned with

[50] Pressure of space and the existence of the nigh-definitive work of David Stevenson on the subject of Scottish military intervention in 1640s Ulster have limited the coverage given to Irish–Scottish contacts – see Stevenson, *Scottish Covenanters and Irish confederates*.

[51] This, of course, is not to deny the importance of factoring in other geographical dimensions, for example the crucially important continental European context of the confederate movement in Ireland.

the interplay of centre and locality, the impact of networks as well as institutions across geographical (and, in this case, constitutional) boundaries, the interaction of ideas and contexts and of social conditions and high political manoeuvres.[52] 'Multi-centred' history can surely be read across kingdoms as well as within them. In the case of the Protestants of Ireland, created from a 'British' mix in an Irish environment, there is perhaps no other option.[54]

The second set of questions concerns the nature, as well as the goals, of the Protestant community in 1640s Ireland. The last decade has seen a miniature renaissance in mid-seventeenth-century Irish history,[55] but little detailed work specifically on the Protestants of Ireland, beyond 1641, has been published.[56] The Protestants of Ireland appear in this present work in their variety and division. Indeed the question of whether there was a 'community' to be defended at all, or a 'Protestant interest' to be advanced, surfaces throughout. The Wentworth years, perhaps even the last several decades, had been fissiparous in tendency, splitting Protestant Ireland by national origin, religious proclivity, regional habitation and even the faction and malice of insiders against outsiders.[57] In particular it had set English against Scots, weakening the emergent 'British-ness' of Protestant Ulster. It had also parted the Protestants from what might have appeared their natural support and focus of their ambitions, the Protestant state. By 1641 that community had developed, if not a political language, then a lexicon, or perhaps an arsenal,

[52] Peter Lake, 'Retrospective: Wentworth's political world in revisionist and post-revisionist perspective', in Merritt (ed.), *Thomas Wentworth*, p. 282.

[53] Lake, 'Retrospective: Wentworth's political world', pp. 275–7.

[54] For the claim that some issues can be understood only in 'the multi-dimensional context of the three Caroline states' and a model of how to undertake just such a task see Ohlmeyer, 'Strafford, the "Londonderry business" and the "New British history" '.

[55] Heralded by Jane Ohlmeyer's landmark study of Randal Macdonnell, earl of Antrim, a man not merely of three kingdoms, but a player on the continental European stage also, this includes the broad-ranging research into, and subtle analysis of, the 1641 rising itself, notably by Michael Perceval-Maxwell and Nicholas Canny. Impressive studies have addressed the unjustly neglected confederate era in Ireland, with Micheál Ó Siochrú's provocative, engaging, thoroughly researched study of the political and constitutional history of the confederates standing alongside Pádraig Lenihan's detailed pioneering work on the military and administrative history of the Catholic cause, while Tadhg Ó hAnnracháin has fitted a masterly consideration of the political and religious implications of the term in Ireland of the papal legate Rinuccini into a stimulating and erudite interpretation of the Counter-Reformation experience in Ireland. See Bibliography.

[56] The principal exception, of course, is the series of succinct, sophisticated and penetrating essays by Patrick Little, cited throughout the present work. The seminal work of Toby Barnard on Protestant Ireland, while characteristically insightful on the 1640s, gives fuller consideration to the 1650s and later decades. See bibliography.

[57] Perceval-Maxwell, *Outbreak*, pp. 14–15 reckons the New English the 'least' 'cohesive political group' in Ireland.

of political concepts and moves, to be drawn upon in ways to be determined by the interplay of principle and circumstance. The horror and bloodshed of 1641, the anguished uncertainty and disorientation unleashed upon the Protestants, has not gained detailed treatment in the pages which follow.[58] But it was a searing experience. Like the ferocity which the Protestants unleashed in their turn, it served to pull together Protestant state and Protestant society, and all the components thereof. It would embrace the 'humbler' Protestants, whose experience is too easily submerged behind the rhetoric, the skulduggery and the achievements of the pre-war New English elites, but whose very presence perhaps contributed more to the transformation of early modern Ireland.[59] Their story, too, in so far as it can be uncovered, is a critical part of that decisive moment in the history of the 'Protestant interest', and of Ireland, which is the subject of this book.

[58] See especially Perceval-Maxwell, *Outbreak*, chapters 10–11; Canny, *Making Ireland British*, chapter 8.
[59] Cf. S. J. Connolly, *Religion, law and power: the making of Protestant Ireland 1660–1760* (Oxford, 1992), pp. 110–11.

1

Protestant Ireland:
a society at war, 1641–42

On the evening of 22 October 1641, across the planted counties of south and mid-Ulster, groups of armed men took control of a number of forts, castles and gentlemen's houses by force and guile. Within a few hours, in Dublin, Lord Justice Parsons would be roused from sleep to cast a cold eye upon tales of an alleged nation-wide uprising centred upon the seizure of Dublin castle, hub of 'the state' in Ireland. The 1641 rising had begun. But quite what had happened was unclear even to the men in power in Dublin. Their early correspondence with their king, their absentee lord lieutenant, the earl of Leicester, or the privy council of England, expressed an openness to a range of possibilities, or maybe just a gnawing uncertainty as to what they were up against, whether a conspiracy of Lord Maguire 'and some Irish of the kindred and friends of the rebel Tyrone' of south Ulster only or a 'general revolt' in which 'all the counties of the kingdom have conspired'. Of one thing they were certain. Even if regional in origin and, so far, in execution, the conspiracy threatened nothing less than 'the government and kingdom' of Ireland.[1]

The cataclysmic events of 1641 have attracted rigorous and sustained attention from historians. Incisive accounts of elite political manoeuvres, sustained investigations of the complex local patterns of events and careful positioning of the rising in multiple contexts, from the economic gloom of the early 1640s or the wellsprings of Catholic political and religious thinking to the broad-angle perspective of three kingdoms staggering towards collapse, have enormously enriched an understanding of a seminal event.[2] The present chapter will draw heavily upon such writing, but will focus in particular on three inter-connected themes: firstly, the manner in which the rising exposed

---

[1] HMC *Ormonde MSS*, new series (London, 1902–3), ii, 1, 4, 8.

[2] Perceval-Maxwell, *Outbreak*; Clarke, *Old English*; Clarke, 'Genesis of the Ulster rising'; Canny, *Making Ireland British*; Brian Mac Cuarta (ed.), *Ulster 1641: aspects of the rising* (Belfast, 1993); Raymond Gillespie, 'The end of an era: Ulster and the outbreak of the 1641 rising', in Ciaran Brady and Raymond Gillespie (eds), *Natives and newcomers: essays on the making of Irish colonial society, 1534–1641* (Dublin, 1986), pp. 191–213.

the nature, and the weaknesses, of the Irish state; secondly, the contrast between the failed attempts to create a loyal, defensive, cross-religious alignment opposed to the insurrection, and the interaction between local initiatives among the Protestant communities of Ireland and state sponsorship of their efforts, an interaction which shaped a Protestant population into a Protestant society at war; and thirdly, the manner in which 'the state' was captured for an unrelenting approach to rebellion, a stance which in turn was part of, and helped entrench, the polarization of Ireland in 1641–42.

The language used by the Dublin administration to describe the events of October 1641 was conventional, perhaps even traditional. From the first they tended to run together the language of 'conspiracy', 'treason' and 'rebellion'.[3] Of course, what for one person was rebellion, and for another was a defence of faith and liberty, as recent events in Scotland had shown, for yet another could be the pursuit of a good cause by bad means.[4] To pronounce a condition of rebellion had, though, long acted as the signal that the state could take off its gloves – the mailed fist was not only expedient but imperative in such circumstances. It was a notion, too, which had a dangerous potential to categorize people as loyal or rebellious, categories which could overlap with pre-existing religious or national divisions within Ireland. The embattled lord chancellor, Sir Richard Bolton, in the balmier days of 1621, had set out in his collection of the *Statutes of Ireland* his conviction that earlier conventions of dividing Ireland's inhabitants into loyal subjects, '*English* rebels' and '*Irish* enemies', no longer applied. Rather 'the *Irish* are no enemies, but haue the absolute freedom of subiects and the full benefite of the lawes . . . euery man is amesnable to the law, & may be punished for any offence whatsoeuer, by the ordinarie course of comon iustice'.[5] Individuality before the law would take precedence over group identification and blanket condemnation; 'rebels' were such individually, their personal culpability something which needed to be established at law. Yet for many in Irish society there was an anxiety that Dublin might lapse into wholesale categorization and condemnation. The 23 October proclamation announcing the plot of 'some evil-affected *Irish* Papists' caused sufficient protests to have it explained in a subsequent proclamation, on 29

---

[3] Proclamations of 23 and 29 October, in J. T. Gilbert (ed.), *History of the Irish confederation and the war in Ireland, 1641–53* (7 vols, Dublin, 1882–91), i, 226–9, and the early letters in HMC *Ormonde MSS*, new series, ii, 1–6.

[4] Meeting in mid-November, the still largely Catholic House of Commons of Ireland apparently sought to dub the Ulstermen 'discontented gentlemen' instead of rebels and in the end adopted the 'uselessly abstruse' distinction of referring instead to persons who had 'traitorously and rebelliously raised arms': Clarke, *Old English*, p. 173; *CJI*, i, 294.

[5] Bolton, *Statutes of Ireland*, 'Epistle'.

October, as being intended to apply only to 'such of the old meer *Irish* in the Province of *Ulster* as have plotted, contrived and been Actors in this Treason'.[6] Even the 'excitedly belligerent' lord president of Munster, Sir William St Leger, was aghast at the reaction locally to the first proclamation.[7]

Language struggled against the protean reality of events. Dublin agonizingly chronicled the geographical seepage of disorder outside the Ulster core, in the process losing its comforting premise of a regionally restricted rising.[8] Recent accounts have validated notions of a rapid spread of insurrectionary activity, at least into Leinster and north Connacht.[9] Moreover, within a month, the rising had changed character, in more ways than one. The 'bloodless coup' intended by the Ulster leadership rapidly degenerated into a violent and vicious assault on the Protestant or English population. If far from being the pre-planned massacre of later legend it included enough killing and robbing, destruction and ejection as to horrify the authorities and terrify Protestants. Not that the privy council were inclined to underplay what was occurring. If at first they reported only claims of intended mass killings, by mid-November they alleged 'many' had been slain, 'thousands' robbed, the 'arts of barbarism and cruelty' practised on the victims.[10] The changing complexion of the participants was also being viewed with trepidation. The state rapidly woke up to the fact that 'certainly this is another kind of rebellion' for, even near Dublin, the 'meaner sort of people of the natives rise up unanimously . . . which kind of spoiling in that manner was not known even in times of the greatest rebellions in former times'.[11] In response the government sought to exploit social and national distinctions among the Catholic population to retain at least some support. The loss of the Old English elite, of the Pale in particular, in December 1641, was thus a pivotal moment. It both changed the nature of the insurrection and, as Aidan Clarke has long since argued, showed that 'rebellion' itself had changed in meaning so as to become the sort of movement such men would join.[12] Yet its impact was just as great upon Dublin, both in how it perceived what was happening and in the manner in which it responded practically.

Sir Francis Willoughby, governor of Galway fort, was given command of Dublin castle in the days following the outbreak in Ulster. Looking back on

---

[6] Gilbert (ed.), *Irish confederation*, i, 226–7, 228–9.

[7] HMC *Egmont MSS*, i, 143–4; Clarke, *Old English*, p. 163.

[8] HMC *Ormonde MSS*, new series, ii, 14.

[9] Perceval-Maxwell, *Outbreak*, pp. 213–27, 246–60; Canny, *Making Ireland British*, pp. 492–5, 501–8, 525–6.

[10] HMC *Ormonde MSS*, new series, ii, 7, 18.

[11] HMC *Ormonde MSS*, new series, ii, 30; cf. Canny, *Making Ireland British*, pp. 502–8, 524 for the role of elite leadership and the force of compulsion by social forces 'from below' in Leinster.

[12] Clarke, *Old English*, pp. 227–9, 231–2.

the early days of the insurrection he recalled his insistence that the privy councillors retreat from the city to the Spartan safety of his charge, where he slept at night on the council table. With only eight old and feeble warders and the lords justices' forty halberdiers under his command, he claimed he would not let down the drawbridge for twenty-four days unless all his forces were assembled at the gates.[13] From within the castle walls, the government issued its orders, though whether they amounted to anything that could reasonably be considered a strategy may be doubted. The contemporary views of external foes and internal critics have shaped later perceptions of the government's role as embodying the actions of the coward, the bully and the opportunist: timidly cowering within the safety of the capital; rejecting plans for rapid military suppression while sponsoring localized brutality (notably Sir Charles Coote's killing sprees in the Dublin hinterland); cold-shouldering efforts to negotiate a resolution to the disturbances and meditating means to entrap as much as possible of Catholic Ireland, toppling its leading representatives from what was left of their hold on political or economic power.[14]

Setting the question of whether the lords justices were moved by 'a machiavellian design to force the country into rebellion for their own profit, or . . . an unreasoning panic arising from their conscious ignorance of the country's true loyalties', Aidan Clarke has suggested that both could be true. If panic dominated their actions in the immediate aftermath of the rising, the more ambitious and scheming response would come into play as the issues and forces involved became reasonably clear and 'there was a definite likelihood of a government victory'. Not only was the council hazily aware that some 'loyal' Catholics might have been – must have been – implicated in earlier royal intrigues and thus hesitant and uncertain about royal responses, but it was alarmingly ill informed about the unfolding of events.[15] The washed-up human jetsam of the popular anti-Protestant disturbances provided much of their information about the spread of the disturbances out from their core in central and southern Ulster. In such a situation Dublin was at least resolved that all the powers at its disposal would be harnessed in suppressing the rising. In such a crisis 'we must vary from ordinary proceedings'. It showed no compunction about resort to martial law or the rack, was aware that a military solution would require substantial reinforcement from England, and empowered Protestant and Catholic grandees to levy supplementary forces and quash rebels by the power of sword and noose. They were clear not only that failure in the short run would necessitate

---

[13] Trinity College, Dublin, MS 840, fos 178–9.
[14] Clarke, *Old English*, pp. 223–6; Micheál Ó Siochrú, *Confederate Ireland 1642–1649: a constitutional and political analysis* (Dublin, 1999), p. 24.
[15] Clarke, *Old English*, pp. 229–31.

a long war with all the welter of mandated havoc characteristic of government campaigns in Ireland, but also of the prospect that failure to act quickly would mean that nothing short of a 'new conquest' would regain the island to a future where 'politic reformation' no longer operated.[16] As 'rebellion' turned to war over the winter of 1641–42, as the country as a whole took to arms, so the position of 'the state' in Dublin changed, in practice if not yet in theory, from enforcer of order to political and military protagonist.

In a situation of civil disturbance, law was order's first line of defence. In 1641 it was a line quickly overrun. On 23 October in Co. Monaghan, the sub-sheriff and clerk of the peace were done to death, while the sheriff fled towards Dublin.[17] The same day, in neighbouring Co. Cavan, the sheriff apparently moved to call out the posse comitatus against the insurgents, but only as a ruse to disarm local Protestants in the rebel interest.[18] The sheriff of Co. Longford acted likewise.[19] The writ of English common law had not run long in Ulster. In the counties of the Pale, common law and the panoply of sheriffs and courts were rooted in the practice of centuries. Here it was to the sheriffs that the Dublin authorities looked to quell disturbances.[20] Yet here, when the local leadership threw in their lot with the Ulstermen in arms, it was through the sheriffs that troops were assembled in the rebel cause.[21] The court system, once so lauded as the epitome of a perfect conquest, buckled and broke. Dublin confessed that it could 'have no sessions held in any county but only the county of Dublin' even to begin the legal process against those in arms. Elsewhere 'the freeholders for the most part are in rebellion'. It had been enacted, under Henry VIII, that where a sheriff could not safely empanel a reliable jury he could 'awarde process' to the sheriff of an adjacent county, a procedure well known to the authorities in 1641–42 but of little use in circumstances where disaffection was considered to be so widely diffused.[22] The collapse of the courts undermined the government's capacity to proceed against 'rebels' by individual trial and conviction, as Bolton had insisted must be done. It threatened the loss both of the opportunity to use legal process to legitimize its actions, and of the legal means to drive forward the conquest by ensuring the property of rebels was delivered over to the crown for reallocation in the English and Protestant interest. In the light of the rising, government supporters would look back

---

[16] HMC *Ormonde MSS*, new series, ii, 3, 9–10, 15.
[17] Raymond Gillespie, 'Destabilizing Ulster, 1641–2', in Mac Cuarta (ed.), *Ulster 1641*, p. 107.
[18] J. T. Gilbert (ed.), *A contemporary history of affairs in Ireland, from AD 1641 to 1652* (3 vols, Dublin, 1879), i, 408, 477–8.
[19] Canny, *Making Ireland British*, p. 503.
[20] HMC *Ormonde MSS*, new series, ii, 4.
[21] Pádraig Lenihan, *Confederate Catholics at war, 1641–49* (Cork, 2001), pp. 36–7.
[22] HMC *Ormonde MSS*, new series, ii, 66, 72, 89; Bolton, *Statutes of Ireland*, pp. 73–4.

upon the pre-rising efforts of MPs to scale back the legal resources of the regime as, at worst, harbingers of the 'plot', at best counsels of folly. Lawyer-MPs had challenged maxims more suited to a land of war, like the claim that those slain in rebellion automatically forfeited their property to the crown, an issue then more obviously relevant to the descendants of past 'rebels' than to the fortunes of future ones. St Leger played with the idea of being present in parliament in alluding to such earlier campaigns: 'No martial law, no governors, no army; train-bands and lieutenants of shires is your only fine government. O that I were with you one half hour to laugh; no plantations, no Justices of the Peace but natives, no punishment of Jurors, no judication but the Common Law'.[23]

St Leger's wry remarks drew attention to the resources of the state, those it considered everyday appurtenances of government, and those stocked for the inevitable emergency. In military terms early Stuart Ireland was bespattered with little garrisons but sat across from an England allergic to the presence of a standing army. The reign of Elizabeth saw a bifurcation in the military organization of the queen's two kingdoms. England witnessed the consolidation of a system of 'trained bands' and county lords lieutenant for home defence alongside a more systematized impressment regime for external service.[24] The defence of Ireland headed in a different direction. Already under Henry VIII Ireland boasted a 'professional' military element unmatched save in the garrisons at Berwick, Carlisle and Calais, a 'standing army'.[25] Boosted by the wars of Elizabeth, then pared back, service under James and Charles was not that of a force grown fat in the years of peace but rather lean and, often literally, hungry.[26] The army swelled up in the crises of the 1620s, as Charles dragged his kingdoms into war with Spain and France, and again in the late 1630s as Lord Deputy Wentworth presided over the creation of his 'new army', potentially 10,000 strong.[27] Again the passing of the crisis, supposedly, saw the collapse back to the old, small-scale and dispersed military formations, if with elements of a higher command as a reminder of the fallen lord lieutenant's schemes. Generally accepted estimates suggest 2,297 foot and 943 horse at the outbreak of the rising, mostly in infantry companies of fifty or cavalry troops of sixty.[28] The common law system collapsed; the army proved a broken reed. Those companies caught

[23] Temple, *Irish rebellion*, pp. 70–1; HMC *Egmont MSS*, i, 143.

[24] Mark Charles Fissel, *English warfare 1511–1642* (London, 2001), pp. 55, 61, 78, 81, 86–8, 105.

[25] Steven G. Ellis, 'The Tudors and the origins of the modern Irish state: a standing army', in Thomas Bartlett and Keith Jeffrey (eds), *A military history of Ireland* (Cambridge, 1996), pp. 131–2.

[26] Canny, *Making Ireland British*, pp. 303–5.

[27] Carte MS 1, fos 181–5.

[28] Temple, *Irish rebellion*, p. 26.

in the first fury of the rising were frequently reported to Dublin as 'surprized' and effectively defunct. Dublin recognized that it simply could not mass such forces safely. Though the council pulled back some horse troops to the defence of the capital, it was clear that it was better to have most companies lodge close to home in castle or fortified town than risk the march to Dublin.[29]

From Munster, St Leger berated the council's pusillanimous response and urged the harnessing of the 'old army' to quash swiftly a largely unarmed and dismounted foe who 'can not stand before horse', perhaps, though, reflecting the less immediate threat in his home territory.[30] He repeatedly referred to his opponents in south Munster as 'naked rogues', highlighting their propensity for plunder and theft, his easy dispersal of larger numbers of enemies and his summary executions of those he captured. What he was describing was not a military campaign but the forceful implementation of martial law. Martial law epitomized the convergence and difference between English norm and Irish practice. In the aftermath of rebellion in early sixteenth-century England, it has been claimed, 'few people were prepared to argue that a provost-marshal ought to be anything other than a hangman; even mid-Tudor lawyers did not dispute the rule that martial law supplanted common law when the King's banner was unfurled'.[31] As the sixteen century progressed martial law was increasingly deployed in time of ostensible peace, and particularly against the 'meaner sort' of 'unruly persons' in Ireland first, but also in the other realms and dominions of the English crown. Yet however loathsome the reputation of post-rebellion provost-marshals in England, the numbers put to death in the violence of Elizabethan Ireland and the allegations, undoubtedly often correct, of corrupt and unjustifiable actions by those entrusted with such powers more than suggest that the use of martial law in Ireland was far more widespread and more brutally aggressive.[32] It also lasted longer.[33] In England provost-marshals were increasingly used as enforcers of the poor laws, and generally uncoupled from the fearsome methods of martial law.[34] Where the latter popped up a grievance in 1620s

[29] HMC *Ormonde MSS*, old series (2 vols, London, 1895–1909), i, 123–7, new series, ii, 4, 17; Temple, *Irish rebellion*, p. 27.

[30] Carte MS 2, fo. 59. Cf. HMC *Ormonde MSS*, new series, ii, 8.

[31] Roger B. Manning, *Village revolts: social protest and popular disturbances in England, 1509–1640* (Oxford, 1988), p. 17.

[32] David Edwards, 'Beyond reform: martial law and the Tudor reconquest of Ireland', *History Ireland 5* (1997), 17–21; David Edwards, 'Ideology and experience: Spencer's *View* and martial law in Ireland', in Hiram Morgan (ed.), *Political ideology in Ireland, 1541–1641* (Dublin, 1999), pp. 132–42, 151–4.

[33] John McCavitt, *Sir Arthur Chichester, lord deputy of Ireland, 1605–16* (Belfast, 1998), pp. 102–3.

[34] Lindsay Boynton, 'The Tudor provost-marshal', *English Historical Review 77* (1962), 445–55; Manning, *Village revolts*, pp. 184, 232–4.

England, it was for its challenge to common law, not for any practice of summary execution.[35] In 1620s Ireland the Graces had conceded both a reduction in the numbers of provost-marshals and, more importantly, an insistence that 'such as may be brought to trial of law are not to be executed by the Marshal except in times of war or rebellion'.[36] The Irish Parliament in 1641 had secured from the judiciary an apparently direct statement that 'they know no ordinary rule of law by which the subjects of this kingdom are made subject to martial law in time of peace', though this was coupled with an insistence on the validity of such a power, 'derived out of His Majesty's regal and prerogative power for suppressing of sudden and great indolencies and insurrections'.[37] By July the Irish Commons had appointed a committee 'to draw up a Bill, to explain how far the Martial law shall be extended upon his Majesty's Subjects of this Kingdom in Time of War'.[38] It is possible that convergence was in sight.

But even wartime England would witness nothing like the exercise of martial law in Ireland from 1641. Existing holders of such powers, like Sir Charles Coote, provost-marshal of Leinster, or St Leger as lord president of Munster, were to act according to the powers long vested in them, and with devastating effect. Martial law could plug the gap left by the collapse of the common law courts, but it could also function as a form of government terror.[39] St Leger was clear that his quarry in the early days of the insurrection was 'this rabble' who had crossed from Co. Wexford to Co. Waterford 'and do there spoil and pillage'. Some he killed, others he carried captive to Waterford city, 'where we intend to execute them.'[40] In Co. Wicklow, Coote 'apprehended', 'executed' and 'hanged' women as well as men for 'receiving their neighbors goods from Rebells and for helping to robb and pillage the English'.[41] For St Leger or Coote there would have been no need to defend such actions as a response to 'massacre'. What they were doing was implementing the requisite punishment for capital offences in conditions of rebellion. Quite emphatically, too, they were aware that martial law would generally not be used against those who had more to lose than their lives. St Leger would later admit that 'albeit I make no difficulty to hang the common sort by martial law, yet freeholders I am told by those that better understand

---

[35] Lindsay Boynton, 'Martial law and the Petition of Right', *English Historical Review* 79 (1964), 255–84.

[36] Clarke, *Old English*, pp. 48, 249.

[37] Patrick Darcy, 'An argument', ed. C. E. J. Caldicott, *Camden Miscellany XXXI*, Camden Society, 4th series, 44 (London, 1992), pp. 233, 247, 290.

[38] *CJI*, i, 273, including not only the likes of Patrick Darcy but also Sir Charles Coote.

[39] Cf. Edwards, 'Beyond reform'.

[40] HMC *Egmont MSS*, i, 153.

[41] Gilbert (ed.), *Irish confederation*, i, xxxii.

the lawes would thereby save their lands . . .'.[42] Though Dublin had overseen the execution of 'some notable offenders', in general it resolved to 'forbear it towards men of any estate'.[43] Martial law was being implemented in accordance with Irish government norms, in its association with rebellion, but also in its social dimension, and in its widespread and perhaps undiscriminating application. Recourse to martial law in this fashion demonstrated how surface similarities to conditions in England concealed the gulf between government norms there and in Ireland. Where the earl of Huntingdon, for example, had 'two or three' of those caught up in the 1607 rising in the English midlands 'brought before him with halters about their necks', yet 'thought it fit to spare their execution for that time', this was hardly the preferred method of Sir Charles Coote.[44] Martial law, however employed in line with Irish precedent, appeared to negate efforts to secure Ireland as a kingdom regulated by process of law. In the 1570s–1580s leading figures in Ireland had sought to dissociate themselves from martial law proceedings as liable to tarnish their reputation and honour.[45] For some of their successors, in 1641–42, it even contributed to an assessment that the state's vision for Ireland was further from such a goal than the aspirations of the insurgents.

Martial law powers were not confined to experienced Protestant enforcers like Coote, but awarded to leading Catholic and Protestant peers and gentlemen in 1641. John Bellew, Catholic gentleman and parliamentarian from Co. Louth, received his commission as early as 30 October, this allowing him to dispense summary execution upon any in rebellion or found 'robbing and spoiling'. These should be 'men of mean fortunes and the most active', though of persons of 'quality' caught up in the unrest 'some must be executed for terror to others'. A swathe of newly named county governors, Catholic and Protestant, were also granted authority to kill, by martial law, 'Traitors, and their Adherents . . . according as it hath been accustomed in time of open rebellion'.[46] The commissioning of military governors was part of Dublin's attempt to obtain supplementary armed support in the emergency conditions of late 1641. The diminished standing army in Ireland stood alongside no trained band system on the English model, but was supplemented only by means of a disparate collection of older and more

---

[42] James Hogan (ed.), *Letters and papers relating to the Irish rebellion between 1642–46* (IMC, Dublin, 1936), p. 29.

[43] HMC *Ormonde MSS*, new series, ii, 72.

[44] Victor Stater, *Noble government: the Stuart lord lieutenancy and the transformation of English politics* (Athens, Georgia, 1993), pp. 9–10.

[45] Edwards, 'Beyond reform', p. 20.

[46] Temple, *Irish rebellion*, pp. 50–3; Harold O'Sullivan, *John Bellew, a seventeenth-century man of many parts* (Dublin, 2000), pp. 24, 26.

recent rights and obligations. In plantation territories land conferred military responsibility, blending the traditional duties of property with the revolutionary upheaval in land ownership. Under the terms of the 1609 plantation orders for Ulster, for example, undertakers were required not only to build fortified dwellings but to obtain 'a convenient Store of Arms, wherewith they may furnish a competent number of able men for their Defence, which may be viewed and mustered every half-year, according to the manner of England'. Those to be armed and mustered were to be of the 'British nation'.[47] In some other parts of the country old obligations to participate in the 'general hosting' or 'rising out' persisted into the earlier part of the century, though attempts to stage a general hosting of the Pale in 1618 collapsed. The international situation by 1625 prompted the unusual step of considering a system of trained bands for Ireland. Controversy concerned the inclusion of the Old English to guard against invasion and the 'tumults of the malcontent mere Irish'.[48] But though the English privy council gave the green light to such moves the plans were eventually killed by the council in Dublin, more than a little uneasy at the prospect of arming even a segment of Catholic Ireland.[49]

If hostile witnesses like Temple and St Leger are to be believed the demand for defence to be placed in the hands of 'Trained Bands of their own Nation' re-surfaced in parliament in 1641.[50] Certainly it would figure as a confederate demand in the peace talks of the mid-1640s.[51] On paper, in terms of powers and duties, it is not so obvious why English-style lords lieutenant should have been preferred to Irish-style governors. With powers over counties, districts, towns or forts, governors were warranted with well-nigh a plenitude of powers resting upon a royal grant. English lords lieutenant, too, though, were established upon the shifting sands of the prerogative. Their powers and duties were, on parchment, every bit as formidable as those which historians have made much of when applied to Irish governors. And such powers were directed to the same ends, including acting 'against all and singular rebells, traytors, and other offendores and theyr adherentes . . . and to slay, destroy, and put to execucion of death such and as many as you shall thinke meet'.[52] The letter kills where the spirit gives life. English lords lieutenant had formidable powers but in practice, much of the time, their

---

[47] George Hill, *An historical account of the plantation in Ulster* (Belfast, 1877), pp. 82–3, 85.

[48] Aidan Clarke, 'The 1641 rebellion and anti-popery in Ireland', in Mac Cuarta (ed.), *Ulster 1641*, p. 148.

[49] Aidan Clarke, 'The army and politics in Ireland, 1625–30', *Studia Hibernica* 4 (1964), 31, 36–8.

[50] Temple, *Irish rebellion*, p. 71; HMC *Egmont MSS*, i, 143.

[51] Gilbert (ed.), *Irish confederation*, iii, 128–33.

[52] 1603 commission to the earl of Hertford, W. P. D. Murphy (ed.), *The earl of Hertford's lieutenancy papers, 1603–1612*, Wiltshire Record Society 23 (1969 for 1967), pp. 17–19.

yoke was easy. They did intervene in riot situations, but as often to mediate as to quash; power of death might be threatened but not often used. Even more importantly, lieutenancy was 'fully integrated into the fabric of society'. Invariably conferred upon the leading peerage families (though Catholic families fared less well), it held military experience at a discount, social prestige at a premium. Trained bands often served social and political functions as much as, if not more than, military ones, reflecting society's structures and compromises back to itself through a military haze.[53] Of course, such a picture can appear too neat and unspoilt.[54] But local conflicts were still battled out within recognizable social norms. In Ireland the whole notion that the upholding of order was a common aim and a task shared between royal government and the natural rulers of localities – a European commonplace – was rendered null. Unless, of course, the alliance of land and arms came through Protestant hands where, as like as not, service of arms preceded entitlement to estate, rather than flowing from it.

What was striking about the government's position in the first days after the outbreak of the northern troubles was the extent to which it sought to give the impression of securing just such a marriage of social, economic, legal and military power. The first precise evidence for warrant to levy counter-force was, indeed, directed to Protestant grandees in Ulster, the seat of rebellion. The 27 October order from the council empowered them 'to levy . . . and put in readiness . . . all or any the forces as well footmen as horsemen of the British nation', to act against those 'assembled together in a warlike and rebellious manner'.[55] But within days, albeit in the words of the less than reliable Temple, government had moved to enroll elsewhere 'chief Persons of quality . . . for the defence of the country . . . made choice of without distinction of Religion'.[56] On the face of it, Dublin was appealing to the forces of social order, mobilizing the elite of Ireland against tumult from below. It was not an impossible aspiration. The restoration of order would remain a priority for Catholic notables even as they evolved alternative government structures.[57] It later suited neither reluctant rebels nor

[53] Stater, *Noble government*, pp. 11–16, 25, 46, 64–5.

[54] Thomas Cogswell, *Home divisions: aristocracy, the state and provincial conflict* (Manchester, 1998).

[55] T. W. Moody and J. G. Simms (eds), *The bishopric of Derry and the Irish society of London, 1602–1705* (2 vols, IMC, Dublin, 1968–83), i, 242–3.

[56] Temple, *Irish rebellion*, pp. 51–3.

[57] Ó Siochrú, *Confederate Ireland*, p. 42. For all the earlier denunciations of government application of martial law terror, the first confederate general assembly in October 1642 saw measures to authorize every sheriff to double as a provost-marshal with power to execute for 'murther, man-slaughter, burglary, theft, robbery or other capital offence' any 'layman not worth five pounds': Gilbert (ed.), *Irish confederation*, ii, 78.

embarrassed statesmen to set much store by the 'Old English moment' when the Dublin regime, with whatever reservations, conferred extensive powers upon such individuals.

The possibility existed for supplementing such direct authorization of the use of force to suppress rebellion with local defence arrangements. The two-day session of the Dublin Parliament, grudgingly conceded by the council in November, with a large Catholic presence, voted an 'Ordinance of this present Parliament' whereby it would be lawful for each county to provide itself with munitions for its own defence and appoint commanders for forces raised. Sheriffs were to assemble lords, gentlemen and freeholders 'for the speedy Accomplishment' of such plans.[58] Such county defence schemes appeared, on the face of it, the most apt means to harness local resources and the legitimacy of established county structures and hierarchies, especially if topped with the organic leadership of a local magnate as military governor. Urban Ireland had a long legacy of loyalty, latterly demonstrated in the wars of the 1590s, albeit alongside tensions and distrust between towns burdened with billeted soldiery and a government griping at lack of enthusiasm in footing bills.[59] Yet towns and cities also retained at least residual control of some aspects of their own defence. In 1641–42 efforts were made to mobilize armed force with the expressed intention of defending towns against external threats. In June 1642 the mayor and deputy governor of Youghal ordered constables to enforce attendance by 'all inhabitants' in 'due course' at the watch, with sword, pike and musket.[60] In Waterford the mayor mandated 'seaven Captaines, and everi Captaine to looke well to the English of his owne parish'.[61]

Dublin appeared to be appealing for assistance by elevating national and social axes of identity above religious distinctions. Yet state action had for decades elevated religion as the defining mark of allegiance within Ireland even as it undercut the social power of the Catholic landed elite. Mutual suspicion, the adoption of state terrorization, the comparative attractiveness of the demands of the 'rebel' leadership for the Catholic elite and the pressure of a mass of external forces sank plans for a broad-based defence of the Protestant kingdom. Aidan Clarke gives priority in explaining the association of the Old English leadership with the insurgents to their discovery of a common political position but draws attention, too, to the pressures exerted by the intrusion of armed force from 'rebel' Ulster. Nicholas Canny has emphasized the more immediate context of disaffection within their own

[58] *CJI*, i, 294.

[59] Anthony Sheehan, 'Irish towns in a period of change, 1558–1625', in Brady and Gillespie (eds), *Natives and newcomers*, p. 108.

[60] M. D. O'Sullivan, *Old Galway* (Cambridge, 1942), pp. 169, 171, 186, 421; Richard Caulfield (ed.), *The council book of the corporation of Youghal* (Guildford, 1878), pp. 98, 220–1.

[61] Gilbert (ed.), *Irish confederation*, ii, 7–8.

sphere of influence.[62] From the start Dublin let slip to London its suspicions and anxieties: 'we must of necessity put arms into the hands of the English Pale' if the Irish 'generally rise'; it was the 'safest way to avoid suspicion of our jealousy of them'.[63] Catholic elite assistance was bound up with the prospect of negotiation with the insurgents and a preference for an 'internal' resolution from within Ireland, neither prospect holding much appeal for the beleaguered Dublin regime.

In late November a 'private advertisement' to Leicester from an inner group within the council denounced the plans of Thomas, fourth Viscount Dillon, to lay before the king a document 'signed by many Papists of the nobility and gentry of the kingdom', offering 'of themselves by their power to repress this rebellion without the aids of men forth of England'. Were Dillon to persuade the king that such aid from England was unnecessary, the letter claimed, the few remaining English and Protestants would be overwhelmed. The authors did not deny that 'when we have an army of some strength, many of the old English here may be fit to be put into it and will doubtless fight well with us' in suppressing the rebellion, but as yet 'we cannot judge whom we may trust'.[64] Dillon had received terms from insurgents in Co. Longford, seeking to lay their grievances before the Irish Council and thence the king. Dillon was present at a brief meeting of the Irish Parliament, where it was resolved to open negotiations with the insurgents, while a group of leading Catholics determined to send Dillon to England to inform the king of their support in return for concessions.[65] The authors of the private dispatch instead urged the advantages of English aid to secure 'a more firm and established peace . . . reducing this kingdom to civility and religion, but also in raising a greater and far more considerable revenue here to the Crown than formerly, out of the estates of those who were actors in the present general mischiefs'. The timing of the letter was perhaps as crucial as its contents. With Dillon still in Dublin, were Westminster to condemn his mission on the basis of this dispatch it could render his efforts abortive even before his departure for England.

Yet the contingency behind the collapse of local defence arrangements needs to be kept in focus. Some of the November appointees as governors straddled religious-national divides, being Protestant (or conformist) nobles of Irish or Old English extraction – the marquis of Ormond, most notably, in Co. Kilkenny, but also the earl of Kildare (Co. Kildare), or Viscount Mayo

[62] Clarke, *Old English*, pp. 223, 232; Canny, *Making Ireland British*, pp. 502, 506, 524.

[63] HMC *Ormonde MSS*, new series, ii, 5, 9.

[64] HMC *Ormonde MSS*, new series, ii, 24–7.

[65] Simonds D'Ewes, *The journal of Sir Simonds D'Ewes*, ed. W. H. Coates (New Haven, 1942), pp. 251–3; Gilbert (ed.), *Contemporary history*, i, 367–8; Conrad Russell, *The fall of the British monarchies, 1637–1642* (Oxford, 1991), pp. 396–8; Clarke, *Old English*, pp. 173–5, 190.

(Co. Mayo) – as were some earlier or later appointees, like the earl of Thomond (Co. Clare) or Lord Kerry (Co. Kerry). Most made at least some attempt to draw together armed force, and all saw their efforts collapse. In Kildare newly raised companies instead spearheaded the insurrection.[66] Ormond was an object of rebel scorn in his home county.[67] In Mayo the viscount saw his authority crumble, and by February he had chosen the prudent course of conversion to Catholicism.[68] Thomond determined to steer a course which he felt could hold together his kin and Catholic tenants, and the Protestants of the area, mostly, presumably, his tenants. As governor, he summoned gentry and freeholders and awarded local Catholic figures positions of command or grants of martial law powers. His forces kept the county relatively free from raids, and even sought to regain plundered goods. He was dissuaded from hanging 'Irishmen of the common sorte' found stealing cattle save, interestingly enough, two 'strangers'. Problems emerged when he sought to impose cess and billeting to support his new forces and to take arms for them from local Protestants. Refusing to hand over their weapons or allow levies to be foisted on them, the local English population fled to fortified bases with their arms. By February Thomond was caught between his notional subordinates, insisting on their authorization to take possession of strong points in the county and his ongoing support for some of the, by now besieged, groups of English. By the summer his authority had collapsed and he gave up the struggle and took to the snug security of his castle at Bunratty, condemning the state for its failure to back his pleas with military hardware.[69] Catholic landowners, in the Pale and elsewhere, had proved more adept than the likes of Thomond in their efforts to acquiesce in, yet steer, popular political drifts. Allying with their social subordinates rather than attempting to stand against them could appear the most apt means to cap popular disorder and to pursue their own political goals.[70] Shrieval initiative and elite co-ordination were implemented instead to mobilize forces for the Catholic cause.[71] Along the way, county defence schemes had been shattered, with those furthest from the range of either the early insurgent

---

[66] Lenihan, *Confederate Catholics at war*, pp. 26, 46.

[67] David Edwards, 'The poisoned chalice: the Ormond inheritance, sectarian division and the emergence of James Butler, 1614–1642', in Toby Barnard and Jane Fenlon (eds), *The dukes of Ormonde, 1610–1745* (Woodbridge, 2000), pp. 55–6, 81–2.

[68] Raymond Gillespie, 'Mayo and the rising of 1641', *Cathair na Mart: Journal of the Westport Historical Society* 5 (1985), 38–44.

[69] G. U. Macnamara, 'Bunratty, Co. Clare', *Journal of the North Munster Archaeological Society* 3 (1913–15), 270–86; Maurice Cuffe, 'The siege of Ballyally castle', in *Narratives illustrative of the contests in Ireland in 1641 and 1690*, ed. Thomas Crofton Croker, Camden Society 14 (London, 1841), pp. 1–11.

[70] Ó Siochrú, *Confederate Ireland*, pp. 25–6, 42.

[71] Lenihan, *Confederate Catholics at war*, pp. 33–8.

forces or violent state-sponsored intervention holding together in local, relatively non-aligned, 'loyal' defence for longest.

The loss of government control in some of the traditional urban outposts of English Ireland was likewise a protracted process, several towns passing through neutralist or pro-government defence arrangements before landing themselves in the confederate camp. In some cases, as at Galway and Limerick, government troops stationed in the adjacent citadel came into conflict with the urban population before the latter, with outside help, emerged victorious.[72] In Waterford, by March 1642, sentiment was moving towards the rebel cause, and the mayor's summons to 'gather all the Captaines and companyes of the citty' to repel advances yielded only twenty-five men.[73] Those towns which remained secure to the state tended to be related to plantation schemes, in some cases as new foundations, or were towns where the garrison presence could swamp opposition. Those in the latter category could endure a long drawn process of increasing tension and distrust. In his 1642 account of events in Drogheda, Dean Bernard claimed that at the outbreak of the rising the corporation had managed to assemble no more than forty men armed with pitchforks and 'Birding-pieces' despite the town's ability to gather 'many Hundreds well armed . . . upon Muster Days'. He recounted a catalogue of suspicion worrying away at Governor Tichborne and other leading Protestants, directed against the Catholic-infiltrated 'two half standing companies' located in the town, and the townspeople. Catholic soldiers apparently deserted or asked leave to depart on grounds of conscience. In December Tichborne 'instantly disarmed the Town Forces' of pikes and muskets, and by early 1642 an 'emptying of the Town of the Papist Towns-men . . . who had been found tampering with the Rebels' had occurred.[74]

Dublin intoned the message that if the Pale elite 'had done their parts, as became good subjects' they could have defended the territory and protected Protestant neighbours and tenants, contrasting their inaction with the vigorous efforts of Protestant figures.[75] Arthur Chichester, governor of Carrickfergus castle and one of the east Ulster commissioners, had, on hearing of the outbreak, ordered the firing of beacons and the beating of drums; Protestants had flocked in, to be armed from the castle arsenal, and 'marshalled in companies' under the 'principal gentlemen' of Co. Antrim.

---

[72] O'Sullivan, *Old Galway*, pp. 237–41; James Hardiman, *The history of the town and county of the town of Galway* (Dublin, 1820, reprint, Galway, 1975), pp. 108–22; Kenneth Wiggins, *Anatomy of a siege: King John's castle, Limerick, 1642* (Bray, 2000), pp. 55–87.

[73] Gilbert (ed.), *Irish confederation*, ii, 18, 20–1.

[74] Nicholas Bernard, *The whole proceedings of the siege of Drogheda in Ireland* (Dublin, 1736), pp. 3, 14, 27–8, 33, 71.

[75] HMC *Ormonde MSS*, new series, ii, 36–7.

Under the authority of Chichester and his associates a rash of captains broke out over the vicinity.[76] In some parts of Ulster warrant to gather forces, issued by Dublin, was overtaken with commissions issued by Charles I himself to named individuals, to raise regiments of 1,000 or 500 foot, or troops of horse.[77] Smaller contingents were assembled across the west and south of the province. The Phillips brothers in north Co. Londonderry pulled together forces of horse and foot; so, in Co. Cavan, did commissioners Sir James Craig and Sir Francis Hamilton, garrisoning castles with 100 and 230 fighting men respectively and ranging as far afield as Co. Leitrim. Urban companies were assembled in Derry and Coleraine.[78] Outside Ulster, too, local defensive and offensive initiatives emerged. Among others Captain George Graham of Ballilenan, Queen's County, gave refuge to neighbouring English and Protestants and 'armed as many of them as he was able',[79] while Lady Dowdall at Kilfiny castle, Co. Limerick, gathered fifty foot and thirty horse.[80] Other evidence from Munster suggests small-scale musters and the establishment of castle wards, though at some point St Leger did pull together a regiment.[81]

The failure of the Dublin government to provide adequate arms and ammunition to those it called to rally to its defence became a common complaint. Thomond, Mayo and Clanricard claimed that they were stymied by such niggardly behaviour. Future confederates would erect a conspiracy upon such failures, alleging that combining the assignment of severe powers with the lack of means to back them up left them open to doom from one side or another. Certainly Dublin proved far from generous in allocating arms, and hasty in recalling weapons from Catholic hands. It would have been little comfort to such figures to know that the council was equally grudging in issuing arms to Protestant commanders. St Leger bemoaned his want of weapons. Outside the corporations he had not arms for 200 'allowing every gentleman to leave at home for the defence of his house two or three pieces, which is a very slender proportion'. If he had arms, he claimed, he 'could draw together three or four thousand good Protestants on whom we

[76] J. S. Reid, *History of the Presbyterian church in Ireland* (3 vols, Belfast, 1867), i, 315–16.

[77] Carte MS 2, fos 51–5; Hogan (ed.), *Letters and papers*, p. 2; George Hill (ed.), *The Montgomery manuscripts* (Belfast, 1869), pp. 158–9.

[78] HMC *Ormonde MSS*, new series, ii, 109–10, 110–12, 161–2, 164; Hogan (ed.), *Letters and papers*, pp. 1–17, 45–7, 119–21; Reid, *Presbyterian church*, i, 348–50; Gilbert (ed.), *Contemporary history*, i, 468–70, 473–5, 478, 491, 497.

[79] Hogan (ed.), *Letters and papers*, pp. 101, 102–3; HMC *Ormonde MSS*, new series, ii, 178–9.

[80] Gilbert (ed.), *Irish confederation*, ii, 69.

[81] Hogan (ed.), *Letters and papers*, pp. 33–4; HMC *Egmont MSS*, i, 150–1, 157, 161. The earl of Cork gathered together rather more substantial forces: HMC *Ormonde MSS*, new series, ii, 114.

might have relied'.[82] If the Pale received no more than arms for 1,700 men, east Ulster was sent arms for only 400, proportionate to one of the Pale counties.[83] To lack of supplies could be added a virtual collapse in communication. Contact between Dublin and the more distant parts of the island was soon rendered hazardous and infrequent. Audley Mervyn, in the north-west, claimed the assembled forces there 'never received one syllable' from Dublin between November 1641 and May 1642 and 'conceive the state in Ireland are as doubtful of our condition in those parts'. That did not prevent the regiments assembled there from developing a vigorous and successful strategy over the winter months.[84]

Local power blocs established their own networks of communication, a two-way process as some external authorities took note of provincial Protestant Ireland, or were reminded of its existence. Royal commissions to raise forces were supplemented by like authorization from the absent lord lieutenant, Leicester,[85] or from the parliament of England.[86] By January 1642 representatives of the leading figures in Co. Antrim were negotiating with the authorities in Edinburgh for purchase of 1,000 muskets, 2,000 swords, 540 pikes, weapons for 500 cavalry and three field pieces, at their own expense.[87] Authorities in Derry city claimed that 'all the arms within his majesty's store here were shipped to Dublin last summer; and nothing left here but old decayed calivers', while the council had sent nothing more than thirty barrels of powder in six months. In their case old-established contacts with London paid off in terms of foodstuffs, but also in artillery pieces for the defence of the city.[88] Sir Robert Stewart later claimed that the king had sent over muskets, pikes, powder, 'backs, breasts and pots' to north-west Ulster with the offer to draw upon the arsenal at Dumbarton for more supplies.[89] By the early summer regional forces were dispatching agents to London to appeal to the Parliament of England for logistical support.

Dublin's role became increasingly that of enlisting such forces, formally incorporating them into the 'list' of the king's army in Ireland alongside 'old' units and the new regiments sent from England. The efforts of the Dublin government to find them a place on the army list worked successfully for

---

[82] HMC *Egmont MSS*, i, 144–5, 148.

[83] Temple, *Irish rebellion*, p. 53.

[84] Gilbert (ed.), *Contemporary history*, i, 465, 468–70, 473–5, 478, 491, 497; HMC *Cowper MSS*, ii (London, 1888), 298–300.

[85] Viscount Claneboy (1,000 foot and 100 horse): HMC *Ormonde MSS*, new series, ii, 126.

[86] Viscount Conway, Sir John Clotworthy.

[87] Reid, *Presbyterian church*, i, 542–4; Hill (ed.), *Montgomery manuscripts*, p. 156, note 11.

[88] Reid, *Presbyterian church*, i, 350, 358–60; Hogan (ed.), *Letters and papers*, pp. 3–4, 8–12, 12–14.

[89] HMC *Cowper MSS*, ii, 298; Stevenson, *Scottish Covenanters*, pp. 51–2.

such scattered units as those commanded by one of the Phillips brothers, Graham and Hamilton, now formally awarded the command of a company or troop with, in theory at any rate, the requisite pay.[90] In parts of north-east Ulster where no regimental commissions had followed the original warrants to commissioners, the latter took it upon themselves to form the men into regiments as early as December, though they were unable even to notify Dublin earlier than the following March. As they reported, the adoption of regimental and garrison formations meant 'they may be the better trained and Coumanded', while when in 'scattered Troopes & Companyes in the Countrey we could not by any meanes draw them together from their owne Townes either to assist one another or to oppose the Enemye'.[91] In and around Dublin efforts were made to create new regiments. Both the privy council and, once he had reached Dublin, Ormond in his capacity as lieutenant-general issued commissions for the raising of fresh regiments for the defence of Dublin and Drogheda.[92] A rationalization of existing forces saw old and new companies garnered into regimental order.[93] Inclusion and exclusion ran in parallel. As early as December 1641 a series of musters was undertaken in the capital to ascertain the numbers of 'natives' (578) and 'papists' (140) identifiable in the forces of the crown.[94] From Drogheda, the newly appointed governor Sir Henry Tichborne endeavoured 'with as little apparence as may be, of distrustinge ye Papistes' to ascertain the proportions of Protestants and Catholics among his garrison.[95] Temple noted that 'many of the *English* who came stripped and despoiled out of the North listed themselves' in the new regiments. The regiment raised by the Palatine veteran (and future Eastern Association officer) Lawrence Crawford was to be from 'such Townsmen as were fit to bear Arms', but 'none were to be admitted into it but Protestants'.[96]

Protestant-dominated towns could be readily incorporated into official defence networks. Urban forces in Derry and Coleraine have already been mentioned. In Bandon, later to reap a vigorous, if not notorious, Protestant reputation, the 'captains of the bands or companies of men of that corporacion' were to be taken into pay as four foot companies;[97] so were

---

[90] HMC *Ormonde MSS*, new series, ii, 161–3, 164; Hogan (ed.), *Letters and papers*, pp. 12–14, 101–3; Gilbert (ed.), *Contemporary history*, i, 497.

[91] Carte MS 2, fos 203, 407.

[92] The council planned to raise 3,000–4,000: HMC *Ormonde MSS*, new series, ii, 17. For early warrants see Carte MS 2, fos 94, 104.

[93] Hugh Hazlett, 'A history of the military forces operating in Ireland, 1641–1649' (2 vols), PhD dissertation, Queen's University of Belfast, 1938, i, 229–39.

[94] Gilbert (ed.), *Irish confederation*, i, 230–2.

[95] Carte MS 2, fo. 47.

[96] Temple, *Irish rebellion*, pp. 41–2, 126.

[97] Hogan (ed.), *Letters and papers*, pp. 111–12.

two companies at Youghal.[98] In Belfast, in June 1642, the town sovereign was to provide 'a list of the men that are to be of the Traine Bande of the Towne . . . that they may be then enrolled as Souldiers'.[99] Oaths and other bonds could reinforce solidarity, as they did in Catholic-controlled towns.[100] Dean Bernard alleged that the mayor and aldermen of Drogheda refused a protestation and oath framed merely to 'endeavour the Defence of this Town' against the 'Catholic army', though, interestingly, he had noted at the very outset of the insurrection his efforts to draw together, apparently almost secretly, the Protestants in the town, so that together they could seek pardon for their sins and enter 'into a solemn Vow, and Covenant with God' to serve him better if preserved.[101] In Derry city a pledge by the officers of the newly raised forces to 'a voluntary oath to be true to the King and State, and to keep the city to the expense of his life' ran alongside a 'League' for defence including the resolve to 'expel all such Irish out of the city, as we shall conceive to be needful for the safety of this city'.[102]

The earl of Cork noted that those engaged in armed support of the government had 'such desire of revenge, as every man hath laid aside all compassion'.[103] Revenge delivered the propulsion power of Protestant society to the government drive towards repression. The grim question of massacre and atrocity has often threatened to overwhelm any study of the early months of the insurrection and war in Ireland, but a lack of detailed consideration here should not be taken as underestimating the decisive impact of such brutality, received and delivered, upon the Protestants of Ireland. Though the initial rising was not directed at mass killings and not undertaken through organized massacres, it was accompanied by a considerable degree of violence, demonstrating the depths of hostility in at least some localities.[104] The estimates by Hilary Simms that 500 to 1,300 perished among the British and Protestants in Co. Armagh in November 1641 – May 1642, while vastly less than the thousands of contemporary claims, suggest that as much as 10–25 per cent of the total British population of the county could have perished by violence, a finding which remains, or should remain, startling.[105]

---

[98] *Private journals*, iii, 364.
[99] Robert M. Young (ed.), *The town book of the corporation of Belfast 1613–1816* (Belfast, 1892), p. 23.
[100] Hardiman, *Galway*, note to p. 111.
[101] Bernard, *Whole proceedings*, pp. 5, 31–2.
[102] *A true copy of a letter sent from Doe castle* . . . (London, 1643) E84 (46), p. 3.
[103] Cork to earl of Warwick, 25 February 1642, quoted in Caulfield (ed.), *Youghal*, p. 1.
[104] Canny, *Making Ireland British*, pp. 541–2, 547.
[105] Hilary Simms, 'Violence in County Armagh, 1641', in Mac Cuarta (ed.), *Ulster 1641*, pp. 134, 137.

Violence begat greater violence, and the importance of local spirals of violence and revenge cannot be underestimated. The notorious mass drowning of Protestants at Portadown has been linked to the insurgents' defeat at Lisburn, and later killings near Armagh followed the capture of Newry by Protestant forces with mass killings there.[106] The hazy evidence for a mass killing of British combatants after surrender near Augher in November 1641 may be linked to the unwonted resistance which had set in, stalling the relatively easy early progress of the Irish forces.[107] The massacre of forty-odd Protestants in Sligo gaol in January 1642 came in the aftermath of the extension of Sir Frederick Hamilton's brutal campaigning to the edges of the county.[108] Sligo was soon followed by the killing of a Protestant refugee column at Shrule, on the borders of Co. Mayo and Co. Galway.[109] On the Protestant side, too, defeat and revenge could spur atrocity. As hostilities mounted in Co. Cavan, it was claimed that the Catholic sheriff's killing of sixty Protestants at Belturbet bridge left Hamilton and Craig 'resolved on revenge, they going forth in severall parties, killing and hanging prisoners'; 'thus were all of the rebells used who after that time fell within their power'.[110] In north Antrim, Archibald Stewart, agent on the Catholic earl of Antrim's vast domains, armed the Protestant tenants from his master's arsenals but, soon afterwards, felt confident enough to enlist the 'natives' also.[111] In January 1642 Catholic recruits under Alastair MacColla attacked their sleeping Protestant colleagues at Portna, killing sixty to ninety of them before moving on to join local insurgents in attacks on Protestant outposts. It was a turning point: as one local deponent, Coll McAllester, was to recall in 1652, thereafter 'without any difference or distincion the Irish killed all the English & Scotts they could lay hands on, & the English and Scotts did the like unto the Irish, except some few Irishmen who shewed mercy', whereof, unsurprisingly, he was one. Particularly harrowing is the testimony of Donell McGillmartin, an Irishman serving under Captain Upton at Templepatrick. On guard duty he witnessed the night-time departure of a party of horse under Lieutenant Garvan and its return the following morning bearing plundered goods, among which he recognized the clothing of his womenfolk. Garvan and his

---

[106] Simms, 'Violence in County Armagh', pp. 124–30; Canny, *Making Ireland British*, pp. 484–5.

[107] Michael Perceval-Maxwell, 'The Ulster rising of 1641 and the depositions', *Irish Historical Studies* 21 (1978–79), pp. 157–8.

[108] Mary O'Dowd, *Power, politics and land: early modern Sligo 1568–1688* (Belfast, 1991), pp. 105, 119–20.

[109] Canny, *Making Ireland British*, pp. 499–500.

[110] Gilbert (ed.), *Contemporary history*, i, p. 492.

[111] Jane H. Ohlmeyer, *Civil war and Restoration in the three Stuart kingdoms: the career of Randal MacDonnell, marquis of Antrim, 1609–1683* (Cambridge, 1993), pp. 106–7.

associates disarmed and threatened to shoot McGillmartin and his fellow Irish soldiers, and though Upton intervened he could win them no more than a safe departure from the town, under escort. As they passed through Ballymartin the families of the Irish soldiers were found, dead.[112]

Mass expulsions of Protestants from at least some parts of Ireland occurred from the very outset of the insurrection.[113] Where Protestants concentrated upon fortified holds which then fell to Catholic forces, further mass movements could occur – refugees from the last two castles to hold out in Co. Cavan trekked to Drogheda in June 1642, those from now-fallen Carlow to Dublin the following month.[114] Catholic populations also took flight, as in east Ulster in the aftermath of the killings in early 1642 and, more especially, the arrival of a Scottish army in April.[115] When the Protestant garrison of Drogheda was not only relieved from the desultory winter's siege but burst forth to harry the northern Pale, large numbers of local Catholics fled west. The Protestant clergymen George Creighton was a witness to how

> all the inhabitants of the countie of Dublin, Meath and Lowth fled with all their goods into the countie of Cavan: daie and night there came through Virginia greate droves of cattell of all sorts, great carts laden with trunckes and all kindes of good howsholdstuff, great store of wheate and malt. They filled all the emptie howses of Virginia full of inhabitants, three or fowre families makeing shift with one poore howse.[116]

Dublin could be unblinking in contemplation of what it had authorized, or of what was perpetrated in its name. Its graphic recounting of rebel atrocities contrasts with the chilling language sometimes used to describe its counter-terror. In February 1642 the earl of Ormond, lieutenant-general, set forth to secure the hinterland of Dublin with instructions to 'kill and destroy all the men there inhabiting able to beare armes'.[117] By June the council could describe how its army acted 'against the rebels, their adherents, relievers and abettors, . . . with fire and sword, the soldiers not sparing the women and sometimes not the children, many women being manifestly very deep in

---

[112] Trinity College, Dublin, MS 838, fos 32b, 139, 160, 181.

[113] Canny, *Making Ireland British*, chapter 8.

[114] Gilbert (ed.), *Contemporary history*, i, 494–6, 788; HMC *Ormonde MSS*, new series, ii, 168; St John D. Seymour, 'The church under persecution', in W. A. Phillips (ed.), *History of the Church of Ireland* (3 vols, Oxford, 1933–94), iii, *The modern church*, pp. 76–7. Estimates include 1200–1340 departing from Cavan, of which 800–1000 eventually travelled on to Dublin, and 400–500 from Carlow.

[115] Ohlmeyer, *Civil war and Restoration*, pp. 113–14.

[116] Gilbert (ed.), *Contemporary history*, i, 536.

[117] Thomas Carte, *History of the life of James, first duke of Ormonde* (2nd edition, 6 vols, Oxford, 1851), v, 294–5.

the guilt of this rebellion'.[118] It did not elaborate upon children's culpability. On the government side a particularly brutal form of warfare not only was adopted, but came burnished with the precedent of 'total war' advocated and practised in Elizabeth's wars.[119] Of course Dublin was sensible enough to insist that corn should not be burnt in the field where it could be brought in.[120] Even when orders to plunder and destroy were given they were not indiscriminate. Lord Justice Parsons's little notes to Ormond listed properties to be spared in his expeditions. Whether Parsons had an eye to the welfare of the present owner or a possible future proprietor is a moot point, but in Co. Westmeath, for example, he did note those to be 'spared' on grounds of loyalty or because 'the English in those p[ar]tes' had testified to some individuals' 'great comfort to them'.[121] But as confidence mounted to the summer of 1642 plans were formulated for a co-ordinated destruction of resources to secure victory by famine.[122] Local Protestants testified to the rapid escalation of conflict. Sir Robert Stewart later referred to the capture of Strabane, where the troops 'putt the ward . . . to the sword' and an ongoing policy of destruction of 'all houses and corne', noting that the Catholic forces also advanced 'burning all the waye till night'.[123]

The Protestant military presence in 1641–42 was much more widespread than a glance at some maps might indicate. Zones of control might be restricted to most of Ulster and coastal stretches in east and south, but what might be thought of as zones of disruption were scattered across much of the island. In May 1642 the privy council instructed Ormond to order all garrisons 'not to hould any correspondence, treatie, intelligence or intercourse with any of the Irish or Papists dwelling or resideing in any place neere about', giving no protections without licence and admitting none save such as labourers to cut turf, servants bringing corn or fishermen delivering their catch.[124] Local realities might not match Dublin's stringent demands, but many garrisons were indeed islands in a sea of religious and national hostility, whether that was more the perception from inside the walls than, necessarily, the unvarying outlook of local inhabitants. They survived by plunder mixed with occasional enforcement of supply.[125] Trade collapsed. Protestant-held towns could become overburdened with soldiers, Dublin

---

[118] HMC *Ormonde MSS*, new series, ii, 130.

[119] Ciaran Brady, 'The captains' games: army and society in Elizabethan Ireland', in Bartlett and Jeffrey (eds), *Military history*, pp. 139–40, 158–9; McCavitt, *Chichester*, pp. 10–15.

[120] Parsons to Ormond [?May 1642], Carte MS 3, fo. 235.

[121] Carte MS 3, fo. 291; other examples, Carte MS 3, fo. 289, MS 4, fo. 228.

[122] Hogan (ed.), *Letters and papers*, pp. 98–101; HMC *Ormonde MSS*, new series, ii, 205.

[123] HMC *Cowper MSS*, ii, 299–300.

[124] Gilbert (ed.), *Irish confederation*, ii, 45–6.

[125] Lenihan, *Confederate Catholics at war*, pp. 61–2; Hogan (ed.), *Letters and papers*, p. 82 (Galway fort); Gilbert (ed.), *Contemporary history*, i, 392 (Cavan forts).

especially so. Unpaid troops mutinied and spread disorder. In and around Dublin the spillover from garrisons allowed for some troops to be stationed on land from which they would appear to have drawn sustenance, though Dublin was slow to award custodiums, temporary possession of 'rebel' land to allow crops to be secured.[126] Tichborne recalled how his Drogheda garrison survived on prey over the winter of 1641–42. By the summer, with the siege raised and Dundalk in his hands, he noted the abundance of corn in the neighbouring country, 'which I allotted to the several Companies, to be reaped by themselves, towards their present Relief and future Subsistence'.[127] In Ulster, where most of the province was more or less safe Protestant ground by the summer of 1642, the farmer-soldier may have been a much more common sight. In the regiments of Viscount and Sir James Montgomery the first companies were supplemented with 'the drawing together oftymes of our whole tenantry', forces being sustained 'by help of his [Lord Montgomery's] tenants, whom he gave allowance in rent for it'. Sir James Montgomery had secured for himself a lieutenant-colonel and major who had had 'hono[ura]ble imploym[en]t in forraigne service (as indeed most of the officers of my regiment also)', but his son later recalled him awarding commissions to 'Gentlemen of the better sort, who had lands or estates in the Ardes, . . . charging them to raise a quota of their tenants to serve in their companys; and he proceeded accordingly with the subalterns, whom he choosed out of fee farmers, or other substantiall men'.[128]

Military service was becoming an economic necessity for increasing numbers of a Protestant population displaced or detached from their previous agricultural, manufacturing or trading livelihoods. Dublin insisted that when men enlisted in the capital out of economic necessity this still left their families destitute – unsurprisingly given the inadequate pay and supply of the armed forces.[129] Nor was this confined to the rank and file. Dublin's clamour on behalf of Irish-based peers and gentlemen for officers' posts, particularly in regiments to be raised in England, was grounded upon their being cut off from their landed income. Dublin was keen to stress how some such were commanders of 'old army' companies, while others 'have been in the late wars' or served abroad; all were needed until English arrivals 'can be enabled to endure the air and nature of the country'. Their first tranche would include lords Baltinglass, Lambert, Blaney, Folliott and Docwra, whose 'estates are

---

[126] HMC *Ormonde MSS*, new series, ii, 122–3, 140–1, 165–6. For organized 'threshing of the Protestants' corn' in Catholic-controlled Co. Meath in 1642, see Br'd McGrath, 'County Meath from the depositions', *Ríocht na Midhe* 9 (1994–98), 32.

[127] Sir Henry Tichborne, *A letter of Sir Henry Tichborne to his lady, of the siege of Tredagh . . .* (Dublin, 1734), p. 189.

[128] Carte MS 2, fo. 193; Hill (ed.), *Montgomery manuscripts*, pp. 154–5, 163, 347.

[129] HMC *Ormonde MSS*, new series, ii, 75–6, 92, 183–4.

utterly ruined by the rebels and whose fathers were eminent servitors at the last war'.[130] It had been suggested that the prestige of peacetime military command was an important consideration for the rising Protestant elite.[131] Such considerations may hold in wartime, and the claim that such men of local experience had more to offer the service may be true,[132] but mere sustenance by the sword was surely crucial.

Protestant Ireland was becoming reliant upon the state as the state was becoming ever more reliant upon it. In sponsoring local military initiatives ahead of, and alongside, armed intervention from England and Scotland, government was, if inadvertently, binding Protestant groups and communities, often rather isolated or indeed displaced, to the structures of the state. If the Elizabethan army in Ireland had acted as a social skeleton for a Protestant presence in the island at large,[133] a kind of reverse process was now occurring whereby the people were flocking to the army, incorporating themselves in the armed wing of the state. Large numbers of officers and soldiers were drawn from the Scottish population, a striking fact in light of the alienation of this community in recent years and the attempts by the insurgents to keep English and Scots apart.[134] Moreover, the sheer scale of this incorporation is at times boggling. If estimates for the Protestant population of pre-rising Ulster are even reasonably accurate, and reckonings of Ulster Protestants in state service by 1642 bear any semblance of reality, then a huge proportion of adult males were now under military discipline. Perhaps 14,500 adult British males were present in Ulster about 1630, that is, ahead of the substantial migration, particularly from Scotland, of the 1630s; alternatively perhaps a total British adult population of 40,000 to 45,000 existed in Ulster by 1641.[135] If the forces voted to be raised in the province had met their quotas this would have put approximately 11,000 men in arms.[136] Of course such figures are best considered aspirational,[137] but there is no doubt about

---

[130] HMC *Ormonde MSS*, new series, ii, 11.

[131] Raymond Gillespie, 'An army sent from God: Scots at war in Ireland, 1642–9', in Norman Macdougall (ed.), *Scotland and war AD 79–1918* (Edinburgh, 1991), p. 123.

[132] Hogan (ed.), *Letters and papers*, p. 32.

[133] Cf. Canny, *Making Ireland British*, pp. 180, 305–6; Brady, 'Captains' games', pp. 153, 156–8.

[134] Michael Perceval-Maxwell, 'Strafford, the Ulster-Scots and the Covenanters', *Irish Historical Studies* 18 (1972–73), 524–51; Perceval-Maxwell, 'Ulster rising', pp. 159–62; Canny, *Making Ireland British*, pp. 291–7, 478–83.

[135] Philip S. Robinson, *The plantation of Ulster* (Dublin, 1984), pp. 104, 106; Michael Perceval-Maxwell, *The Scottish migration to Ulster in the reign of James I* (1973; Belfast, 1990), pp. 313–14; Perceval-Maxwell, *Outbreak*, p. 31.

[136] Hazlett, 'History of the military forces', i, 164–9.

[137] Though Coleraine, for example, claimed to have forwarded to Dublin a muster book recording the 600 enrolled there: Hogan (ed.), *Letters and papers*, p. 11.

large-scale enlistment. This is not to make any assertions about the military effectiveness of such forces. Rather it is to suggest the potential for social transformation where most civil structures of authority were bending or broken and where military authority could often be buttressed by the economic and social clout of landed commanders. If a high proportion, even a majority, of men were under military authority and they and their families at least partially dependent upon military provision, direct or indirect (pillage, occupation of land), for sustenance, then Protestant-controlled zones, in Ulster at least, were indeed slipping into a condition of a society in arms.

Both in the provinces and at the heart of government, opinion had been divided over whether security could be best obtained by maximizing or minimizing the gap between the Protestant and British population and those among whom they dwelt. Dublin had remained wary of casting the elite of the Pale completely into outer darkness even as its support drained away. The council's reluctance to take the initiative in actually issuing any 'proclamation for proclaiming them rebels' lest they 'anticipate any direction of his Majesty's' would chime with Aidan Clarke's supposition about their unease as to the king's position with regard to those leading Catholics he had recently seemed to favour.[138] Instead they pressed Charles to proclaim the rebels and produced a draft proclamation for him, one which 'is so framed that their laying down of arms shall not wipe away all their former offences'.[139] Once the king had appended his consent to their proclamation, they had locked him into a policy of defining rebellion broadly and applying the law rigorously so as to clear the ground for a new order where such deeds would not be repeated because they could not be repeated.[140] With the pithy royal proclamation in their hands they proved quite willing to supplement it with a lengthy and detailed proclamation of their own directed against named persons 'according to the custom of this Councell Board' and setting out rewards for the heads of rebels.[141] With the king on side the trap could be sprung, so to speak. From stalling on any negotiation with the insurgents Dublin could move to outright refusal. It could act as barrier to

[138] HMC *Ormonde MSS*, new series, ii, 48; Clarke, *Old English*, pp. 229–31.

[139] HMC *Ormonde MSS*, new series, ii, 43–5.

[140] This action would mean 'those great countries of Leinster, Ulster and the Pale lie the more open to His Majesty's free disposal and to a general settlement of peace and religion by introducing of English': HMC *Ormonde MSS*, new series, ii, 43.

[141] Dated 1 January, the royal proclamation appears to have been received by 20 January and proclaimed in the Pale by 8 February and as far off as Youghal by 1 March: Gilbert (ed.), *Irish confederation*, ii, 24–8; Richard Caulfield (ed.), *The council book of the corporation of Kinsale* (Guildford, 1879), pp. 217–18. The more detailed proclamation issued by Dublin is dated 8 February: Gilbert (ed.), *Contemporary history*, i, 383–93.

any approach to the king and toss aside any appeals to its mercy, for it was engaged on a work where such compromise could prove awkward and messy.[142]

James Butler, earl of Ormond and lieutenant-general of the king's forces, has generally been regarded as the pole around which an alternative perspective might have coalesced.[143] Not that he was hesitant about adopting the military option. Indeed his later admirers suggested that his military initiative was curbed by cautious and malign forces on the council eager to let the rebellion grow. Certainly he was inhibited from marching too far from Dublin, despite his protests, and his discretion in receiving surrenders severely curtailed, while it was clear on occasion that alternative commanders were preferred.[144] If this bespeaks a lingering suspicion of their own senior officer, it also fits with contemporaneous orders to as reliably bellicose an officer as Coote to restrain his forward march, perhaps remembering the fate of Elizabethan expeditions which ventured too far from secure bases.[145] But from early on Ormond was telling the king that, for all his suspicion of how far the rising might extend, and of how religion was acting as a bond among rebels, that did not mean that all those engaged were seeking to shake the king's government.[146] By the following summer he was setting forth his opinion that Dublin was failing to make distinctions between the more and less guilty, treating all precisely as the letter of the law would suggest, with all the fearsome implications of such an ascription. From Connacht the Catholic loyalist Ulick Bourke, earl of Clanricard, lamented that there, where the sin of blood had not often accompanied rebellion, government rigour would lead to desperation. He warned that the innocent would perish and of the dangers of having the 'king's mercy totally bound up'.[147] In the early months of 1642 Clanricard had thrown his energies into plans to mediate a remonstrance, from insurgents and others, to the king, in the context of a cessation, all the while keeping a firm hold on Co. Galway.[148] He also maintained contacts with the canny lord president of Connacht, the Protestant Viscount Ranelagh, boxed into Athlone and frustrated with Dublin's narrow interpretation of 'submissions and protections'.[149] In June

---

[142] Clarke, *Old English*, pp. 204–10; Ó Siochrú, *Confederate Ireland*, pp. 28, 37–8.

[143] Cf. the argument in Edwards, 'The poisoned chalice', pp. 57, 70 that Ormond was already considered 'immoderation personified' in his home territory.

[144] Carte, *Ormonde*, v, 296, 298–9, 360–3; Carte MS 2, fo. 398.

[145] Parsons to Ormond, 9 May, Carte MS 3, fo. 128; Clarke, *Old English*, pp. 229–31; John McGurk, *The Elizabethan conquest of Ireland* (Manchester, 1997), p. 225.

[146] Gilbert (ed.), *Irish confederation*, i, 232.

[147] Carte, *Ormonde*, v, 318–21, 322–3, 324–34.

[148] Ó Siochrú, *Confederate Ireland*, pp. 29–35, 37–9. See also Patrick Little, ' "Blood and friendship": the earl of Essex's efforts to protect the earl of Clanricard's interests, 1641–6', *English Historical Review* 112 (1997), 927–41.

[149] Carte, *Ormonde*, v, 323–4.

the council sought to withdraw protections issued in counties Dublin and Meath to allow supply of foodstuffs to market, alleging these had been abused; in August it sought to curb protections issued in Ulster.[150] Such questions stood at the nexus of the logistical and the political, determining how the king's cause was to survive and who could or should be embraced by it.

Dublin had taken the bit between its teeth in terms of legal proscription. Having spent much time spelling out to official audiences in England all the sorts of obstacles to indictment and conviction,[151] by the summer it found that its initiative, and its new confidence, had triumphed over many of these obstacles. Indictments and outlawries were now undertaken in a number of counties, principally, it seems, Dublin, Kildare, Wicklow, Meath, Down and Cork.[152] In all bar the latter two counties it appears that indictments were filed in the court of king's bench, and outlawry then proclaimed in the county in question. Down and Cork held sessions to indict, though the sheriff of Down was clear about his inability to enforce the outlawries.[153] The seemingly omnicompetent earl of Cork had, as custos rotulorum for Cork and Waterford, presided over the indictments of as many as 1,100 individually named persons, not all residents but all allegedly found in rebellion in the county.[154] Dublin had circuitously returned to the personal definition of treason implied in Bolton's legal reasoning, but only after securing royal approval for categorical condemnation of all rebels and their 'adherents and abettors'. The common law courts could now slot back into the battery of anti-insurgency measures. Individuals rammed through the legal process could now face lose of estate as well as life. The process of transmuting rebel resources into the future stock of a reformed and secure kingdom was underway.

By the spring campaigning season few corners of Ireland had the luxury of working out their political salvation without the intrusion of angry orders or hungry forces from one or other armed camp. The war party within the administration had won, and could scent victory with all the benefits for the project of an English Ireland. The only genie who could escape to cause havoc to their plans was the king himself. Having boxed him into a condemnation of all in arms, Dublin then cautiously joined Charles's English opponents in

[150] Robert Steele (ed.), *Bibliotheca Lindesiana: a bibliography of royal proclamations of the Tudor and Stuart sovereigns* (Oxford, 1910), ii, part 1, 44.

[151] HMC *Ormonde MSS*, new series, ii, 66, 72, 84, 88–91, 103–4, 131.

[152] R. C. Simington and John MacLellan (eds), 'Oireachtas library list of outlaws, 1641–1647', *Analecta Hibernica* 23 (1966), 317–67, especially pp. 319–23. Some evidence exists for such proceedings in no fewer than seventeen counties: see *17th report of the deputy keeper of the Public Records of Ireland* (Dublin, 1885), appendix 1, pp. 13–15.

[153] Gillespie, 'Destabilizing Ulster', p. 109; HMC *Ormonde MSS*, new series, ii, 75.

[154] Charles Smith, *The ancient and present state of the county of Cork*, ed. Robert Day and W. A. Copinger (2 vols, Cork, 1893–94), ii, p. 77; Caulfield (ed.), *Kinsale*, pp. 328–37.

seeking to block off the monarch from a personal intervention in Ireland in April 1642.[155] It was a prospect which the king, ever sanguine about his personal political pulling power, had embraced believing it would prompt a widespread turning to the crown, across the political and religious divide.[156] It was a hope derided by the council in Dublin.[157] A royal visit fed the hopes of Clanricard and the fantasies of humble insurgents and offered a chink of light for those Old English Catholics whose efforts to reach out to their monarch were being systematically shut down by Dublin.[158] But it was not to be.

Instead the path from terror to security for Protestant Ireland was to be charted through solidarity and a solid and sole grasp on as many instruments of power as came to hand. The danger of the Old English campaign to strengthen the Irish legislature in 1640–41 had, for them, lain in the broader, long-term pattern whereby that institution was being modelled into a Protestant-dominated institution.[159] That danger came to pass with a vengeance in 1642. Even in late 1641 Catholic MPs had felt uneasy in the brief session called in response to the rising. By the following year most, if not all, had departed. When the Irish Parliament met in June 1642 it hammered home that position. The Houses listed forty-one MPs who being 'in open Rebellion, or stand indicted of high Treason . . . are conceived and adjudged to be rotten and unprofitable Members, fit to be cut off', and were duly 'expelled and excluded'.[160] It was resolved that all MPs must take the Oath of Supremacy or be expelled, and plans were broached for an act to confirm that ruling.[161] Parliament issued a declaration categorizing the rising as the result of earlier failures to suppress the anti-Christian popish religion, and as being directed at the expiration of Protestantism and all its professors (English, Scots, Irish) and the casting off of English government. It called for a 'thorough reformacion of religion', the enforcement of recusancy laws and the extension to Ireland of the much tougher English recusancy legislation.[162] By August plans were afoot for an 'Act, authorizing Statutes to be made in the present Parliament concerning the abolishing of Popery, and attainting of Rebels'.[163] The rump parliament of Ireland would have a limited role to play

---

[155] See below, Chapter 2.
[156] Nicholas to Ormond, 13 April 1642, Carte MS 2, fo. 64.
[157] HMC *Ormonde MSS*, new series, ii, 117–20.
[158] Clanricard to Ormond, 19 May 1642, Carte MS 2, fo. 194; Carte, *Ormonde*, v, 313–15, 321–2.
[159] Clarke, *Old English*, pp. 151–2.
[160] *CJI*, i, 295, 299.
[161] *CJI*, i, 297–9, 301; Hogan (ed.), *Letters and papers*, pp. 52–4; HMC *Ormonde MSS*, new series, ii, 162.
[162] Hogan (ed.), *Letters and papers*, pp. 54–6.
[163] *CJI*, i, 303.

in the war years ahead, but it remained a forum for the vocalization of Protestant opinion and assumptions.

Protestant Ireland had evolved a distinct political geography by the summer of 1642. The Scottish Covenanters in 1638–41 had won the triple prize of gaining physical control of the bulk of Scottish territory, of securing possession of the legitimate institutions of state, such as privy council, parliament and law courts, and of creating an effective and efficient alternative state structure, with local committees of war and parliamentary interim committees. Irish confederates had managed only the first and last of these desiderata, and even then their territorial control was much less complete. In England the warring camps contested territory and legitimate institutions, and on both sides, but especially Parliament's, new modes and methods superseded the old. In Protestant-held parts of Ireland the pattern was strikingly different. Territory was largely lost, though the capital, several important towns and much of Ulster were retained. Few new institutions were created, and control took on a very military tinge as orders were transmitted through town governors and garrison commanders, and decisions taken by councils of war. But 'the state' remained in Protestant hands. A royally approved privy council replete with lords justices remained at the top of the political pyramid. Law courts could be operated to condemn opponents even if their rulings could not be enforced. And a parliament remained in being. The 'natural' alignment of Protestant state and Protestant population, shaken during the Wentworth years, had been restored.

The methods deployed by Dublin demonstrate something of the nature of the kingdom, suspended between the notion of an English kingdom of law and a country subdued by force, between one where all subjects stood equal, at least in their sins, before the law and one where categorization in 'loyal' and 'rebel' camps could be neatly mapped on to old-established religious and national blocs. The war transformed Protestant society. The state had armour-plated a community. It had enhanced the already existing tendency to harness military with social or economic power. It had provided through military service a lifeline for the poor and bedraggled refugee as for the displaced aristocrat. It had incorporated local defence arrangements into an armed wing of the state, the 'list' of the king's army. But the identity of state and community was not destined to last. Deep political, religious and national divisions from before 1641 appeared to have disappeared in the new world post-rising. But they had not. Partly from logistical pressures, but mostly as a result of the intrusion of the king and the English Parliament, state and society would be rent apart, old divisions revived. It is with these processes, and the effect Ireland had upon the English quarrel, that the following chapters will be concerned.

2

The king, the Parliament and the Irish rebellion, 1641–42

Robert Sidney, earl of Leicester and lord lieutenant of Ireland, was not a man made for the eye of a political storm. Prone to think deeply, read widely and tread warily, he was the epitome of the politician of the middle ground, open to consensus or to dither.[1] On the morning of 1 November it fell to him to convey to a startled House of Commons the news of 'a great Treason, and general Rebellion, of the *Irish* Papists in *Ireland*'. As reported, his own gloss was that 'some of the Rebels confess, That all the Protestants were to be cut off, and not to save any *Brittish* Men, Women, or Children alive . . . That there must be a speedy course taken . . . that there be timely supply from *England* with Men and Money which will enable us to do great things to save *Ireland*; for the safety of *England* depends upon it'.[2] Charles I had already learnt that some had 'risen up in arms' in his western kingdom.[3] In Scotland since August, he had ceded further control of his Scottish kingdom to the Covenanter regime which he had so signally failed to dislodge, albeit with a last desperate attempt to preclude negotiation by force.[4] Despite all the anxieties and allegations about royal involvement in the Irish rising, there is little reason to doubt the genuineness of Charles I's efforts to secure the suppression of the insurrection there. A king as allergic to sedition in all its forms as Charles would not fail to recognize rebellion when he saw it. He duly gave his attention to efforts to secure armed intervention from Scotland, and to sponsor assistance to Protestant Ulster.[5]

At Westminster, shock was followed by an energetic and united response. In the year since the assembly of the present Parliament in November 1640 the grievances arising from the years of Charles I's 'personal rule' had largely

---

[1] Jonathan Scott, *Algernon Sidney and the English republic, 1623–1677* (Cambridge, 1988), chapter 3.

[2] *CJ*, ii, 300; John Rushworth, *Historical collections of private passages of state . . .* (8 vols, London, 1721), iv, 398.

[3] *CSPI, 1633–47*, p. 341.

[4] Russell, *Fall*, chapter 8.

[5] Stevenson, *Scottish Covenanters*, pp. 43–52.

been redressed, yet the depths of distrust between the king and his most unflinching critics at Westminster remained all too apparent. A widening gulf was evident, too, between those who pressed for ever more stringent guarantees to shackle the king to his concessions, and called for 'further reformation' of the English church, and those within Parliament ever more inclined to turn back to their chastened monarch as a lesser threat to social, political and religious order than their rivals. Ireland did not divide England as Scotland had done in recent years.[6] The notions that what was occurring in Ireland was a rebellion which must of necessity be suppressed, and that forces would need to be deployed to that purpose, provided the parameters within which alternative policy options would be battled out.

That is not so say that the hearts of all men looked as one upon events in the neighbouring island. As Ethan Shagan has reminded us, it is crucial to take into account not only what happened in Ireland, but how England read Ireland at this time, drawing upon pre-existing 'symbols' and vocabulary used in English political debate.[7] Yet, unlike Scotland, Ireland was securely within the sphere of operations of the crown of England; unlike the Covenanters, those in Ireland were perceived as undoubtedly engaged in rebellion, and were securely 'papist'. Broad patriotic-Protestant assumptions conditioned Parliamentmen to oppose what was happening in Ireland, and there is an inherent danger in prising apart threads of a web of ideas which contemporaries would have woven together. It was perfectly possible to abhor the Irish rising both as a merciless attack of papists upon Protestants and as an assault upon the authority of the English crown. It did not take the ghost of James I to remind political England in 1641 that 'popery' was inherently political, or indeed inherently disloyal. Puritans had no prerogative on anti-popery, 'part of the instinctive intellectual equipment of ordinary Englishmen', if they were more inclined to a belief that 'Antichrist [was] . . . manifesting himself . . . as a hideous and largely concealed conspiracy at the very heart of government' and more susceptible to definitions of 'popery' as a phenomenon which had oozed beyond the Roman church to infect the established Church of England.[8] Ireland could, and did, divide English opinion, but principally when Irish events were read on to an English plane, as when reportage of events in Ireland was linked to claims of 'popish plots' in England, or even to allegations of royal involvement.[9] Lodging Ireland within the

---

[6] Russell, *Fall*, pp. 83–5, 166–7.

[7] Ethan Howard Shagan, 'Constructing discord: ideology, propaganda and English responses to the Irish rebellion of 1641', *Journal of British Studies* 36 (1997), 4–34.

[8] Conrad Russell, *The causes of the English civil war* (Oxford, 1990), pp. 75–81; Russell, *Fall*, pp. 228–30, 416; John Morrill, *The nature of the English revolution* (London, 1993), p. 270.

[9] Shagan, 'Constructing discord', pp. 23–31.

commonplaces of English political discourse did not defuse its danger; it brought that danger closer to the heart of English political imagination.

That oracle of the rebellion, Owen O'Connolly, who had not only informed the Irish regime of the Dublin plot but acted as interpreter of events in Ireland to the Parliament of England, gave his imprimatur to the broadest of interpretations of the insurrection. The drawing up of 'interrogatories' for his examination was committed to a small 'close Committee' of Clotworthy, Denzil Holles, Oliver St John and John Pym, staunch future parliamentarians to a man. O'Connolly was asked, 'What have you heard any priests, or others, say, concerning the promoting of the Romish religion?' and 'Have you heard of any design of the like nature in England or Scotland?' His answers matched the presumed intention, alleging that 'all the places of strength in Ireland' were aimed at; that aid was expected from Spain; that like events were expected in England and Scotland; that the Irish had their favourers in high places in England.[10] Yet the triumph of one interpretation, that which would magnify events in Ireland and depict them in the most polarized of terms, was not complete. The declaration put out by Parliament on 4 November still left room for an 'Old English window', like that left ajar by Dublin. Though it suggested a priest-instigated rebellion to deprive the king of his governance of Ireland it still depicted an intended massacre directed against both 'all Protestants' and 'other His Majesty's Loyal Subjects of *English* Blood, tho' of the *Romish* Religion . . . who have always in former Rebellions given Testimony of their Fidelity to this Crown'. While positing rewards for service in land (to '*English* or *Irish*' who served against the rebels) it also sought to 'commend' the use of pardon 'to all such as within a convenient Time . . . shall return to their due Obedience'.[11] In the changed circumstances of February 1642 Charles, charged with permitting named papists to travel to Ireland, reminded the Houses that the lords justices had so far trusted some Catholic 'Noble men' with arms and that 'so great a trust reposed in some of the Lords of that Religion was not disapproved by the Parliament here'.[12]

Parliament drew itself up to a response which promised men, money and supplies to the beleaguered Dublin government,[13] albeit in conjunction with a battery of measures against a suspected Catholic 'fifth column' in England.[14] Over the weeks that followed, Westminster would keep in step with the

---

[10] *CJ*, ii, 302; D'Ewes, *Journal*, pp. 67, 73–5.

[11] *LJ*, iv, 422; D'Ewes, *Journal*, pp. 82, 103; Richard Cox, *Hibernia Anglicana: or the history of Ireland from the conquest thereof by the English to the present time* (2 vols, London, 1689–90), ii, 81–2. While Bishop Williams delivered the document to the Lords, it was Pym who read it in the Commons and Clotworthy who pressed for it to be sent.

[12] [Edward Husbands], *An exact collection of remonstrances* (London, 1643), p. 72.

[13] *LJ*, iv, 416–18, 421–2.

[14] Russell, *Fall*, pp. 418–22.

requests detailed from Dublin for men and money, committing itself to the dispatch of at least 10,000 English troops.[15] Letters from the king, read in the Houses on 4 November, had sought 'present advice, by what ways and means best to suppress this dangerous rebellion'. But when the king added that the Lords had been so informed 'that, by joint counsels, some vigorous and speedy course may be taken for suppressing this great evil and relieving his loyal subjects in Ireland' he had, if unwittingly, sold the pass on the question of executive military action, for the Houses chose to interpret his letter as having 'delegated [the] royal prerogative' over active intervention.[16] In the next few weeks, with the king still absent, Parliament 'came nearest to being an effective government', not least on the back of its Irish initiatives. Ordinances were approved enabling the earl of Newport, master of the ordnance, to issue munitions, and the earl of Leicester to nominate officers to raise volunteers, both for Irish service, the peers stating that they did so not only because of the king's absence but 'for that his Majesty hath especially recommended the Care of the Preservation of that Kingdom unto both Houses of Parliament'. When Leicester proved scrupulous, doubting whether he could act without a commission under the Great Seal, both Houses voted on 9 November that their ordinance was sufficiently valid.[17] Operating through the great officers of state was a stance which could be considered safe both in terms of constitutional legitimacy and in terms of the political security derived from reliable figures.[18]

Safety was not assured, though, to those whose perception of the rising's extra-Irish connections carried the threads close to the king. This presumably formed the context for the rather odd episode of the 'Additional Instruction' to be appended to those to be sent to Parliament's commissioners in Edinburgh, and asserting that unless evil counsel was removed, Parliament would not aid the king in Ireland or, as modified, would also take a course to secure itself.[19] The incident belongs to the unfolding challenge to Charles's unfettered right to his choice of counsel, and indicates how Ireland, embedded within the developing English constitutional crisis, contributed to the escalation of that debate. In passing it might simply be noted that the second,

---

[15] *CJ*, ii, 311–13; *LJ*, iv, 434–5; HMC *Ormonde MSS*, new series, ii, 7–13; D'Ewes, *Journal*, pp. 121, 124.

[16] HMC *4th report* (London, 1874), p. 104; Little, 'English Parliament', pp. 108–9; Russell, *Fall*, p. 402. On 2 December Falkland referred to the letter as having 'given us authoritie to proceed in this busines', yet when read it appeared 'hee did onlie require our advice': D'Ewes, *Journal*, pp. 223–4.

[17] *CJ*, ii, 306, 308; *LJ*, iv, 424–5, 429, 444.

[18] Russell, *Fall*, pp. 416, 472; cf. Russell's account of the Houses' response to the first army plot, pp. 298–9.

[19] S. R. Gardiner (ed.), *The Constitutional documents of the Puritan revolution* (reprint of 3rd edition, Oxford, 1979), pp. 199–201.

'moderate' version, to offer to intervene in Ireland and yet also take action to 'the securing of ourselves' and confiding aid for Ireland 'to the custody and disposing of such persons . . . as we have cause to confide in', was in some ways the more radical. As D'Ewes noted, 'that wee would not give his Majestie aide without a redresse of our grievances it is noe more then the ancient and undoubted rite of Parliament', and could be construed as the kind of tactic employed in earlier conflicts.[20] That it was the later version which in the end prevailed suggests, if no more, the strength of feeling behind maintaining a commitment to Ireland; for whatever reason, it was a threat too far for the Lords.

Division at Westminster would raise its head more obviously whenever the third kingdom was factored into the English–Irish equation. David Stevenson has convincingly recounted the prolonged and cumbersome negotiations whereby a 10,000-strong Scottish army was mandated to serve in Ireland, as a separate army, though with a rather ambiguous subordination to the authorities in Ireland.[21] The Scottish regime, of course, had its own agenda in Ireland – a need to protect itself from a potentially hostile Ireland, a sense of fellow feeling with the Scottish population in Ulster, an allergy towards the 'erection of a popish kingdom in so near a neighbourhood'.[22] Charles was much less uncomfortable with the notion of a Scottish army in Ireland than many of those who would become his staunchest English supporters. Having only recently secured the exclusion of armed Scottish intervention in England, they were presented with the prospect of renewed, and possibly permanent, armed Scottish interference in what they considered English concerns. Among much else, the saga of negotiation is worth noting for its demonstration of the potency of the control of committees and of correspondence within Parliament. By 13 November, for example, proponents of Scottish involvement had faced two days of stonewalling, or open resistance, to Scottish offers of 10,000 troops for Ireland. At that juncture Pym presented a letter sent by the vice-treasurer Sir Adam Loftus from Dublin, depicting a threat to the lives of 100,000 Protestants as well as loss of control of Ireland, and conveniently mentioning that there was 'Nothing soe terrible to the apprehensions off the Rebels as a considerable force from the Scotts'. Immediately Sir John Hotham was able to report the pre-secured recommendation of the committee for Ireland[23] that 6,000 Scots be called

---

[20] D'Ewes *Journal*, p. 100.

[21] Stevenson, *Scottish Covenanters*, pp. 48–65.

[22] Quoted in Perceval-Maxwell, *Outbreak*, p. 268.

[23] For the committees for Ireland see Robert Armstrong, 'Ireland at Westminster: the Long Parliament's Irish committees, 1641–1647', in Chris R. Kyle and Jason Peacey (eds), *Parliament at work: parliamentary committees, political power and public access in early modern England* (Woodbridge, 2002), pp. 80–1.

for, a move doubtless strengthened by his own earlier opposition to the idea. The Commons agreed to re-open the debate, and ultimately agreed to the increased numbers.[24] Similar co-ordination of news and committee votes would recur as the tortuous negotiations proceeded.[25]

Over the winter of 1641–42, as Parliament rapidly accumulated votes and resolutions on Ireland, actual aid was slow to arrive. The November votes took place in a situation where England not only had no troops to send, but had no money with which to send them. Even Parliament's offer, the very day it heard news of the rising, to send £20,000, was made in a context where only £11,000 was actually 'in hand'. It took the negotiation of a costly scheme to mandate merchants to transport Spanish coin to Ireland to secure the sum. For the next few months Parliament could rely only on loan money, including £50,000 from the London authorities, and sums from the merchant adventurers and from MPs themselves, to keep aid to Ireland flowing. It did not matter that the Commons could be persuaded to up the totals it was willing to devote to Ireland, or even to resuscitate a moribund act for a £400,000 taxation of England, if ready cash could not be dispensed to get troops moving. In this context, Parliament's achievement of dispatching early quotas of troops in December–January should not be underestimated. As money came in, so it went out, to captains and colonels to assemble and dispatch volunteer soldiers. By the first week in March something of the order of 3,400 infantry and at least 300 cavalry had been sent across to Dublin. Along the way Chester had clogged the system as the same bottleneck it had been in Elizabeth's days, as shortages of shipping, adverse winds and lack of small, but essential, sums of money all proved enemies to rapid deployment, some units being stranded there for weeks.[26] Cash, if never enough, continued to be shipped to Dublin, and a commissary of victuals was appointed to channel supplies.[27]

December was a frustrating month. As the minutiae of the early arrangements were tidied up deadlock appeared to ensue on negotiation with the Scots and on an impressment act to speed levies. Meanwhile some within Parliament were making serious moves both on the policy for a future Ireland and on the escalation of direct intervention. The 'Dillon mission' of early December, noted above, was effectively scuppered when the prompting

[24] D'Ewes *Journal*, pp. 90–4, 119, 124–5, 130–1, 137–8; *CJ*, ii, 314–15.

[25] The Lords finally agreed to the full quota of 10,000 Scottish troops on 21 December, the same day the Commons passed up to them the petition of 'divers Lords and Gentlemen' of Ireland, which laid particular emphasis on the importance of sending such a number of Scottish soldiers: *CJ*, ii, 351–3; *LJ*, iv, 484–6.

[26] Robert Armstrong, 'The Long Parliament goes to war: the Irish campaigns, 1641–3' (*Historical Research*, forthcoming); cf. McGurk, *Elizabethan conquest*, chapter 6.

[27] *CJ*, ii, 362.

of an inner group within the Irish Council led to Pym's detailing the plan to the Commons. The upshot was a resolution to deny toleration of Catholicism in any of the king's dominions. Those who spoke against the declaration warned of the prospect of alienating 'many Papists that held with the rest of the good subjects of that kingdome'. Conversely proponents insisted that non-toleration did not mean 'extirpation'. Sir Benjamin Rudyerd, hardly a firebrand, urged the declaration forward, but remarked that 'When we deny the Irish a Toleration, we do not withdraw the eases and favours they have heretofore enjoyed, Greater, I am sure then they would afford us, if we were in their power'.[28]

The declaration tied together two non-negotiable aims of 'the junto', the core group of the future parliamentarian leadership: the view, shared by Lord Justice Parsons and his allies in Dublin, that the rising must be suppressed not pardoned,[29] and the demand that no ground be given to Catholicism in England. This second point needed stating out loud as, the same day as Pym read the calls for toleration from the Irish, the Lords heard the French ambassador's pleas to show clemency to convicted Catholic priests in England 'the rather for it may concern the settling of Affairs in *Ireland*'.[30] Over the next few days the declaration's accretion of clauses reflected the religious dynamic which propelled it. The Irish committee successfully recommended a statement to 'vindicate' the queen, by her condemnation of 'all those that shall engage ther lives for the meyntenance off the popysh Religion by insurrection', while pressure from the floor secured calls for public prayers and fastings tied to relief measures. A rebuff from the Lords in matters ecclesiastical preceded the inclusion of an Irish committee condemnation of the bishops 'and looser clergie' for their earlier loud denunciations of 'the King's good subjects of Scotland' and their silence over Ireland's rebels. The declaration went through the Commons and on to the Lords, apparently with a blisteringly anti-episcopal speech from Holles. Having wrapped their declaration in anti-episcopal garb they could not expect an easy passage for it. Toleration, the reprieve of the condemned priests and the attack on the bishops led to frayed tempers in the upper house. For the moment the peers' greater compromising instincts held good. Their heterogeneous committee on the documents scrapped the preamble but also postponed an attempt to insist that none but the 'established' religion be tolerated.[31]

---

[28] D'Ewes, *Journal*, pp. 254–5; Rushworth, *Historical collections*, iv, 456.

[29] HMC *Ormonde MSS*, new series, ii, 42–4.

[30] *LJ*, iv, 466. In his speech on 14 December, the king cautiously upheld the convicted clergy. For delays over other anti-Catholic legislation, see Anthony Fletcher, *The outbreak of the English civil war* (London, 1981), pp. 164–5.

[31] D'Ewes, *Journal*, pp. 277–88, 281–2; *LJ*, iv, 473, 476, 479, 480; Fletcher, *Outbreak*, pp. 168–9; HMC *Buccleuch MSS*, i (London, 1899), p. 289.

As always, Ireland would divide whenever interpretation of events there drew Parliamentmen into pondering problems and implications closer to home. They were on safer ground when they tackled the practicalities of military aid. On Monday 27 December the committee report on the examination of Viscount Dillon was delivered alongside a plethora of correspondence, perhaps the largest consignment to date, concentrating on the prospects of calamity in Munster and ill tidings from Connacht. In what seems to have been a carefully co-ordinated effort the spur to action and the threat of betrayal from within were neatly dovetailed. The following day a whole spate of proposals were put forward. Large numbers of soldiers and munitions were voted for Munster, to be co-ordinated by a new committee. A further expansion in troop numbers was designed to safeguard the western province via Dublin, while a 'general' warrant was now to be sought to expedite all necessary issues of arms for forces raised in Ireland or in England. To fill such numbers would all but round out the proposed 10,000-strong English expeditionary force.[32]

To meet that quota meant raising troops at the very moment when the control of armed force was wrenching apart the king and majority opinion in the Commons. Russell has noted the intensity of the struggles over the power to command the small numbers of troops involved in providing a 'guard' for king or Parliament, a struggle which coincided exactly with the question of raising several thousand soldiers for Ireland. From the moment the news of an Irish rising had reached Parliament, plans had been laid for an impressment bill. Concern for the threat such a measure posed to the 'liberties' of the subject had quietly subsided, but contention remained over the possible threat to a royal prerogative of raising forces.[33] With the bill stalled, the king, 'very sensible of . . . the Blood which hath already been spilt by the crueltie and barbarousnesse of those Rebels', offered to 'take care, that by Commissions which he shall grant, ten thousand English Voluntiers shall be speedily raised . . . if so the House of Commons shall declare that they will pay them'.[34] If it appeared to be the only obvious route to supplying the reinforcement, Charles's offer was made even while crowns in London were clashing with officers in royal pay and days before the king arrived in the Commons with a tail of disbanded and disgruntled soldiers at his heels to arrest five of his most persistent opponents on charges of treason. In fact, the impressment bill, as finally drafted, did more than just address a constitutional dilemma, for it offered a safe method of raising troops in practice, vested in JPs on the basis of orders transmitted from

[32] *CJ*, ii, 357–9, 360–1, 365, 380; *LJ*, iv, 495–6, 500; D'Ewes, *Journal*, pp. 349–54.
[33] Russell, *Fall*, pp. 417, 434–5, 439–47.
[34] [Husbands], *Exact collection*, p. 33.

the king and the two Houses.[35] Charles's offer of 28 December could be considered anything but safe, and the Houses seem simply to have stalled on it. It was, however, accompanied by a pertinent concession. Within days the king had authorized a proclamation for dispatch to Ireland, openly condemning the insurgents as 'rebels and traitors'.[36] It was one of those demands which had joined the 'popular' party at Westminster and the more rigorous members of the Dublin government. The latter had argued that their own proclamations were inadequate, given rumours of royal support for the uprising, though they were careful to note that they did not seek an offer of pardon on the laying down of arms, lest this promote future restiveness.[37] Charles was foreclosing a political option which he had as yet left open. For the moment he had retreated on policy towards Ireland accompanied by a hardened position on the potent question of the control of military force.

If English politics ever stymied adequate military engagement in Ireland, then it was in these bitter and tense weeks of December and January. Yet it must be borne in mind not only that involvement with Ireland never faltered completely, but that co-operation between king and Parliament never entirely collapsed. Even in the dire days of early January the Commons persisted with their efforts to supply the precise wants of the pro-government forces in Ireland. In the Commons on 6 January, only two days after Charles's attempts to seize the 'five members', orders for the dispatch of munitions were voted, if 'in such haste as they woulde not permit the Clarke to reade them for wee had new Alarums given us of the comming downe of armed persons upon us'. No fewer than three committees with some Irish responsibilities were authorized to meet during the 6–10 January adjournment.[38] Warrants for munitions would still secure royal assent, with future royalists like Viscount Falkland and Sir John Culpepper to the fore in the process.[39] The soldiers mustered at English ports were gradually sent across as funds were made available.[40]

Yet the general perception of a response slower and less substantial than needed to quell Irish assertiveness and English anxieties was an accurate one. The necessary complications in a large-scale logistical exercise were

[35] Gardiner (ed.), *Constitutional documents*, pp. 242–5.

[36] [Husbands], *Exact collection*, pp. 33–4; *Calendar of the Clarendon state papers*, ed. O. Ogle et al. (5 vols, Oxford, 1869–1970), i, 222.

[37] HMC, *Ormonde MSS*, new series, ii, pp. 43–5.

[38] *CJ*, ii, 369; D'Ewes, *Journal*, p. 387; Ralph Verney, *Verney papers: Notes of proceedings in the Long Parliament*, ed. John Bruce, Camden Society 31 (London, 1845), p. 140.

[39] *Private journals*, i, 45, 68; *LJ*, iv, 507–8, 511, 514–15, 518.

[40] Schedules and musters, PRO SP 17/H/7; Hazlett, 'History of the military forces', i, pp. 186–8.

dragged on to the floor of a Commons ready to seize upon and censure delays and inefficiency.[41] When, in January, London refused to advance a further £100,000 loan for the relief of Ireland, its allegations of a bleak economic situation were not a partisan excuse, but showed how inextricable were the economic downturn in the capital (and beyond), the loss of political confidence (indeed lapses into political panic) and disgruntled reactions to the slow response to Ireland. It did not need an all-embracing 'popish plot' analysis, such as Pym had to hand, to explain all this, though that helped.[42] Instead, interaction between press and public, often running along well-defined channels, bore fruit in a smattering of petitions anxious about affairs, and worried at delays over Ireland. Concern for Protestant sufferings in Ireland, for the upholding of the English interest against international popery as much as against international rivals, and concerns for English popish plots or invasion bled into each other. Ireland inserted itself into disparate fears.[43] At this level, Ireland served to shape a shared, patriotic-Protestant discourse, one which retained its dominance in early 1642. Yet in another sense it was being embedded within a 'parliamentarian' variant of that discourse, shared with many in Dublin, which would prove unrelenting to those engaged in insurrection, unrepentant in casting the net widely to embrace invasion of, or uprising in, England, and unremitting in reading Ireland on to English political controversies, not least in its agenda of 'further reformation' and the combating of 'evil counsel'.[44] It would consequently be important for the king and his new-found friends to assert an alternative reading from such shared presuppositions. For now, those assuming control at Westminster were poised to secure their interpretation of a shared political language, and to make the running in securing practical engagement with the insurrection.

From the nadir of January 1642, it was possible to climb back in terms of intervention in Ireland. In January Charles departed from London, not to return until the eve of his trial in 1649. In the coming months many of those who sought to argue his position within the Houses abandoned the struggle

---

[41] For example, the debates on 24 January leading to the emergence of a committee to 'inquire where the Remoras and Obstacles have been': *Private journals*, i, 144–57; *CJ*, ii, 391.

[42] *LJ*, iv, 537–43.

[43] Fletcher, *Outbreak*, pp. 200–4, 210–13; Keith J. Lindley, 'The impact of the 1641 rebellion upon England and Wales, 1641–5', *Irish Historical Studies* 18 (1972–3), 145–61; Shagan, 'Constructing discord', pp. 7–17. Joseph Cope has argued that Henry Jones's *Remonstrance . . . concerning the church and kingdom of Ireland* at once presented the Protestants as 'a homogenous group, united in their sufferings' and 'the rebels as a diverse if not conflicted assembly of Irish and popish malcontents', threatening in religious, political and ethnic terms: Cope, 'Fashioning victims: Dr Henry Jones and the plight of Irish Protestants, 1642', *Historical Research* 74 (2001), 370–91.

[44] Fletcher, *Outbreak*, pp. 213–14, 217–22; Lindley, 'Impact of 1641', pp. 152–4.

to join his peripatetic court. Yet from late January those remaining at Westminster not only regained the momentum of at least incremental progress on Ireland, but secured royal consent, reluctant or otherwise, where necessary. Detailed schedules of officers had been approved by early February, but not before extensive excisions had been made, and the choice of senior officers remained problematic.[45] An ordinance to secure payment, by Parliament, for merchants who delivered supplies to secure ports in Ireland and a resolution to permit export of provisions to Ireland to pass free of customs were passed.[46] Parliament got to grips with negotiations with merchants for the supply of vessels to guard the coasts of England and Ireland – five were accepted by late January.[47] Even the deployment of a Scottish army in Ireland made progress. Despite agreement on a 10,000-strong army in December, the Scots commissioners' submission of wide-ranging proposals on the army's conditions of service had prompted lengthy and contentious debates on such questions as the surrender of garrison towns in Ulster (notably Londonderry), the powers of the lord lieutenant over the Scots and a Scottish role in future plantations.[48] Then, on 24 January, the emergence of an interim plan for the immediate dispatch of 2,500 troops opened the prospect of at least circumventing a possible deadlock. It was accepted by both Houses, only to encounter a royal refusal to allow the inclusion of the delivery of Carrickfergus as part of the interim plan. It was an unfortunate, and uncharacteristic, decision by the king, who, for his own reasons, was far more open to Scottish intervention in Ireland than many of his future supporters. Significantly it was the peers at this point (27 January), albeit 'after a long Debate', who appointed seventeen of their number to investigate the issue, including the role of the king's advisers, who were voted to be 'Enemies to the King, and both Kingdoms'. In this situation the king relented, that very day pleading his wish not to hinder the relief of Ireland.[49]

Royal support was forthcoming for the initiation of goodwill measures, notably the fast days for Ireland, with attached sermons, and the associated 'Contribution' for distressed victims of the insurrection. The re-awakening of the impressment bill in the Lords on 27 January saw it ready for royal approval by 7 February and duly secured one week later.[50] Influential voices

[45] No fewer than thirty-one exceptions were made from one list, while three of the seven colonels recommended to Leicester by the king were considered 'altogether unfit' on the basis of their actions on 4 January: *CJ*, ii, 398–9, 411; *Private journals*, i, 192–3, 243–5, 248, 260–1.

[46] *CJ*, ii, 395, 405, 412, 418; *LJ*, iv, 546.

[47] *CJ*, ii, 378, 398–9; *Private journals*, i, 173, 188, 200–1. For a cynical interpretation, see *CSPD, 1641–3*, p. 274.

[48] Stevenson, *Scottish Covenanters*, pp. 55–61, 64–5.

[49] *LJ*, iv, 530, 534, 544, 546–7, 548; *CJ*, ii, 399, 400, 433.

[50] *Statutes of the realm*, ed. A. Luders et al. (11 vols in 12, London, 1810–28), v, 138–9, 141–3.

around the king were urging him to hold a line of legality, 'moderation' and 'solicitude for Ireland'.[51] Charles's statements continued to lament slow proceedings over Ireland and project his own co-operativeness.[52] Royal statements and declarations condemned a 'horrid and odious' rebellion of 'mischevious and wicked rebels' or 'barbarous rebels' and lamented the 'great calamities, and unheard of cruelties Our poore Protestant Subjects . . . have undergone', and lauded the notion that 'a Protestant King' should 'venture and engage His Person for the defence of that Profession, and the suppression of Popery' in the interests of the 'security' of 'the Protestants of Christendome'.[53] Royal consent was also obtained for two decisive measures, which would shape the constitutional and political engagement of the Parliament of England with Ireland across the 1640s, the so-called 'Adventurers' Act' and the commission for the affairs of Ireland. Both sets of measures addressed pressing problems of the moment, set the parameters for parliamentarian involvement in Ireland across the 1640s, and set Irish precedents for approaches adopted for and adapted to the English war.

The emergence of the 'adventure' proposals, their constitutional impact and the fallout for Anglo–Irish relations of a commitment to mass confiscation and re-distribution of Irish land have received sustained historical treatment.[54] Only a few points will be addressed here. Firstly, as presented to Parliament on 11 February, the propositions concentrated on an offer to 'tender at their own charges considerable forces to be added to the new forces'. It was not envisaged that the provision of arms would be other than from the 'state stores', but the propositions did seek to lay claim to the powers of impressment and requested the right to appoint officers. It was thus a measure for the 'privatization of war'.[55] By contrast, the eventual legislation concentrated much more on the generation of revenue for the Irish war in general. Moreover, by early April, the Commons had intruded themselves into the process by the appointment of a permanent committee, including all MP-adventurers, to dispose of adventure stock, though the adventurers themselves could elect their own representatives to attend the

[51] See Russell, *Fall*, pp. 480–1; B. H. G. Wormald, *Clarendon: politics, history and religion 1640–1660* (Cambridge, 1951), pp. 56–61, 78, 80–2, 103.

[52] Rushworth, *Historical collections*, iv, 533–4, 535–8; Edward Hyde, earl of Clarendon, *The history of the rebellion and civil wars in England*, ed. W. D. Macray (6 vols, Oxford, 1888), i, 589–90, 591–2; ii, 2–3, 5–6.

[53] [Husbands], *Exact collection*, pp. 71–2, 107, 133–4, 144.

[54] Karl S. Bottigheimer, *English money and Irish land: the 'adventurers' in the Cromwellian settlement of Ireland* (Oxford, 1971); J. R. MacCormack, 'The Irish adventurers and the English civil war', *Irish Historical Studies* 10 (1956–57), 21–58; Keith Lindley, 'Irish adventurers and godly militants in the 1640s', *Irish Historical Studies* 29 (1994–95), 1–12.

[55] *CJ*, ii, 425, 435–6; *Private journals*, i, 369–71; cf. Russell, *Fall*, p. 476.

parliamentary body.[56] The 'adventure' located its sponsors within what might rightly be considered the mainstream of recent English policy towards Ireland. It is true that 'continuous plantation' had not won an unchallenged triumph as the mode of 'civilizing' or 'Anglicizing' Ireland, but it had won the ongoing support of Dublin administrations, Strafford's as much as his successors'.[57] The final draft propositions for the adventure envisaged as a prospective outcome 'That, for the Erecting of Manors, Settling of Wastes and Commons, Maintaining of Ministers, Creating of Corporations, and Regulating of the several Plantations, One or more Commissions be hereafter granted by Authority of Parliament'.[58] Selling the adventure meant not merely elaborating the combination of public good and private gain, but the prospects of royal benefit from a more secure revenue in the kingdom of Ireland. The Irish committee's sub-committee on the adventure displayed considerable interest in the permanent financial prospects envisaged by the scheme, whether through increased royal rents, increases in customs or decreases in military costs.[59] In his speech to the Lords, Bulstrode Whitelocke pointed out how the propositions could assuage English discontent at the large sums otherwise necessarily raised through taxation; in the longer term he emphasized how the lands to be allotted to the adventurers would not only profit them but also add £30,000 to £40,000 in reserved rents to the royal revenue in Ireland, 'which never yielded much, and altogether would scarce defray the charge of that Crown'.[60] Thus confiscation could feed not only the hopes of Thomas Edmundes that 'then land will surely be cheap in Ireland' and open 'to settle to posterity' by efforts 'to extirpe and extinguish the papist' but also the view of Henry Kinge that rent on the newly distributed land 'will make his Maty [sic] a greater revenue than any before him ever had'.[61] Whether realistic or not, the adventure addressed itself to pressing concerns of both the Dublin administration and the more imaginative of the English 'patriot' MPs in rebuilding royal finances to ensure a glorious and gloriously safe Protestant kingdom, in England and Ireland. The temptation of building on the ruin of the enemies of such a vision was one which had

---

[56] *Statutes of the realm*, v, 168–72; *CJ*, ii, 500, 506, 511; Bottigheimer, *English money*, pp. 77–8. Changes appear to have been thrashed out in a sub-committee of the Irish committee: *Private journals*, i, 369–71, 387, 395.

[57] Treadwell, *Buckingham and Ireland*, pp. 302–5; Canny, *Making Ireland British*, chapter 5, especially pp. 275–98; Perceval-Maxwell, *Outbreak*, pp. 157–9.

[58] *CJ*, ii, 435.

[59] *Private journals*, i, 369–70, 387.

[60] *The speech of Bulstrode Whitelocke* . . . (London, 1642) E200 (30), p. 6.

[61] Edmundes to Perceval, 8 February 1642, HMC *Egmont MSS*, i, p. 163; Kinge to Martyn Calthorpe, 17 February 1642, in Charles McNeill (ed.), *The Tanner letters* (IMC, Dublin, 1943), p. 140.

already enticed English MPs; with the outbreak of war there it was a temptation they could not resist. Finally, as Patrick Little has shrewdly noted, Charles's approval of the adventure legislation meant that 'he not only invited parliamentary involvement in the war, he voluntarily agreed to assign to parliament his prerogative rights over the making of war and peace in Ireland'.[62]

The 'commissioners and council' for the 'government and defence' of Ireland, seven peers and fourteen members of the Commons, took that war-making in hand. At one level their commission, issued under the Great Seal, was a direct response to all the delays and defects of the previous months. The commissioners were explicitly granted authority to ensure full recruitment and reinforcement of forces voted for by Parliament, and to provide them with foodstuffs and clothes, weapons and equipment and shipping. They were empowered to set out a sea guard, and had control over all expenditure resulting from their prescribed duties.[63] Their emergence was the culmination of repeated attempts to obtain a structure for military supply free from the convolutions inherent in conditions of disputed authority. In particular the powers were clearly similar to the repeated calls for a 'general warrant' or 'warrant dormant' for the issue of munitions or the transport of troops.[64] Agitation for such a measure easily elided into calls for a body of commissioners to meet such a need.[65] The commissioners had fixed times and place of meeting (thrice weekly, Star Chamber), and paid employees, including auditor and secretary.[66] In their executive powers they resembled such wartime bodies as the Committee of Safety or the Committee of Both Kingdoms – certainly more so than Parliament's large and loose committees of defence – but set on an altogether more secure and legitimate constitutional foundation.[67] In form and function closer to a committee of the privy council than to one of a parliamentary committee, the commissioners stood apart from king and Parliament.[68] Constitutionally,

---

[62] Little, 'English Parliament', p. 110.

[63] *Private journals*, ii, 404–5.

[64] For example, *CJ*, ii, 360–1.

[65] On 16 December, Sir Philip Stapleton had called for a commission to 'some Persons, agreed upon by both Houses, for the Considering and Disposing the Affairs of *Ireland*'. Instructions had apparently been drafted by 29 December: *CJ*, ii, 348; D'Ewes, *Journal*, pp. 309, 363.

[66] *Private journals*, ii, 139, 407–8. The minutes of the commissioners are printed in *Private journals*, ii, 403–67; iii, 363–409.

[67] Wallace Notestein, 'The establishment of the Committee of Both Kingdoms', *American Historical Review* 17 (1911–12), 477–95; Lotte Glow, 'The Committee of Safety', *English Historical Review* 80 (1965), 289–313.

[68] The commission made clear that they were 'appointed and nominated' by the king, but 'by the advice' of Parliament. They were to observe any further instructions received 'from us by the counsel and consent of our high court of parliament': *Private journals*, ii, 403, 406.

they were a living blueprint for the kind of institutional arrangements which appealed to many at Westminster, combining practical autonomy with legally impeccable credentials, and a membership of aristocratic grandees and their allies. The January origins of plans for the commission and for the measures which would take shape as the Militia Ordinance and the Nineteen Propositions were hardly coincidental.[69]

The commissioners held responsibility for ensuring the observation of all articles and agreements made with the Scots, and advisory powers over the best use to be made of the ally's army. Advisory duties were also granted vis-a-vis the lord lieutenant, lords justices and 'other governors and commanders' in Ireland as to 'what you conceive to be needful for the prosecution of the war'. To an extent the commissioners' relations with Leicester, while he remained in England, were problematical. Obviously communication was easy with his attendance, but relative powers were not fully worked out. By early May, at least, the commissioners had assumed directive power over the lord lieutenant's issuing of funds, while he could at least pressure them as on the delivery of arms.[70] Since the commissioners were to 'so order and provide that you be duly informed' of the condition of Ireland and the progress of the armies, they resolved to inform all those 'to whom any of his majesty's provinces, towns, castles, and forts in Ireland were committed' to address their dispatches to them.[71] Perhaps as a result of this, the Irish privy council had, by 7 June, begun direct correspondence which not only included the usual pleas for aid but added that if this was forthcoming it would need 'present and particular direction for the prosecution of the war and the execution of His Majesty's justice upon these unnatural and unthankful rebels'.[72] At the least, the king had consented to the insertion of an English authority, tied to Parliament, into the affairs of the other two kingdoms.

Finally, there is the matter of the first article of the commissioners' instructions, which mandated them to

> be careful to inform and advise us how the true reformed Protestant religion may best be maintained, practised, and professed in that kingdom, idolatry, ignorance, and superstition diminished and suppressed, and to perform and execute all things requisite for the effecting thereof according to the laws and

---

[69] For timing, and for 'aristocratic conciliarism' and its legalistic basis, see Fletcher, *Outbreak*, pp. 262–3; Morrill, *English revolution*, pp. 11–13; Russell, *Fall*, pp. 471–4; J. S. A. Adamson, 'The baronial context of the English civil war', *Transactions of the Royal Historical Society*, 5th series, 60 (1990), 93–120.

[70] *Private journals*, ii, 429–30.

[71] *Private journals*, ii, 421–2. Cf. the intelligence-gathering function of the Committee of Safety: Glow, 'Committee of Safety', pp. 291–2.

[72] HMC *Ormonde MSS*, new series, ii, 128–41, especially 130–1.

statutes of that kingdom with such gentleness and moderation that all our loving
subjects who have been seduced and misguided may discern our princely care
not only to protect their persons and estates according to the rules of justice
and the laws of that kingdom but likewise to provide for their souls and
consciences to be instructed in the ways of salvation.

This could be seen as no more then the conventional inclusion of matters
religious at the head of declarations and manifestos. But from the first the
commission was envisaged as containing power 'to consider of the matters
of religion in Ireland' as well as to provide a focus for military planning.[73]
For all that it spoke of 'gentleness and moderation' the article was clear
that what was aimed at was execution of the penal legislation. As such it
was in line with the attempts to put into operation the laws against the
Catholics of England[74] and with plans for expansion of Irish legislation to
bring it into line with the more stringent English laws against Catholicism.
It carried an ideological charge to the heart of a severely practical and
logistical arrangement.

Royal approval of the commission was secured on 2 April; it got to work
within days. With the coming of spring, the stalled expedition to Ireland
had been re-started. Once adventure funds came on stream in April,
Parliament ensured they were diverted ('lent') to the expanded main
expedition mandated back in December.[75] With a secure officer list and,
more importantly, money, it was possible to begin further recruitment. As
in late 1641, once commissions and cash were out there, troops could
assemble relatively quickly. Musters were underway at Chester and Minehead
by late April, and most troops were reported gone by the end of May.[76] In
addition, by 7 April there were already almost 3,000 men from the Scottish
army mustered in Ulster; 1,119 officers and 10,042 soldiers would be listed
by the beginning of August.[77] At the end of March the Houses resolved to
approach the adventurers for sponsorship of even more 'additional forces',
an approximation to the original proposals which would evolve into plans
for a self-contained expedition to the southern province of Munster.[78] The

---

[73] *Private journals*, i, 274. Cf. the repeated suggestions in Parliament of the introduction of
'commissioners' at either central or local level, to oversee changes in the English church: Russell,
Fall, pp. 185, 193–4; Anthony Fletcher, 'Concern for renewal in the root and branch debates
of 1641', *Studies in Church History* 14 (1977), 279–86.

[74] See e.g. Nineteen Propositions, *Private journals*, ii, 494–7; Fletcher, *Outbreak*, p. 247.

[75] The December votes, noted above, were to give effect to November resolutions to dispatch
a 10,000-strong English army, only the first quota of which had actually been levied.

[76] Schedules and musters, PRO SP 17/H/7, fos 20–2; Leicester's warrants, April 1642, PRO
SP 28/1B, fos 444–50, 524; *CJ*, ii, 515, 520, 524, 555, 584–5; *Private journals*, ii, 269–70, 364.

[77] Stevenson, *Scottish Covenanters*, p. 72.

[78] *CJ*, ii, 506; *CSPI, 1633–47*, p. 361.

commissioners also showed energy in getting to terms with the practicalities of supplying food, clothing and munitions. Within days of their first meeting they would be unveiling ambitions for extensive supply of key outposts in Ireland, and plans for substantial additional reinforcements.[79]

On 8 April, the king detonated his bombshell. In his message to Parliament he offered to go in person to Ireland, to raise 2,200 troops as a guard to accompany him, with arms from the Hull magazine, and to leave the militia secured by bill in his absence and the country under commissioners, though with the continuation of Parliament.[80] The notion of such a visit had been mooted some time earlier; on 14 February the king let it be known that he might 'venture his own Royal Person in that War, if His Parliament shall think it convenient', as well as promising to 'leave nothing undone for their Relief, which shall fall within His possible Power'. It was a promise which would be drawn on to collect his assent to the adventure proposals, and had been repeated since.[81] With the king's choice of commanders for the forces raised in England for the Irish war over-ruled, it is worth pondering that his commander-in-chief in Ireland, Ormond, was passing on to Edward Hyde (increasingly prominent in the circle around the king) assurances of the 'right inclinations' of prominent officers in the government forces already there, and pointing out that it would be worthwhile to advance assurances of royal favour.[82] Hyde's retrospective claims that the king's resolution to venture to Ireland was a decision 'very suddenly taken' may more accurately reflect the exclusion of Hyde's own circle of royalist converts from the king's plans.[83] The timing may have owed something to the recent declaration of the lord lieutenant that he would not be in a position to travel to Ireland at this juncture[84] but more, probably, to the recent establishment of the commissioners. In Parliament's response they urged Charles to allow the new commissioners to act.[85] Again taking away even as he gave, the king seemed poised to subvert the very institution he had created. Yet there is little reason to doubt the king's claims that he would 'spare no paines nor hazard for the full and finalle suppressing of that Rebellion and punishment of the Rebells in such sort as wee hope thereby to settle that kingdome in present peace and quietnesse, which is our principall care'.[86] Suppressing rebellion was always amenable to Charles; the question was of how he would do it.

[79] *Private journals*, ii, 409–20.

[80] *LJ*, iv, 709–10; [Husbands], *Exact collection*, pp. 133–5.

[81] *LJ*, iv, 580–1; [Husbands], *Exact collection*, pp. 74–5, 86–7, 107.

[82] *Calendar of the Clarendon state papers*, i, 223 (8 February).

[83] Clarendon, *History*, ii, 41–2; Wormald, *Clarendon*, pp. 103–7.

[84] *LJ*, iv, 679.

[85] [Husbands], *Exact collection*, pp. 141–3.

[86] Nicholas to lords justices, 13 April 1642, PRO SO 3/543.

That Charles's actions would prompt fear of some form of conjunction with Catholic forces was hardly surprising, despite his promises that he intended the suppression of rebellion, the denial of toleration and the security of the adventurers.[87] But what was he trying to accomplish? A sideways glance at the actions of that ever-adaptable courtier and warlord Randal MacDonnell, earl of Antrim, is perhaps illuminating here. Antrim claimed royal approval for his mission to Ulster which wove together three rather disparate threads. Though with little practical success, he engaged in parleys with the insurgent leader Sir Phelim O'Neill even while speaking against the insurgents' conduct, sent relief to the besieged Protestant town of Coleraine, and attempted to make contact with both the newly arrived Scottish forces and their local allies.[88] Antrim's actions contained all the elements, in miniature, of the kind of all-embracing plan for Ireland the king may have wished to implement. For one thing it diminished the gap between possible Irish and Scottish strategies open to him.[89] Control of the Scottish army in Ireland, whether through political manipulation in Scotland or in Ulster, would bring a valuable asset. Essentially Charles was trying to make room for himself, to burst through the constrictions forged by Parliament. Disparate aspirations, like the linkage of a royal expedition with a cessation and perhaps a receipt of insurgent grievances, or the mobilization of neutral opinion, could all compete for the attention of a monarch set loose.[90]

Charles was reasserting the expansiveness of monarchy. In part this may have reflected his always sanguine hopes for the effects of his personal intervention,[91] his obstinate conviction of his capacity to reconcile apparently incompatible policies or his awareness of the advantages of keeping open mutually exclusive options, in part, too, the more hard-headed assumption that success against rebels could be best secured by a flexible yet strong monarch. His attitude from the first had been not unlike that in 1640 when he hoped that Parliament would supply the resources he needed for his fight with the Scots without interfering.[92] So in 1641–42 he wished that they would

---

[87] He would 'never consent (upon whatsoever pretence) to a Toleration of the Popish Profession there, or the Abolition of the Laws now in force against the Popish Recusants in that Kingdom': [Husbands], *Exact collection*, p. 134. Cf. the position of the queen, anxious about the Scottish army, which might mean that Charles 'cannot join the army of the Catholics nor approach Dublin . . .': Henrietta Maria, *Letters of Queen Henrietta Maria*, ed. M. A. E. Green (London, 1857), p. 66.

[88] Ohlmeyer, *Civil war and Restoration*, pp. 111–12; T. H. Mullin, *Coleraine in by-gone centuries* (Belfast, 1976), pp. 87–8.

[89] Russell, *Fall*, pp. 490–4.

[90] Nicholas to Ormond, Carte MS 3, fo. 64.

[91] 'We cannot conceive that the Rebels are capable of a greater Terrour, then by the presence of their lawfull King in the head of an army to chastise them': [Husbands], *Exact collection*, p. 145.

[92] Russell, *Fall*, pp. 78–9, 155–6, 248–9, 303–4.

sustain armies he would raise and leave to him to suppress, pardon or condone.[93] Instead combined pressure from the seats of power in all three of his kingdoms was exerted against the king's plan.[94] That his Parliament of England and his governments of Scotland and Ireland should all oppose his plan reflects how far he had slipped, as well as the level of distrust he had generated. Looking at Ireland makes sense of that old concern that however much the king conceded there was always something he was keeping up his sleeve. For all that he appeared to have ceded practical control of the war there, and curtailed his own policy options, he was slowly cooking alternative sets of arrangements. None of his parliaments or governments could close him down – 'Neither can it be understood', he asserted, 'That when We recommended the Managing of that warre to you, That We intended to exclude our Selfe, or not to bee concerned in your Counsels, That if We found any expedient (which in Our conscience and understanding we thought necessary for that great worke) Wee might not put it in practice'.[95] In Alan Orr's words, the English conflict was 'a struggle for sovereign power – sovereign power understood as a cluster of loosely defined positive powers, themselves contested'.[96] For Charles to cede the marks of sovereignty was to surrender the ideological battle itself. And those marks embraced the power of pardon no less than the power of the sword.[97] As with Ananias, however much Charles gave there was always something kept back; there had to be. Charles's initiative at this point showed two abiding characteristics – a canny appreciation of power gained from control of armed force, and a willingness to think beyond the bounds of any one of his kingdoms in enforcing his will within it. The planned journey was still rumoured into May 1642.[98] For the moment, though, its ripples moved out to the broader question of the 'militia controversy'.

'No one quarrel led so inexorably to war' in England 'as that over the . . . Militia Ordinance'[99] wherein Parliament, in March 1642, named lords

---

[93] Thus it would be perfectly possible to condemn those in arms as rebels, yet regain authority with selective pardons, and meet the promise not to grant toleration, while not upping the level of persecution.

[94] [Husbands], *Exact collection*, pp. 141–3, 148–9; *Register of the privy council of Scotland*, 2nd series, ed. David Masson and P. Hume Brown (8 vols, Edinburgh, 1899–1908), vii, *1638–43*, pp. 250–1.

[95] [Husbands], *Exact collection*, pp. 145–6.

[96] D. Alan Orr, 'Sovereignty, supremacy and the origins of the English civil war', *History* 87 (2002), 475.

[97] As Clarendon would later have it, the adventure bill meant blocking 'the interposition, shelter, and mercy of the sovereign power' to protect 'that whole people' the Irish, from 'their cruel enemies': quoted in Bottigheimer, *English money*, p. 43.

[98] Henrietta Maria, *Letters*, pp. 66, 68; *CSP Venice, 1642–43*, p. 46; *Private journals*, iii, 19; Gillespie, 'Destabilizing Ulster', p. 114.

[99] Austin Woolrych, *Britain in revolution, 1625–1660* (Oxford, 2002), p. 215.

lieutenant to command England's local and voluntary armed forces, the trained bands, in defiance of the monarch. Charles made a strategically sound decision when he linked concessions on control of the trained bands with the potentially threatening prospects of his raising of soldiers for Ireland and, indeed, of securing control of the substantial magazine lodged in Hull.[100] The militia bill which he dispatched to Westminster was welcomed in the Commons on 19–20 April, even by supporters of the recent Militia Ordinance. By contrast, the resolution in response to the proposals for an Irish visit, as sponsored by Pym, not only rejected the thinking behind the expedition but insisted that any troops so raised would be resisted.[101] It would often be the case, for the king and for his opponents, that matters needed to be kept together which the middle ground would have wished to address separately, and thus resolve. With Parliament's condemnation of the proposed journey and his repulse before the walls at Hull by a defiant Parliament-appointed governor, Charles in turn repudiated his proffered, if now amended, bill.[102] The parliamentary leadership's attempt to secure control of armed force, without alienating too many of its potential supporters, had required not merely a strict legality, but reconciling two rather mismatched principles. One was that such measures had more to do with denying force than with harnessing it, binding the hands of anyone (for the moment, the king) who might wish to use force to no good end, the other the need to plug loopholes, to ensure that any arrangement, even a temporary one, was watertight.[103] It was this that the king was determined to resist. A straw in the wind had already blown in over impressment. Since the recent Act meant that impressment was not legal save under defined conditions, it is worth noting that Charles, on 1 March, a mere two weeks after giving his assent to the act, had issued a commission to Leicester to raise 6,000 troops who 'shall voluntarily undertake the same service by accepting of prest money'.[104] He needed to combine the bill with a gap for raising troops by other means, and his opponents needed to plug that gap.

While the hope persisted that some agreed and legal means could be found to raise troops for Ireland, many within Parliament sought a show of joint

[100] Fletcher, *Outbreak*, pp. 231–2.
[101] *Private journals*, ii, 169–72; [Husbands], *Exact collection*, pp. 141–3. For a more extreme draft version, see Russell, *Fall*, p. 489.
[102] Fletcher, *Outbreak*, p. 232. For the subsequent debate over the bill, see [Husbands], *Exact collection*, pp. 157–60, 171–3, 173–8.
[103] Cf. Burgess, *Ancient constitution*, pp. 197–9, 204.
[104] PRO SO 3/540 (p. 270b). This was one day after his offer to issue commissions to lords lieutenant named by Parliament or, if additional powers were sought, to accede to an Act of Parliament which vested powers in the crown first, then in the appointees. His insistence that thus would such powers be defined could still allow for a gap for additional prerogative powers outside any such legislation: [Husbands], *Exact collection*, pp. 90–2.

king–Parliament validation, while covertly transferring real power from the monarch. Meanwhile, as any officer could verify, raising an initial army was one thing, but a constant supply of recruits was essential, especially given the horrific wastage rates experienced by the English forces in 1640s Ireland.[105] The 15 April vote that any who advised the king's raising of 'forces for Ireland, or otherwise, . . . is an enemy to the state' was not an attempt to shut down recruitment, since it coincided with the delivery of a request from the commissioners for Ireland that their instructions be amended to permit them to oversee the recruitment of up to 10,000 fresh troops for Ireland.[106] Presumably encompassed within this were the ongoing plans for adventurers to sponsor their own expedition, under officers of their choosing, with parliamentary approval, and a further scheme for an 'additional' or 'sea adventure' restricted to the coasts of Ireland. The Houses processed the various measures during April, and dispatched to the king for his approval the draft warrant for the levying of troops by the commissioners, and a draft commission for the sea adventure.[107]

As the military stand-off within England escalated it was hardly surprising that, on 16 May, the Houses learnt that the king had spurned the amended instruction for the commissioners. Instead he issued yet another warrant to Leicester, to raise 4,000 soldiers, significantly, again, volunteers. Leicester denied seeking such a mandate, and the Commons appointed a committee to prepare an order for raising troops for Ireland.[108] It was in this context that the Commons took the decisive step of themselves drafting ordinances mandating the raising of troops for the adventure expeditions.[109] The Lords needed to be persuaded, though, and persuaded through recourse to some legal mandate. Though the Impressment Act had earlier been advanced as grounds for the planned extension of the commissioners' powers, the Commons now turned to a convoluted interpretation of the adventure legislation. This was presented as authorizing the expenditure of funds on the sending and supply of troops until Parliament declared that Ireland was duly 'reduced'; logically, this could not be accomplished until such forces were raised, and so Parliament's duty under the Act would be thwarted unless it had power to raise the requisite soldiers. As Serjeant Wilde argued, 'At common law if a tree be sold to any person, he hath liberty to come and cut it down and carry it away'. It was enough to persuade the majority of the remaining peers. Their decision lodged in Parliament ample power over

[105] Lenihan, *Confederate Catholics at war*, pp. 58–62.

[106] *Private journals*, ii, 412, 419–20.

[107] *CJ*, ii, 531, 533, 536, 540–1, 546, 554, 562–3; *LJ*, v, 5–6, 12, 15–16, 33–4, 56–7; *Private journals*, ii, 198–9, 213, 227, 244, 305–6.

[108] *LJ*, v, 65–6, 73; *CJ*, ii, 582; *Private journals*, ii, 322, 351, 456.

[109] *LJ*, v, 82; *CJ*, ii, 583; *Private journals*, ii, 362.

military intervention in Ireland, at least to their own satisfaction. Yet that same day, 28 May, when the upper house learnt from Leicester that the king was willing to amend the terms of his recent warrant for 4,000 volunteers, they seized the opportunity offered and voted to ask the monarch for a further warrants for 6,000 more men.[110] The royal warrant to Leicester was seized upon by the commissioners as a means of topping up depleted units in Ireland.[111]

Westminster was still straining for a legal framework for its Irish war, one which, for the parliamentary leadership, incorporated the king but blocked him from acting unilaterally. Yet across June and July the parliamentarian alliance which had stood together as recently as the Militia Ordinance was collapsing. Conservative peers who were willing to take aggressive force out of the hands of the king were not willing to place it in the hands of his opponents.[112] The growing numbers of those who were not willing to tarry for the magistrate in assembling volunteer bands for national defence in England were no more willing to delay over Ireland. Royal rejection of the commission for the sea adventure, itself the venture of a ginger group beyond the main body of subscribers,[113] had prompted the Lords to urge the king to re-consider, but eventually the Houses were persuaded actually to launch the venture on the basis of an ordinance, albeit with Leicester entering his protest.[114] By 5 July the vote on the raising of the main adventure expedition had also been transmuted into an ordinance for immediate action.[115] Westminster was only days away from authorizing the raising of a volunteer army for service in England.[116] The ongoing needs of the war in Ireland had been entwined with the broader debates on armed force in England at every step.

The adventure legislation could also be used to stymie policy options. The king had been accused of discouraging the adventurers with his proposal to travel to Ireland, and claims that some had stalled their subscriptions

---

[110] *LJ*, v, 88–9, 91; *Private journals*, ii, 383. Separate authorization was secured to beat the drum for 1,000 volunteers for the sea adventure on 31 May: *LJ*, v, 92, 95.

[111] *Private journals*, iii, 386, 404–5.

[112] Russell, *Fall*, pp. 511–7; Richard Tuck, ' "The Ancient Law of Freedom": John Selden and the civil war', in John Morrill (ed.), *Reactions to the English civil war 1642–1649* (London, 1982), pp. 152–3.

[113] Robert Brenner, *Merchants and revolution: commercial change, political conflict and London's overseas traders, 1550–1653* (Princeton, 1993) pp. 403–9.

[114] C. H. Firth and R. S. Rait (eds), *Acts and ordinances of the interregnum 1642–1660* (3 vols, London, 1911), i, 9–12; *LJ*, v, 102, 105, 114–15, 140, 142, 143–5; *Private journals*, ii, 19–20, 89, 91, 93–4. At one point the Commons had even urged the expedition to sail ahead of its commission, which was to be sent afterwards on a pinnace.

[115] *LJ*, v, 181.

[116] Fletcher, *Outbreak*, pp. 338–40.

may well have been correct.[117] The commissioners had long considered it a priority to attempt to sustain strategically vital but isolated fortresses like Duncannon (in the south-east), Limerick and Galway (in the west).[118] In June they learnt that Galway had been received into terms by the local grandee, Clanricard, in conditions which raised the possibility of a neutrality based on toleration.[119] The lords justices were cautious enough not to condemn Clanricard's action, while noting that they would not have taken such a course, and would prefer its dissolution. Parliament rose to the challenge and condemned the articles on the basis of the adventurer legislation, voting to move the king to revoke the protection granted to Galway and to call on the lords justices to summon it to surrender 'absolutely' to the King's mercy.[120] The Dublin authorities had added a call for advice on how to transform recent successes into an offensive war, and a request for direction on the 'execution of his majesty's justice upon these unnatural and unthankful rebels'. Likewise they reported their expulsions of Catholic clergy from Dublin and wondered whether they should consider the preparation of bills 'for confirming here all laws in force in England against Jesuits, priests, friars etc., as also against Papists'. For the moment they had forborne to expel all Catholic inhabitants, though if king or commissioners 'shall adjudge it fit to be now done, we shall readily do it'. One at least of the commissioners was more than ready; Oliver Cromwell had it agreed that the commissioners should consider the issue of the estimated 10,000 Catholics in Dublin, whose presence was deemed to demand the deployment there of a garrison of equal size.[121]

Galway raised questions of policy, Limerick of strategy. The besieged castle there was a prime target for an energetic 'forward' policy.[122] As summer passed, it became clear that the presence in Ireland of English and Scottish armies, each 10,000 strong and accompanied by even more numerous local allies, had raised expectations in some quarters which had not been met. One informed observer in London noted that some there thought 'little service had been done of moment, considering the great stoar of forces nowe at Dublin and in Leynster'. It would 'not be beleiued here, that there is any want of victualls or other necessaries there to keep the army in the feild to

---

[117] [Husbands], *Exact collection*, pp. 141–3; *Private journals*, ii, 178–9, 185; MacCormack, 'Irish adventurers', p. 34.

[118] *Private journals*, ii, 409–28.

[119] For Clanricard, see Ó Siochrú, *Confederate Ireland*, pp. 37–9.

[120] HMC *Ormonde MSS*, new series, ii, 148–51; *LJ*, v, 164, 166, 167; *CJ*, ii, pp. 640, 643; *Private journals*, iii, 384, 119–20, 126, 131–2, 133, 135.

[121] HMC *Ormonde MSS*, new series, ii, 138–40; *Private journals*, iii, 134.

[122] In fact, the castle had fallen four days before the Commons heard the letter from Inchiquin, acting lord president, detailing its imminent capture: Hogan (ed.), *Letters and papers*, pp. 42–3.

pursue the reables'.[123] Westminster had agreed to take into its support the extensive local forces raised in Ireland to supplement the old standing army.[124] Limerick's fate prompted unrealistic calls for the diversion of existing forces from Leinster and Ulster to the relief of Munster. It is perhaps no coincidence that such calls were being made just a few days ahead of the moves to divert the adventure expedition, designed for just that end.[125]

By 25 July rumours were circulating of the re-deployment in England of the adventurer regiments.[126] Five days later came the raid on the adventure funds for the support of the English army, at the instigation of the Committee of Safety, the executive body of a Parliament now bereft of the king's supporters and gathering an army in defiance of their monarch. To this end, the main adventure expedition was to be re-deployed to Essex's English army. D'Ewes alleged that it was perpetrated at a packed and 'thin' meeting of the adventurer committee.[127] Yet there is little evidence of a deep-laid plan for the diversion of resources. Spokesmen for the MP-adventurers were soon calling for the repayment of the 'loan'.[128] The commissioners had persisted with their efforts to send supplies to Ireland right up to the last moment. One adventurer regiment, under Lord Kerry, was indeed dispatched to Ireland, arriving in Munster in October. A £100,000 loan secured from the city companies for the Irish war was indeed collected, and spent on Ireland, outweighing the sums diverted from the adventure coffers. Though the king was handed a huge propaganda coup he was hardly above blame. Royalist seizures of supplies destined for Ireland may have been of limited value but were realistically presented as sufficiently threatening to close down the major supply lines overland from London to Chester or Bristol.[129] Nor could he take much credit from diverting the last of the navy's vessels off the Irish coast, especially given that the insurgents were now beginning to see some much-needed sustenance from continental Europe.

If those left at Westminster believed the line they had spun on Ireland over the previous year, then what they faced there was but one theatre of war upon Protestant England. What they had done, on such a reading, was to re-deploy resources to where the need was greatest in the war on popery. In turn, the

[123] Valentia to Eustace, 20 July 1642, Carte, _Ormonde_, v, pp. 339–41.

[124] _Private journals_, iii, 378–9; _CJ_, ii, 662–3.

[125] _CJ_, ii, 675, 677; _Private journals_, iii, 190, 399, 221–3; _LJ_, v, 226–7. Cf. the August proposals to send the 'whole body' of the Scottish army to the vicinity of Limerick, _Private journals_, iii, 424.

[126] _CSP Venice, 1642–43_, p. 107.

[127] _CJ_, ii, 698; _Private journals_, iii, 301 and note 2. The Committee of Safety also drew upon the clothes obtained by the adventurers to supply Essex's army: _CSPD 1641–3_, pp. 366, 274.

[128] _Private journals_, iii, 331–2.

[129] _CJ_, ii, 736. D'Ewes describes the Commons' consideration of the incident as being among 'other trivial things': _Private journals_, iii, 316–17.

language of royal condemnation is instructive. That the king should ask 'whether they who divert the Men and Money collected for the Relief of distressed *Ireland*, to raise forces against their Prince . . . do not joyn with the Popish and Jesuitical Faction in the bloody Massacre of many thousand Protestants in that miserable Kingdom?' betokened the fact that he and his supporters too were reading or at least inscribing the Irish conflict within a "Protestant war" characterized by priestly malice and 'bloody Massacre'.[130] From a shared language of rebellion had sprouted a shared reading of massacre and religious conflict. It was one which resonated with public opinion, at least as conveyed through petitions and publications. Of course it covered divergences, quite sharp in cases, over the most appropriate policies for dealing with Ireland, whether in moral or material terms. But it made it hard for the king and his supporters to claw back a position which represented flexibility and adaptation as virtues in the Irish conflict. Only the eventual equation of Irish with English rebellion allowed the king some room for an alternative ideological position.

Ireland caused the English political nation to pull together and to pull apart because it abutted so clearly on to issues at the heart of the English political debate. At least rhetorically, all shades of opinion needed to commit themselves to 'reducing' the rebellion, and almost certainly did so with a will. The 'constitutional royalist' Sir John Culpepper made his call for a political lexicon sensitive to the presence of loyal Catholics, but he countered the 'additional instruction' with a forthright insistence on the need to intervene in Ireland, and spearheaded the Houses' efforts to provide troops and supplies for Munster in December–January 1641–42. And, for whatever reason, he urged Charles to concede the Impressment Act.[131] Leicester, a stickler for legal propriety, had hesitated over acting to raise troops until he had royal as well as parliamentary validation. Yet he had proved reliable in his support of Scottish intervention, in his concern for a 'general warrant' or for the appointment of the commissioners, and in his disclosure of the details of the Dillon mission. In 1642 Charles seemed to trust him enough to urge him to Ireland, and only after his protests are there hints at dismissal. Yet throughout May and June he went beyond even the conservative upper House in standing out against actions without legal warrant, sometimes as a lone voice. In June–July he remained sufficiently trusted at Westminster to have his reasons for delay accepted, and money voted him for his own expenses and to pay the army in Ireland.[132] Then on the verge of departing for Ireland, he headed to York for the king's approval.

---

[130] Rushworth, *Historical collections*, iv, 767, 775.

[131] D'Ewes *Journals*, pp. 98–9, 254–5; *CJ*, ii, 360, 362; *Private journals*, i, 45, 99; David L. Smith, *Constitutional royalism and the search for settlement, c. 1640–1649* (Cambridge, 1994), p. 88.

[132] *LJ*, v, 95, 123, 129–30, 143, 227; HMC *Buccleuch MSS*, i, p. 298. Leicester also dissented from votes to raised forces in England.

Such a middle road was one which Protestant Ireland, as a whole, was keen to tread. Yet the reality of its situation was that it was those who remained with Parliament who had taken the burden not merely of logistical support but of the solid commitment to victory over popery and the Irish which most of them would espouse. They had their own leverage within the Houses. Clotworthy was everywhere, from the breakthrough measures to the most minor votes on munitions or cash disbursements. It was he who presented the interim plan for immediate Scottish intervention in January, he who sponsored the measures for merchant delivery of supplies to safe ports; Clotworthy was there as the adventure proposals were sifted and formed into legislation and always on hand with fresh news from Ireland.[133] The point is not that he was a one-man lobby for Ireland; plenty of other MPs did sterling work in forwarding the practicalities of armed engagement. But he symbolizes the ongoing involvement of Protestant Ireland in England's Irish war, of the new colony with its calls for aid, its bank of support and its ideological affinity with the ends of the war.[134]

[133] For a smattering of examples, see *CJ*, ii, 342, 357, 392; *Private journals*, i, 16, 147, 162–3, 169, 395.
[134] Cf. Perceval-Maxwell, *Outbreak*, pp. 273–4.

3

Making loyalists,
fighting 'papists', 1642–43

As England stumbled into war in the summer of 1642 both armed camps
could not but be aware of the formidable armed might of Protestant Ireland.
Westminster, Dublin and Edinburgh had co-sponsored the build-up of arms
in pursuit of a war to victory to which the king too appeared to be bound.
As the English polity imploded, it was the king who adopted the more
pragmatic approach to Ireland, one concentrated on securing control of
armed force, one justified in terms of logistical realities and one determined
by broad strategic priorities. Troops could be withdrawn from an unwinnable
war in Ireland if they could safely be deployed to quash rebellion in England.
Parliament retained the more 'ideological' stance, committed to maintaining
the war effort in Ireland as part of a grand campaign against popery. At the
same time it was an approach which had the potential to reach out to allies,
in Ireland and in Scotland, drawn to professions more principled than royal
realpolitik. Protestant Ireland, for the most part, remained resolute in standing
aside from the quarrels in England, if with a certain amount of hand-wringing,
and concerned at being abandoned to defeat at the hands of an increasingly
well-organized and militarily effective Catholic enemy. It fell to the council in
Dublin to make decisions which would inexorably align it with one or other
English armed camp. Its reluctance to declare such an allegiance saw English
political labels foisted on it in accordance with its preferred policy for Ireland,
a neat reversal of the way in which Parliament would increasingly describe
the English war in terms originally applied to Ireland. This chapter will
concentrate on the evolution of those divergent policies by king and
Parliament and the crucial struggle for control of Dublin, its government
and its army.

The spring and summer of 1642 had seen the success of Protestant arms in
all the main theatres of war in Ireland. Locally raised forces alongside the
newly arrived forces from Scotland (to Ulster) and England (to Dublin and
Munster) had won a spring of victories. Outside Ulster, though, the ability
to control territory proved more problematic, with armies being fielded at

once too large for the outposts retained in the winter of 1641–42 to sustain, but not large enough to hold and garrison expanding blocs of territory. As the summer passed, Protestant forces faced the 'destabilizing' prospects of reduced supplies from an England drifting to war, and the 'pressure on the uneasy Protestant alliance' of English divisions. Their Catholic opponents benefited from military reorganization, under the influence of returned veterans of continental service, and attained a degree of political unity and structural coherence with the emergence of the oath-bound 'confederate Catholics', whose first representative general assembly met in October 1642.[1]

If any bridge remained between the Irish policies of king and Parliament then it was girded by such constitutionally impeccable institutions as the lord lieutenancy, the commission for Ireland and, from the other shore, the privy council in Dublin. The strength of the commission was also its weakness, for the political heavyweights who had diligently attended its proceedings were soon drafted on to Westminster's new executive Committee of Safety, or dispatched to stir up the cause beyond the confines of the Houses.[2] Despite a reduced quorum, meetings became less frequent and less well attended, yet criticism from the adventurers in the Commons ran up against the indispensability of the commissioners' mandate under the Great Seal of England. The upshot was the formation of a hybrid body of all commissioners, all MP-adventurers and other named MPs, to meet when the commissioners could not.[3] The new 'committee for the affairs of Ireland' would in practice take primary responsibility for the ongoing sustenance of the war in Ireland for the next six months, acting in conjunction with a new eleven-strong London adventurers' committee.[4] Regular meetings are recorded, several times weekly, from 4 October.[5] It was the beginning of a process whereby the minutiae of Irish business were overseen by a succession of select committees with limited executive functions, liable to competition from other bodies as each succeeding emergency spawned further deliberative bodies. While numbers of MPs would be named to such committees, active

---

[1] Jane Ohlmeyer, 'The civil wars in Ireland', in John Kenyon and Jane Ohlmeyer (eds), *The civil wars* (Oxford, 1998), pp. 75–7, 81–3. The confederate organization was topped with a powerful Supreme Council. The divisions within the confederate ranks would become apparent in the years ahead.

[2] Thus six of the seven peers were appointed to the Committee of Safety, and Pym, Holles, Marten, Vane and Evelyn were also in regular attendance there: Glow, 'Committee of Safety', p. 313.

[3] *LJ*, v, 303; *CJ*, ii, 723, 726, 750; *Private journals*, iii, 332–3.

[4] *CJ*, ii, 780.

[5] The minutes of this committee survive as BL Additional MS 4,782. The committee was granted the right to receive copies of all orders and resolutions relating to Ireland; the order-book is printed, from the MS in the Bodleian Library, as 'Rawlinson manuscripts, class A.110', in *Analecta Hibernica*, iv (1932), 1–98. The Lords appear to have failed to respond to the establishment of the new body: *CJ*, ii, 808, 810, 812; *LJ*, v, 400.

participation was increasingly confined to a small caucus within the Houses and their associates in the City. The attendance lists for the 1642 committee, dating from February 1643, show that those in regular attendance were few, with a core group based around the chairman, John Goodwyn (or Goodwin), two 'commissioners' recently returned from a stint in Dublin, Robert Reynolds and Robert Goodwyn, the three Irish-based MPs Clotworthy, Arthur Jones and William Jephson, all of them only episodically in London, and a handful of adventurer-MPs.[6]

The replacement of the commissioners by a body lodged within the English Parliament's institutional framework, and with an outlier in the City of London, was a not unimportant shift in the relationship between Westminster and Dublin. Not that Westminster would not strain to incorporate the legitimist claims generated by both the commission itself and the adventure legislation for years to come.[7] The other constitutionally impeccable link between England and Ireland, the office of lord lieutenant, was also suffering a slow death as Leicester fretted away the months. By mid-August Parliament had resorted to harrying and threatening him to push him to Ireland, while he protested his 'not being yet dispatched, by reason of his Majesty's commands'.[8] Instead the Commons responded to a further initiative from the adventurer-MPs on 29 August, a proposal to send two MPs to Ireland 'to be of the Council of War, and in Commission with them that are of that Council' with the London adventurers having the option of adding two further members 'to be assistant to these Committees'. There were even suggestions that the lower House discuss 'the nomination of a Captain General of all the Forces in *Ireland*'.[9]

Across September the Commons busied themselves with arrangements for the departure of the commissioners, eventually naming Robert Reynolds and Robert Goodwyn for the posts, while the London adventurers took up their option of nominating a member, Captain William Tucker.[10] Leicester, back at Westminster, found his champions in the upper House, particularly among 'peace lords' like Northumberland and Holland. The peers voted their satisfaction with his conduct, and amended the commissioners' instructions to ensure they did not trench upon the honour of the lord

[6] BL Additional MS 4,782; Armstrong, 'Ireland at Westminster', pp. 83–8.

[7] Little, 'English Parliament', pp. 111–12.

[8] *CJ*, ii, 721, 734. On 15–16 August the Houses had insisted that Leicester be at Chester within a week, 'And if he shall fail herein, that then both Houses may consider of chusing another'.

[9] *CJ*, ii, 742. Debate on a captain-general bore no fruit, though it seems that Leslie, commander of the Scottish army in Ulster, was mooted as a possible candidate: *CJ*, ii, 755, 757, 765; *A Perfect Diurnall*, 5–12 September 1642, E239 (17), p. 3; *Perfect Diurnall*, 12–19 September 1642, E240 (5), p. 6.

[10] For Tucker see Brenner, *Merchants and revolution*, pp. 118–20, 184, 186, 188, 189, 190, 195, 414, 449; Keith Lindley, *Popular politics and religion in civil war London* (Aldershot, 1997), pp. 68, 208–9, 274.

lieutenant, to whom 'the Ordering of the war belongs'.[11] Voices in the Commons ranged from those, like Henry Marten, who laid an array of sins to Leicester's charge, from obstructing plans for Ireland to failing to implement the Militia Ordinance in Kent, to cool proponents like St John who alluded merely to the delays which would ensue were Parliament to challenge him in his position.[12] It was the commissioners who were dispatched first, accompanied by £20,000 and supplies for the beleaguered Dublin government.[13] Leicester had been pressed to disclose the instructions he had received from the king, but even then his departure was delayed and he set off in November, with the Commons' approval, but not their money.[14]

Leicester retained a residual importance as a hinge around which a joint royal-parliamentarian policy towards Ireland could swing, but he retained the full confidence of neither party. For the moment, an aristocratic lord lieutenant cursed with a capacity to see both sides to a dispute was being secluded behind humble committeemen boosted with the 'Credence, Power, and Esteem, of a Committee sent over thither by the Advice and Authority of . . . Parliament', to whom all Irish officials, from the lord lieutenant down, should give 'their best furtherance and Assistance'.[15] Their instructions, embedded among the speeches in the Commons and the opinions of the London newsletters, set out the parliamentarian agenda for Ireland. In terms of the war itself, confidence of victory rubbed shoulders with concern over inefficiency, corruption, lack of zeal and even treachery. The commissioners were to advise themselves of all things concerning the state of the war and vote on all debates on its conduct; to combat promotion by 'indirect Means' and ensure officers were 'well-affected'; and to report such civil officials as merited commendation.[16] Knowledge of 'the certaine truth of the condition' of Ireland was at a premium in an atmosphere of heightened rumour, including claims of Spanish intervention in Ireland.[17] Shortly

---

[11] *LJ*, v, 357–9, 360, 370, 373. Northumberland was Leicester's brother-in-law and long-term ally. Leicester's letters to him were printed by the Houses: see [Robert Sidney, earl of Leicester], *A letter from the Lord of Leicester* (1642) E118 (48); R. W. Blencowe (ed.), *Sydney papers* (London, 1825), pp. 363–8.

[12] *CJ*, ii, 781; Walter Yonge, *Walter Yonge's diary of proceedings in the House of Commons 1642–1645*, ed. Christopher Thompson (Wivenhoe, 1986), i, *18 Sept. 1642–7 March, 1643*, pp. 16–17.

[13] *CJ*, ii, 756, 760, 782, 787, 793; HMC *Portland MSS*, i (London, 1891), 65; HMC *Ormonde MSS*, new series, ii, 219–20.

[14] Leicester eventually allowed his instructions to be placed in Pym's hands. They were copied but not read in the Commons: *CJ*, ii, 795, 797, 798, 802, 811, 812, 823, 835; *LJ*, v, 389, 393, 394, 432, 433; BL Additional MS 31,116, fo. 6b.

[15] Firth and Rait (eds), *Acts and ordinances*, i, 32–3.

[16] *LJ*, v, 364–5.

[17] *A Continuation of Certain Speciall and Remarkable Passages*, 29 September–1 October 1642, E240 (17), p. 3. *Perfect Diurnall*, 19–26 September 1642, E240 (13) saw the committee as needed specifically to try the truth of O'Neill's alleged commission from the king.

before his departure Reynolds vented the latest 'news' from Dublin, D'Ewes recording allegations that Dublin forces 'had trifled away ther time this summer' and of unreliability or treachery at the highest levels, notably claims that Lord Lambert, governor of Dublin, 'was soe Irishified as hee cared not much for ther safetie', that there was a 'popish' paymaster and that 'recusants are admitted to the councell table'. By contrast, the Scottish general, Leslie, was lauded as successful in Ulster.[18]

News from Lord Forbes, commander of the piratical sea adventure, devastating the western and southern coasts of Ireland, were placed before the Commons by Hugh Peter, fresh from the scene. Forbes was clear that '5 or 6000 men will take Limerick and Galloway [Galway] and ende the warre before xmas'. This sanguine assessment, and the highlighting of the region in question – 'the strength of the rebellion lies here, and ther would be no difficultie in subduing the rest' – kept alive the summer's scheme for the recapture of Limerick. Reynolds and Goodwyn pressed such a strategy, however unrealistic, on the more hard-headed Dublin executive during their stint in Ireland.[19] They would also advance with full force other elements of their mandate. They were to pursue the improving of revenue and the reduction of costs, 'by Way of Adventure, or otherwise', and were warranted to pursue a systematic programme of anti-Catholic measures. The Commons had long since resolved that Catholics in Dublin 'and thereabouts' be disarmed, and that 'principal Papists' be 'secured'.[20] Now the commissioners were to ensure that all garrisons and the army were to be cleared of Catholics; that steps be taken against all who claimed neutrality; that all penal legislation should be enforced and the conviction of 'rebels' secured.[21]

Across the winter of 1642–43 London newsbooks and pamphlets jostled together accounts of the 'miraculous' victories of Protestant forces in Ireland and the nigh-desperate conditions endured in the Protestant quarters.[22] This reflected a Parliament where perceptions of Ireland were constantly poised between hope and despondency. Garrisons and armies were under pressure,

---

[18] BL Harleian MS 163, fo. 383b. The letter which Reynolds claimed to cite called for a committee to be sent to Dublin to tackle the problems outlined. Cf. *Speciall Passages*, 13–20 September 1642, E118 (10), p. 45; *Speciall Passages* 20–27 September 1642, E119 (2), p. 51; *Continuation*, 21–4 September 1642, E240 (9); *Perfect Diurnall*, 26 September–3 October 1642, E240 (19), p. 2.

[19] *CJ*, ii, 808 (14 October); *A true copie of two letters brought by Mr. Peters . . . from my L. Forbes* (London, 1642) E121 (44).

[20] *CJ*, ii, 735 (24 August).

[21] *LJ*, v, 364–5.

[22] The decline in published pamphlets recorded by Lindley ('Impact of 1641', p. 44) was offset by the coverage of Irish events in the proliferating parliamentarian newsbook publications. See for example the sequence of letters reportedly from Kinsale printed in *Speciall Passages* for January–February 1643: see e.g. nos 22 (E84 (36)), 25 (E86 (39)), 27 (E89 (17)).

from Derry to Duncannon, with money and munitions in especially short supply. Across Ireland, Protestant forces had long since built up networks of contacts, supplementing or by-passing Dublin, in the search for sustenance and validation. Westminster had become a point of convergence for agents representing, and lobbying for, provinces, garrisons, even regiments. Displaced clergymen like Robert Barkley, dean of Clogher, rubbed shoulders with seconded officers, or the influential lords and gentlemen whom the Dublin government sought to tap in its interests.[23] Yet the new Irish committee was saddled not only with the massive 'loan' to the English war effort, which it unsuccessfully fought to have repaid, but with a plethora of inherited debts for supplies sent but not paid for, and no fresh sources of revenue.[24] It struggled manfully just to get some supplies afloat to Ireland, even as delayed repayment on merchants' certificates threatened to sink the system completely.[25]

Among those dispatched to London in the hope of obtaining supplies were three senior Ulster officers, colonels Sir James Montgomery, Arthur Hill and Audley Mervyn and, from Munster, Lieutenant-Colonel Sir Hardress Waller.[26] They secured the permission of the Committee of Safety to petition the king 'so to reflect upon the bleeding condition of that perishing kingdom, that timely relief might be afforded'. The king's reply, written by Falkland, breathed sympathy while dodging commitment. He offered to receive specific requests for assistance, and insisted that 'the present miserable condition and certain future loss of Ireland to be one of the principal motives most earnestly to desire that the present distractions of this kingdom might be composed'. The incident is indicative of how king and Parliament were positioning themselves over the Irish war. The colonels brought the matter back before Parliament with their 'Conceptions'. These were, firstly, the overriding need for an English accommodation if Ireland was to be delivered. Second came the need for immediate war supplies. Lastly, failing this also, they hoped Parliament would 'allow them a favourable Construction' if they were forced to accept harsh terms from their enemies.[27] The following day John Goodwyn, chairman of the Irish committee, did manage to squeeze through the Commons a long-delayed report on Irish supplies, but since it dealt only with debts already incurred it offered little in the way of

---

[23] By 27 May 1643 the Irish committee had to insist that officers in London should elect one agent to represent each province in the distribution of provisions, an attempt to curb the proliferation of representatives: BL Add. MS 4,782, fo. 190.

[24] BL Additional MS 4,782, fos 5a–b, 17a–b, 64a–b.

[25] Armstrong, 'Protestant Ireland', appendix 3, pp. 340–8.

[26] For recent resolutions on supply for Ulster and Munster, see for example BL Additional MS 4,782, fos 14a–17a, 27a, 34b–35a, 35b–37b; *LJ*, v, 482.

[27] *LJ*, v, 483–5; Clarendon, *History*, ii, 491–2; *The petition of the committees for Ireland to His Majestie: with His Majesties answer thereunto* (Oxford, 1642).

encouragement for the pursuit of the war there. Instead the surrounding debate witnessed incredulous MPs demanding that Goodwyn 'give an account how things came to such & such prices'. Overall the comments of the four officers 'were not relished by ye ho[use]' as leaning towards 'an accommodacon yt might be pr[e]judiciall to ye Privil[ege] of Parliam[en]t, Religion & Lib[er]ties of ye Sub[jec]t'.[28]

Parliament blended a commitment to unrelenting war with anguished incredulity over the likely costs. Meanwhile the king had retreated only to wriggle free of the bands in which Parliament had bound him over Ireland. His ability to rinse his hands of blame and generously dollop out sympathy was to prove useful in gaining the hearts and hands of Protestant forces in Ireland, a stratagem focused on the bloated garrisons in and around Dublin, and helped forward by Ormond as lieutenant-general. In the summer a petition had been drafted by two senior officers, Sir Thomas Wharton and Sir Robert King, to be sent from the officers in Ireland to king and to Parliament with the expressed intention of promoting reconciliation in England. Ormond intervened to secure a wording leaning less towards Parliament, with the result that the petition was withdrawn. He posted it to the king anyway, adding assurances of the good affection, valour and wants of the army.[29] By September, rumours were circulating that Charles intended to summon the English army back from Ireland. More empirically grounded reports noted how he had summoned individual officers from their Irish commands.[30] In September, too, he had granted Ormond a commission securing his command of the army in Ireland even in the event of the arrival of his superior, Leicester.[31]

The position of the Dublin army was certainly bleak. In the depth of winter it was marched forth explicitly to keep busy any disaffected minds or idle hands, and in the hope of garnering resources.[32] Parliament's newly arrived commissioners got to work with a will, and not without a warm reception in Dublin for some items on their agenda. Bills to 'abolish Popery, and to attaint the Rebels' had already been raised, albeit unsuccessfully, in the Dublin Parliament,[33] and the commissioners were committed to re-launching such initiatives. They also spurred forward a proclamation from the Irish Council

---

[28] BL Additional MS 31,116, fo. 14a; *CJ*, ii, 883–4.

[29] Carte, *Ormonde*, ii, 297–300; Carte MS 3, fos 282, 289, 376ff., 378–9; MS 63, fo. 108.

[30] See *Speciall passages*, 20–27 September 1642, E118 (45), pp. 49–50 for instances of officers withdrawn from Ireland.

[31] This followed a lengthy quarrel between Leicester and Ormond over appointments to military commands: Carte, *Ormonde*, ii, 287–97, 347–9.

[32] HMC *Ormonde MSS*, new series, ii, 225–6; see also [J. Skout], *Exceeding certain and true newes . . .* (London, 1643) E84 (26) for conditions in Dublin.

[33] *LJI*, i, 181–3.

for mustering of troops under oath to prevent fraudulent returns, and advanced
an Irish 'adventure' as a means of assuring officers of future remuneration of
their arrears.[34] Wharton and King, tellingly, took the lead in seeking to
adventure their pay at once, but met with divided counsel among the English
commissioners. Reynolds was willing to pledge 'under his own hand' that
their subscriptions would be honoured, despite the concern of his more cautious
colleagues, given the failure, thus far, to pilot a bill through the Dublin
Parliament.[35]

Yet the commissioners soon met with a backlash, and one they could be
forgiven for believing to have been far from spontaneous. On 19 December
army officers set a petition before the council outlining their grievances:
lack of pay, corrupt distribution of such funds as were available and the
challenge to their integrity implicit in oath-bound musters. The security of
arrears was raised, and the right to have these paid in money, not in
subscriptions 'which they conceive to bee a hard condition for them to venter
their lives on'. Indeed they raised the possibility that they might 'deserve the
rewards in lands without other price, as well as in former rebellions in this
kingdome others have done'.[36] This petition (or remonstrance) was
precipitated by the return to Dublin of Major Henry Warren, a professional
soldier of long standing sent by the officers to put their case before king and
Parliament.[37] Warren may already have been engaged in conveying
clandestine correspondence from the king to Ormond, perhaps concerning
the prospects for a truce.[38] Certainly the message he brought seriously
damaged the credibility of the commissioners in Dublin and the Houses at
Westminster, for he alleged that a 'principal person' on the Irish committee
had said that if £500 would save Ireland they would not spend so much.
Warren may have 'brought noe answer at all, but framed one, as he pleased,
from some particular persons' but the damage was done.[39]

The council appears to have concocted a relatively satisfactory reply to
the army petition, though its anxiety can been seen in its order that all citizens
deliver half their plate to pay the army; a mere £1,200 was collected.[40]

---

[34] Hogan (ed.), *Letters and papers*, pp. 168–70; Carte, *Ormonde*, ii, 392–3; see PRO SP 63/
260/78 proclamation for oath-bound musters (18 November).

[35] Tucker's journal, printed in Gilbert (ed.), *Irish confederation*, ii, 176, 185.

[36] Carte, *Ormonde*, v, 395–7.

[37] For Warren see P. R. Newman, *Royalist officers in England and Wales, 1642–1660* (London,
1981), p. 398.

[38] Charles to Ormond, 12 January 1643, Carte, *Ormonde*, v, 1. See William Kelly, 'John
Barry: an Irish Catholic royalist in the 1640s', in Ó Siochrú (ed.), *Kingdoms in crisis*, p. 148,
note 44.

[39] Gilbert (ed.), *Irish confederation*, ii, 177; cf. *CJ*, ii, 984.

[40] Raymond Gillespie, 'The Irish economy at war, 1641–1652', in Jane H. Ohlmeyer (ed.),
Ireland from independence to occupation, 1641–1660 (Cambridge, 1995), p. 167.

Ormond, who had acted as a conduit for the petition in Dublin, dispatched a copy to Oxford and won words of concern from the king.[41] By January a second petition was in circulation, reaching the major outlying garrisons in Leinster, such as Drogheda and Dundalk. It sought to promote an appeal directly to the king since Parliament had failed the officers.[42] Quarrels erupted at the council board over the choice of Major Michael Woodhouse as an agent to the king but Ormond won his dispatch over the opposition of the English commissioners and, it would appear, the lords justices.[43] A fight was on for the allegiance of the men of war in Dublin. The stakes would soon be raised when, on 11 January, the king issued a commission to Ormond and others to treat with the confederate Catholics.[44] If acted upon, it would breach the solid front erected by Dublin and Westminster a year earlier. Ormond relayed to his monarch the discontent such news brought to the some on the privy council, and to the English committee. Meanwhile there were hints, as yet kept private, that the king intended Ormond to take upon himself greater authority within the realm.[45]

In the meantime, successful implementation of the royal design meant blocking opposition within Dublin. Ormond expressed concern that Parliament's commissioners were attempting to woo the out-garrisons so as to construct an anti-treaty power within the armed forces.[46] As the Dublin army geared itself up to an expedition to the south-east the lords justices and the commissioners were perceived to be advocating vesting command not in Ormond, but in the youthful Philip Sidney, Viscount Lisle, son of the absentee Leicester.[47] The leading confederate, Richard Bellings, in his later account of the period, claimed that the motivation behind such a move was not only that victory would cast doubt on the advantage of proceeding with negotiations with the confederates, but that Lisle would receive the honour of the enterprise and 'soe winn upon the souldier enriched by the spoyles of the country under his command, as to affect him beyond the Marquis of Ormonde'.[48] Ormond's motives in seeking command of the expedition

---

[41] Carte, *Ormonde*, v, 399–400, 381–2.

[42] Carte, *Ormonde*, v, 398–9; HMC *Ormonde MSS*, old series, ii, 225.

[43] Carte, *Ormonde*, ii, 400–2; Gilbert (ed.), *Irish confederation*, ii, 187–9.

[44] Carte, *Ormonde*, v, 380–1. For the king's instructions to Ormond on terms, see Carte, *Ormonde*, v, 1–3.

[45] See Ormond to Charles, 31 January 1643, Carte, *Ormonde*, v, 432–3.

[46] Carte, *Ormonde*, v, 393. Carte claimed they also attempted to stir up the population to protest against any treaty: Carte, *Ormonde*, ii, 402.

[47] Ormond denounced Lisle as an obstructer of royal designs and a supporter of Parliament: Carte, *Ormonde*, v, 394.

[48] Gilbert (ed.), *Irish confederation*, ii, 123–4. He adds that this was so that the army could be persuaded to intervene on the side of Parliament against the king, which is unlikely, at least in the short term. Bellings's account of these years was apparently written in the 1670s.

doubtless included keeping the army with him through success in the field, but also increasing his bargaining power with those with whom he was commanded to treat, but whom he clearly regarded as rebels, even if with some cause. Bellings provided a convincing portrait of Ormond setting himself forth as patron of, and one among, the army commanders, the defender of their interests with the government, not as privy councillor but as lieutenant-general.[49] Perhaps he was always more at ease donning the mantle of the noble warrior, hallowed by family tradition and social prestige.[50]

Ormond's opponents were disposed to attribute to him the killing-off of the plan to fuel the war through extending the adventure to those already serving in Ireland. It was later claimed that subscriptions to the value of £35,000 had been obtained but that expressions of dislike from the king sunk the scheme. A later tract contended that it had been Ormond who had procured Charles's disavowal.[51] Then, in mid-February, the commissioners found themselves barred from the council table on royal orders, procured by Ormond,[52] though supporters on the council[53] ensured they departed from Dublin ahead of orders for their arrest, furnished with a letter of commendation and escorted by one of only two pinnaces available to the Dublin government.[54] The king was candid about the impossibility of his sending supplies to Ireland but insisted that Ormond overcome Protestant support for the lords justices' refusal to implement the commission for negotiation.[55] This division of opinion over whether or not to accept peace short of total victory was emerging as the primary one within the Irish executive. During the commissioners' stint in Dublin, they had already aligned themselves with the uncompromising element, even if a firm commitment to Parliament had not been secured in return.

[49] Gilbert (ed.), *Irish confederation*, ii, 125–7.

[50] T. C. Barnard, 'Introduction: the dukes of Ormonde', in Barnard and Fenlon (eds), *Dukes of Ormonde*, pp. 2–3, 10–11.

[51] BL Harleian MS 164, fo. 329a. The MS version of 'Ormond's Curtain Drawne' (BL Additional MS 4,819, fos 320a–b) includes a claim that Ormond gained the king's disavowal through the agency of Captain Yarner; certainly Yarner was at Oxford in late January with correspondence from Ormond: Carte MS 4, fos 342, 347.

[52] Carte, *Ormonde*, v, 393, 392.

[53] Not all of the eight signatories (Parsons, Borlace, Sir Adam Loftus, Sir Gerard Lowther, Temple, Sir Thomas Rotherham, Sir Francis Willoughby and Sir Robert Meredith) appear as later parliamentarians, but only Willoughby seems to have been much involved in the early treaty negotiations. Notable by their absence are five other councillors, whose signatures appear on another letter dated 21 February – Ormond, Brabazon, Lambert, Ware and Wentworth: HMC *Ormonde MSS*, new series, ii, 236.

[54] Charles to the lords justices, 3 February, Carte MS 4, fo. 349; to the lords justices and Ormond, 1 March 1643, Carte MS 4, fos 432, 435; see *The true state and condition of the Kingdom of Ireland . . .* (London, 1642 [1643]) E246 (31) for the committee's account.

[55] Carte, *Ormonde*, v, 3–4.

But how committed was Parliament to the furtherance of the war in Ireland? Westminster had spent the winter months suspended between equally fervent and occasionally raucous calls for immediate peace or for a more sustained and determined war in England. Irish adventurers were 'strongly represented' in the ranks of the 'militant' petitioners.[56] Their prescriptions for the war in England – the avoidance of 'destructive counsells of accommodation' not based on 'honourable and safe conditions' but permitting 'delinquents' to escape punishment (and the application of their estates to repay City contributors to Parliament), and the move to immediate battle by the earl of Essex – all were clearly analogous to proposals made for Ireland in late 1642.[57] Within the Houses voices had been heard casting doubt on Parliament's continued engagement with Ireland. The king's repeated failures to allow Leicester to depart prompted the Lords to agitate for a resolution that the king be pressured to send him, or provide an appropriate alternative, 'else they shall not be able to save that Kingdom'. As voted on in the Commons, the component of threat had apparently transmuted to a charge that without such a resolution 'both Houses must give over the Care of the Management of these Affairs'. The motion was voted down in January, but presumably Henry Marten was not the only MP of the opinion that the Houses should not 'take any further care of Ireland but declare to the world that during these troubles at home wee cann doe nothing to releive that kingdome'.[58]

The alternative was surely to pour more resources into the Irish theatre. January had seen Parliament approve an ordinance drafted by John Goodwyn for the Irish committee, which established a new 'loan and contribution' scheme. Aimed at the supply of the armies in Ireland, it was directed towards the United Provinces as well as England and Wales, and to the proffering not just of money but of 'any Victual, Arms, Ammunition, Goods, Wares, or Commodities fit and necessary', for which repayment was promised, in money or Irish land, at adventurer rates.[59] Implementation of the measure was rapid and the first payments were being made from it by mid-February, albeit rather predictably to repay debts. Yet it was progress. A regional framework for the collection and valuation of goods offered under the ordinance was set up, and the Goodwyn committee was given power to collect and spend arrears from earlier funds for Ireland.[60] Deliveries were still being made to outposts from

[56] Lindley, *Popular politics*, p. 308. For militant and pro-peace pressures upon parliament from London see Lindley, *Popular politics*, pp. 304–10, 337–48.

[57] *The True and Original Copy of the First Petition which was delivered by Sir David Watkins* (London, 1642) E130 (26).

[58] *LJ*, v, 518, 577; *CJ*, ii, 905, 946–7; BL Harleian MS 164, fo. 284a.

[59] Firth and Rait (eds), *Acts and ordinances*, i, 70–3.

[60] BL Additional MS 4,782, fos 88a–b, 102b–103a, 105a–b, 118a–b, 120a–123b, 162b; *CJ*, ii, 994, 996. A second ordinance on May 17 clarified procedures for collections: *LJ*, vi, 50–1; Firth and Rait (eds), *Acts and ordinances*, i, 158–60.

Ulster to Munster, with large shippers dispatching everything from ammunition to Colonel Mervyn's consignment of Madeira wine.[61]

February saw further new proposals on the table. Clotworthy presented a plan for a £200,000 loan from the United Provinces, sponsored by 'the Lords, Knights, Gentlemen and other Protestants, late Inhabitants in the Kingdom of *Ireland*', with the claim that he knew of 'diuerse of the dutche marchants whoe will contribute that waye', while the long-standing demand from the adventurers for compulsory collection of unpaid adventure subscriptions was aired in the Commons.[62] As so often, fresh measures had been pushed through on the back a potent mixture of exhilaration and terror which comprised the 'news' from Ireland. Knowledge of the king's commission to treat with the confederates reached Parliament even as it trudged through the morass of propositions and position papers that was the 'Treaty of Oxford', the lengthy attempt to begin moving towards an English settlement. John Goodwyn gibed that the king 'intends to make peace with his best subiects first', and the Commons resolved to prepare a declaration of protest and to 'think of some letter of Encouragement to the Justices and Committees at *Dublyn*'. The battle for the control of the Irish government was out in the open. Parliament was in effect 'encouraging' the Dublin regime to open defiance of the royal will.[63] The king was well aware of the connection between peace-making in England and Ireland. As he informed Ormond, 'no lesse power than his, who made the worlde of nothing, can draw peace out of thease articles' delivered by the English rebels.[64] Though the propositions advanced by Parliament did not explicitly deal with Ireland a tough line was implicit. The proposed Act of Oblivion excluded not only all who had committed offences in relation to the Irish rebellion, but all who had offered 'counsel, assistance or encouragement', a sweeping demand given Parliament's propensity to cast such a slur in recent months, while efforts were made to translate Charles's earlier promises of hostility to 'popery' into potent anti-Catholic legislation.[65] Simultaneously approval had been given to the suggestion of the commissioners in Dublin for expulsion of Catholics from the Irish capital.[66] As one newsletter summed it up, the talks were designed to ensure a people

[61] BL Additional MS 4,782; Armstrong, 'Protestant Ireland', appendix 3, pp. 340–8.

[62] *CJ*, ii, 970, 973; Yonge, *Diary*, p. 319; BL Harleian MS 164, fo. 307a; BL Additional MS 4,782, fo. 29a–b.

[63] *CJ*, ii, 965; BL Harleian MS 164, fos 296b–7a; BL Additional MS 31,116, fo. 25b; Yonge, *Diary*, p. 311.

[64] Carte, *Ormonde*, v, 3.

[65] Gardiner (ed.), *Constitutional documents*, pp. 262–7.

[66] Hogan (ed.), *Letters and papers*, pp. 168–70; *CJ*, ii, 914. The proclamation of 1 April issued by the Dublin government suggests economic as much as political motivation in so far as it covers the expulsion of both Catholic and Protestant arrivals to the city, the latter to go to England: Carte MS 5, fo. 37.

'enjoying our Religion without innovation, and our Liberties without violation; the Papists extirpated his Majesties Dominions, *Ireland* subdued and planted with honest English Protestants . . .'.[67]

The commissioners' return to England was effected soon afterwards, and they quickly entered into the shaping of Irish policy at Westminster. News of their expulsion had run ahead of them and their account of events was conveyed to the Commons on 28 February, a day already earmarked for a full debate on the Irish situation. The commissioners' report alleged that 'the labour is on both sides the Sea, to make the Rebels appear strong and considerable, and to put difficulties and impediments upon our Military proceedings, the better to bring on a most horrid pernitious peace . . .', whereas in fact the confederates 'will ere long (if you do not exceedingly abandon this service) disband, starve, and cut-throats among themselves'. Clotworthy followed this dispatch with a letter from his brother-in-law John Chichester, lately released from imprisonment in beleaguered Athlone. His letter had a bleaker tone, asking for help 'That we may not dye in a ditch, and starve, which is the condition threatening us all'. But his worries were compounded by the fact that what was being squandered through inadequate support was 'a probable way of reducing these miscreants for ever'.[68] It was now decided to proceed with the plan for compulsory adventure subscriptions in the form of an Act, a procedure which would provide security for land ownership but would of course necessitate royal approval.[69] A sub-committee of John Goodwyn's committee negotiated the legal minefield presented by the bill, for the Commons were exceedingly wary of the very principle of compulsion. Allowing payees to regain their rights to land sweetened the pill considerably, and the Commons approved the requisite bill on 13 April.[70] Parliament had been locked into a system which sought to legitimate its demands by placing them under the rubric of 'loans', forced or otherwise, a situation which sapped efforts on the English as much as the Irish front. It was only now, after all, that Westminster was easing itself to overt acknowledgment of its acquisition of taxation powers to fight its English war.[71] Again at the prompting of 'divers *English* Gentlemen, Inhabitants of *Ireland*', early March saw the Commons respond

---

[67] *Speciall Passages* 27, 7–14 February 1643, E89 (17), p. 225.

[68] *CJ*, ii, 970; *The true state and condition of the Kingdom of Ireland* . . .; Yonge, *Diary*, p. 338.

[69] *CJ*, ii, 981, 988; Yonge, *Diary*, pp. 337–8; BL Harleian MS 164, fos 309b, 311a–b.

[70] *CJ*, iii, 6, 27, 43–4; Yonge, *Diary*, pp. 341–3; BL Harleian MS 164, fo. 332b; BL Additional MS 31,116, fo. 39b.

[71] James Scott Wheeler, *The making of a world power: war and the military revolution in seventeenth century England* (Stroud, 1999), pp. 101–6. Weekly assessment was introduced in February.

positively to the idea of a 'national adventure' by the whole kingdom of England, to the tune of £200,000.[72]

The 28 February debate had also seen the launch of a new committee to consider what 'may be most necessary and requisite for the speedy Supply and Safety of the Kingdom of *Ireland*'.[73] The experiment of a new committee was not a happy one.[74] Though it co-operated with Goodwyn's committee in a plan to supply all forces in Ireland with six weeks' provisions, at a cost of £28,000–£30,000, it showed little patience with the methodical efforts and book-balancing mentality of the older committee. Even less consideration was shown to the hard-pressed Dublin executive. Having presented a particularly excruciating letter from the Dublin authorities on their final and 'inevitable Ruin' on 17 March, Vane, chairman of the new committee, delivered the reply which his committee had drafted, confidently assuring Dublin 'that wee had provided 6 weekes provisions to be sent away to severall parts of Ireland' and adding a recommendation that, in the short term, trade be used to generate supplies by the encouragement of the resort of merchants to Dublin.[75] A month on, Vane responded to Goodwyn's attempt to spring funding legislation from the latest Dublin lamentations by 'reproveing' Goodwyn and alleging Dublin's claims of imminent ruin 'to bee a mere threatening of us'.[76]

While Westminster urged war, but toyed with supply, Dublin braced itself both to talk, and to fight, with confederate Ireland. If these alternatives were to be embraced as some kind of twin-track strategy, then both tracks needed to be traversed under Ormond's direction. The outcome of the planned spring campaign into the south-east would be vital, politically even more than strategically. Despite hostile allegations, there is no doubt that Ormond worked hard to ensure military success, neglecting the negotiations in order to win a better position by battle, a stance he was to take up again in the autumn.[77] With his departure from Dublin, the lords justices and other privy councillors made their last bid to deflect the king, the very day before the scheduled meeting with the confederate delegates at Trim. Their 16 March letter is a key statement in the developing 'massacre' legend, advancing the subsequently much-cited figure of 154,000 'British and Protestants' slain between October 1641 and March 1642. The strategy adopted was one which

---

[72] Apparently the money would be raised 'by way of Subsidy': *CJ*, iii, 10–11.

[73] *CJ*, ii, 984.

[74] Armstrong, 'Ireland at Westminster', pp. 85–8.

[75] *CJ*, iii, 6; BL Additional MS 4,782, fo. 118a; BL Harleian MS 164, fo. 332b; HMC *Ormonde MSS*, new series, ii, 239–41.

[76] *CJ*, iii, 47; BL Additional MS 31,116, fo. 44a; BL Harleian MS 164, fo. 370.

[77] See, for example, Ormond's efforts to co-ordinate with Esmond, governor of Duncannon, and to obtain naval assistance for the operation: Carte MS 4, fos 438, 439, 463, 467, 469, 471. For accusations of treachery set flying in all directions see Kelly, 'John Barry', p. 147.

elided the Old Irish of Ulster and the Old English Catholics of the Pale. All could be condemned for barbarism, for settled hatred of the English and of Protestantism and for explicit rejection and usurpation of the king's rights and authority. The authors' vision was quite openly that of a final and complete solution to the problem of rebellion in Ireland. Peace was to be wished for, but 'the settlement of it in this kingdom will be of a different consideration from the rest'. The authors claimed that 'if peace should now be granted them before the sword or famine should have so abated them in numbers as that in reasonable time English Colonies might overlap them, ... the English do plainly foresee it can never be safe for to cohabit with them, secure for England to enjoy them, or likely that themselves ... can ever digest into a people good to themselves, or profitable to their king or country'. It was a searing vision of peace through destruction, for all the signatories' protestations that 'the utter extirpation of the nation ... is far from our thoughts'.[78]

It was their last real chance to defend an unrelenting agenda, and it failed. In the meantime they could take little comfort from the confederate documents of 17 March which openly named those they considered liable for the troubles of Ireland, with Sir William Parsons at the head of the list.[79] Though Ormond declared himself happy neither with the terms submitted, nor with the lords justices' opposition to the treaty,[80] his return premised an alteration in the balance of forces. Pamphlets celebratory of his victory at Ross honoured the general, who showed 'both his valour and his inveterate hatred against his kinsmen and Countrymen for their Rebellion', but did not attempt to disguise two facts. One was the poor condition of the troops, whose return to Dublin was a disaster for both them and the populace. The other was that 'much more might be done, if wee had but more men to make good the places that would be gotten in, which now we cannot doe for feare of weakning our Army'.[81] The military option had failed, but Ormond's credibility had been enhanced. The privy council was quite clear that it now had more to fear from its own army than from any external enemy. The

---

[78] HMC *Ormonde MSS*, new series, ii, 244–53. The ten signatories (Parsons, Borlase, Archbishop Bulkeley, Lambert, Loftus, Shirley, Lowther, Temple, Rotherham and Meredith) insisted that 'a safe and lasting peace' could come only when 'the sword have abated these rebels in number and power'.

[79] Gilbert (ed.), *Irish confederation*, ii, 226–42. Sir Adam Loftus, Clotworthy and Arthur Hill were also singled out, as was the late Sir Charles Coote.

[80] See Carte MS 5, fo. 17 for Ormond's draft comments.

[81] G. T., *Truth from Ireland* (London, 1643) E99 (12); [Robert Cole], *A full and true relation of the late victory* ... (London, 1643) E96 (6). Cole, who claimed to have served on the expedition, reported how rumours that the army was to turn back to Dublin were greeted with disdain by the troops, loath to 'so soone part with their plenty to eate shotten herrings without bread, and cold water instead of hot water' back in the capital: [Robert Cole], *The true coppies of two letters* (London, 1643) E94 (20).

officers turned to petition the Irish House of Lords in April, and were sharply critical of how monies sent for the army had been handled. The upper House unsuccessfully sought to escape an order from the lords justices to prorogue the session to November so as to consider the petition.[82]

Members of the council itself were breaking with the justices' control. On 1 April eight councillors signed a letter to the king pointing out the misery of the army and population in direct terms, and awaiting the king's opinion on what they should do. They admitted that a motion at the council board to make known their condition in these terms had not met with 'that approbation which in our judgements it ought'.

Most of the signatories would be at the heart of the cessation plans.[83] On 22 April the council responded to the 17 March letter from Vane's committee at Westminster. The fatuousness of the notion that they would build up funds through the encouragement of trade was duly exposed. Whatever about the situation in peacetime, they asserted, since the rising the 'rebels' had become 'masters of all the native commodities in the country' and all that the 'good subjects' had left was an inconsiderable number of hides taken from captured cattle. The authorities admitted to having themselves plundered Dublin's merchants and retailers. Their needs were so great that any merchant who thought to bring goods to Dublin for Irish products faced a government 'constrained . . . either to force those provisions from those that shall bring them, or from those to whom they shall sell them, and from both without any payment of money for them'. It was an accurate assessment of the condition of things, not only in the capital but also, for example, in Munster, where Inchiquin had resorted to seizure of tobacco, cattle and herrings from merchants.[84] While government forces had maintained a solid record of victory in the field in the earlier part of 1643, and while control of Ulster was consolidated, there was an increasing vulnerability to the attrition wrought by ever more capable and increasingly well-equipped confederate forces. As Protestant holds fell, the loss of territory which could be drawn on for supplies, alongside the reduction in external logistical resources, reduced the capacity of even the more successful Protestant forces to undertake large-scale expeditions or secure permanent gains.[85]

An alternative response to the plight of the Protestant forces was generated

---

[82] *LJI*, i, 196–8; HMC *Ormonde MSS*, new series, ii, 265, 269–70; Carte, *Ormonde*, ii, 452–7; v, 439, 440–1. The petition was duly forwarded to the king.

[83] Carte, *Ormonde*, v, 432–4. Of the signatories, only Lambert also signed the 16 March letter above – the others were Bolton, Ormond, Brabazon, Bishop Martin of Meath, Willoughby, Ware and Wentworth.

[84] HMC *Ormonde MSS*, new series, ii, 266–70, 272; Smith, *Cork*, ii, 82; Carte, *Ormonde*, iii, 6.

[85] Stevenson, *Scottish Covenanters*, pp. 127–8, 130–2, 136–8; Lenihan, *Confederate Catholics at war*, pp. 60–71.

from Oxford. Charles wrote privately to Ormond on 23 March that he must conclude a cessation so as to bring his army over for service in England.[86] Public documents followed. On 31 March the order was issued to dismiss Parsons as lord justice, replacing him with that staunch and unrelenting soldier Sir Henry Tichborne, who had won plaudits for his defence of Drogheda and harsh harrying of the Pale. It was followed on 23 April by the dispatch of a new commission for the negotiation of a one-year cessation with the confederates. As Micheál Ó Siochrú has perceptively noted, the king now referred to 'our subjects, who had taken up arms against us' rather than, as in January, to 'rebels'.[87] Finally, there was a public letter dated 29 April in which the king encouraged the army 'to make such a shift yet for a while for subsistence as possibly you shall be able to effect with your united forces and counsel' until he could give succour. He blamed Parliament, to whom he had 'commended the care of the country . . ., the only means of reducing the rebels to obedience'.[88] As in the past and the future, Charles was at his most successful when at his most impotent. Parliament could be blamed for all the harm done to his faithful soldiery, whose welfare was always on his mind. Yet the royal stance of upholder of the army in Ireland was being chipped away concurrently by dispensations to prominent individuals. A succession of officers were diverted to commands in his English armies, probably not unwillingly.[89]

Meanwhile Oxford dispensed a stream of rewards, large and small, to reliable persons in and around Dublin.[90] Army petitions had condemned the allocation of custodiums, grants of temporary possession of 'rebel' property, but among the recipients of such royal bounty now were William Hilton, baron of the exchequer; Sir Maurice Eustace, king's serjeant and speaker of the Irish Commons; two men close to Ormond, Sir Francis Butler (who was later to present the charges against Parsons) and Sir Patrick Wemyss; and Sir Robert Hannay, who, like Wemyss, acted as a conduit between Oxford and Dublin at this time. Offices were also awarded; the governorship of Meath, with pay and custodiums attached, had gone to Sir Henry Tichborne a few days before his promotion to the chief governorship, and the post and pay of major general to the privy councillor Sir Francis Willoughby.[91] The king

---

[86] Carte, *Ormonde*, v, 5.
[87] Ó Siochrú, *Confederate Ireland*, pp. 61, 64 and note 35. Tellingly the 'public letter' spoke differently.
[88] *CSPI, 1633–47*, p. 381.
[89] Officers included Major Woodhouse, captains Edward Molesworth and Edward Boughton: Carte MS 4, fos 384, 460, 549, 553; Newman, *Royalist officers*, pp. 44, 421.
[90] A number of the recipients were personally present in Oxford, as well as Dublin, at this time, surely aiding their chances of securing rewards.
[91] *CSPI, 1633–47*, pp. 377, 378, 379, 380, 381, 383, 385.

and Ormond were winning the battle for control of the Irish government. On 3 May, two days after the reading of Charles's commission for a cessation, eight senior figures signed a 'Consultation' to work to that end: Ormond, Lord Chancellor Bolton, Sir Francis Willoughby, Sir Thomas Lucas, Sir James Ware, Sir George Wentworth, Justice Donnellan and Sir Maurice Eustace.[92] It was not as if they, least of all Ormond, had any notion of capitulation, but in opening themselves up to the conscious pursuit of a halt in the conflict they had set themselves on a collision course with Westminster.

Efforts at a peace in England had collapsed in a welter of disillusionment and frustration. The aftermath was no better for Parliament as the spring and early summer of 1643 saw its cause battered all across England. Defeat in the field was bad enough, but between March and June the parliamentary side found itself riddled with plots and defections, real or suspected. Parliament needed moral and logistical rejuvenation.[93] On 9 May, it learnt that the king had refused his assent to the bill for unpaid adventure subscriptions, carried to court by the hands of three serving officers in the forces in Ireland, William Jephson, Sir Robert King and Arthur Hill. The king raised concerns over the details of the legislation, in the interests of the subscribers, but the thrust of his argument was that he could not trust that any money so collected would not be diverted in the manner of the July 1642 'loan'. He ended rather pointedly, noting that Ireland could best be served by an outbreak of peace in England.[94] What broke out in the Commons over the next few days was anything but the language of peace. Allegations were already being aired of royalist atrocities in Buckinghamshire perpetrated by 'Irish, Walloons and Papists' when Jephson rose to draw attention to his recent experience of royalist Oxford. There, he claimed, great store was set by the lords Taaffe and Dillon, who he claimed had been in correspondence with the Munster confederate leader, Lord Muskerry, assuring him of royal approval for his stance. Stapleton reportedly 'seconded' Jephson, 'shewing that we have fostered the Papists too long, letting them have a quiet being amongst us, while they by all meanes labour our ruine'. It was resolved that all counties should rise up at the coming of the earl of Essex to oppose the establishment of popery in England and Ireland. More specifically, all papists under arms, or found to have aided the enemies of Parliament with arms or money, were to be proceeded against as traitors.[95] Papists, *en masse*, were deemed to be Englishmen worthy of being treated as Irish. It was but a prelude

---

[92] Gilbert (ed.), *Irish confederation*, ii, 268.

[93] Robert Ashton, *The English civil war* (London, 1978), p. 188; J. H. Hexter, *The reign of King Pym* (Cambridge, Massachusetts, 1941), pp. 111–20.

[94] *LJ*, vi, 36–7. The message was composed by Falkland.

[95] BL Additional MS 31,116, fo. 51a; *CJ*, iii, 91; *Perfect Diurnall* 49, 15–22 May 1643, E249 (8).

to the specific condemnation within a few days of the most notable Catholic in England, the queen herself.[96] To render secure the 'popish plot' interpretation a committee was named to issue a declaration proving 'That the Rebellion in *Ireland*, and this in *England*, spring from one Head; and are managed with concurrent Counsels to one End; for the utter Overthrow and Extirpation of the Protestant Religion'.[97]

Before that statement could emerge, the Commons were confronted with another declaration, specifically replying to the royal denial of the recent bill. Though some in the Commons opposed the intention of addressing the king, insisting that Parliament no longer dispute with the monarch any legislation presented to him, such stalwarts of the Irish interest as Reynolds and Robert Goodwyn pressed the case for a declaration answering old charges about diversion of funds which 'had brought a scandal upon the Parliament in forraigne parts' long since. An attached schedule set out claims that the £73,346 diverted from the adventure (not £100,000 as the king constantly alleged) was dwarfed by the £279,207 19s 3d the Houses had overspent on Ireland, £123,382 14s 9d since the July 1642 'loan'.[98] Parliamentarian newsbooks made great play of the claims advanced.[99] Combining enthusiasm for war and for classical allusion, the first issue of *Mercurius Civicus* reminded its readers 'that the very Heathen Romans, when Italy was over-run with a powerfull invading Army, and *Hannibal* marched even to the gates of Rome, even then they sent supplies into Sicilie'.[100] Lest the moment be lost, a new committee was formed on 29 May, empowered to investigate the present and future condition of the armies in Ireland 'as also, their Opinions, how they may be disposed, for the future, to the better Advantage'. A meeting of all MP-adventurers was called at Grocers' Hall for 1 June with a full assembly of all adventurers in London set for the following day.[101]

As the proposals gestated, news broke which, in D'Ewes's words, 'made my heart and I believe the hearts of many more to ake [ache]'. Intercepted letters were laid before the Commons from Leicester, still lord lieutenant in

---

[96] *Mercurius Aulicus* 21, E105 (12), pp. 271–2, contrasted the inclusion of the queen with the exemption of Essex's half-brother Clanricard from sequestration – it was safer to be a 'friend of some potent member' than the queen of England. Cf. Little, 'Blood and friendship'.

[97] In addition, a six-man committee headed by Jephson was allotted the task of collecting such informations as they deemed relevant to such a consideration of the rising: *CJ*, iii, 91–2.

[98] *CJ*, iii, 96, 102–3; BL Harleian MS 164, fos 392b–393a; BL Additional MS 31,116, fo. 53a. The declaration, which may have been drafted by Clotworthy, does not appear to have emerged from the Lords: *LJ*, vi, 81, 95.

[99] *Perfect Diurnall* 49, 8–15 May 1643, E249 (5); *The Kingdomes Weekly Intelligencer* 18, 2–9 May 1643, E101 (4), p. 143.

[100] *Mercurius Civicus* 1, 4–11 May 1643, E101 (15).

[101] *CJ*, iii, 109, 110; printed circular summoning adventurers to a meeting at Grocers' Hall, E104 (23).

name, and from Parsons, alongside letters sent to Reynolds from unnamed
correspondents in Dublin. Taken together, they could be used to demonstrate
to MPs just how imperilled Ireland was, and that by royalist treachery and
malice. Leicester confided to his daughter that the king had prohibited him
from travelling to Ireland because Charles 'entended to agree with the Rebells
of Ireland that hee might trust them and that hee [Leicester] had told his
Ma[jes]ty plainely that they would cheate him of his Kingdome'. Parsons's
language was hardly designed for parliamentary ears: he sought to secure his
restoration, since he was 'no Roundhead after ye New Appelacon, nor no
Puritan after ye old'. But Reynolds's Dublin informant nonetheless dubbed
him 'an enemy to the Rebells and a favourer to the Parliament of England' and
claimed that he was to be charged with treason, the charges to include his aid
to Reynolds and Goodwyn. He added that 'the whole frame of the government
was now likely to bee altered there' and that the king intended 'to receive the
Rebells there into his favour'.[102] The news had tumbled into Parliament only
five days after the announcement of 'Waller's plot', an alleged plan to betray
London to the king. MPs could be forgiven for seeing nigh-incomprehensible
betrayal at every turn. In a fresh declaration mandated on 16 June the Houses
insisted on the religious basis of the Irish war and pledged themselves again to
drive forward supply for Ireland 'considering what courses are set on foot at
Oxford'. When they reissued their declaration a week later they were able to
hitch to it a whole sequence of votes and resolutions.[103]

The results of the recent consultations of adventurers and MPs were unveiled
on 19 June. The adventure was to receive new life from two pieces of legislation.
In a 'doubling' ordinance, those who upped their original payments by an
additional quarter were to receive double their original allocation of land. A
completely new adventure was to be launched, to be redeemed from the
confiscation of urban property at Waterford, Limerick, Galway and Wexford.
It was set down that the requisite ordinances would be followed up with
confirmatory Acts of Parliament in both England and Ireland. In addition
Parliament promised to send a commander-in-chief to Ireland 'such as the Kingdom
will have good cause to confide in' and to name committees for each province in
Ireland for the keeping of intelligence. All was to be watched over by the 29 May
committee in harness with a newly named London adventurer committee.[104] If

---

[102] *CJ*, iii, 115; BL Harleian 164, fos 395a–396a; BL Additional MS 31,116, fo. 55a. Sir John
Temple was later accused of communicating with Reynolds and Goodwyn at this time, Carte:
Ormonde, v, 518–20.

[103] *A Declaration of parliament concerning the miserable condition of Ireland* . . . (London,
1643) E55 (1); *A Declaration of parliament* . . . *whereunto are added the propositions made by
the committees* . . . (London, 1643) E55 (20).

[104] *CJ*, iii, 135–6; *LJ*, vi, 104–5. The old parliamentary and London committees were
empowered to 'sit and vote with this committee'.

implemented, it would be the largest initiative undertaken since the outbreak of the war in England. Not all the measures set in motion in recent weeks came to fruition, but July saw the passage of ordinances for 'doubling' and the urban adventure, and for the Dutch benevolence, piloted through by such stalwarts of the cause of Ireland as Clotworthy, Jephson and John Goodwyn.[105]

Those making the running at Westminster were out to ensure Parliament was re-charging itself ideologically and re-equipping itself financially for a long war, in both England and Ireland. The despondency which had touched even such as Reynolds was to be banished by an act of will – the hold on Ireland would not be loosened. This was the moment when Parliament pledged itself anew in its 'Vow and Covenant' and when the summoning of the Westminster divines began the process of reshaping the English church in the puritan image. The capstone of ideological re-commitment and military revival would of course be the emergent alliance with covenanting Scotland. In May it was decided to dispatch a parliamentary committee to Scotland to deal with the question of the Scottish army in Ulster, though its greater task would turn out to be the negotiation of an Anglo–Scottish alliance.[106]

Across 1642–43 the army in Ulster had provided a point of contact between Westminster and Edinburgh, even if usually in terms of Parliament's neglect of its responsibilities to sustain the troops.[107] Back in November 1642, in naming an agent, John Pickering, to lay its case before the Scottish Council, Parliament had located that army in a war raised 'by the Practice of the Papists . . . for the Destruction of Religion'.[108] It was a reading every bit as potent in the months to come. Pickering's contacts over the winter of 1642–43 included one individual well attuned to anti-popery and 'godly reformation' in all three kingdoms, Sir John Clotworthy. Pickering informed him of opinion in Scotland favourable to intervention to 'rescue the King out of captivitie' to malignants, and motivated by the vision not only of 'unity of Religione' but of 'putting downe the masse in England'.[109] Clotworthy, writing from Antrim, passed back to London word

[105] Firth and Rait (eds), *Acts and ordinances*, i, 192–7, 220–1. The proposed ordinance for £200,000 for Ireland appears to have fallen by the wayside, though it was still under consideration in August (*CJ*, iii, 121, 213, 218–19), as does the ordinance replacing the rejected bill to compel adventure subscriptions to be paid. For Dutch aid see Ole Peter Grell, 'Godly charity or political aid? Irish Protestants and international Calvinism, 1641–1645', *Historical Journal* 39 (1996), 743–53.

[106] *LJ*, vi, 59–60, 62–3, 68.

[107] Stevenson, *Scottish Covenanters*, pp. 139–45.

[108] *LJ*, v, 469.

[109] HMC *Hamilton MSS, supplementary report* (London, 1932), p. 67. Scottish pulpits were exercised in denunciation of the earl of Newcastle's reception of Catholics into his northern royalist army. Cf. P. R. Newman, 'Catholic royalists of northern England, 1642–1645', *Northern History* 15 (1979), p. 95.

of the latest doings of the earl of Antrim, still captive in the hands of the Scottish army.[110] By the end of January Clotworthy was back at Westminster having passed through Scotland. It seems unlikely that he had not touted such news there also.[111] If it was too cold to produce much response, or if the processes of Scottish politics were not ready to react, the doings of Antrim would produce a storm within a few months. By the early summer the escaped Antrim's latest schemes included the harnessing of confederate and royalist resources in Ireland not merely against the Scots in Ulster but also to set Scotland in flame. With Antrim captured once again by Monro in Ulster, word of his deeds was released. The impact on opinion in Scotland cannot easily be exaggerated. 'To many, it was further proof that the papist, with a letter of approval from the King, was on the march in the three kingdoms'.[112] Those sympathetic to the position of the English Parliament had already orchestrated the summoning of a convention of estates in Edinburgh ('a body identical in membership to parliament but with more limited powers'), on the grounds of providing supply for the army in Ireland. The convention duly succumbed to the full force of the Antrim revelations. Full-scale alliance between Edinburgh and Westminster would soon be cemented.[113]

The ideological fire of 1643 was still largely fuelled by the sense of a great papist threat to uproot Protestantism throughout the king's realms, and spearheaded from Ireland. It was epitomized in the latest, and fullest, declaration on Ireland brought forward in the Commons on 4 July and requiring half an hour to read. In its final form it passed the Commons ten days later, guided throughout by Robert Reynolds.[114] As printed it ran to sixty-three pages, including forty pages of supporting documentation. As a work of propaganda it was a notable achievement, carefully and, within its own terms, convincingly weaving together threads of testimony into a coherent account of a grand 'popish' design. (Even such witnesses as the voluble John Dodd, late of Cavan, were drawn upon to prove the presence of named Irish 'rebels' at Oxford. D'Ewes had remarked that his earlier testimony to the Commons that 4,000 Irish had joined the king at Oxford was 'farre stretched beyond all possibility of truth'.[115])

---

[110] HMC *Hamilton MSS, supplementary report*, pp. 68–9.

[111] See *Certain Informations* 3, 30 January–6 February 1643, E88 (17), p. 18 for Clotworthy's journey south through England 'disguised and disfigured'. If he shared nothing else with Antrim, both men gained a reputation for travel incognito.

[112] John Scally, 'Constitutional revolution, party and faction in the Scottish parliaments of Charles I', *Parliamentary History* 15 (1996), 66. For a full account of the Antrim schemes see Ohlmeyer, *Civil war and Restoration*, pp. 117–22.

[113] John R. Young, *The Scottish Parliament, 1639–1661: a political and constitutional analysis* (Edinburgh, 1996), pp. 60–3; David Stevenson, *The Scottish revolution, 1637–44: the triumph of the Covenanters* (Newton Abbot, 1973), pp. 142, 283–8.

[114] *CJ*, iii, 154, 166; BL Harleian MS 165, fo. 115b; BL Additional MS 31,116, fos 61b, 63a.

[115] BL Harleian MS 164, fo. 233a.

The declaration drew together allegations of evil plans to subvert Protestant Ireland from the beginning of Charles's reign, through the activities of the parliamentary commissioners in Dublin (given a worthy defence) to the Antrim revelations, duly slotted in.[116] It set Parliament's stamp on claims for 154,00 Protestant deaths in Ireland recently articulated in Dublin. It was a signal that parliamentarian self-definition remained firmly locked into anti-popery. More than that it very neatly made that popish threat one to all of Charles's kingdoms, and one countenanced by those closest to the king ('the Queen with her Romish priests . . . have been principall Actors and Sticklers therein'). Such an undertaking as the rising would be 'so rash . . . without being encouraged, incited, nay commanded from *England*, with an assurance of connivence and assistance too', and was to be followed up with 'a Designe to pardon them, and to bring them into *England* to do the like'. The declaration rounded itself out in ringing assertions 'That no earthly power is likely in humane reason to withstand this damnable Plot, but the power of the Parliament of *England*' and that 'honest and moderate English Protestants' must no longer act alongside international popery lest 'this Renowned Kingdom be no more a Nation'.[117]

All the declarations at Westminster could not turn the tide of affairs in Dublin. Ormond was clearly committed to securing the truce that the king desired. His critics made the valid claim that it was he who prompted the confederates to petition for a cessation (the only honourable means to initiate one).[118] Yet if he was to bargain from strength and, as importantly, if he was to carry enough of the Irish Council with him to make any ceasefire hold, he needed to uphold the Protestant military position. On 22 June he put it to the Irish Council that if it found a cessation dishonourable, 'unsafe' and 'dangerous' it should take its case to the king, offering an alternative. If £10,000 in cash and supplies could be gathered within the next two weeks he would give up negotiations and march on Wexford.[119] Of course it could not. With the excise proclaimed in Dublin on 24 June a last but inadequate expedient, he was determined to squeeze from the confederates an undertaking to support the forces so recently at war with them.[120] Inchiquin,

---

[116] Cf. *A declaration of the Lords of His Majesties Privie-Councell in Scotland* . . . (London, 1643) E56 (9) and, for Monro's examinations, released to Parliament, HMC *Portland MSS*, i (1891), 120–3.

[117] *A Declaration of the Commons* . . . *concerning the rise and progress of the grand rebellion in Ireland* . . . (London, 1643) E61 (23).

[118] Algernon Sidney to the countess of Leicester, 18 June 1643, in Gilbert (ed.), *Irish confederation*, ii, xlix; Kelly, 'John Barry', pp. 148–9.

[119] McNeill (ed.), *Tanner letters*, pp. 161–2; cf. Ormond to lords justices, 24 June 1643, Carte MS 5, fo. 569.

[120] *Ireland's excise* (London, 1643) E62 (10); Gilbert (ed.), *Irish confederation*, ii, 284–5, 287, 306.

the commander in Munster, had swung round to the idea of a cessation, whether regional or national, as vital to survival in the southern province after a contingent of his men went down to defeat at Fermoy.[121] Logistical arguments were Ormond's strongest card, but it was not as if a strong counter-argument could not be mounted. Fighting and negotiation could be presented as alternative routes to the essential objective of securing the year's harvest. Sir John Temple expressed shock that the officers should so readily support a ceasefire, believing that the Irish would contribute to their upkeep, a notion he considered ludicrous.[122] Parsons reminded Ormond that however ill Parliament had served Ireland, it would give nothing after a cessation and, more pertinently, that survival by pillage would no longer be possible.[123] While Parsons had his own reasons to oppose negotiation, June saw Sir Philip Perceval, later a signatory of the deal, and later still a defender of the cessation on grounds of necessity, in a sceptical frame of mind about the benefits to the army.[124] Irish-based Protestants now in London blended threat to promise as they sought to persuade Ormond of the imminence of parliamentary aid, but only if negotiations were halted.[125] But at Westminster the Irish committee was all too aware that it could not now respond as rapidly as was needed to the Dublin council's frantic requests, the only realistic means to avert a deal.[126]

The cessation was concluded in September, though Ormond admitted that the Antrim scare had almost scuppered a deal.[127] In return for a bare halt to the war, Ormond won the promise of a contribution of £30,800 to sustain his troops.[128] The four leading anti-cessationists on the Dublin council, Parsons, Temple, Sir Adam Loftus and Sir Robert Meredith, had been isolated and, in August, were arrested. It was laid to their charge that they had supported the English Parliament against the king and sought to promote such a stance among the army.[129] English political allegiances had become the stuff of Dublin Protestant politics. With the cessation in place Ormond introduced an oath to bind the Dublin forces to the king's

[121] Karl S. Bottigheimer, 'The English interest in southern Ireland, 1641–1650', PhD dissertation, University of California, Berkeley, 1965, pp. 94–7.

[122] Temple to Dr Thomas Temple, 16 June 1643, in Gilbert (ed.), *Irish confederation*, ii, xlvii.

[123] Parsons to Ormond, 22 June 1643, Carte MS 5, fo. 541.

[124] Perceval to Sir Robert King, 17 June 1643, Carte MS 5, fos 478–9.

[125] Ranelagh's letters, Carte MS 5, fos 425 (13 June 1643), 492 (20 June 1643), 611 (27 June 1643); Clotworthy to Ormond, 25 July 1643, Carte MS 6, fo. 116; Sir Thomas Wharton to Ormond, 29 August 1643, Carte MS 6, fo. 281.

[126] HMC *Ormonde MSS*, new series, ii, 296–9; BL Additional MS 4,782, fo. 233a; Carte MS 6, fos 213, 281.

[127] Ormond to the king, 11 July 1643, Carte, *Ormonde*, v, 456–8.

[128] Gilbert (ed.), *Irish confederation*, ii, 365–76.

[129] Carte, *Ormonde*, v, 519–20; HMC *Portland MSS*, i, 125–6.

cause.[130] In Parliament, reports from Ireland were interpreted to show the dangers of a ceasefire with the rebels, and how the demise of Protestantism in Ireland and the flight of the Protestant population was the unavoidable outcome.[131]

A year on from the outbreak of war in England it had been mandated, at the highest levels, that the guns fall silent not in England, but in Ireland. Over the course of that year the two kingdoms had been inextricably bound together. Information had been deployed and manipulated in all directions to re-commit, re-orientate or disorientate the various protagonists. Over most of Ireland Protestant leaders, forces and communities had striven to avoid overt commitment to the warring protagonists in England. In Dublin it became all but impossible to avoid entanglement with English divisions as alternative policies for Ireland were developed. It was the king and Ormond who had taken the initiative, escaping the restrictions on action set by Westminster and Dublin and their attempt to depict their chosen strategies as the only valid Protestant and English policy towards Irish 'rebels'. Ormond and his royal master had proved adept at winning power where it mattered in Dublin, and had demonstrated how honeyed words and a sane combination of combat and negotiation could trump the parliamentary hand of belligerence plus parsimony.

Parliament had gone through the mangle in 1642–43. That it had emerged committed to fight on in England and in Ireland was the real story of the year, casting in the shade the limited practical steps taken to make that struggle possible. To keep going it had kept close to its core values, or perhaps rather to its core antipathies, to 'popery' and its implicit challenges to 'The Protestant Religion, The Parliament, Liberties and Lawes of England'.[132] Yet pressure of events had been at work to remould those values. Shared hostilities had brought together the revolutionary regimes in London and Edinburgh but their alliance would challenge the assumptions of both parties. Reliance upon radical opinion and aid, and upon the zeal of plebeian supporters, had troubled the minds and consciences of solid parliamentarians, and tipped some overboard.[133] The

---

[130] Rushworth, *Historical collections*, v, 950. As early as June Viscount Lisle was aware of rumour of an oath 'but am of opinion that I shall not like it': Gilbert (ed.), *Irish confederation*, ii, lx.

[131] *CJ*, iii, 213; BL Additional MS 31,116, fo. 72a.

[132] *A Declaration of the Commons . . . concerning the rise and progress of the grand rebellion in Ireland . . .*, p. 23.

[133] Andrew James Hopper, ' "Fitted for Desperation": honour and treachery in Parliament's Yorkshire command, 1642–1643', *History* 86 (2001), 138–54. Cf. David Wootton, 'From rebellion to revolution: the crisis of the winter of 1642/3 and the origins of civil war radicalism', *English Historical Review* 105 (1990), 654–69.

Scottish alliance would shake up the relations between Parliament and Protestant Ireland almost as much as Ormond's Dublin coup. Thus far the effects of English division had been sharpest close to the centre of power in Dublin castle. The next year would see Protestant Ireland, stretched out in garrisons and holds across the island, face its own challenge of popular politicization, spurred on by developments in all three of Charles Stuart's kingdoms.

4

The cause of the Covenant, 1643–44

On 8–9 April 1644 the parishioners of Holywood, Co. Down, were sworn into the Solemn League and Covenant. At least seventy of them had 'sworne, subscribed and sealed with marks' a printed copy of the Covenant, part of an Edinburgh print run published at the behest of the regime in Scotland.[1] It is not known how many of those present did so with the tears of remorse for past, coerced, repudiation of Covenanting, or in spiritual response to a movement of religious revival, but both these responses were present in Ulster in 1644.[2] Instead the signatures and marks indicate a community incorporating itself in the most solemn manner in a pledged commitment to the reform and renewal of three kingdoms. Whatever their motivations, these individuals were being given their due, their share in a great endeavour. It epitomized a moment that would have lasting consequences, rending the Protestant community of Ireland yet also firing part of it with a new zeal, and bringing some of its members in as active participants in a cause which, for the moment at least, was drawing together politically and religiously charged individuals and groups in England and in Scotland. The Solemn League and Covenant was proclaimed within days of the proclamation of the cessation in Ireland. Those two events would dominate the political fortunes of Protestant Ireland over the next year, and set the parameters for those in Britain engaging with the conflict in Ireland, for they carried with them questions of war and peace, of the role of Scotland in Ireland and of the nature of the cause to which Protestants in Ireland were to give their allegiance.

At Westminster, it had taken a last-minute intervention from Sir John Clotworthy to secure the inclusion in the text of the Covenant of a pledge to reform the Church of Ireland in the same manner as that of England. Some

---

[1] David Stevenson, 'Copies of the Solemn League and Covenant', *Records of the Scottish Church History Society* 25 (1995), 181–2.
[2] Adair, *True narrative*, pp. 102–18.

of the opposition to his move had come from MPs concerned at making any alterations without Scottish approval, a telling indicator of the importance some within Parliament already attached to the goodwill of their new allies.[3] The Convention of Estates in Scotland in the summer had been stirred up by news from Ireland of the planned cessation, interpreting it as liable to 'strengthen and ayde the popisch and prelaticall partie' in England. Despite efforts both at Westminster and in Edinburgh to sustain the Scottish army in Ulster, its situation in 'that desolate land' was considered bleak. In July the Convention had insisted that the English meet their treaty obligations either by sustaining the army in better fashion or, if they were disposed to recall it, by matching their promises on pay arrears. The English commissioners who negotiated the Anglo–Scottish alliance in Edinburgh duly advanced the notion of withdrawing the Scottish army, but the terms they offered were frowned on by the Scottish executive Committee of Estates, and scorned by the army itself.[4]

As the cessation loomed it was met with predictable condemnation by Parliament. Westminster confronted Dublin's plans with what had become its standard 'constitutional' argument for its own involvement, alleging the 'power that is in the Houses of Parliament' of England by virtue of the 1642 commission and the adventurer legislation.[5] Dublin's failure to seek 'advice or counsell', it was alleged, dishonoured Parliament, and was 'no more but to make the Houses of Parliament the commissaries of victuall, armes and ammunicion and treasurers for money, but not to participate in your counsell of warre and peace'. Logistical arguments for the ceasefire were dismissed with less than compelling claims that Westminster had indeed sent supply and that pursuit of the war against a weakened enemy was still feasible. Instead the 'true causes' of the negotiations 'were the wicked practices of those that have cast this kingdome into such combustions', the papists, who having 'given us an unparalleled example of their cruelty in time of peace, so now they have of their craft and subtility in time of warre'. The truce was a 'Trojan horse' which could only usher in the toleration of Catholicism in Ireland. Yet, even as the deal was done, Westminster presented itself as confident that Dublin would reject the cessation, salting its declaration of opposition with an offer of 'such a weekly contribucion' as would sustain its forces.[6] When confirmation of the cessation came through in October the

[3] BL Harleian MS 165, fos 163b–164a; *CJ*, iii, 224, 230; Gardiner (ed.), *Constitutional documents*, pp. 267–71.

[4] *The Acts of the Parliament of Scotland*, ed. T. Thomson (12 vols in 13, London, 1814–75), vi, 8–9, 15–17, 17–18, 37–8, 48–50; Stevenson, *Scottish Covenanters*, pp. 144–7.

[5] Cf. Little, 'English Parliament', pp. 110–12.

[6] *LJ*, vi, 238–40; *Analecta Hibernica*, iv, 84–7; *A declaration of . . . Parliament shewing the present designe . . . for a cessation . . .* (London, 1643) E69 (16).

Houses resolved that 'the warr be vigorously prosecuted, notwithstanding this cessacion'. Those 'whose eyes shalbe opened upon the discovery of the treachery and ruine attending this cessacion' and who maintained the struggle and their allegiance were promised 'a setled course for the maintenance' of their forces and, with full victory, that everyone 'according to his condition and meritt shalbe plentifully rewarded in land'.[7]

Such offers were to be made to the Scottish army in Ulster as well as to local forces. Into the autumn Parliament had pressed ahead with searching out some additional supplies for the Scottish forces in Ireland. Two ordinances were rushed through parliament in September for the support of both the Scottish army in Ireland and the new Scottish army intended for service in England, drawing upon the sequestered property of Parliament's enemies in England.[8] If the Scottish army in Ulster were not to be dangerously isolated then Parliament must take seriously reports from Scotland that locally raised forces in Ulster would accede to the cessation.[9] Back in August the Convention of Estates had professed itself solicitous for the well-being not only of the Scottish army but of 'other good cuntrey men and christianes' in Ulster and had asked whether it was likely that the 'Scottis and Inglisch' there 'wilbe content to concurre and joyne' in the Covenant.[10] By October, with resolutions taken to impose the Solemn League and Covenant upon the populations of England and Scotland, Westminster resolved with regard to the Scots that 'the Covenant may be taken by all the Officers, Soldiers, and Protestants of their Nation in *Ireland*: As likewise, this House will take care, that the *English* Protestants, Commanders, and Officers in *Ireland*, shall take the Covenant also'.[11] It was a momentous decision. It not only extended to Protestant Ireland the personal opportunity and obligation of Covenant participation, but did so by sifting the national mix and implicitly conceding to the kingdom of Scotland an obligation for its nationals in Ireland.

The 1641 rising had seen the revival of the language of 'British-ness' in Ireland, and particularly with regard to Ulster. 'British' became, particularly for Parliament, the conventional designation for locally raised forces in the province, drawn as they were from Scottish as well as English plantation populations, and was echoed back in petitions and other productions from within the community. But existing Anglo–Scottish tensions were not easily papered over, even if some among the local elite perceived a greater cleavage between the 'new Scots' of Monro's army and the 'ancient' inhabitants of

---

[7] *Analecta Hibernica*, iv, 91–2; *CJ*, iii, 294, 295; *LJ*, vi, 289.

[8] Firth and Rait (eds), *Acts and ordinances*, i, 311–15, 322–7; cf. Stevenson, *Scottish Covenanters*, pp. 142–8.

[9] *LJ*, vi, 274–6.

[10] *Acts of the Parliament of Scotland*, vi, 49–50.

[11] *CJ*, iii, 277.

both British nations. The Covenant would expose and provoke religious and political division within Protestant Ireland, but for many contemporaries its impact was to be interpreted in 'national' terms, depicting it as a Scottish initiative, driven forward principally by the Scots of Ireland. For now, Westminster mandated a letter to be sent to the Ulster forces to stir them to continue the fight despite Ormond's truce with promises of aid. The sentiments were familiar, if given more strident expression, calling on the province's soldiers to act for 'the ridding of it [Ulster] of those wretches who were a burdan to the earth' and describing the supporters of cessation as 'shamefully apostasised'. The messenger bringing the letter, none other than Owen O'Connolly, would also deliver the Covenant to them, and 'the only expedient which will aboundantly satisfy both Houses' was to be their swearing it alongside Monro's men. This letter was to 'be read to the souldiers under your comaund the first and fittest opportunity', with the possibility of binding the soldiery directly into Parliament's schemes.[12]

Westminster and Edinburgh were designing a solid bank of support within Ireland, calling upon some of the Protestant forces there to repudiate the commands emanating from Dublin. Dublin, however, was loath to repudiate Parliament publicly. On 28 October the council took the trouble to produce a massive statement of its position as a rebuttal of Parliament's accusations. It insisted that it accepted Parliament's power 'to advise and direct the managing of the war', but complained of the failure of the Houses and the commissioners both in advice and in the practical matter of supply, the latter claim buttressed with detailed information on Dublin's repeated pleas for supply and the meagre provisions received.[13] The validity of such claims arguably constituted the strongest argument for the cessation in Protestant eyes,[14] despite Westminster's failure to produce a response.[15] Instead such arguments were trumpeted from Oxford, where the council's letter was published by the university printer at the king's command.[16] It had been preceded by an edition of the cessation terms, prefaced with a brief argument that the king 'thought Our selfe bound in duty and Conscience, since it was not in Our power otherwise to preserve

---

[12] *Analecta Hibernica*, iv, 92–4; *CJ*, iii, 298; *LJ*, vi, 292–3.

[13] HMC *Ormonde MSS*, new series, ii, 320–32.

[14] Cf. the 'Vindication' produced by Sir Philip Perceval, then commissary in Dublin, in 1646, which provides detailed evidence of money and supplies sent to argue that 'nothing but want and necessity . . . and the exceeding great discontents of the army . . . did or could compel his consent to the cessation . . .': Carte, *Ormonde*, iii, 6–22; HMC *Egmont MSS*, i, 270–7.

[15] *CJ*, iii, 307. Cf. Parliament's sponsorship, in November, of *A true and exact relation of the most sad condition of Ireland since the cessation . . .* (London, 1643) E76 (4), designed to show the hardships in post-cessation Dublin.

[16] *A copy of a letter from the speakers of both houses . . . together with the answer of the Lords Justices and Counsell* (Oxford, 1643) E78 (25), dated 18 November, also includes Parliament's 4 July letter to the council.

that Kingdome from utter ruine, at least to admit any expedient, which with Gods blessing might be a meanes to preserve that people . . .', casting on Parliament the odium for failing to sustain the government forces. Reference to Oxford's correspondence from the army and the 'state' in Dublin was thrown in the mix to back up the royal claims, and the prospect of engagement in negotiations with Catholic Ireland played down.[17]

Royal propaganda was just as reticent about the withdrawal of troops from Ireland for service in England, though numbers of such men would begin landing in November, undertaking far from unworthy service in the north-west and south-west of England.[18] Protestant Ireland was not to be completely denuded of troops. In letters to Secretary Nicholas shortly before and after the cessation, the council in Dublin urged the necessity of a supply of munitions, for 'we be not too believing in the undertaking of an enemy whose wounds of distrust given us are not yet healed, but rather . . . that the enemy through our want may not be emboldened to a breach, but that by His majesty's power and greatness they may be so awed as not to dare to attempt a breach'. The king recognized the necessity, pressed on him by Ormond, of retaining adequate garrison forces.[19] The cessation terms had made some evacuation all but unavoidable. The arrangement, considered from the confederate point of view, has generally been reckoned a good deal for the Protestants, sparing them the attacks of an increasingly threatening foe, now capable of reducing fortified posts through newly acquired artillery, granting them safe quarters and topping this up with generous offers of money and foodstuffs to the value of £30,800, commitments which the confederates struggled to meet. Yet even if paid in full, such offers could not sustain the bloated forces under Dublin's authority. The quarters assigned the Protestants were narrow, and though they might reflect accurately enough the territory under Protestant control they were far short of what might be

---

[17] *The grounds and motives inducing his Maiesty to agree to a cessation* . . . (Oxford, 1643) E71 (20), which also includes the 15 September statement from seventeen lords, officers and officials in the government ranks supporting the cessation explicitly on the basis that all other means of sustaining the army had been attempted and that prosecution of the war required 'large supplies, whereof they can apprehend no hope nor possibility in due time' (pp. 21–2).

[18] Ronald Hutton, *The royalist war effort 1642–1646* (London, 1982), pp. 116, 124, 127, 138; John Lowe, 'The campaign of the Irish royalist army in Cheshire, November 1643–January 1644', *Transactions of the Historic Society of Lancashire and Cheshire* 111 (1960), 47–76; M. D. G. Wanklyn, 'Royalist strategy in the south of England 1642–1644', *Southern History* 3 (1984), 69–70; Joyce Lee Malcolm, 'All the king's men: the impact of the crown's Irish forces on the English civil war', *Irish Historical Studies* 21 (1978–79), 239–64.

[19] HMC *Ormonde MSS*, new series, ii, 309–10, 311–13; Ormond to Nicholas, 28 September 1643, Edward Hyde, earl of Clarendon, *State papers collected by Edward, earl of Clarendon*, ed. R. Scrope and T. Monkhouse (3 vols, Oxford, 1757), ii, 155–6; Charles to lords justices and Ormond, 7 September 1643, Carte, *Ormonde*, v, 465–7.

termed the zone of disruption where government forces could wreck considerable, and often sustained, devastation over confederate lands.[20] The departure of substantial numbers of forces was a necessity under the new dispensation.

In the longer term the cessation could have only one of two outcomes: either a negotiated settlement which must involve concessions to the confederate Catholics, or the renewal of the war. 'From early 1643 onwards, . . . confederates of all political persuasions sought an accommodation with the state'[21] and, as far back as July, the king had been clear that a successful ceasefire would result in the dispatch of confederate commissioners and government advisers to Oxford. The latter duly set out in November.[22] By then Dublin had witnessed the emergence of a new petitioning movement. Its immediate request was quite modest, that four agents also be admitted to the royal presence at Oxford. Their task was to 'manifest the truth' of the petitioners' interpretation of recent events in Ireland, the by now standard reading of an unprovoked and barbarous uprising aimed at the 'utter extirpation of the Protestant Religion and all the British professors thereof'. But the agency was geared towards securing a future Ireland where 'the Protestant religion may be restored throughout the whole kingdom to its lustre, that the losses of your Protestant subjects may be repaired in such manner and measure as your Majesty in your princely wisdom shall think fit, and this your kingdom may be so settled, as that your said Protestant subjects may hereafter live therein under the happy government of your Majesty . . . with comfort and security'. The petition, with its formidable list of signatories, did not represent an anti-cessation movement.[23] But it was indicative of a movement to ensure that Protestant interests would be safeguarded in any possible negotiations. As they claimed, the petitioners reflected the 'Protestant subjects of the several provinces' of Ireland. They also included leading military figures whose influence would only grow as the English-raised army departed from Ireland over the winter of 1643–44. In a one-day session of the Irish Parliament in November the Commons busied themselves with a Remonstrance to the king, which appears to reflect the same initiative, though the move was soon shut down by prorogation. Charles

---

[20] See the map in Ó Siochrú, *Confederate Ireland*, p. 31 for some sense of 'Protestant controlled' and 'disputed' territory.

[21] Ó Siochrú, *Confederate Ireland*, p. 243.

[22] Carte MS 6, fo. 12; HMC *Ormonde MSS*, new series, ii, 313–15, 334–5, 337.

[23] Further signatures were sought: HMC *Ormonde MSS*, new series, ii, 316–17, 319, 341–4; Samuel Luke, *Journal of Sir Samuel Luke*, ed. I. G. Philip, iii, *1 November 1643–29 March 1644*, Oxfordshire Record Society (Oxford, 1953), pp. 212–13. The four agents were named as Captain MacWilliam Ridgeway, Sir Francis Hamilton, Captain Michael Jones and Fenton Parsons.

had earlier planned to dissolve and replace the parliament, and though Ormond had urged its continuance as reassuring to the Protestants royal permission had been given for a one-day meeting only at this time.[24] If Oxford was nervous about the proclivities of a Protestant parliament in Dublin, it was also engaged in shoring up the executive power in Ireland. On 18 November the king ordered the installation of Ormond as lord lieutenant of Ireland, replacing the lords justices, though delays in transmission meant the changeover occurred only in January.

In Ulster, the combined actions of the Scottish army and the locally recruited forces had produced a much more favourable military position than elsewhere in advance of the cessation. With the exception of the fortress at Charlemont, most of Ulster, bar the far south of the province, had become clear ground for Protestant forces in the course of 1642, albeit at the cost of considerable devastation. The campaigns of 1643 had banished any substantial confederate field army, the 'Ulster army' under Owen Roe O'Neill going down to defeat at Clones in June. Lack of success in Ulster had pressed the confederates towards a cessation; conversely, it made the truce less appealing to the Protestants of Ulster.[25] The terms of the cessation were vague regarding the northern province, merely providing that the territory in the hands of either party be retained for the duration of the accord. Colonel Arthur Chichester, on behalf of the local 'British' forces, unreservedly accepted the cessation but insisted, to his delegates to the meeting with the Irish forces, that the Ulster Protestant army 'doe clayme all Ulster for their quarters (Charlemont and such other holds . . . only excepted)', a concession in itself, he argued, since these were 'straitly besieged' at the date of the signing. Nothing should be done which would prejudice this claim, which delegates were sent to Dublin to uphold.[26]

Before long sentiment in the province was moving beyond a determination to squeeze the cessation for the best terms. On 8 November eighteen signatories headed by Robert Thornton, mayor of Derry, set out their concerns in a letter to the lord chancellor and government of Scotland. Not only had Dublin failed to provide adequate securities for the present condition in north-west Ulster. The letter openly showed a pro-war sentiment, its signatories claiming that if their suit for immediate supply of ammunition and victual was successful, they would 'want neither affection nor zeal to the prosecution of these rebels, so long as there runneth a drop of warm

---

[24] *CJI*, i, 314; HMC *Ormonde MSS*, new series, ii, 313–15; Carte MS 6, fo. 12; Clarendon, *State papers*, ii, 155–6.

[25] Stevenson, *Scottish Covenanters*, pp. 127–30, 136–7, 146; Lenihan, *Confederate Catholics at war*, pp. 67–8.

[26] Gilbert (ed.), *Contemporary history*, ii, 554–9.

blood in our veins'. They required assurances that Monro's Scottish army would remain in Ireland and sought pressure on Parliament for further supply.[27] This crucial document signalled a break in the ranks of Protestant Ireland, outside the narrow confines of Dublin council politics.

As the leaders of Protestant Ulster sought to interpret the action to Dublin, some resorted to claims that popular sentiment needed to be steered but could not be overcome. Sir James Montgomery offered assurances concerning the assent of colonels Sir William and Sir Robert Stewart to the letter, urging that 'their ends are good and that he cannot misdoubt of their affection and fidelity to His Majesty'. Responding to seditious stirrings in their absence, 'to gain time and to stop the current, and the better to divide them' the Stewarts 'thought fit to seem to comply with the multitude, and to concur in a letter, and having qualified it all they could, did sign it with the others'. Montgomery, though, sent his own letter to Chancellor Loudoun which proclaimed his loyalty to the king, yet added that he could see no better way of serving the king than against the Irish rebels. He at least claimed to have blocked another letter intended for the English Commons.[28] However much a brake was being applied, what was unmistakable was that pressure was building in Ulster to resume the war. Reports circulated of a 'band' to join with Monro against all cessations, and of the inclination of many in the ranks of the local forces to join in the bond of the Covenant, a tendency ascribed to the Scottish nationality of the troops in question. The Covenant itself appears to have reached east Ulster by 6 December, at the hands of Owen O'Connolly. It had not been needed as a catalyst for pro-war sentiment, but was instead being sought out by the 'giddy multitude'.[29] The appeal from leading Ulster Protestants to the Scottish regime was indicative not merely of the profile of the planter population, but of provincial contacts maintained with Scotland since the outbreak of the rising for the severely practical purposes of securing military aid. For all that the Edinburgh regime was now aligned against its, and their, monarch, it retained a claim to legitimacy, as the king's government there, which Westminster could not claim.

The pro-war camp was insistent on the need to retain Scotland's army in the province, though Ormond also sought such an outcome, following royal preferences against allowing that force to be re-deployed in Great Britain.[30]

[27] Carte MS 7, fo. 383; HMC *Portland MSS*, i, 148–50.
[28] Lords justices and council to Nicholas, 19 December 1643, HMC *Ormonde MSS*, new series, ii, 339–40; Montgomery to Ormond, Carte MS 8, fos 249–50.
[29] Robert Thornton to Ormond, 28 December 1643, Carte MS 8, fos 231–2; Stewarts [to Ormond?], Matthews to Ormond, 7 December 1643, Carte MS 8, fos 32, 55. Matthews to Ormond, 19 November 1643, Carte MS 7, fo. 527; Robert Stewart to Ormond, 21 December 1643, Carte MS 8, fo. 179.
[30] Stevenson, *Scottish Covenanters*, pp. 145–6, 159–60.

That army had done more than alter the military balance within Ulster; it effected a seismic shift within the religious balance of the island of Ireland. The sponsorship of Presbyterianism in Ulster by Monro's army attracted the attention of contemporaries and has drawn the curiosity of historians. Institutionally, Presbyterian structures in Ireland grew from the army presbytery formed from the chaplains and officer-elders of the Scottish army.[31] But it was a two-way street. It was not inevitable that a Scottish presence in early seventeenth-century Ireland would result in a Presbyterian church, though the tendency of Wentworth's regime implicitly to brand all Scots as disaffected Covenanters undoubtedly helped the process forward.[32] Ulster had witnessed the growth of a popular Protestantism with distinctly puritan and revivalist tendencies in the 1620s, a plant which would bud again in the circumstances of the 1640s.[33] Anti-episcopal petitions had circulated in Ulster in 1641; from 1642 a sequence of petitions would be directed to successive General Assemblies in Scotland seeking ministerial provision in terms which signified the export of the Presbyterian movement to the province.[34] Certainly not all Ulster Protestants shared religious commitments of the kind that would, in England, make for supporters of Parliament, but there was a bedrock of reformist religious sentiment which would affect both the external alliances and internal divisions of the northern province. This was soil in which the Covenant would sprout.

Despite Westminster's resolution back in October, the Solemn League and Covenant had not been enforced in Ulster. The Convention of Estates which met in Edinburgh in January 1644 was keen to ensure that the bond be duly pressed in both England and Ireland.[35] The Dublin government, perhaps prompted by reliable senior figures in Ulster, had already issued an order forbidding the swearing of the Covenant in the army, followed up with a formal proclamation.[36] In early January Ulster's senior 'British' officers met in Belfast to consider the Covenant. They resolved that the league was as yet only proposed, not pressed; given this, and the widespread support for it, not

---

[31] Edward M. Furgol, 'The military and ministers as agents of Presbyterian imperialism in England and Ireland, 1640–1648', in John Dwyer at al. (eds), *New perspectives on the politics and culture of early modern Scotland* (Edinburgh, 1982), pp. 103–10.

[32] John McCafferty, 'When reformations collide', in Allan I. Macinnes and Jane H. Ohlmeyer (eds), *The Stuart kingdoms in the seventeenth century: awkward neighbours* (Dublin, 2002), pp. 186–203.

[33] Marilyn J. Westerkamp, *The triumph of the laity: Scots–Irish piety and the Great Awakening 1625–1760* (Oxford, 1988), pp. 23–42; Alan Ford, 'The origins of Irish dissent', in Kevin Herlihy (ed.), *The religion of Irish dissent 1650–1800* (Dublin, 1995), pp. 24–9.

[34] Perceval-Maxwell, *Outbreak*, pp. 113–15.

[35] *Acts of the Parliament of Scotland*, vi, 70.

[36] Carte MS 8, fos 114, 134; Sir Robert Stewart to Ormond, 10 December 1643, Carte MS 8, fos 80–1.

least among private soldiers, it would cause greater 'distraction' to proclaim the Covenant, as instructed, than to let it go ahead. They thus suggested a respite of the order.[37] Ormond's information suggested that the Ulster colonels' desire to resume the war extended to a willingness to receive supply from Parliament, though privately they sought to avoid the Covenant or the imposition of a Scottish commander-in-chief in the province.[38]

The idea of awarding command of all Protestant forces in Ulster to the commander of the Scottish army in the province had been mooted as far back as July 1643, when the Scottish Convention of Estates had raised it as a question worthy of discussion with the representatives of the English Parliament.[39] The rumour mills of London and Oxford had re-cycled it as a topic for consideration in the autumn, but it had taken centre stage only in December when Westminster received the terms which its commissioners in Edinburgh had agreed with the Scottish government.[40] Alongside a series of practical propositions for the supply of money, foodstuffs and clothing, and a pledge to support local 'British' forces opposing the cessation, was the resolution 'That the chief commander of the Scots Army in Ireland shall also command the rest of the British forces there'.[41] The ensuing debates would spark the first serious divisions over policy for Ireland to confront Westminster since the outbreak of the English war, if the rearguard action against an ongoing tendency to mismatch strong sentiments with niggardly supply is left aside. Indeed the division prompted by the Scottish command was both to wrench apart the small world of the 'Irish lobby', those with a genuine commitment to the pursuit of the Irish war, and to play itself out as a sub-plot in the realignment of parliamentary politics brought about by the Scottish alliance.[42]

The Anglo–Scottish coalition sealed in the Covenant was neither inevitable, nor ever easy. If the wartime Long Parliament had been beset with its fair

---

[37] British officers to lords justices and Ormond, 16 January 1644, Carte MS 8, fo. 510. The thought that the departing Scots might draw with them numbers of their own troops was a concern for the colonels, who issued an order to prohibit departure of their men on 11 January 1644, apparently to limited effect: HMC *Ormonde MSS*, new series, i, 71; Stevenson, *Scottish Covenanters*, p. 151.

[38] Lieutenant-Colonel Matthew (Chichester's regiment) to Ormond, 13 January 1644, Carte MS 8, fo. 480.

[39] *Acts of the Parliament of Scotland*, vi, 17.

[40] As early as 10 November 1643 Digby was able to inform Ormond of the dispute over whether Monro or Lisle should have the command: Carte, *Ormonde*, v, 503–5.

[41] *CJ*, iii, 335, 338–9; McNeill (ed.), *Tanner letters*, p. 165. The Scottish army in Ulster had given prior support to the proposal to have one commander for both armies. For their November terms see PRONI MS T525/4 (Wodrow transcripts), Stevenson, *Scottish Covenanters*, pp. 147–8.

[42] For more detail see Armstrong, 'Protestant Ireland', chapter 5.

share of faction and division in 1642–43, the emergence of the Scottish alliance deepened tensions within the parliamentarian camp and pushed forward issues, principally of religious reform and the shape of a post-war settlement, which would fatally fracture any unity at Westminster.[43] Not that the impact of the Scottish alliance was consistent over time. Many of the foremost proponents of the alignment in 1643 – supporters as they were of vigorous war in England, and suspicious of too soft an accommodation with the king – would become leading critics of the Scots by 1645, alienated by Scots calls for Presbyterian uniformity between the nations, dismissive of the efforts of the Scottish army in England and, in some cases, riled at the activities of the under-supplied Scots soldiers in the north of England.[44] The process worked in reverse too, for it was alleged, with good grounds, that the leading opponent of the Scottish command at this juncture was none other than that past and future pro-Scot, and persistent proponent of Protestant Ulster, Sir John Clotworthy.[45]

Consideration of the Edinburgh terms was referred to three committees, John Goodwyn's parliamentary Irish committee, the London adventurers' committee and the new committee for Scottish affairs, based at Goldsmiths' Hall in London. It was a telling combination, for two of the three could be readily won over to Scottish interests. The London committee had already come out in favour of a Scottish command in a petition which was referred to John Goodwyn's committee in October and never re-appeared, perhaps buried by Clotworthy.[46] The Londoners repeated their preference at the joint meeting of the three committees where approval of the proposals as a whole was duly secured, with the adventurers bound into the plans to float financial advances to the Scots.[47] There was already a noticeable overlap between London figures prominent in the adventure and those operating the new machinery to transmit funds from sequestered property in England to the Scots, for their armies in both England and Ireland. A nexus was forming

---

[43] For political developments see especially M. P. Mahony, 'The Presbyterian party in the Long Parliament, 2 July 1644–3 June 1647', DPhil dissertation, University of Oxford, 1973; Valerie Pearl, 'Oliver St. John and the "middle group" in the Long Parliament, August 1643–May 1644', *English Historical Review* 81 (1966).

[44] David Scott, 'The "Northern Gentlemen", the parliamentary Independents, and Anglo–Scottish relations in the Long Parliament', *Historical Journal* 42 (1999), 350–1, 353, 356–7.

[45] See in particular PRONI MS T525/4 (Wodrow transcripts), an unsigned and undated document setting out a series of charges designed to show Clotworthy's 'disaffection to the Scots both in England & Ireland'. See also Michael Perceval-Maxwell, 'Ireland and Scotland 1638 to 1648', in John Morrill (ed.), *The Scottish national Covenant in its British context, 1638–1651* (Edinburgh, 1990), pp. 202–3; Armstrong, 'Protestant Ireland', pp. 121–6; Stevenson, *Scottish Covenanters*, p. 148.

[46] *CJ*, iii, 286; PRONI MS T525/4, article 6; HMC, *Portland MSS*, i, 143.

[47] McNeill (ed.), *Tanner letters*, pp. 169–71; HMC, *Portland MSS*, i, 164; *CJ*, iii, 349–50.

between radical London, the Scots and confiscated property in both England and Ireland, one doubtless fuelled by a combustible combination of zeal and self-interest.[48] Sir Henry Vane the younger delivered the resolutions agreed by the committees to the Commons on 28 December, prompting a 'very vehement & earnest debate' over the proposed Scottish command. Vane, St John and Mildmay spoke in favour, Vane claiming that he believed that otherwise Scotland would withdraw its army and Ireland would be 'quite lost'. On the other side claims were made for the appointment of 'some English nobleman' by those stalwarts of the Irish war, and of the parliamentary Irish committee, Reynolds, John Goodwyn and Clotworthy, the latter urging the adverse effect of such a Scottish appointment on 'neare upon 12000 English' in Ulster who would 'all disband and bee gone' rather than accept such a command. Approving the appointment of one, Scottish, commander-in-chief by a margin of fifty-seven to twenty-five, a majority of MPs appeared willing to value the favour of their new allies over the possible adverse effects of the vote upon relations with locally raised forces in Ireland.[49]

Within days, though, the Commons approved a move to assemble all London adventurers to consider the case of the 'British' forces in Ulster. The promised 'convention' duly took place on 4 January, though of MPs only Clotworthy, Reynolds and John Goodwyn were recorded in attendance.[50] It had been preceded by resolutions passed by Goodwyn's committee and the London committee, now sitting as a joint committee, which showed a concerted effort to put the 'British' of Ulster back on the agenda. Assuming they would cross the threshold of the Covenant 'when it shalbe tendered them' and came out against the cessation, the meeting urged adequate supply for the 'British' forces as well as for Monro's army, particularly by means of a six-month

---

[48] The treasurers under the ordinances to supply the Scots from sequestrations were the prominent adventurers Michael Herring and Richard Waring. The leading adventurers Sir David Watkins, Jerome Alexander, Samuel Moyer (all on the London adventurers' committee), Richard Shute and William Thompson were all active on the Goldsmiths' Hall committee; the group also appears to have been identical with the subcommittee at Turners' Hall which co-ordinated supplies for the Scottish army in England and possibly the army in Ireland too: *Calendar of the proceedings of the Committee for Compounding 1643–1660*, ed. M. A. E. Green (5 vols, London, 1889–92), i, 8, 16, 23–4, 30, 781; Firth and Rait (eds), *Act and ordinances*, i, 802–3; Lindley, 'Irish adventurers'.

[49] *CJ*, iii, 350; BL Harleian MS 165, fos 254–5. The command was vested in the commander of the Scottish army, nominally the absentee Leven; in practice Monro held the command. The question of whether the command extended to 'British' forces outside Ulster 'was left ambiguous' though 'in practice' the Scots 'accepted that they had only been given command' of locally raised forces in Ulster: Stevenson, *Scottish Covenanters*, p. 158.

[50] *CJ*, iii, 353; undated circular for London clergy to read the order summoning all adventurers, E79 (28).

assessment levied upon England. A full-scale programme for the immediate implementation of the adventure in Ulster was put forward, with confiscation, survey and plantation of 'rebel' lands, and agreed by the 'meeting' of the body of adventurers.[51] A petition outlining at least some of the new plans was delivered to the Commons by seventeen citizens and as many of the 'Lords and Gentlemen of Ireland as may have notice'.[52] Measures to sustain the Irish war were more talked about than effected. Plans for an assessment give the impression of being repeatedly re-directed to the back-burner, though in early February the committee was sufficiently confident of progress that it moved to collect money and supplies on the credit of such an ordinance.[53] In the interim the joint committee of MPs and adventurers (to be revamped by the addition of new members chosen by the 'body' of adventurers) grasped at control of the only ready resource to hand, supplies bestowed on Ireland by sympathetic subscribers in the Netherlands.[54] Such co-operation had not submerged the differences arising from the divisive Scottish command. Opponents claimed that Clotworthy and his allies sought to use the assembly of adventurers to subvert the measure on the basis that 'it would bring all the busines into confusion if an english man did not comand these apart by themselfes'.[55]

Efforts to sustain the war in Ireland were being caught up in the tangles of factional politics at Westminster, where charges and counter-charges can all too easily ravel into knots of accusation and speculation. It was laid against Clotworthy, an active proponent of a settlement between king and Parliament at this time, that he was engaged in correspondence with Oxford, even that he was involved in attempts to deliver London to the king.[56] Critics of his stance over the command of anti-cessation forces in Ireland claimed that he

---

[51] BL Additional MS 4,771, fos 4–7v. These elaborate plans failed to catch fire.

[52] *CJ*, iii, 368, 370; BL Additional MS 4,771, fo. 9; BL Harleian MS 165, fo. 278v.

[53] BL Additional MS 4,771, fos 17v–18v. This proposed assessment was the measure previously mooted as a 'national adventure' by the kingdom of England, since the adventurers' joint committee intended that any locality which delivered more than its quota of funds would be entitled to draw Irish land to the value of the surplus: BL Additional MS 4,771, fo. 4.

[54] The supplies intended for 'poore distressed Protestants' were to be directed to the soldiers of the 'British and Scottish Armies poore ynough and too much distressed': BL Additional MS 4,771, fos 4v, 10v–11v, 16–17, 22v–23; Grell, 'Godly charity', pp. 746–53.

[55] PRONI MS T525/5. When challenged about his use of the term 'English' to describe 12,000 local forces, Clotworthy reverted to the term 'British' claiming a common animosity towards the Scottish army among Ulster English and 'old' Scots.

[56] B. M. Gardiner (ed.), 'A secret negociation with Charles I', *Camden Miscellany VIII*, Camden Society, new series, 31 (London, 1883), pp. 13–17; Pearl, 'Oliver St. John', pp. 512–13. For Clotworthy's general political position, see Mahony, 'Presbyterian party', p. 98; Lawrence Kaplan, *Politics and religion during the English revolution: the Scots and the Long Parliament 1643–1645* (New York, 1976), p. 43.

justified continued contacts with Leicester, based at Oxford. But Leicester was, albeit nominally, still head of the Irish administration until Ormond formally received the sword of state in January 1644, and, tellingly, Clotworthy was supposed to have supported as the 'fittest man' for the post of captain-general none other than Leicester's son Philip Sidney, Viscount Lisle.[57] Though the various allegations may have had more or less truth in them, there was a certain logic to securing a candidate who could be at once energetically pro-war regarding Ireland and without too much partisan baggage regarding England. Stances adopted on matters Irish cannot readily be plotted on to any map of 'party' alignments at Westminster. Fluidity of alignment as well as fixed points determined by particular policy positions, by regional interests or by factional associations, continued to characterize political life within Parliament. In a reverse of David Scott's depiction of the political preferences of the 'northern gentlemen' – MPs from the north of England drawn to a Scottish alliance at least in part as a means to secure their home territories – those MPs most associated with the Irish war saw in the Scottish alliance not only a dangerous diversion of resources from other forces in Ireland, but a threat to the prospect of winning the allegiance of local troops. Too many barriers should not be laid in the way of bringing the settler forces back on side.

Instead Scottish influence over the direction of the war in Ireland was to be consolidated, through new institutional arrangements and the influence of those MPs most supportive of the alliance. Vane, at this stage a prominent advocate of the Scots, had managed to secure some measures to assist the Scottish army in Ulster over the winter of 1643–44, working through Parliament's Scottish committee.[58] But in January 1644 the Scottish Convention of Estates resolved that its army should be permitted to return from Ireland if English promises were not met by a February deadline.[59] By February the Houses were consumed by the struggle for the implementation of the legislation establishing the new executive Committee

---

[57] PRONI MS T525/5, articles 13, 19. It was further charged against Clotworthy that he had promoted to Leicester the candidature of his brother-in-law Colonel John Chichester for the post of governor of Derry. Certainly Chichester had been at Oxford and secured the support both of the Westminster committee for Irish affairs and of Ormond. The importance of the post is evident from the struggles to secure a successor after Chichester was drowned en route to the city in early 1644.

[58] BL Harleian MS 166, fo. 18; *Calendar of the proceedings of the Committee for Compounding*, i, 3, 779.

[59] *Acts of the Parliament of Scotland*, vi, 72–3. It had been agreed in November that the minimum quota of supplies would be delivered to the Scots in Ulster between December and February, but by the latter date these terms had not even been ratified fully by Westminster. On 20 February the Scottish government resolved to persuade the regiments to remain in Ireland until March in hope of supplies: Stevenson, *Scottish Covenanters*, pp. 151–2, 155.

of Both Kingdoms.[60] The ordinance establishing the committee empowered it 'to advise, consult, order and direct, concerning the carrying on and managing of the war for the best advantage of the *three* kingdoms . . .'.[61] The assumption that one war was being conducted, embracing Ireland too, was hitched to the vesting of that war in a binational body, with four Scottish delegates eventually joined with seven English peers and fourteen English commoners. The Committee of Both Kingdoms rapidly, and successfully, pressed for the ratification of the terms agreed between the two countries' commissioners back in November, including the controversial joint command.[62] News that elements of the Scottish army in Ulster, stretched beyond breaking point, had begun to depart back to Scotland gave added impetus to their efforts, and a sub-committee of the Committee of Both Kingdoms, including the Scottish commissioners, drew up an additional set of proposals, designed to translate commitments into action.[63] Aided by the Committee's reports to the two Houses which incorporated reports and requests from the Scottish commissioners,[64] the additional proposals, which included a commitment to the long-hoped-for assessment for Ireland, were passed in early April.[65] This time some action does appear to have followed. Problems with the diversion of sequestration revenue to aid the Scottish army in Ulster were overcome, though the cash-bearing ships set sail only in June.[66] To the Scottish command were added plans to name an Anglo–Scottish committee to reside in Ulster, and a resolution finally to determine 'the Manner of tendering and taking' the Covenant in Ireland.[67]

Scottish involvement was written in at all points in the conduct of the war in Ireland. Clotworthy and Reynolds continued to formulate plans to relaunch the war, arguing that adequate supplies would bring local Protestant forces back on board.[68] A report delivered to the Commons on 2 April from the Revd Mr Traile realistically depicted the plight of both 'British' and Scottish forces but also alleged 'their good Affections to the Parliament of *England*;

---

[60] J. S. A. Adamson, 'The triumph of oligarchy: the management of the war and the Committee of Both Kingdoms, 1644–1645', in Kyle and Peacey (eds), *Parliament at work*, pp. 101–27.

[61] Gardiner (ed.), *Constitutional documents*, pp. 271–3; my italics.

[62] The terms were almost all accepted in early March, lingering difficulties being absorbed into the supplementary proposals in April, *CJ*, iii, 418; BL Harleian MS 166, fos 25v, 28; *LJ*, vi, 458, 463–4; McNeill (ed.), *Tanner letters*, pp. 172–3.

[63] *CSPD, 1644*, pp. 61–2, 64, 79–80.

[64] McNeill (ed.), *Tanner letters*, pp. 173–4; *LJ*, vi, 499–500; *CJ*, iii, 448; HMC *6th report* (London, 1877), p. 8.

[65] *CJ*, iii, 452, 456; *LJ*, vi, 511–12.

[66] *CSPD, 1644*, pp. 123–4, 133, 189.

[67] In addition both kingdoms were to be involved in nominating treasurers for the new assessment revenue and for aid received from the Netherlands: *CJ*, iii, 456.

[68] BL Additional MS 4,771, fos 27v–28; *CJ*, iii, 443; BL Additional MS 31,116, fo. 128v.

and their Inclination to take the solemn League and Covenant; and their Disaffection and utter Dislike of the Cessation; and of any Peace that shall ensue thereupon'.[69] Yet it is hard to avoid the impression that proponents of the 'British' of Ireland had a less ready ear at Westminster than the Scots. Clotworthy challenged the intention of providing £4,000 per month each to the Scottish and to the 'British' forces, 'more in number', urging a proportionately greater sum for the latter 'lest they should otherwise grow into discontent'.[70] Reynolds and Clotworthy were outside the political grouping then in the ascendant in Parliament – both were in fact named to an alternative Committee of Both Kingdoms being considered by the factional opponents of the new executive in May.[71] As the months unfolded relations soured within the joint committee, with the London committeemen distancing themselves from the committee's activities and increasingly at odds with Clotworthy and his associates over control of resources and access to provisioning contracts.[72] The rise of the Committee of Both Kingdoms in turn sidelined the joint committee. The Committee of Both Kingdoms focused its support on the London component of the joint committee, even installing it as one of its own sub-committees, significantly enough meeting at Turners' Hall, also the location of the London committee supplying the Scottish army in England.[73]

Behind the complex tussles and personal animosities at Westminster what was the larger political pattern of the months when Parliament was passing though its 'Scottish moment'? For one thing, tensions were generated within the Irish lobby at Westminster which, if patched over, were never fully resolved. Conflicts of interest between influential adventurers and figures with pre-existing connections in Ireland would erupt intermittently in the months and years ahead. Scottish interests had come to the fore in discussion of the war in Ireland, and that war had been re-cast as an Anglo–Scottish joint venture. Parliament would in time retreat from those commitments, even as it would back out of its tentative progress towards confederal arrangements in Great Britain,[74] while the priority in awarding resources to the Scottish army in Ireland remained largely a matter of paper commitments or long-delayed recompense to Scotland for resources advanced by that kingdom.[75] Yet the Scottish alignment sharpened the division between royalist

[69] *CJ*, iii, 444; BL Harleian MS 166, fo. 42v.

[70] BL Additional 31,116, fo. 131.

[71] BL Harleian MS 166, fo. 58v.

[72] BL Additional MS 4,771, fos 43–9; *CJ*, iii, 564.

[73] *CSPD, 1644*, pp. 169–70, 181, 210, 227, 229, 256, 346; *CSPD, addenda, 1625–49*, pp. 659–61; Armstrong, 'Ireland at Westminster', pp. 88–90. I am heavily indebted to unpublished work by Dr Patrick Little for my interpretation of events at Westminster in 1643–44.

[74] Little, 'English Parliament', pp. 114–17; Scott, 'Northern Gentlemen', pp. 365–70.

[75] Stevenson, *Scottish Covenanters*, pp. 158–9, 201–2.

and parliamentarian over Ireland, as would be apparent in the forthcoming peace negotiations at Uxbridge.[76] Moreover, it was within the political and religious matrix of a Covenanter Britain that Protestant Ireland would be re-integrated into the war of the three kingdoms.

Despite the belligerent rumblings emanating from the Protestant quarters in Ulster, the senior officers in the province were slow to commit themselves to war under a Parliamentarian-Covenanter banner. By February they were willing to justify to Ormond their receipt of supplies from Westminster. They framed their answer in response to the recent dispatch of confederate delegates sent to talk peace at the royal court in Oxford, arguing that they must maintain their strength lest the confederates impose terms upon the king, though they also noted that the king had devolved the conduct of the Irish war to the Parliament of England.[77] They gave expression, in a more advanced form, to a mood of dissatisfaction with the present and fear for the future which had settled upon the scattered Protestant garrisons across Ireland over the winter of 1643–44. In Connacht, discontent with quartering arrangements had emerged within weeks of the proclamation of the cessation, and rumours of impeding renewal of war were abroad by December.[78] If the cessation terms which specified that Protestant forces be supplied with money and cattle placed a not insubstantial burden upon the confederates, the pessimists on the Protestant side had also been right in their predictions of the dangers of reliance upon an enemy for food supplies in place of a previous recourse to plunder.

Munster soon felt the sapping effects of seemingly interminable disputes dependent upon the attempt to implement the cessation arrangements. Inchiquin, in command in Munster, took a vigorous part in the dispatch of troops to England, though he soon found his resources so straitened as to make this difficult.[79] Over the winter months he and his subordinates sought to exert pressure, directly or indirectly, to secure provisions peacefully from confederate quarters.[80] Disputes mounted over the possession of territory from which to draw sustenance. Covert shifts of allegiance were alleged to have occurred, bringing property into enemy hands. Thomas Bettesworth, one of the commissioners appointed to settle disputes in Munster, could put

---

[76] See below, Chapter 5, for a discussion of the Uxbridge negotiations.

[77] British officers to Ormond, 5 February 1644, Carte MS 9, fo. 104; cf. Arthur Hill to Ormond, 15 February 1644, Carte MS 9, fos 199–200.

[78] Clanricard to Ormond, 3 October 1643, 3 December 1643, in Carte, *Ormonde*, v, 473–4, 532–4.

[79] Inchiquin to Ormond, Carte MS 7, fo. 91 (10 October 1643); Carte, *Ormonde*, v, 498–500 (29 October 1643), 522–3 (23 November 1643); Carte MS 8, fo. 139 (18 December 1643).

[80] Inchiquin to Ormond, 18 December 1643, Carte MS 8, fo. 139. Hardress Waller to Ormond, 6 February, 9 February 1644; undated draft of Ormond to Waller, Carte MS 9, fos 125, 163, 568.

it forward as 'a received opinion' even in October 1643 that 'the cessation will be sooner ended than the controversies that arise from it'. One local garrison commander, Thomas Reymond, had no doubt that his 'condition is far worse than in the time of open hostility', for the wheels of negotiated redress ground very slowly, and the outcome was slight advantage, compared with the possibilities of armed restitution.[81]

To anxiety at the prospect of being slowly ground away, of losing in one year what could not be regained in seven,[82] should be added a sharper distrust of the intentions of recent enemies and a nurtured bitterness over recent wrongs. Leading figures in Munster retained an interest in the depositions taken in the aftermath of the rising in 1641, being concerned at their dispersal and keen to ensure that they be 'kept safe'. Sir Philip Perceval, one of the Dublin government delegation to Oxford, asked to be sent 'notes of the murders about Cashell and Goolan Bridge'.[83] The idea of a future reckoning remained alive.[84] The arrival of a confederate delegation in Oxford in March 1644 spurred Protestant Ireland to take its battle to court. When the Dublin Parliament briefly reassembled in February it picked up its agenda from the previous November. The Commons nominated agents to argue before the king a position redolent of the stance adumbrated the previous autumn, with no compromise offered in peace terms, and a concern lest 1641 come again. That they mandated an elaborate structure to provide funding for the agents, on a provincial basis, is a reminder that some sort of national structure could be sustained for Protestant political expression; not all politics were regional politics.[85]

In Ulster the partial departure of the Scottish army in the spring, with three regiments transporting themselves to Scotland by March, had caused considerable concern. The senior officers of the British forces were entangled in strategic and political dilemmas. The very presence of the Scottish army constituted a standing challenge to the combination of social, economic, military and political leadership exercised by the Ulster Protestant elite, in the east of the province at least.[86] Still, its departure not only ran up against a royal preference to keep it in Ireland (and so not available for use against the

---

[81] HMC *Egmont MSS*, i, 190–1, 195.

[82] Thornton to Ormond on the cessation, 28 December 1643, Carte MS 8, fos 231–2.

[83] HMC *Egmont MSS*, i, 192, 194–5, 201–3, 209–10. Cf. Aidan Clarke, 'The 1641 depositions', in Peter Fox (ed.), *Treasures of the library: Trinity College Dublin* (Dublin, 1986), pp. 114–16, 120.

[84] Likewise Henry Jones and his associates among those commissioned to take depositions chose November 1643 as the moment to issue a second remonstrance summarizing statements, emphasizing the malice and barbarism of the rebels: Clarke, '1641 rebellion and anti-popery', pp. 151–7.

[85] *CJI*, i, 317.

[86] Gillespie, 'Army sent from God' pp. 123–4.

king in England), but posed a threat that the local Protestant front would crumble as rumours circulated of popular intentions to disband or flee in the wake of Monro's forces.[87] Yet retaining the Scottish army only added the dangers of attack by the confederates, for by the spring it was known that they were mustering against the Scots.[88] Local forces could not but be caught up in the crossfire. By 1 March, Sir Robert Stewart, a solid king's man in the north-west, asserted that some local officers had promoted a 'band' to break the cessation in the hope that this would stay the Scots army.[89] Word from Scotland was not long in coming. Orders to stay Monro's army were conveyed to Ulster by Sir Frederick Hamilton, also mandated by Lord Chancellor Loudoun to contact the well-affected 'British' in Ulster. Loudoun's approaches to local figures were met with a letter, dated 26 March, which repudiated the cessation, indeed condemned it as dishonourable to God, the king and the people of Great Britain and dangerous to the Protestant remnant. It pledged concurrence with Monro in offensive and defensive actions, but insisted that nothing could be undertaken without supplies.[90] Early April then saw the delivery not only of money and provisions for the Monro's Scots, but also of Dutch aid for local units.[91]

Yet rather than easing local forces into an uncomplicated return to war, the hitching of war to supply, and of supply to a Covenanter agenda, threatened to derail the whole process. Sir Robert Stewart blamed Hamilton for winning over the Derry populace to the 'cause' and the Covenant in the absence of Sir William Stewart and himself, and promised to oppose such moves from his base at nearby Culmore fort.[92] Evidence for the spread of the Covenant is stretched between the reports to Ormond of senior Ulster officers, who alleged that the soldiery and country were won to the noxious document more by the pleadings of their stomachs than by their consciences,[93] and the reading of the process by Presbyterian ministers, who highlighted the spiritual

---

[87] For example, Hill to Ormond, 15 February 1644, Carte MS 9, fos 199–200.

[88] Ohlmeyer, *Civil war and Restoration*, pp. 137–8; Pádraig Lenihan, 'Confederate military strategy, 1643–7', in Ó Siochrú, *Kingdoms in crisis*, pp. 161–2.

[89] Stewart to Ormond, 1 March 1644, Carte MS 9, fo. 391.

[90] Thornton to Ormond, 14 March 1644, Carte MS 9, fos 530–1; Loudoun to Derry civil officials, to officers in north-west, Carte MSS 9, fo. 348, 10, fo. 271; copy for Ormond (unsigned) of letter to Loudoun, 26 March 1644, Carte MS 10, fo. 269. The reply echoed the language of Loudoun's letter.

[91] British officers to Ormond, 7 April 1644, Carte MS 10, fo. 153, 14 April 1644, Carte MS 10, fo. 207.

[92] Stewart to Ormond, 17 April 1644, Carte MS 10, fo. 261. Hamilton himself later boasted that he was 'the immediate instrument, and best help to the ministers, who were intrusted with the Solemn League and Covenant, to get it taken by the citizens of *London-Derry*, the Regiments and Countrey thereabouts': *The humble remonstrance of Sir Frederick Hammilton* [*sic*] (London, 1643) Wing H477B.

[93] Audley Mervyn to Ormond, 22 April 1644, Carte MS 10, fo. 336.

enthusiasm of the Covenanting dynamic.[94] No doubt the responses of the populace spanned the spectrum in between. The Covenant could indeed act as a defensive bond or a means of plugging Ulster into a current of, primarily Scottish, military energy.[95] But Covenanting in Ulster bore the hallmarks of a genuinely popular political movement, and one with a recognizable ideological edge.

Dublin's campaign against the Covenant had extended to the Irish Parliament, where, in another brief session in April, a letter from the speakers of the two Houses had been produced commending the council's proclamation against the Covenant. Plans were laid to formulate a full-scale repudiation of the Covenant's terms.[96] Back in Ulster, though, Sir James Montgomery and Viscount Ards reported the impossibility of overcoming the Covenant, popular within and without the forces, and both men sought leave to depart.[97] Chichester, Blayney and Hill, commanders of the regiments drawn from the 'English' population of east Ulster, reported on 25 April that they had read the proclamation against the Covenant, but against their better judgement, and argued that the vast majority of soldiers in the province had accepted it. They claimed that if they had not proclaimed the Covenant they would have been in a better position to obtain supplies, alleged that soldiers would desert for those regiments where they could be supplied, and admitted that they too considered 'shifting for our selves' the wisest option. By 29 April, Chichester had heard rumours of Monro's being awarded the chief command in Ulster; he saw this, in combination with the Covenant, as leading to the handful of loyal subjects being 'utterly ruined'.[98] In the hub of the north-west Ormond had moved to replace the late compromise candidate for the city's governor, John Chichester, with Sir Audley Mervyn, prompting division among the civic authorities. Though the latter had waged a campaign to retain civilian control of the city, the mayor, Thornton, now accepted that the 'sedition' associated with the Covenant demanded a military figure, even as others quailed at the prospect of a 'great royallist' in command. Mervyn had already pondered the re-modelling of local forces to ensure loyalty,[99] but he could not stem the Covenanting tide. Local commanders argued with the

[94] Adair, *True narrative*, pp. 102–18.
[95] Perceval-Maxwell, 'Ireland and Scotland', pp. 204–6; David Miller, *Queen's rebels: Ulster loyalism in historical perspective* (Dublin, 1978), pp. 14–16.
[96] *CJI*, i, 324, 325, 326, 328–9; *LJI*, i, 206, 207, 208, 210.
[97] Sir James Montgomery to Ormond, 23 April 1644, Carte MS 10, fo. 350; Sir James and Viscount Montgomery to Ormond, 23 April 1644, Carte MS 10, fo. 355.
[98] Carte MS 10, fos 391, 395–6, 472–3.
[99] Mervyn to Ormond, 17 February, 21 February 1644, Carte MS 9, fos 217–18, 269. Mervyn claimed to 'love not' national distinctions, yet pointed to the English origin of his own forces.

Scottish ministers who sponsored the Covenant that it would break Protestant unity, only to be met with the response that it was their failure to subscribe which was in breach of a united front.[100]

In the east of the province the senior officers planned another summit in Belfast in early May, reputedly to discuss Monro's claims to the chief command. The location was significant, for Belfast had been targeted by Ormond to be secured against those who, as he put it, would urge religion against their king.[101] In fact the meeting was overtaken by Monro's capture of the town, with assistance from officers and men of the local forces, on 14 May. The bulk of the officers were quick to come to terms with Monro, issuing a declaration on 17 May that 'this warr against the Irish Rebells is a most iust warr' and one in which they would join, as enabled,[102] and in turn receiving assurances of supply and that the Covenant would not be enforced. Chichester, though, fled to Dublin, while 'his' town of Belfast staged its own miniature coup, repudiating the Chichester governance under colour of the Covenant.[103] In south Ulster and north Leinster 'English' garrisons fortified themselves against a repetition of the Scottish coup. That they looked to Owen Roe O'Neill and the demonized Ulster Irish for supplies, while within the framework set by the cessation, was hardly likely to sit easily with Protestant opinion at large.[104]

The Covenant wrenched Protestant Ireland apart. Outright violent conflict was avoided, but only by an unusual deployment of restraint and good sense. As a political community it would re-form, but not entirely re-integrate, for the Covenant remained an awkward and jarring element in its political culture. The Presbyterian ministers who had presided over the subscriptions had blended a voluntarist appeal to popular participation with a justification

[100] Ormond to the Derry authorities, 17 April 1644, Carte MS 10, fo. 265; Mervyn to Ormond, Thornton to Ormond, both 22 April 1644, Carte MS 10, fos 336, 338; Scots ministers to aldermen Lawson and Osborne, 25 April 1644, Carte MS 10, fo. 361; Thornton to Ormond, Mervyn to Ormond, both 25 April 1644, Carte MS 10, fos 401, 409–11; Sir Robert Stewart to the Scottish clergy, 26 April 1644, Carte MS 10, fo. 407; Mervyn to Ormond, 26 April 1644, Carte MS 10, fos 411–12; Mervyn to Ormond, 24 May, Carte MS 10, fo. 789; R. Stewart to Ormond, 26 May 1644, Carte MS 11, fo. 3. Mervyn was the last of the west Ulster colonels to avow the Covenant (in his own manner), and 'the soldiers who had taken it before cried out – "Welcome, welcome, Colonel!" ': Adair, *True narrative*, p. 116.

[101] Ormond to Chichester, 2 May 1644, Carte MS 10, fo. 509; Ormond to Lieutenant-Colonel Matthews, commanding at Newry, whom he urged to hasten to Belfast, 2 May 1644, Carte MS 10, fo. 502; Stevenson, *Scottish Covenanters*, pp. 161–3.

[102] Moore to Ormond, 18 May 1644, Carte MS 10, fo. 688; Matthews to Ormond, 19 May 1644, Carte MS 11, fo. 54. The declaration was produced by the officers of the three 'English' regiments (Chichester's, Conway's and Hill's) upon which any Ormondist hopes of resistance to the Covenant had been based.

[103] Gillespie, *Colonial Ulster*, p. 185.

[104] HMC *Ormonde MSS*, new series, i, 76–9.

based on the interlocking arrangements put in place between England and Scotland. Neither layer was likely to appeal to the entrenched leadership of Protestant Ulster.[105] The proponents of the Ulster British at Westminster had been wise in their calls to limit the barriers to participation in renewed war. Their critique had not extended to the enforcement of the Covenant, and though that proved the greatest obstacle for the elite it was one safely hurdled by numbers of the soldiery and the 'country'. When Westminster did receive a formal call for aid from an assembly of 'British' officers, it was couched in suitable language, laced with claims that they had long been willing to renew the war, but were restrained only by their fear of the Scots' departure. The officers' resolution to fight again, they claimed, was a result of reassurances that the Scottish army would stay and that supplies would arrive, but they insisted that their delegates' requests for further supply were vital, else disbandment threatened.[106]

Westminster's response was rather at once ostensibly generous and griping. A new committee was to:

> consider of the Propositions this day presented to the House, from the distressed *Brittish* Regiments in *Ulster*; and to bring them as low as possibly they can; and . . . to take notice of the Votes formerly passed in this House, concerning the carrying on of the War, that nothing may interfere with those Votes: And are to consider what Commanders and Officers are fit to be removed; and of Raising of Monies for carrying on the War; and of lessening the Charge.[107]

The Ulster British would be supported under Scottish patronage. The practical outcome would not be fruitless, but even here the timing was poor. For within a week, news of the defection of Munster would open up a second front in Ireland, and one with no unfortunate complications involving the Scots.

Protestant Munster's decision to resume war was preceded by months when relations between the armed camps in the south had been worn ragged and mutual suspicions had been caught in a downward spiral of distrust. In February Inchiquin had travelled to court to plead the province's cause, and his own, for he was in pursuit of his father-in-law St. Leger's old post as lord

---

[105] Mervyn's constitutionalist past comes out in his assertion of the need to 'defend ye independeancie of this Government upon a forraigne Kingdom': Mervyn to Ormond, 25 April 1644, Carte MS 10, fos 409–11. Cf. Robert Armstrong, 'Viscount Ards and the presbytery: the politics of the Scots of Ulster in the 1640s', in John R. Young (ed.), *Scotland and Ulster* (Dublin, forthcoming).

[106] The letter's signatories included leading figures from locally raised regiments with both Scottish and English identities, and commended agents newly dispatched, 'taking there to their Assistance Colonel *Clotworthy*': CJ, iii, 560; LJ, vi, 621, 622–3.

[107] CJ, iii, 574.

president of Munster.[108] He was unsuccessful on both counts, returning 'as full of anger as his buttons will endure'.[109] Oxford had merely become another site for the provincial struggle over loyalty; the confederate delegates, at some point, even produced for the king a list of Protestant garrisons and commanders they considered unreliable.[110] Sir Hardress Waller, in command in Inchiquin's absence, noted that the outcome of the latter's visit would determine for him 'what sail to bear'.[111] Waller considered the situation all but desperate, with his forces down to just over 1,000 infantry and 200 cavalry, and was unsure how he could keep even this remnant together.[112]

As spring turned to summer, such concerns grew more intense. Confederates claimed concern at possible parliamentary landings on the south coast.[113] Their charges of surreptitious contacts with Parliament are unlikely to have been baseless.[114] Inchiquin, in turn, later alleged 'a plot laid to take these garrisons, under pretence of a suspicion they had of my intention to bring in the parliament shipping and forces', charges, it would seem, also not without foundation. Broghill, the other leading figure in Protestant Munster, pointed to the provocation entailed in the raising of new forces by the confederates.[115] Inchiquin's 'defection' to Parliament has been seen as not embracing any ideological 'espousal of the tenets of parliamentarianism on the part of the Munster Protestants generally'.[116] Perhaps it is not irrelevant in this regard that contacts appear to have been established with the parliamentarian cause in the south-west of England, where Essex and Robartes were campaigning with notable lack of success, more ably supported at sea by the earl of Warwick, all three of them associated at this juncture with Essex's 'policy of a settlement negotiated on lenient terms' with the king.[117] The declarations issued by the Munster leadership, to both king and

[108] In September 1642 the English Commons' resolution to grant him the post was blocked by the upper House, who declared that with him 'being an *Irishman* born, and many of his kindred out in Rebellion, it might be prejudiciall to make him Provost', though not, it seemed, to retain him in provincial military command: *CJ*, ii, 787; *LJ*, v, 376, 377; Yonge, *Diary*, p. 25.

[109] Arthur Trevor to Ormond, 19 February 1644, Carte, *Ormonde*, vi, 38.

[110] Gilbert (ed.), *Irish confederation*, iii, 162–5.

[111] Waller to Bettesworth, 12 February 1644, HMC *Egmont MSS*, i, 199.

[112] Waller to Ormond, 6 February 1644, Carte MS 9, fo. 125.

[113] Gilbert (ed.), *Irish confederation*, iii, 205–8.

[114] See, for example, Richard Bellings to Ormond, 10 April 1644, Carte MS 10, fos 165, 169.

[115] Inchiquin to Clanricard, 26 July 1644, *Letter-book*, p. 102; Broghill to Clonmel corporation, 26 July 1644, Gilbert (ed.), *Irish confederation*, iii, 216–17. John A. Murphy, 'The expulsion of the Irish from Cork in 1644', *Journal of the Cork Historical and Archaeological Society* 69 (1964), 126, accepts the reality of a plot to seize Cork.

[116] John A. Murphy, 'The politics of the Munster Protestants, 1641–49', *Journal of the Cork Historical and Archaeological Society* 76 (1971), 10.

[117] See M. L. Baumber, 'The navy and the civil war in Ireland, 1643–1646', *Mariner's Mirror* 75 (1989), 262–4; Adamson, 'Triumph of oligarchy', p. 114.

Parliament, expressed the hope that the situation in Ireland would push forward a peace in England, but were unrelenting in an insistence that the signatories would 'die a thousand deaths rather than condescend to any peace with these perfidious Rebels' in Ireland.[118]

It would be some weeks before the Covenant arrived in Munster, prompting not a little unease and heart-searching.[119] In the first glow of their re-alignment, expressed almost with an air of defiant liberation, a freedom to fight, there was a hope that Ormond could be pressed to join in the plan of English peace and Irish war.[120] As late as 14 September Inchiquin was offering Ormond the command of his forces, though by now he was obliged to undertake the invidious task of attempting to gloss the Covenant as a 'loyal' document, as was Audley Mervyn, at the other end of the island.[121] From the baron Inchiquin to the parishioners of Holywood, questions of allegiance were worked at, and worked out, within ideological, political and, indeed, emotional contexts which swirled around all three Stuart kingdoms. Across the land of Ireland political decisions, for Protestant communities, were framed by two alternative paths to settlement, the prospective peace-talking between confederate Catholics and the court and that which loomed between royalists and the Covenanter alliance.

[118] *A letter from the right honourable the Lord Inchiquin . . . to his Majestie . . .* (London, 1644) E8 (37); *A manifestation directed to the honourable house of parliament . . . from the Lord Inchiquin . . .* (London, 1644) E6 (1).

[119] Murphy, 'Politics of the Munster Protestants', p. 11.

[120] 'The Unanimous Declaration of His Majesties Subjects of the Province of Munster' ends: 'Then though we lose our lives in this cause, we shall give our friends occasion to rejoice, and our Enemies to envie at so blessed an end': *A manifestation . . . from the Lord Inchiquin . . .*, p. 10.

[121] Inchiquin to Ormond in Clarendon, *State papers*, ii, 168–9 (undated), 170–1 (23 July 1644), 173–5 (19 September 1644); cf. Sir Thomas Wharton to Ormond, 19 July, Clarendon, *State papers*, ii, 169–70. For attempts at equivocation or 'interpretation' in the taking of parliamentarian oaths see Edward Vallance, 'Protestation, Vow, Covenant and Engagement: swearing allegiance in the English civil war', *Historical Research* 75 (2002), 417–21.

5

Quests for peace, 1644–45

Oxford was many things during the war years of the 1640s: royal headquarters, garrison and magazine; hub for royalist propaganda; site for an attenuated but busy little court, for a depleted crown administration and for an occasional, and slightly bewildered, 'parliament'. It was also the location for intermittent diplomacy and sporadic episodes of treaty-making. In the early spring of 1644 agents of the confederate Catholics of Ireland finally got their chance to present their terms to their monarch.[1] Edward Hyde, future earl of Clarendon, a man on the spot, would later claim that the king's intentions from the time of the cessation had been 'to have made a good peace there, and to have had the power of that united kingdom to have assisted in suppressing the rebellion in this'.[2] When he came to the point Charles always preferred the assistance to the unity and peace of Ireland. Certainly the confederate delegates returned home with little sense of achievement. The king offered little more than promises and assurances, offering a lenient application of penal legislation rather than its abrogation, and deployed the language of legality and parliamentary rights to avoid commitment to confederate demands; he remitted negotiations to his lord lieutenant in Dublin, Ormond.[3] The episode gives all the indications of a court loath to make any concessions of substance for fear of the possible backlash in England. But if compromise was ever on the cards there were voices from Ireland to expostulate loudly against it. Hyde described the stance of the Dublin government representatives at court as an insistence

> that there could be no other security for the Protestants in that kingdom but by leaving the Irish without any capacity or ability to trouble them, . . . and therefore

---

[1] Gilbert (ed.), *Irish confederation*, iii, 128–33; also printed in Curtis and McDowell (eds), *Irish historical documents*, pp. 152–6.
[2] Clarendon, *History*, iii, 445.
[3] Gilbert (ed.), *Irish confederation*, iii, 175–8, 198–9, 208–10; Ó Siochrú, *Confederate Ireland*, pp. 72–3.

they must either be put into such a condition by being totally disarmed that they should not be able to do any mischieve, or that all the Protestants must leave the kingdom to the entire possession of the Irish; and whether that would be for his majesty's service and security they must refer to his own wisdom.[4]

The Irish councillors' extended commentary on the confederate terms was an unrelenting reading, a security-dominated counter-agenda.[5] Yet even they were not the hardliners.

As discussed in Chapter 4, a considerable segment of Protestant opinion in Ireland had insisted on securing its own voice at court through the appointment of 'Protestant' agents. Their mandate was not only to stand against the treaty with the confederates, but to put the case for a forward Protestant policy, of a bolstered confessional state, a reinvigorated plantation policy and full and rapid restitution for Protestant sufferings and losses.[6] They were content to admit that the king was in no position to enforce such a solution, but gave the ready answer that if he were to make peace with his English Parliament, together they could 'send over such assistance to Ireland as would quickly settle that kingdom'.[7] Neither set of Protestants left Oxford secure and happy. Sir Philip Perceval, one of the Irish councillors, gave vent to a sense of exclusion and disillusionment, claiming that he and his fellows were not given adequate opportunity to engage with the confederate stance. Had he but known it, the word back to Ormond was that his colleagues were reckoned to have 'played ye fooles notably', being too opposed to the Catholic terms, while Perceval himself could have passed for a 'Roundhead'.[8] By 1 June one of the 'Protestant' agents, Captain William Parsons, nephew of the ousted lord justice, was to be found addressing the Commons at Westminster. He claimed that his delegation, having had enough trouble getting out of Ireland, reached Oxford too late to confront their Catholic rivals. These, though, had, during their stay, 'frequent accesse & dayly discourse w[i]th ye K[ing] in his Garden, when the Protestant Agent stood aloof, & had no Countenance nor Respect at all'; they had not even received a proper answer to their proposals, which 'were discountenanced with the

---

[4] Clarendon, *History*, iii, 447–8.

[5] HMC *Egmont MSS*, i, 212–29.

[6] Gilbert (ed.), *Irish confederation*, iii, 143–8; Curtis and McDowell (eds), *Irish historical documents*, pp. 156–8.

[7] Clarendon, *History*, iii, 448. For criticism of the 'Protestant' agents as opposed to any negotiated settlement see Digby to Ormond (6 May), Radcliffe to Ormond (16 May 1644), Carte MS 10, fos 532–3, 651.

[8] Perceval to Ormond, Carte MS 10, fo. 747; Sir George Radcliffe to Ormond, 11 June 1644, Carte MS 11, fo. 172.

Title of Unreasonable, and the Propositions of Madmen'.[9] The four 'Protestant' agents were offered a sequestered and re-furnished house in London, the ministrations of the 'Irish lobby' within Parliament and the ear of the Committee of Both Kingdoms. Within a few weeks some of the Irish councillors late at Oxford would join them.[10]

The failed royal peace initiative had done little more than keep the embers of Catholic hopes alive while fanning the flames of Protestant anxiety. Ulster had been braced for a large-scale confederate campaign designed to quash Monro and his allies in the summer of 1644, but the resulting debacle not only sent the Catholic camp into spasms of recrimination and accusation, but left the Scottish general burnished with 'the honours of the 1644 campaign', both his own march into Leinster in the early summer, his 'largest, . . . longest, . . . and . . . most successful' operation, and his defensive blocking of the confederate assault, its own kind of slightly accidental victory.[11] Ulster officers picked up on the moves towards peace negotiations in the English war, driven forward by the Scots, and hoped that the latter might broker a settlement there. Major George Rawdon of Lord Conway's 'English' regiment expressed his hopes of an English settlement but claimed that all officers, given reports of renewed fighting in Munster and Connacht, hoped Ormond would resist pressure for an Irish peace settlement, or even for another cessation.[12] Audley Mervyn, still claiming to serve Ormond under cover of the Covenant, reported that no form of cessation could please Ulster, and the only acceptable peace was one based on Catholic surrender.[13] If Ormond had any doubts on this score they would have been nailed with the receipt of a belligerent petition from Ulster which set out to rebut any idea of a peace necessitated by Protestant weakness. If the king were deceived into such a settlement it could only mean 'quarter graunted us, and iron chaines of slavery, and Antichristian bondage'. Instead Ormond should follow the example of the Munster forces, who 'find it high tyme rather to study unity among our selves then peace with them', since 'theise inhumaine natives are incapable of any mercy or pardon, but such as shall gratiouslie flowe from his Majesty and his greate Counsell, without capitulacion'.[14]

[9] *CJ*, iii, 513–14; BL Additional MS 31,116, fo. 141b.

[10] *CJ*, iii, 520, 525–6, 560.

[11] Stevenson, *Scottish Covenanters*, pp. 191–201; Lenihan, *Confederate Catholics at war*, pp. 81–2.

[12] Rawdon to Edmund Matthews, 23 and 27 August 1644, Carte MS 12, fos 173, 204. The Ormondist Matthews, lieutenant-colonel in Chichester's regiment, was in active command at Newry, where he had readied himself to oppose Monro in arms. Cf. Stewart to Sir Patrick Wemyss, 31 August 1644, Carte MS 12, fo. 229.

[13] Mervyn to Ormond, 6 September 1644, Carte MS 12, fo. 305.

[14] Gilbert (ed.), *Contemporary history*, i, 602–5.

Instead, on 6 September, Ormond and his negotiating team embarked on their first bout of talks with the confederate treaty delegation. It was the beginning of a fraught, fatiguing, yet occasionally fruitful series of negotiations, in person and on paper, which would stretch over the best part of the next year and a half, before eventually yielding a treaty between the king's lieutenant and his Catholic subjects in arms.[15] Ormond embarked with his eyes open. Back in early July his letter to George, Lord Digby, the king's secretary of state, noted that, if even those in England who wished well to the king 'haue such a reluctancy to a peace with the Irish, . . . how can it be possible that the English heere, who for the most part haue felt those iniuryes and affronts, which the other soe much pitty and recent, will be induced to aquiessye to a settlement not held fitt to be avowed on that side . . .'.[16] The king himself had written of passing over the treaty to Ormond lest, though he 'should doe that heere, which perhaps may be necessarye there, . . . it might, thorough indispositions heere, be of dangerous consequence to the maine of my affaires'.[17] The lord lieutenant's friends at court criticized the 'cautious councillors' there who would not even venture to send Ormond instructions, leaving all to his discretion, a stance which could be cynically interpreted as avoiding all contamination from the Irish negotiations. As Arthur Trevor put it, 'the councell will putt the stocke into your hand, and stand themselves behind the hangings. I presume the marquess of Ormonde will thinke it proportionable to reason, that they goe their shares, if they expect a profitt in the returne'.[18]

The first round of negotiations in September 1644 produced a hefty quota of position papers and critiques.[19] Indeed the principal gain, for either side, may have lain in a careful and illuminating probing of positions and agendas by two groups of capable and experienced individuals. The committee of the Irish Council assembled by Ormond provided considerable legal expertise.[20] On the confederate side, negotiations fell into the hands of leading members of that wing of the movement most eager to secure a settlement with their monarch, a development which might ultimately allow progress in talks, but not only threatened to open a gap between the negotiators and their more

---

[15] The successes and failures of the treaty negotiations are considered, from different perspectives, in Ó Siochrú, *Confederate Ireland*, chapter 2; Robert Armstrong, 'Ormond, the confederate peace talks, and Protestant royalism', in Ó Siochrú (ed.), *Kingdoms in crisis*, pp. 122–40.

[16] Ormond to Digby, 9 July 1644, Carte, *Ormonde*, vi, 154.

[17] Charles to Ormond, 17 July 1644, Carte, *Ormonde*, v, 7.

[18] Trevor to Ormond, 20 August 1644, Carte, *Ormonde*, vi, 197–8; Daniel O'Neill to Ormond, 13 August 1644, Gilbert (ed.), *Contemporary history*, i, 594–8.

[19] Gilbert (ed.), *Irish confederation*, iii, 278–329.

[20] Gilbert (ed.), *Irish confederation*, iii, 278: Lord Chancellor Bolton, Chief Justice Sir George Shurley [Shirley], justices Thomas Dongan and Sir William Ryves, and Sir Maurice Eustace, king's serjeant and speaker of the Commons.

unbending colleagues but even raised 'the danger of a disjunction between the main body of the association and its official representatives'.[21] For now, as the talks petered out, Ormond recognized that the answers from the Irish Council, 'after much debate, weare agreed to be in substance the same with those received [by the confederates] at Oxford'.[22] Ormond's goals were the restoration of royal authority in, and over, Ireland, and aid for his majesty in his difficulties in the other two kingdoms. Those were the king's goals, too, if not necessarily in that order. They determined Ormond's stance during the peace negotiations, a stance essentially reactive,[23] sometimes grudging, occasionally obstructive. He can hardly be accused of an imaginative response to the confederate agenda, but that was hardly to his purpose.[24] Instead three sets of considerations may be said to have affected the position of the royal negotiators, Ormond especially, over the next several years: the balance between necessary and dangerous concessions within the treaty itself; the balance between formal treaty and alternative routes to attaining the royal purposes; the positive vision for the kingdom of Ireland within the Protestant royalist tradition.[25]

As will be seen, the months and years ahead would see significant concessions offered and received, not least as the changing political fortunes of the participants put pressure on the king to offer more, and on the confederates to ask for more. Yet there remained limits beyond which it became counter-productive for Ormond to cede ground. It was already clear that offers which might win Catholic Ireland back to the crown could push Protestant Ireland into the embrace of the crown's foes. It was not only the case that the Protestants of Ireland were the community from which the crown's negotiators were drawn, nor were they merely an irritant boxed into corners of Ireland; rather their enclaves were potential outposts for a tri-kingdom alliance more threatening to Charles I than the confederate Catholics could be. If sufficiently alienated they could contribute to the loss of the island as a whole to an aggressive Covenanter alliance. Digby had already urged an Irish peace to make possible united action against the 'traitors of the covenant [there], so much more dangerous than any other, as they are more firmly linkt unto the rebells here' in England.[26] More than

---

[21] Ó hAnnracháin, *Catholic Reformation*, pp. 30–1.

[22] Ormond to Digby, Gilbert (ed.), *Irish confederation*, iii, 329–33.

[23] In practice, the agenda for the peace talks was largely set by the propositions presented by the confederate agents: Gilbert (ed.), *Irish confederation*, iii, 128–33, 324–7; for propositions presented by Ormond on behalf of the king, the Church of Ireland and the 'Protestant party', see Gilbert (ed.), *Irish confederation*, iii, 319–20, 321, 312–13.

[24] For the view that Ormond's 'tactics . . . provided the greatest obstacle to a peace settlement' see Ó Siochrú, *Confederate Ireland*, pp. 76–7, 82.

[25] This case is argued in much more detail in Armstrong, 'Ormond . . . and Protestant royalism'.

[26] Digby to Ormond, 22 July 1644, Carte, *Ormonde*, vi, 174.

that, there lurked the possibility that the negotiations could subvert the whole purpose of a settlement from the royal, or royalist, point of view, by further undermining the monarchical, English and Protestant nature of the Irish polity rather than regaining Catholic allegiance to it by what could be presented as appropriate, and gracious, concessions.

The treaty was of crucial importance to all political actors in Ireland, but it was never the only option pursued by confederates or by royalists. The confederate agents returned from Oxford with what they considered a crucial additional concession, a royal offer of military co-operation against the opponents of the cessation. On 1 July the Supreme Council wrote to Ormond to activate such an initiative,[27] with all that it promised in terms not only of resources but also of implicitly regaining the status of the 'faithful and loyal subjects' that confederates had always claimed to be. The flip-side lay in the confederates' inclusion in their treaty propositions of demands that Ormond actively condemn those who refused the cessation or who swore the Covenant. Such miscreants should be 'proclaimed Traitors and prosecuted accordingly'; counties and corporations which rejected the cessation should be barred from electing to Parliament; those who assisted the king's enemies in England should be subject to impeachment and attainder, with forfeiture to the king, while those of 'our partie' with estates held by the Scots or Parliamentarians should 'be recompensed out of the estates of those malignants in this kingdom'.[28]

Other voices were calling for Ormond to declare himself. In August he received a letter addressed to the king and signed by a small but significant group of mostly western-based grandees, Clanricard, Dillon, Taaffe, Ranelagh and Thomond among them, which presented loyal Ireland as trapped between 'two powerful armies' of confederates and Covenanters, and insisted that a negotiated peace was necessary. In the short term, though, it was the Scots who should be publicly declared the king's enemies, for 'to subsist in this divided condition, without joining or receiving help from one party or other, we conceive utterly impossible'.[29] It reflected the outlook of individuals who had sought to steer a middle course in 1641–42, and would again, but for the moment it was telling which enemy they considered the greater danger to king and country. Ormond resisted all siren calls. He ordered his officers to try to protect pro-cessation Catholics from the Scots,[30] but he

---

[27] Carte MS 11, fo. 328.

[28] Gilbert (ed.), *Irish confederation*, iii, 324–7.

[29] *Letter-book*, pp. 93–5. The letter was drawn up in mid-July but finally dispatched to Ormond on 18 August by Clanricard, Dillon and Taaffe after long-drawn-out, but futile, attempts to secure Inchiquin's support: *Letter-book*, pp. 95–101, 103–4.

[30] Ormond to Tichborne and Moore, 12 July 1644, Carte MS 11, fo. 435.

firmly rejected the idea of taking arms against the latter, a course of action which would see him 'suddainely and totally deserted by all the protestants'.[31] Digby, in turn, glossed the royal offer of co-operation with the confederates; its exercise was left to Ormond's discretion, and should be used only in extremity or in the event of a settled peace.[32]

Ormond, too, though, would increasingly look outside the parameters of the formal negotiations. To him, after all, the confederates were arrant rebels who should be on their knees in quest of royal forgiveness. That he was not so unyielding as to seek to punish them all and to the uttermost did not detract from his obvious intention to seek the complete overthrow of the confederate organization. To ingest it back into the body politic was one route, but to disrupt and dismantle it through defections and defeats was another acceptable option, and one Ormond would pursue with some energy in the months ahead.[33] Royalism, in Ireland as in England, was apt to stigmatize rebels but retained the potential to receive them back, duly pardoned and cleansed for royal service.[34] One route to redemption was to aid the king by harnessing Irish resources to his British wars. As Tadhg Ó hAnnracháin perceptively noted, 'none of the protagonists during this period . . . believed that a settlement in Ireland would not lead to an intervention in the English civil war'.[35] For the king and those closest too him, though, the enticing prospect was that of intervention before settlement. Jane Ohlmeyer has demonstrated how the marquis of Antrim pursued the goal of Irish armed engagement in the king's cause in both Scotland and England in advance of any peace settlement, supportive as he was of the treaty negotiations. To that end he was willing to sow disruption in confederate ranks and, knowingly or not, accept the risk that concessions were less likely to be offered if the confederates would raise and send soldiers without them.[36] How much more would Ormond not also favour such endeavours to cut though the tangles and deliver aid while it could still do good.

Finally, there remains the question of what, if any, broader vision directed the specific positions adopted by Ormond and his increasingly small band of comrades in the seemingly interminable pursuit of a settlement. It was an essentially restorative commitment to a rejuvenated version of the Irish kingdom which was already in existence before the disruption of 1641, not

---

[31] Ormond to Digby, 9 July 1644, Carte, *Ormonde*, vi, 153–9; 17 July 1644, Carte MS 11, fos 484–6.

[32] Digby to Ormond, 13 August, Carte, *Ormonde*, vi, 192–5.

[33] See below, Chapter 6.

[34] Armstrong, 'Ormond . . . and Protestant royalism', pp. 126–30.

[35] Ó hAnnracháin, *Catholic Reformation*, p. 30.

[36] Ohlmeyer, *Civil war and Restoration*, pp. 129–37.

the 'new', or perhaps more accurately, the 'fulfilled' Ireland sought by confederates or Covenanters.[37] At its most blunt it could be summed up in the first of the demands submitted by Ormond on the king's behalf, for the restitution of all cities, towns, counties, castles, forts and munitions taken and held by the confederates, and the end of their jurisdiction. All their military strength was to be placed under the lord lieutenant's control. Similar demands would open the crown's case in past and future English negotiations.[38] But more was at issue than the blunt assertion of civil and military authority. Only two elements can be briefly mentioned here, the attachment to the legal-constitutional and to the religious perceptions of the realm.

The 'rule of law' was another catch-call of royalist negotiators, in England as in Ireland.[39] In the Irish case, it could be deployed to block confederate demands to overturn at a stroke actions against confederates and their supporters in the Protestant 'rump' of the Irish Parliament or the residual components of the legal system. It was an argument which could intrude into deliberations on such lofty matters as the powers and autonomy of the parliament of Ireland, or such specific, miscellaneous grievances as the status of the recent plantation in Wicklow.[40] Royal negotiators refused to countenance resolutions which would undermine prior actions undertaken, by proper procedure, in duly constituted institutions, according to the existing letter of the law. (For confederates, of course, procedural correctness weighed less heavily than a blatant lack of neutrality within both law courts and parliament.) Yet this was not merely a negative response. Flexible alternatives could be considered to achieve at least some of the ends sought by the confederates, but not through the disruption of the legal and constitutional continuity of royal government. Thus, for example, the Irish Parliament's attempt to expel all MPs who would not swear the Oath of Supremacy could be deemed inherently illegal, since lacking statutory authority, and in due course a royal directive to have the order vacated was secured.[41] Legality, in form as well as content, was a core value, and among those around Ormond it could be combined with an attachment to 'constitutionalist' values, such as a sturdy understanding of the Irish Parliament, which might be a handy response to the threatenings from a Westminster Parliament now in defiance

---

[37] Of course, confederates saw their future Ireland in a restorative light, healing the breach between king, community and faith. But the end result of their ambitions would be a 'kingdom of Ireland' discontinuous with the main drift in direction since the declaration of the kingdom in 1541.

[38] Gilbert (ed.), *Irish confederation*, iii, 319, 321–3; Gardiner (ed.), *Constitutional documents*, p. 286.

[39] Cf. Smith, *Constitutional royalism*, p. 318.

[40] Gilbert (ed.), *Irish confederation*, iii, 176–7, 279–81, 294–6, 316–17. For the use of parliament and the courts against insurgents in 1641–42 see above, Chapter 1.

[41] Gilbert (ed.), *Irish confederation*, iii, 315–16; Carte MS 13, fo. 503.

of the common monarch, but which contained elements of a genuinely held set of values shared with at least some on the confederate side.[42] Religious commitment, too, was more than a cloak for the eagerness of Protestant clerics to regain their tithes, glebes and churches. For some churchmen at least a commitment to a 'national' church, on theological and even pastoral grounds, was every bit as pressing as for their Catholic counterparts.[43] For Ormond, no zealot, the king's religion was intrinsically bound up with the king's rule.[44] From the Dublin royalist perspective, some degree of accommodation of Catholicism was not impossible, but the public face of the Irish polity must remain resolutely Protestant.

Such clashes of principles and such jarring of strategies lay, for the most part, in the future. For figures like Clanricard and Taaffe, close to the centre ground of politics, the brief duration of the autumn talks was little short of disastrous.[45] Clanricard may have begun his attempts to break the deadlock almost at once.[46] In the meantime Ormond had worries close to home. Having sent two close associates, Sir Henry Tichborne and Sir James Ware, off to Oxford with details of the negotiations,[47] he worried about both the reduced numbers of the Irish Council and, more especially, about disaffection in its ranks.[48] It had been reported that one of his own negotiating team had made plain to his opposite numbers at the talks his frustration at being 'checked now at this Board by rebels'.[49] Protestant support continued to ebb from Ormond. By the autumn of 1644 the Covenant was winning adherents in the Protestant port towns of south Munster and the strategic south-eastern outpost of Duncannon.[50] Anti-cessation Protestants in Connacht devised an oath pledging the subscribers to take commands from, and hold posts for, the king and Parliament of England.[51] Though Inchiquin protested to Ormond that the Covenant did not betoken rebellion, he too tried to formulate an alternative oath, including a pledge to accept no peace not warranted by both

[42] Clarke, 'Colonial constitutional attitudes in Ireland', pp. 359–61.

[43] Robert Armstrong, 'Protestant churchmen and the confederate wars', in Ciaran Brady and Jane Ohlmeyer (eds), *British Interventions in early modern Ireland* (Cambridge, 2005) pp. 230–51.

[44] Raymond Gillespie, 'The religion of the first duke of Ormond', in Barnard and Fenlon (eds), *Dukes of Ormonde*, pp. 101–13.

[45] Clanricard to Ormond, 29 September 1644, Carte, *Ormonde*, vi, 200–1; *Letter-book*, pp. 108–9, 114–17.

[46] [William Usher to Perceval], 4 October 1644, HMC *Egmont MSS*, i, 239.

[47] [William Usher to Perceval], 8 October 1644, HMC *Egmont MSS*, i, 240.

[48] Ormond to Digby, 19 October 1644, Carte, *Ormonde*, vi, 207–8. He was duly granted authority 'to suspend from the councell board, which you will make such use of as in your wisdome you shall thinke fitt': Carte, *Ormonde*, vi, 221.

[49] [William Usher to Perceval], 4 October 1644, HMC *Egmont MSS*, i, 238, referring to Chief Justice Shirley.

[50] HMC *Portland MSS*, i, p. 188; Murphy, 'Politics of the Munster Protestants', p. 11.

[51] Gilbert (ed.), *Irish confederation*, iv, 31.

the king and the English Parliament.[52] Inchiquin's position bore some resemblance to that of Audley Mervyn, who squirmed at unequivocal acceptance of the Covenant, at first attempting to swear to the 'title' rather than the contents of the oath, then to interpret it, in its defence of religion, the 'honour and happiness' of the king and the 'peace and safety' of the three kingdoms, as at one with commitments made under the Oath of Supremacy.[53]

Drogheda, the most important of Ormond's garrisons after Dublin, was the site of a series of overlapping initiatives, from October to the following January, designed to loose the town from the lord lieutenant's grasp. Plans were laid to establish contact with Inchiquin, with Monro's forces to the north and with Westminster itself. The final stage envisaged was the surprisal of the town by its garrison, the plunder and expulsion of the Catholic inhabitants and co-operation with Monro until assistance could arrive from Parliament. Delays and betrayals foiled the enterprise, and resulted in a spate of arrests in early January, though the plotting continued at nearby Dundalk.[54] Ormond felt unable to exercise his instinctive preference for making an example of those involved, given 'the number of the ill affected, the distance wee are yett at with the Irish, and the weakness and wants of such as stand right . . .'.[55] Among the plotters, the dowager Lady Moore alleged that the earl of Antrim had informed her that 'one condicion of the peace was that their party was to have one church and ours another, and that this tolleracion was to be assented unto by our Councell as well as by theirs' and that Alderman Nugent of Drogheda had claimed that a peace would allow assenting Protestants to repossess their losses but any opponents to be 'proclaimed traitors and rebells with the Lord of Inchiquin and the Scotts . . .'.[56] That such relatively modest reversals could be brought forward as grounds for the breach with Ormond is indicative of how deeply entrenched Protestant hostility to a peace had become. Ormond could perhaps take some comfort, though, from the plotters' evident distrust of the Scots. Plans for co-ordinated operations beyond the town walls foundered on concerns that the Scots would appropriate an unfair share of the booty,

[52] Gilbert (ed.), *Irish confederation*, iv, 49–50. The oath referred to the king's placing the prosecution of the war in the Parliament of England but made no reflections on the English war and included only a general religious commitment to extirpate popery, schism and heresy.

[53] Mervyn to Ormond, 4 February 1645, HMC *Ormonde MSS*, old series, i, 91; cf. Adair, *True narrative*, pp. 107, 113, 116.

[54] Carte, *Ormonde*, iii, 147–53; Stevenson, *Scottish Covenanters*, pp. 215–16.

[55] Carte, *Ormonde*, vi, 243.

[56] Lady Moore also alleged a more grudging interpretation of the peace as voiced by Sir Nicholas White, who reportedly told her that her late husband's actions against the insurgents meant that no reparation could be expected by any of his kin: Gilbert (ed.), *Irish confederation*, iv, 131–3.

while the final plan, drawing upon Scottish assistance after taking the town, stimulated anxieties that Monro would break the deal and seize control.[57]

Ormond lamented to Digby that 'I haue long feared our wants, ioyned to the generall aversion the English heere haue to a peace with the Irish, and the large promises that are made from London, would at length produce some such designe . . .'.[58] At Westminster, the Committee of Both Kingdoms had indeed responded promptly to news of Munster's defection in the late summer, but promissory commitments yielded little practical assistance – as late as December it was still struggling to dispatch an interim advance of £1,000 to the province.[59] Of more use to the province was the commitment to assume the costs of foodstuffs dispatched thence by merchant interests, and the arrival there of Dutch aid. Even so, the word from Cork by year's end was that they were holding out on supplies of beans and rye bread, which might be stretched to last three weeks only.[60] Petitions and agents were desperately dispatched, but in the meantime Inchiquin was obliged to resort to a new round of short-term cessations with his provincial counterpart, Viscount Muskerry, extending into April 1645.[61] The outpost at Duncannon was not so lucky, being subjected to confederate siege from January, and would eventually surrender in March.[62]

Parliament had, though, put its Irish war on a new footing with the passage, in October, of the long-awaited assessment ordinance.[63] At the Committee of Both Kingdoms it was resolved that the £80,000 yield would be carved up as £42,000 for Ulster, £10,000 for Munster, £5,500 for Connacht and £2,500 for Duncannon, the rest held in reserve. Orders could be placed on the credit of the ordinance, with loans to bridge the gap to collection, and widespread consultation was undertaken over the details of expenditure, drawing in adventurers and representatives of all the Irish provincial interests. The upshot was the award of a series of supply contracts, for all the Irish theatres, to John Davies, Ulster merchant and close associate of Sir John Clotworthy.[64] It was

---

[57] Late in the day, Monro was urged to scale back the number of troops he would send to Drogheda: Stevenson, *Scottish Covenanters*, pp. 215–16.

[58] Carte, *Ormonde*, vi, 243.

[59] *CSPD, 1644*, pp. 415, 476; *CSPD, 1644–5*, pp. 105–6, 166, 176, 202; *CJ*, iii, 587.

[60] Hodder to Perceval, 30 December 1644, HMC *Egmont MSS*, i, 243; *CSPD, 1644–5*, pp. 44, 55; *CJ*, iii, 668, 671, 673.

[61] HMC *Egmont MSS*, i, 243–7; Bottigheimer, 'English interest', pp. 152–5.

[62] See Lenihan, *Confederate Catholics at war*, pp. 179–89 for a detailed account.

[63] Firth and Rait (eds), *Acts and ordinances*, i, 531–3. Clotworthy was involved at every stage of the process up to its delivery to the Lords on 10 October.

[64] *CSPD, 1644–5*, pp. 61–2, 85–6, 104–6; *CSPD, addenda, 1625–49*, p. 669. Cf. the investigation of the two men by the Committee of Accounts, largely relating to 1644–45, PRO SP 28/253B, part ii, 'Depositions in connection of an examination of abuses in the Accounts of Sr John Clotworthy and Mr. Davies'.

a landmark not only in the rise of Davies but of the fall of the London adventurer nexus, which lost even its token contract to supply Duncannon.[65] In the years ahead Davies would dominate the potentially lucrative provisioning of the Irish war, in connection with business contacts outside the charmed circle of the London adventure committee.[66] His rise to prominence reflected, too, the growing influence of the spokesmen, nominated or self-appointed, of the Protestants of Ireland.[67]

Over the winter of 1644–45 the long haul of putting together the largest consignments of supplies to date continued. Davies's goods were dispatched between January and April 1645 aboard two ships for Munster and six ships for Ulster and Connacht.[68] As Duncannon struggled for survival a relief expedition was put together, with munitions and supplies, but too slowly.[69] The decision was even taken, on 21 November, to allow the shipping of food, clothes and fuel to Dublin on the basis that Protestant citizens might perish while Catholics received aid from the countryside. In this case the matter was scuppered from the other end, as Ormond refused the offer to let supplies pass to the Irish capital, denying he had any need of such assistance.[70] Ulster remained the main focus of attention, no doubt in part owing to the Scottish presence on the Committee of Both Kingdoms, though even there the situation remained bleak. The demands made of the local inhabitants by the hard-pressed Scottish army for food and money 'were increasingly severe', and further seepage of veteran soldiers back to Scotland occurred, prompted by the successes of Montrose's royalist forces against the Covenanter regime.[71] In so far as Westminster engaged in strategic thinking at all, it took the not unrealistic choice of seeking to exploit the potential surplus of armed manpower in Ulster to relieve the other provinces, with schemes to dispatch 1,500 troops south-west into Connacht and, much less realistically, to send another 2,000 by sea to Munster. Since the Scots would not countenance their troops' participation, these were marked down to the local 'British' forces.[72] More telling in the long term was the emergence, months after being first mooted, of commissions for lords president in both Munster and Connacht. Inchiquin finally attained his commission, if little else, in January, while a tardy Commons continued to process the award of the western command to the younger Sir Charles Coote, son of the much loathed, and

[65] *CSPD, 1644–5*, pp. 68, 164.
[66] For a list of Davies's London associates, see PRO SP 28/139/8.
[67] e.g. *CSPD, 1644–5*, pp. 171, 172, 183–4, 195.
[68] PRO SP 17/H/10, fos 170–80.
[69] *CSPD, 1644–5*, pp. 183, 190, 193, 242, 249, 272, 291, 294–5, 309, 320, 327.
[70] *CSPD, 1644–5*, pp. 62, 106; *CJ*, iii, 701; Carte MS 12, fos 508, 510, 513.
[71] *CJ*, iv, 2–6; *CSPD, 1644–5*, pp. 175, 201–2; Stevenson, *Scottish Covenanters*, pp. 203–6.
[72] *CSPD, 1644–5*, pp. 200, 271–2, 291, 294.

occasionally lamented, Sir Charles Coote who had perished in 1642 on foot of his punitive campaigns in the Dublin hinterland.[73]

As Westminster's Irish war machine creaked into operation, the notions which underlay this Anglo–Scots commitment to war in Ireland were being fleshed out in the peace talks with the king's representatives at Uxbridge.[74] Peace propositions, and the position papers and debates surrounding them, remain an under-utilized resource in interpreting the ideologies of the disputants of the 1640s.[75] The propositions delivered to the king in November 1644, in the name of the two Houses and their Scottish allies, ranged over the whole field of disputed issues. But when Westminster came to determine the format of negotiations in January, it resolved to concentrate debate on just three issues – the church, the militia and Ireland.[76]

For Charles, peace negotiations in Britain and in Ireland were designed to run along parallel tracks – headed in the same direction, but never meeting, linked only by the presence of the monarch and those to whom he chose to open his mind. The parliamentarian naval presence in the Irish Sea had delayed the departure of Ormond's agents for court, an instance of a recurring royalist nightmare. Their report to the king was probably not in advance of the reception of the terms from the Covenanter alliance.[77] Yet in the gap before the Uxbridge talks began, the king and Digby found themselves cheered by the informal offer of terms submitted by the leading confederates Muskerry and Browne. Charles sought to keep up the momentum of the Irish negotiations. In a series of letters to Ormond he urged a quick deal so that he could repudiate Parliament's demands on Ireland at the upcoming talks, and posited the idea of using a threat of royal acquiescence in England to push the confederates to a settlement. More constructively he offered the present non-execution of the penal laws if peace were made, and kept, in Ireland, and the 'repeale of them by a law' in the future in return for Irish aid in England.[78] By late February he was prepared to countenance some new concessions,

[73] *CSPD, 1644–5*, pp. 201, 234, 237, 272, 285, 294; *CJ*, iii, 647; iv, 19, 27, 44.

[74] A much more detailed comparison of the peace talks in Dublin and at Uxbridge is to be found in Armstrong, 'Protestant Ireland', chapter 6.

[75] Though, of course, even agreed propositions, such as those advanced by Parliament and the Scots in 1644–45, could disguise the deep divisions among their sponsors: David Scott, *Politics and war in the three Stuart kingdoms, 1637–49* (Houndmills, Basingstoke, 2004) pp. 44–7, 91–2.

[76] *CJ*, iv, 11, 31. The terms are set out in Gardiner (ed.), *Constitutional documents*, pp. 275–86; for a useful account of the negotiations, see Smith, *Constitutional royalism*, pp. 120–4.

[77] Carte, *Ormonde*, vi, 211, 214; S. R. Gardiner, *History of the great civil war* (4 vols, London, 1893), ii, 85.

[78] Carte, *Ormonde*, v, 8–9, 9–10, 10–12; vi, 219, 233–4; Ó Siochrú, *Confederate Ireland*, p. 81. Charles was also willing, in extremity, to offer Ormond's co-operation against Inchiquin and the Scots.

notably on the suspension of Poynings's law and 'the present taking away of the penal lawes against the papists by a law'. Yet, characteristically, Charles hived off such offers into his 'private' correspondence with Ormond, keeping a tougher line in his 'public' dispatches to the Irish Council and insisting that Ormond both 'conclude a peace . . . whatever it cost' and yet 'make mee the best bargaine you can, and not to discover your enlargement of power till you needs must'.[79] In practice, co-ordination was hard to accomplish. Ormond's returning councillors were taken at sea and their papers captured or destroyed, and word from Oxford appears not to have reached Ormond until March. In the meantime he could only mark time, delaying the renewal of negotiations.[80]

At the Uxbridge talks, the royalist negotiators could only insist that they knew nothing of Ormond's powers to treat in Ireland.[81] When the agenda brought Ireland forward the parliamentarian-Scottish team sought to focus the debate around their thirteenth article, designed to produce an act to nullify the cessation and secure 'the prosecution of the war in Ireland' to Parliament. The result was that the first three-day session on Ireland degenerated into old wrangles about the legality and, particularly, the necessity of the cessation.[82] There were plenty of other matters to tease out. Scottish concerns permeated the agreed propositions from the Covenanted alliance, and extended well beyond calls for religious change in England.[83] In their attack upon their opponents' Irish plans the royalists targeted the increase in Scottish power in the third kingdom, alleging that the king's authority was 'wholly taken away, and in truth, that whole kingdom be thereby delivered into the Hands of His Majestie's Subjects of *Scotland*, which we conceive is neither just, prudent, or honourable to be done'.[84] It was a charge which echoed the

---

[79] Gilbert (ed.), *Irish confederation*, iv, 105–7; Charles to Ormond, 27 February, Carte, *Ormonde*, v, 13. The repeal of Poynings's law, the fifteenth-century enactment which intruded the English privy council into the Irish legislative process, was a significant confederate demand. On 5 March Charles wrote to the queen authorizing her to offer repeal of penal laws against Catholics in England, in return for such assistance in the war as would 'deserve so great a favour', but again counselling the secrecy of such a move, and adding 'I know thou wilt make as good a bargain for me even in this': *The King's Cabinet opened* (London, 1645) E292 (27), pp. 7–8.

[80] Gilbert (ed.), *Irish confederation*, iv, 116, 117, 130; Kelly, 'John Barry', p. 152.

[81] Rushworth, *Historical collections*, v, 898, 902–5.

[82] Rushworth, *Historical collections*, v, 897–8 – and for the papers relating to Ireland, see pp. 897–918, 932–41. Parliament's arguments were, again, grounded in the alleged delegation of the war to Parliament in 1641–42, the cessation being seen as a breach of this arrangement. The proposal added that the war would 'be managed by the joint advice of both kingdoms, and the King to assist and to do no act to discountenance or molest them'.

[83] Little, 'English Parliament', pp. 115–16; Kaplan, *Politics and religion*, pp. 97–107; David Stevenson, 'The early Covenanters and the federal union of Britain', in Roger A. Mason (ed.), *Scotland and England 1286–1815* (Edinburgh, 1987) pp. 170–3, 177–8.

[84] Rushworth, *Historical collections*, v, 902–5, 906–8, 936–7.

king's own reading of events (he told the queen that Parliament had 'transmitted the Command of *Ireland* from the Crown of *England* to the *Scots*, which . . . will clearly shew, that reformation of the Church is not the Chief, much less the only end of the *Scottish* Rebellion'[85]), and was exploited in royalist reportage of the treaty to Ireland.[86] It slotted into the more general royalist repudiation of Scottish involvement in matters English, such as control of the nation's military resources.[87]

The royalists exploited some awkward ambiguities in the parliamentary-Scottish arrangements for Ireland, and doubtless made mileage in propaganda terms. But the inclusion of a Scottish dimension in Westminster's plans, however significant in itself, was but one side of a coin which flipped to reveal an expansion of English, and parliamentary, determination of the future settlement of Ireland. They could validly assert that they had gained Scottish co-operation, 'their Councels and Forces', against a common threat, and assuaged Scottish fears, while vesting the final determination of such matters as control of armed force in Ireland or the appointment of the Irish executive in English institutions, the Westminster Parliament or the new, statutorily mandated and Parliament-nominated English militia commissioners.[88] Likewise, even as the treaty proceeded, the Commons were engaged with legislation to abolish the episcopal hierarchy in England, and resolved 'That the Hierarchy in *Ireland* shall be inserted in this Bill'. A further bill was to be drawn up for the disposal of church lands in Ireland.[89] It was, to say the least, probable that the other measures of religious change raised in the propositions could be extended in like manner, keeping Ireland in step with English developments, and by English legislative enactment.[90]

For the king, though, the clauses on religion were perhaps the most unpalatable of all, and they reflected many of the same distasteful demands he was to encounter, with increasing force in the months ahead, in the path to an Irish settlement. The necessity of retaining 'the dependency of the Clergy

---

[85] Rushworth, *Historical collections*, v, 947.

[86] Radcliffe told Ormond (24 February 1645) that the Scots had 'swallowed Ireland in their hopes', Daniel O'Neill (22 February 1645) adding that Ormond's own estate was marked out for delivery to the Scottish chancellor: Carte MS 14, fo. 131; Carte, *Ormonde*, vi, 249. See also Digby to Ormond, 23 February 1645, Carte, *Ormonde*, vi, 252.

[87] Rushworth, *Historical collections*, v, 881–3; Kaplan, *Politics and religion*, pp. 105–6.

[88] For example, they argued that, while the joint militia commissioners were to oversee armed force, in case of disagreement the English retained authority: Gardiner (ed.), *Constitutional documents*, pp. 281–4.

[89] *CJ*, iv, 43.

[90] At Uxbridge the Directory of Worship and the propositions on (Presbyterian) church government already agreed by Parliament were taken to encompass the terms of proposition 5: Gardiner (ed.), *Constitutional documents*, pp. 268, 275–6; Rushworth, *Historical collections*, v, 897–8.

intirely upon the Crowne, without which it will scarcely sit fast upon the Kings Head . . .' was as much threatened by a parliamentarian bill by which, it was reckoned, 'His majesties ancient and undoubted Power of the *Ecclesiastical Jurisdiction* is wholly taken away' as by the demands for the exercise of Catholic ecclesiastical jurisdiction in Ireland. Calls for the retention of Irish churches in the hands of the Catholic clergy were as abhorrent as the sacrilege and breach of his coronation oath which Charles believed he would commit were he to concede 'any diminution or alienation' of 'the Churches Patrimony' in England.[91] On a more positive note, his willingness at least to consider measures 'for the ease of tender Consciences (so that it endamage not the Foundation)' of the English church settlement could be matched by his concession on the non-enforcement, even repeal, of penal measures in Ireland.[92]

Like their counterparts in Dublin, the royalist negotiators sought to present a case built upon the 'rule of law', the return of power and authority to 'their Ancient channels' and reforms, as in matters religious, to be 'regularly and calmly made'.[93] A whole slate of individuals and groups were singled out for punishment or exclusion from pardon for their various sins in the parliamentarian-Scottish propositions, including all those involved in the heinous Irish rebellion, a stance not replicated in the royalist terms.[94] Indeed, among the texts of the negotiation at Uxbridge, there are few things more striking than the language employed to describe the insurgents in Ireland. The parliamentarian-Scottish harangue on the need for war against 'these execrable antichristian rebels, who have made a covenant with Hell, to destroy the Gospel of Christ, and have taken up arms to destroy the Protestant Religion, and set up Popery, to rend away one of His majesties Kingdoms and deliver it up into the hands of strangers' could be topped only by their final paper on Ireland, which denounced '*any agreement of Peace, and respite from Hostility with such Creatures, as are not fit to live no more than with Wolves or Tygers, or ravenous Beasts, destroyers of Mankind*'. It was left to the royalists to urge that while justice must be done upon those who had broken 'the Laws of God and Man, their Faith, their Allegiance, the Bonds of Charity, Rules of Humanity, and Humane Society' it might perhaps be worth considering 'whether it would not be more agreeable to our Christian profession, to endeavour the binding up of those Wounds, which interests, passions, and animosity have made.'[95]

[91] Rushworth, *Historical collections*, v, 869, 872, 924, 945.
[92] Gardiner, *Great civil war*, ii, 125, 130.
[93] Gardiner (ed.), *Constitutional documents*, pp. 286–7; Rushworth, *Historical collections*, v, 922–5.
[94] Gardiner (ed.), *Constitutional documents*, pp. 278–81.
[95] Rushworth, *Historical collections*, v, 910, 917, 914.

For the royalists the very elevation of the king served to relativize both national and religious commitments. Lifting the monarch above any one of his realms served to liberate him from narrowly national considerations yet, conversely, leave him with room to solve English difficulties without Scottish intrusion,[96] or settle Irish conflicts outside the English negotiations. If they could hardly place the king's cause before the cause of God, it was possible to argue that conflict was not strictly 'religious' at all, that Catholics, too, could be loyal subjects,[97] that Scots and English 'rebels' used religion only as a mask for baser ends. English parliamentarians, Scottish Covenanters, Irish confederates, all needed to make their cause the cause of the nation, all needed to infuse that cause with religious justifications, and all needed to punish those who set themselves against the national good. Anglo–Scottish refusal to countenance peace in Ireland was alleged on the grounds that national and spiritual interests were at stake, too profound to be surrendered.

Protestant Ulster had invested much hope in the Anglo–Scottish negotiations.[98] Ormond would begin another round of peace talks in April, perhaps driven to a more serious engagement with the confederates by the fall-out from Uxbridge.[99] But the winter months had seen him struggle to retain residual support, and if possible extend the king's party, through informal deals, personal connections and private rewards. Ormond deployed Archdeacon Humphrey Galbraith in Protestant Ulster, a man with no end of connections and contacts, who would labour on the lord lieutenant's behalf for months to come, downplaying the cessation throwing the blame for the Uxbridge collapse on Parliament.[100] From the north-west Audley Mervyn plied Ormond with comforting claims that, given that the 'large promises which the Covenant assured them into a belief of performance are failed', the 'Northerne army is so equally poised, that if but one regiment should start it would much weaken the whole'.[101] Yet even in Mervyn's base in Derry city, Presbyterianism continued to provide a populist base for an attack on

---

[96] On the militia, the royalists concluded their argument by urging 'whatever is now, or hereafter be thought necessary to be done, we desire may be so settled, that this Kingdom may depend uppon itself, and not be subjected to the Laws or advice of *Scotland*, as we think fit that *Scotland* should not receive rules or advice from this . . .': Rushworth, *Historical collections*, v, 924.

[97] Cf. G. E. Aylmer, 'Collective mentalities in mid-seventeenth century England, II: royalist attitudes', *Transactions of the Royal Historical Society*, 5th series, 37 (1987), 12.

[98] Rawdon to Matthews, 5 January 1645, Carte MS 13, fo. 265; Sir James Montgomery to W. Usher and S. Mayart, Carte MS 13, fo. 287.

[99] Michael Perceval-Maxwell, 'Sir Robert Southwell and the duke of Ormond's reflections on the 1640s', in Ó Siochrú (ed.), *Kingdoms in crisis*, pp. 237–8.

[100] Carte, *Ormonde*, iii, 161–4; Ormond to Galbraith, 25 February 1645, to Digby, 27 February 1645, Carte, *Ormonde*, vi, 254–5, 258.

[101] Mervyn to Ormond, HMC *Ormonde MSS*, old series, i, 90–5; Galbraith to Ormond, 29 January 1645, Carte MS 13, fo. 568.

the established elite of Protestant Ulster, a covenanted language of criticism. The efforts of Mayor Thornton to curb religious innovations in Derry only prompted a renewal of popular petitioning in favour of a Presbyterian ministerial presence, and a concerted drive to bring the authority of the Westminster Parliament and the Scottish general assembly to bear upon the ecclesiastical arrangements of north-west Ulster.[102] The mayor had long since taken to securing himself with a guard of 'English men . . . armd with long bills' on his ventures to Prayer Book service in the cathedral.[103]

Meanwhile others sought to seduce Ormond, politically speaking, or at least those around him. Swanley, the parliamentary admiral, offered to treat towards 'an honourable complyance with your best friends, the Parliament'.[104] Copies of the intercepted correspondence of the confederate agent in France, Father O'Hartegan, attacking a royal–confederate settlement, were dispatched from London to Dublin, both by Swanley and by Sir Robert King, by now another of the Protestant émigrés in London.[105] The letters were laughed off in Dublin, and in Oxford: Ormond told Clanricard the letters were 'worth your observation, and the most of it may provoke your mirth', while Digby responded that he 'shall need say noe more then of a madman's whose calumnyes cannot wound'.[106] Yet wound they had. The letters were commended to Ormond by his captured councillors, Tichborne and Ware, who had been subjected to the visits of a battery of displaced Protestants in London. Tichborne at least seems to have reconsidered his loyalties.[107] Meanwhile Ormond's schemes to regain Protestant dissidents went nowhere. Despite the opening of a confederate campaign in Munster in the spring of 1645, neither Inchiquin nor his army showed signs of wavering from the course they had adopted. Though their pleas for aid from England grew increasingly insistent as spring turned into summer, Inchiquin failed to respond to the blandishments offered by Oxford.[108] His correspondence

---

[102] Mervyn to Ormond, 1 and 3 February 1645, Carte MS 14, fos 38, 61–2; Thornton to Ormond, 3 February 1645, Carte MS 14, fos 40–1; Mervyn to Ormond, HMC *Ormonde MSS*, old series, i, 90–5.

[103] Thornton to Ormond, 17 October 1643, Gilbert (ed.), *Contemporary history*, i, 792–4.

[104] Swanley to Ormond, 12 January 1645, Gilbert (ed.), *Irish confederation*, iv, 122.

[105] Carte, *Ormonde*, vi, 241, 259–60; Gilbert (ed.), *Irish confederation*, iv, 63–6, 80–8. Thomas Morrissey, 'The strange letters of Matthew O'Hartegan SJ', *Irish Theological Quarterly* 37 (1970), 159–72 argues against the genuineness of the letters.

[106] Ormond to Clanricard, 3 February 1645, Digby to Ormond, 23 February 1645, Carte, *Ormonde*, vi, 241, 251.

[107] Gilbert (ed.), *Irish confederation*, iv, 116; Richard Bagwell, *Ireland under the Stuarts and during the interregnum* (3 vols, London, 1909–16), ii, 75–6; *CSPD, 1644–5*, pp. 337, 340.

[108] Though Muskerry had been accepted as Lord President of Munster, Oxford continued to dangle the prospect of the post before Inchiquin, though perhaps, as Bottigheimer suggests, allowing news of their offer to fall into Parliament's hands, in order to stimulate distrust of Inchiquin: Bottigheimer, 'English interest', pp. 152–5; HMC *Egmont MSS*, i, 248; Carte, *Ormonde*, vi, 286.

with Protestant churchmen in Dublin focused on the necessity of continuing the war in Ireland, and he hinted that he could act as an intermediary if Ormond wanted to make his peace with Westminster.[109]

With plenty of his own problems, Mervyn counselled Ormond that 'if theer be a necessitie to transact such a matter' as a peace 'tis wisdome to have many sharers'. Ormond should turn to the Irish Parliament as a 'buckler' for himself and the king against any retribution by posterity.[110] Ormond was alive to such sage advice. By late April he had sent two draft bills to Oxford, the first, an 'Act for avoiding of all doubts concerning the validity of the late cessation', being designed to provide the imprimatur of the Irish Parliament for that measure, and indemnify royal servants. With it went a bill for an 'Act declaring his Majesties Grace and Goodness' offering secure possession of property, remission of rent and, in Ulster, more acceptable forms of tenure not only to those who had proved their obedience, but to those received into the king's grace and favour. It was designed to be applicable to planter and native, confederate or Covenanter, an enticement to loyalty perhaps open to being used within or outside a formal peace settlement.[111] Like the king and those around him, in the aftermath of Uxbridge, Ormond considered the prospect of winning support with offices and titles, noting that 'there are many considerable persons of the Irish that, I conceiue, might be gained with addition, others with new creations, of honour . . .'.[112] With the talks with the confederates poised to commence, Ormond reckoned his interlocutors set the securing of posts for Catholics above the suspension of Poynings's Act.[113] Again while this was a demand within the peace terms, it was open to exploitation as a parallel track, and one which could undermine confederate unity. For the moment Ormond concentrated on the often-neglected middle ground between the two camps. Oxford mandated the admission of the Catholic Clanricard to the privy council, avoiding the Oath of Supremacy, and the raising of

---

[109] Inchiquin to the bishop of Cloyne, Carte MS 15, fo. 547, and the comments of Dean Boyle to the bishop of Cloyne, 30 August, Carte, *Ormonde*, vi, 317–18.

[110] Mervyn to Ormond, 2 February 1645, HMC *Ormonde MSS*, old series, i, 93–4. Mervyn urged the issuing of writs to fill up vacant seats.

[111] Ormond to the king, 22 April 1645, *CSPI, 1633–47*, p. 401; HMC *Portland MSS*, i, 220–1.

[112] Ormond to Digby, 28 March 1645, Carte, *Ormonde*, vi, 274. The latest royal instructions for peace talks, received by him on 5 April 1645, were accompanied by a royal warrant for Ormond to make promotions within the peerage: Charles to Ormond, 4 March 1645, Carte MS 14, fo. 212.

[113] That is to say an 'equality' of posts now, rather than an equality of access to appointments, the latter much more acceptable to both Ormond and the king: Ormond to the king, 8 May 1645, Gilbert (ed.), *Irish confederation*, iv, 252; Digby to Ormond, 22 May 1645, Carte, *Ormonde*, vi, 287–8.

regiments by Clanricard and Thomond.[114] It was a foretaste of Ormond's summer strategy for the creation of a cross-religious third force to which, ideally, disillusioned confederates and Covenanters could attach themselves.

At a formal level, the Irish peace talks, begun again in April, pursued their course into the autumn of 1645. At one level, substantial progress was made, with agreement reached on a range of awkward issues. Ground was ceded on both sides, in Ormond's case most significantly in eventually agreeing to a repeal of penal legislation against the practice of Catholicism. If rather late in the day, Ormond would defend his delayed response by arguing the royal order to hold off concessions and make the best deal he could, and the practical limitation that the council in Dublin would not agree unless mandated to do so by the king. Charles's, and Ormond's, persistent insistence on siphoning off 'private' concessions from 'public' statements would cause repeated problems for both men.[115] In turn Ormond felt aggrieved by what he considered confederate bad faith in expanding the definition of 'penal' legislation to encompass pre-Reformation laws advancing the claims of the English crown over against the medieval church, moves which prompted him to harry the confederates for a list of the particular statutes for which they sought repeal.[116]

Yet even as the Dublin royalists had fallen out of step with Protestant opinion generally, so a gap was opening up between the confederate negotiators and a strong body of opinion within their own ranks, well represented within the confederate general assembly. Even as debates on the scope of penal legislation were being pursued the question was being overtaken by the rise to prominence of the issues of Catholic possession of captured (or reclaimed) church property and the exercise of Catholic ecclesiastical jurisdiction, matters which had been simmering in the

[114] Charles to Ormond, 13 May 1645, *Letter-book*, p. 161; Charles to Ormond, 22 May 1645, Carte MS 14, fos 562, 579.

[115] Carte, *Ormonde*, v, 13, vi, 280–1. Digby's letter of 21 May 1645 allowed Ormond to divulge his powers in this regard to the privy council when 'seasonable': Carte, *Ormonde*, vi, 287–8. The leak of the earlier 'private' letter to Ormond allowing him to offer repeal had caused much discontent among the confederates (Ó Siochrú, *Confederate Ireland*, p. 93), but Clanricard, Barry and Glamorgan undertook to defend Ormond, arguing that the letter was more a limitation on Ormond than an expansion of his powers: *Letter-book*, p. 175.

[116] The resulting list, of July 1645, stretched back to the reign of Edward III, covering laws Ormond considered 'not concearneing any matter of religion'; the list submitted back in September 1644 had specified leglislation only from Henry VIII onwards: Gilbert (ed.), *Irish confederation*, iii, pp. 289–93; iv, 327–9, 331–5. Charles had already made it clear that though he would agree to the repeal of 'penal statutes . . . all those against appeales to Roome and premvnury [praemunire] must stand': Charles to Ormond, 18 January 1645, Carte, *Ormonde*, v, 9–10. He does not appear to have departed from such a position.

background but were now openly addressed at the assembly in May 1645.[117] It has been recognized that Charles, no less than Ormond, was unlikely to bend on these issues.[118] Writing to Ormond on 29 July he insisted that Ormond not 'grant onto the Irish . . . any thing more in matters of religion than I have allowed you already' save the establishment of chapels in some Catholic parishes.[119] He ordered Digby to write to the confederate commissioners, and the resulting letter expressed angry disappointment that the terms once (privately) offered at Oxford had not been adhered to, and claimed that rational men could not expect the king, in the light of both his conscience and present position, to allow retention of churches.[120] Charles's commitment to his vision of the church, in Ireland as in Britain, was absolute and, hinged as it was on notions of royal supremacy, could not countenance concessions to alternative spiritual authority, whether of Pope or presbytery.[121]

What, then, of the substantial concessions on just such matters offered, in the king's name, by the Catholic earl of Glamorgan, incorporated in a secret treaty with leading confederates in August 1645 (while negotiations on the public treaty with the lord lieutenant persisted) and subsequently repudiated by Ormond? The Glamorgan mission to the confederates has been the subject of more discussion than any single episode in the Irish conflict of these years, and no more than a few comments need be added here.[122] Firstly, it cannot be emphasized too strongly that Glamorgan's mission needs to be located within a sequence of attempts by the king to gain troops from Ireland, clearly the royal priority, and to that end to supplement or circumvent Ormond's efforts to achieve armed support within the treaty framework. The efforts of the earl of Antrim are only the best known (and most successful),[123] but the missions of Oliver Fitzwilliam and Daniel O'Neill shared this primary goal with Glamorgan's mission.[124]

[117] Ó Siochrú, *Confederate Ireland*, pp. 88–92; Tadhg Ó hAnnracháin, 'Rebels and confederates: the stance of the Irish clergy in the 1640s', in John R. Young (ed.), *Celtic dimensions of the British civil wars* (Edinburgh, 1997), pp. 105–10.

[118] Ó hAnnracháin, *Catholic Reformation*, p. 31; Ó Siochrú, *Confederate Ireland*, p. 89 concedes that 'publicly at least, Charles remained firm on the issue' of church property.

[119] *Letter-book*, pp. 179–80; Carte, *Ormonde*, vi, 305–6. The letter was received on 14 August.

[120] Digby to Muskerry et al., 1 August, *Letter-book*, pp. 181–2; Carte, *Ormonde*, vi, 309–10. Clanricard noted that it was not fit to deliver the letter as matters then stood.

[121] Smith, *Constitutional royalism*, pp. 143–56. See below, Chapter 6.

[122] See especially S. R. Gardiner, 'Charles I and the earl of Glamorgan', *English Historical Review* 2 (1887), 687–708; John Lowe, 'The Glamorgan mission to Ireland, 1645–6', *Studia Hibernica* 4 (1964), 155–96.

[123] Ohlmeyer, *Civil war and Restoration*, p. 166, and chapter 5 *passim*.

[124] For Fitzwilliam, dispatched from the queen's court in France, and with experience in raising Irish forces for foreign service, see *The Lord George Digby's cabinet . . .* (London, 1646) E319 (15), especially pp. 44–6, 56; for O'Neill, Gilbert (ed.), *Contemporary history*, i, 655, 656–7; Donal F. Cregan, ' "An Irish cavalier": Daniel O'Neill in the civil wars 1642–51', *Studia Hibernica* 4 (1964), 120–1.

Secondly, there is the question of how Glamorgan's efforts fitted with the characteristic approaches adopted by of the king. It was not just that Charles was apt to set multiple schemes in operation to one end, even if this meant undermining the efforts of those whose loyal support he professed to recognize. The episode also reflected his tendency to cultivate private assurances rather than permit public avowals of tricky concessions, and his incapacity to recognize that if he made what he considered 'reasonable' gestures these would not be accepted.[125] The commissions granted Glamorgan in early 1645, like Fitzwilliam's vague instructions to offer concessions on religious matters, need not necessarily be read as countenancing further advances from those terms Charles authorized Ormond to grant.[126] The most probable solution to Charles's intentions when commissioning Glamorgan is that long since propounded by S. R. Gardiner, namely that Glamorgan was to promise repeal of penal legislation, from which Ormond still held back at that stage, rather than that he make offers on the newly prominent issues of churches and jurisdiction.[127] Charles implicitly alleged this interpretation himself, after the debacle of the exposure of the Glamorgan terms, alleging the necessity of a 'less publique way' to cede the removal of penalties for the practice of Catholicism, and his hope that Glamorgan could assist in securing confederate acquiescence to the offer.[128] Those close to the king, in all his kingdoms, were by 1645 desperately trying to build bridges between the royal mind and the real rebellion-rent world, some form of connection, however flimsy, which would allow grace and pardon to pass in one direction, cash and troops the other, and all the awkward rocks in the road to be avoided. Into this can be slotted not only Glamorgan, but the

---

[125] Cf. his comment to the queen in February 1646 that the Irish had 'fedd me with vain hopes' since they had 'not accepted those conditions which no reason could warrant them to refuse', Charles I, *Charles I in 1646: letters of King Charles the First to Queen Henrietta Maria*, ed. John Bruce, Camden Society 63 (London, 1856) pp. 17–18. For his 'lack of any sense of the impossible' in dealing with the Covenanters in 1638, see Russell, *Fall*, p. 51.

[126] Fitzwilliams's terms ('free use of Religion a free Parliament, and the penall Lawes to be taken off') wholly missed the fundamental questions of whether 'penal' laws extended to the medieval legislation against papal jurisdiction and whether 'free use of Religion' included claims on church property and ecclesiastical jurisdiction. In sponsoring Fitzwilliam, the king could well have allowed himself to believe in the narrower reading of the terms, as much as Fitzwilliam later protested that if he had known the limits of the terms on offer, he would not have bothered to undertake his enterprise: *Lord George Digby's cabinet*, pp. 49–51; *CSPD, 1645–7*, pp. 20–1.

[127] Gardiner, 'Charles I and the earl of Glamorgan', pp. 701–2. Ormond would make the case that the king would not have known of the issues when commissioning Glamorgan (*Letter-book*, p. 177). That, in June, Charles sought to chivy Glamorgan to be gone to Ireland may have signalled his awareness by then of these questions or, as Gardiner suggests, his knowledge that Ormond had still not conceded the repeal of penal laws.

[128] Carte, *Ormonde*, vi, 348.

knot of mainly Catholic royalists – Clanricard, Barry, O'Neill – with whom he operated in the confederate capital.[129]

Thirdly, such efforts necessarily blurred the distinction between shrewd diplomacy and simple bad faith. Of course, by the time Glamorgan was dealing with the confederate negotiators it was necessary to address the matters of possession of churches and ecclesiastical jurisdiction, both of which he would cede in his treaty.[130] If there seems little doubt that the 'peace faction' among the confederates had already proved themselves willing to mislead their brethren in the interests of a deal,[131] then Glamorgan may well have been involved with them in a double- or even a triple-cross. His oath, of which a number of influential confederates would have been aware, appeared to pledge him almost to coerce the concessions from the king, at least at the price of losing the newly raised Irish army, while his ultra-secret 'defeasance' effectively offered an opt-out – he was indemnified if he failed to secure royal approval, by which point he would have got his Catholic Irish army over to England.[132] This does not mean that Glamorgan (or indeed Clanricard) would not have wanted the concessions implemented, nor that he would not have strained to achieve them, but it does look like a canny attempt to square his (or their) ambitions for king and religion, worthy of the earl of Antrim.

Glamorgan, then, wanted to make everyone happy: to let the confederates believe he had as good as got them a deal, to give the king his Catholic army, albeit with a price tag, but then, he hoped, to catch from the king this reward for faithful, and delivered, service, always a better bet with Charles than any show of negotiation between king and subjects. Of course, the end result was the collapse of the house of cards. Speed was of the essence, in both tying up the civil treaty and, even more, getting the troops to England while they might still make a difference. The newly arrived papal nuncio, Rinuccini, had good grounds for his scepticism as to whether Glamorgan could deliver. But that as shrewd an operator as Clanricard could believe that Glamorgan had brought the treaty to 'such a happy and secure condition' and would retire to his home at Portumna for the hunting[133] suggests that a group of

---

[129] Clanricard to Ormond, 23 August 1645, Ormond to Clanricard, 25 August 1645, *Letter-book*, pp. 173–6, 177–9. Cf. Lowe, 'Glamorgan mission', p. 167; Cregan, 'Irish cavalier', p. 121; Kelly, 'John Barry', p. 153.

[130] Printed in *The earl of Glamorgan's negotiations* (London, 1645 [1646]) E328 (9), pp. 17–25; *The Irish Cabinet, or his majesties secret papers* . . . (London, 1646) E316 (29), pp. 3–13.

[131] Ó hAnnracháin, *Catholic Reformation*, p. 78.

[132] Conveniently printed in Gardiner, 'Charles I and the earl of Glamorgan', p. 704. Glamorgan also appears to have amended his oath to include the phrase 'or his [the king's] pleasure known': Lowe, 'Glamorgan mission', p. 182.

[133] Clanricard to Sir George Hamilton, *Letter-book*, pp. 185–6.

clever men had concocted a scheme which they genuinely believed they could sell to their stricter brethren in Dublin, Oxford and Kilkenny. It was, of course, too clever to work.

As Glamorgan and his associates put the last touches to their scheme, the broader picture was of an Ireland slipping inexorably back into war. For all the continuing cessations between Dublin and Kilkenny, the reality was that campaigns were now afoot not only in Ulster, but in the south and west of Ireland too.[134] Protestant support had been haemorrhaging for the last year. The Protestant kingdom of Ireland, the linkage of Protestant state and Protestant people, had been crumbling under pressure of the peace talks. Yet the integration of disaffected Protestants into a wider, three-kingdom, Covenanter coalition had been no easy process. National tensions between English and Scots ran a jagged course from London to Londonderry; Westminster had concocted schemes for tightening its control of Ireland (with or without Edinburgh) but functioned in practice on an ad hoc and sometimes absent-minded manner, relying heavily on émigré Protestants for information and direction and as points of contact. The year ahead, from the summer of 1645 to the summer of 1646, would see the intensity of parliamentary efforts to incorporate at least Protestant Ireland taken to a new pitch, but it would also see a renewed drive, from Dublin, to recapture not only Catholic but Protestant Ireland for a restored Irish kingdom. The battle for the soul of Protestant Ireland had been engaged.

---

[134] Discussed below, Chapter 6.

6

Renewing the war, regaining the Protestants, 1645–46

In October 1645 Ulster British forces, headed for the relief of Protestant garrisons in the western province of Connacht, fell upon a party of Catholic troops mobilized to recapture Sligo. Among the dead was the reforming archbishop of Tuam, Malachy O'Queely,[1] and among the papers of the slain prelate was a copy of the 'Glamorgan treaty', the articles concluded between the earl and confederate representatives the previous August, appearing to grant, in the king's name, far more than religious freedom for Catholics, but rather the secure re-establishment of Catholic ecclesiastical structures, including the retention of church property. The incident stands at the confluence of the principal currents of events in 1645–46, the quest for a royalist–confederate alignment and the emergence of western strategies by all the principal belligerents, from Parliament to Ormond and the confederates. The ripple effect of the capture and publication of the 'treaty' was apparent in the dispositions of all the political players, not least the Protestants of Ireland. But the year between the summer of 1645 and the summer of 1646 was also characterized by contesting attempts to incorporate the inhabitants of Ireland more closely into competing schemes of a revamped kingdom of Ireland or a new-forged Covenanted Britain, and to do so both by enlistment into new institutional formations and, from Parliament at least, by the empowerment which came from the receipt of the resources of war.

With the coming of spring, Westminster foresaw decisive military action in both England and Ireland. If in both cases the armies of their Scottish allies were still considered a vital part of the overall strategic design, in both cases those very allies were the subject of criticism for having 'done little all this while in Ireland' or England, even if this was tempered somewhat by a recognition of the failure to conjure adequate supplies from the sequestration

---

[1] Ó hAnnracháin, *Catholic Reformation*, pp. 59–60, 62–3.

revenue allocated to support the Scottish forces.[2] In Ulster, still regarded as the driving force for a new offensive in Ireland, the balance of power was shifting in favour of the local forces as more and more of Monro's army was withdrawn to Scotland to counter Montrose's campaigns.[3] Parliament moved both to enlist the Ulster forces more closely into its structure and to empower them to act. The last of Davies's supply ships set sail in April, bringing a much-needed material incentive to re-start the war in earnest.[4] April saw the nomination of three commissioners – Sir Arthur Annesley, Sir Robert King and a London representative, Colonel William Beale – to exercise civil and military authority in Ulster, in co-operation with their Scottish counterparts, as envisaged as far back as the April 1644 resolutions for a Scottish command. The appointment was secured in May, alongside the commissioning of Sir Charles Coote as lord president of Connacht.[5] If he did not have much of a province to preside over, Coote was nothing short in his determination to launch a swift and decisive campaign in the Irish north-west. The commissioners, it was hoped, would encourage the army to advance at once in order that 'winter garrisons' be planted by harvest time, while the Committee of Both Kingdoms wrote at once to both Monro and the Ulster British, to win them to the dispatch of a 1,500-strong expedition into Connacht.[6]

With the commissioners held up in London through the want of a small sum to take over as pay for the soldiers,[7] the senior British officers, meeting at Antrim on 17 May, formulated a 'joynt and unanimous Declaration', to establish 'a firme union and order amongst our selves' by a 'generall court of warre' to respond to the commissioners 'and for the better order, administration of justice, good government, and subsistence of the army, and for no other cause'. They insisted that they intended nothing 'destructive or preiudiciall' to the Covenant, nor would they cease to prosecute the war until 'ane safe peace' was concluded with the consent of the king and the English Parliament. They even pledged co-operation with Monro to the extent of obedience to his orders, when in joint operations in the field.[8] The document does not imply that the army was bridling at parliamentary control,

[2] Mark A. Kishlansky, *The rise of the New Model Army* (Cambridge, 1979), pp. 31, 35–6; BL Harleian MS 166, fo. 193a; *Calendar of the proceedings of the committee for compounding*, i, 17–19, 25, 781; Stevenson, *Scottish Covenanters*, pp. 201–4.

[3] Stevenson, *Scottish Covenanters*, pp. 204–5.

[4] PRO SP 28/253B, fos 100–1.

[5] The Ulster commissioners were to act as authorized agents of the powers of the Committee of Both Kingdoms as envisaged under the Uxbridge proposals (including power to dispose of church lands): Firth and Rait (eds), *Acts and ordinances*, i, 677; Gardiner (ed.), *Constitutional documents*, p. 283; Rushworth, *Historical collections*, v, 872.

[6] *CSPD, 1644–5*, pp. 383–4, 475–6, 487.

[7] *CSPD, 1644–5*, p. 505.

[8] Gilbert (ed.), *Contemporary history*, i, 653–5.

but is indicative of ongoing efforts to entrench the political and military leaderships of Protestant Ulster and to maintain their cohesion, as would be made clear in the case of Lord Conway, owner of extensive estates in east Ulster. A defector from Parliament while in England, Conway had been removed from the colonelcy of his Ulster regiment by the Committee of Both Kingdoms, and the command awarded to Lord Blayney. The assembled officers instead upheld the regimental preference for the appointment of Lord Conway's son, Edward, and suggested that without his assistance the regiment could not survive in its wasted quarters.[9] News reaching Ormond from the regiment's acting commander, Theophilus Jones, suggested that the regiment would go over to the lord lieutenant if he awarded the command to the younger Conway. Conway's soldiers largely overlapped with his tenants: Jones claimed they stood by Parliament to prevent sequestration of his lordship's estates, and thereby their own ruin.[10] In a war-ravaged province where clashes over quarters soured relations even between friendly units,[11] there was a premium to be earned from the proprietorial nature of landowner regiments.[12]

If the summer witnessed a 'rather half-hearted attempt' by Monro to capture Charlemont, he could nonetheless 'march through the province at will' with no formidable enemy forces in the field. Coote, on the other hand, assembled 4,500 men from among the Ulster British forces in June, marched upon Connacht, and captured Sligo on 8 July.[13] The cessation had led to 'a chaotic and, according to Clanricard, an almost anarchic situation in Sligo and in north Connacht in general'.[14] Though Clanricard presented some of the disorder as emanating from 'pillagers' of mixed ethnic origins and, apparently, religious allegiance,[15] pro-Parliament sentiment had been waxing among the scattered Connacht Protestant garrisons for some time. The 'king's party' could count securely only on possession of Athlone and the three baronies in Co. Galway under Clanricard's sway.[16]

Both Clanricard and the Ormondist lord president, Thomas, Viscount Dillon, criticized confederate failure to suppress the anti-cessationists in Connacht, and professed themselves unable to offer resistance to Coote. Yet like Ormond they were loath to 'join with or receive the assistance of

---

[9] *CSPI, 1633–47*, p. 402; *CSPD, 1644–5*, pp. 361, 375, 386; cf. Carte, *Ormonde*, iii, 164–6.

[10] Jones to Ormond, 18 April 1645, Carte MS 14, fo. 408; Jones to Ormond, 1 May 1645, Carte MS 14, fos 474–7.

[11] Something of a damper was placed on Jones's offer of defection when his men clashed with some of Gibson's Ormondist garrison at Dundalk over supplies: Jones to Ormond, Gibson to Ormond, both 28 June 1645, Carte MS 14, fos 436, 437.

[12] Gillespie, 'Army sent from God', pp. 123–4.

[13] Stevenson, *Scottish Covenanters*, pp. 221–2; Hogan (ed.), *Letters and papers*, p. 189.

[14] O'Dowd, *Power, politics and land*, p. 127.

[15] Clanricard to Ormond, 10 March 1645, *Letter-book*, pp. 149–50.

[16] Clanricard to Ormond, 29 January 1645, *Letter-book*, p. 138.

the confederates until they were united with us under the king's government'.[17] Instead, on 24 June, Ormond issued a commission to Theobald, Viscount Taaffe, to raise forces against those who 'presume in hostile manner to enter into any of the quarters allotted in Conaght to such as are obedient to his Majestie's governments . . . or doe any hostile act or acts in the said province to the prejudice of his Majestie's said subjects', which could cover both the troublesome Roscommon Protestant garrisons who had spurned Dillon's authority and violated Clanricard's quarters, and Coote's expeditionary forces. Taaffe was empowered to command 'all such forces who shall joyne with you' and to receive into mercy and pardon 'such of the said persons who shall come to you and give obedience unto his Majesties authority', powers with the potential to actively extend the borders of royalist allegiance.[18] If entered into somewhat uncertainly,[19] the Taaffe commission provided the opportunity for a striking experiment by the lord lieutenant and his allies, an attempt to clear a space for a cross-religious royalist alliance, to defend of 'loyal' Connacht and to expand that constituency.

Clanricard permitted forces from his jurisdiction to serve under Taaffe; Dillon recommended, successfully, the adhesion of Sir James Dillon, a confederate colonel, to the new forces; Ormond agreed to the offer by the earl of Westmeath to raise a regiment and a cavalry troop for the king. With Taaffe's own 'English volunteers' and 'some auxiliaries from the confederates', he had the makings of a small army and by 3 August could claim to command 2,500 infantry and 400 cavalry.[20] Ormond continued to refuse Viscount Muskerry's requests for offensive co-operation with confederate forces against Protestant Ulster in the absence of a peace, though admitting a willingness to accept a 'loyall offer' of assistance.[21] Instead he was building just such an alternative force in the midlands without any concessions to, or recognition of, the confederate regime. He had drawn upon families (Dillon, Taaffe, Nugent) from a background very like his own: Old English, sometimes religiously divided, liable to straddle the line between loyalist and 'rebel'. Both Westmeath's father and Sir James Dillon had initially opposed the rising in Co. Westmeath in 1641, while Taaffe and Dillon had hovered between Ireland and the king in 1641–42 in efforts to patch a settlement. Dillon, like Ormond, had been admitted a privy councillor as a

[17] *Letter-book*, p. 169; Dillon to Ormond, 5 July 1645, Carte MS 15, fos 209–10; Carte, *Ormonde*, iii, 169–72.

[18] Gilbert (ed.), *Irish confederation*, iv, 306–7.

[19] Ormond–Dillon correspondence, Gilbert (ed.), *Irish confederation*, iv, 354–6.

[20] *Letter-book*, p. 170; Carte MS 15, fos 240, 244, 285, 291, 339; Gilbert (ed.), *Irish confederation*, iv, 16–17.

[21] Muskerry to Ormond, 18 August 1645, Carte MS 15, fo. 455; Ormond to Muskerry, 19 August 1645, Carte MS 15, fos 467–8.

professed Protestant, though he was to be reconciled to Rome in 1646.[22] With this force, Taaffe made significant gains in August: Protestant outposts at Tulske, Elphin, Castle Coote and Jamestown were taken by force or submitted to his army, and Carrigdrumrusk, Boyle and Roscommon, though untouched, professed renewed obedience to the king's government and the cessation.[23] That Taaffe's army quickly ran into serious logistical problems was only standard for armies in 1640s Ireland,[24] while for a small force such as this any fall in numbers, even through garrisoning, could be serious. But there were bigger problems.

Taaffe had an unfortunate habit of stirring up trouble. As early as 7 August Ormond was worried that confederate dabbling might foment a breach between Taaffe and Viscount Ranelagh, which he laboured to overcome. Much more serious was Taaffe's displacement of the Protestant bishop of Elphin from the castle he had held since the outbreak of the rising. Before the campaign started, Ormond had issued instructions that special regard was to be had for Bishop Tilson.[25] By 14 August, however, the bishop was complaining at the eviction of his garrison in favour of a Catholic one; though he agreed to surrender the castle, he professed himself worried at the safety of his men.[26] Dillon attempted to mediate, and Ormond insisted on restoration, citing the terms of Taaffe's commission on submissions.[27] But the bishop claimed he could not return while Taaffe held command, and wrote to ecclesiastics in Dublin (17 September) of a Catholic religious takeover after his departure from Elphin.[28] Clanricard, like Ormond, was worried lest Taaffe's improvidence 'in a matter of so small concernment not only shake and endanger the good success of that province' but disturb more important proceedings by 'fomenting jealousies and misapprehensions'.[29] For other Protestant garrisons were petitioning Ormond and Dillon on the basis of their displacement from control after submission.[30]

Rumours of the approach of a relief force under Coote left both Dillon and Clanricard anxious, and the latter appears to have hoped for the

---

[22] Taaffe would in time take up a command under confederate authority, and Westmeath's regiment, like Sir James Dillon's, would be absorbed into their Leinster army: Clarke, *Old English*, pp. 119, 188; O'Dowd, *Power, politics and land*, p. 124; G. E. C[okayne], *The complete peerage*, ed. V. Gibbs et al. (new edition, 14 vols, London, 1910–59), iii, 28; iv, 358; Nicholas Perry, 'The infantry of the confederate Leinster army, 1642–1647', *Irish Sword* 15 (1982–83), 234.

[23] Gilbert (ed.), *Irish confederation*, iv, 16–18; Carte MS 15, fos 414–15, 502, 663, 673, 712–13.

[24] *Letter-book*, pp. 182–3, 183–4, 185–6.

[25] Carte MS 15, fo. 373.

[26] Carte MS 15, fos 420, 430.

[27] Carte MS 15, fos 439, 458, 462, 474, 524–5, 545–6, 552.

[28] Carte MS 15, fos 578, 652.

[29] Clanricard to Captain Richard Burke, 21 September 1645, *Letter-book*, p. 189.

[30] For example, Jamestown garrison to Ormond, Carte MS 16, fo. 61.

intervention of confederate forces.[31] Both men, however, showed obvious relief when the retreat of the bulk of Coote's force[32] meant there would be 'no need of them, who will be as destructive as the enemy'.[33] Taaffe was suspected of inclining more to the confederates than his commission warranted, to the prejudice of the government in Dublin; by 21 September Clanricard reported that Taaffe's commission had been withdrawn, largely because of the bishop of Elphin incident, and ordered his own forces to leave Taaffe.[34] Ormond's western strategy had sought to secure the adherence of Catholic grandees and their supporters, not through institutional amalgamation with the confederate organization but through common service under royal authority. (Even as the campaign opened Clanricard, at Kilkenny, wrote to ask Ormond if the latest treaty concessions could be offered to 'well disposed' individuals on the same basis as 'to all in general', a plan apparently acceded to by Ormond.[35])

Yet the submission, and incorporation, of Protestant garrisons was also intended. There was a temporary pay-off in that Coote's relief force was discouraged to find these garrisons held against it,[36] but local hostilities, and perhaps Taaffe's ineptitude, were obviously too great for this to work. The future loyalty of neither the Protestant garrisons nor the Catholic forces was guaranteed. O'Queely's failed, and fatal, assault on Sligo in October had used the remnants of Taaffe's forces, now acting under confederate auspices under the command of Viscount Taaffe's brother, Luke.[37] Clanricard spoke the epitaph of the endeavour: 'I shall hold to my former maxim that until we all serve and obey one master, neither myself nor any under my care shall by my consent undertake any great employments, though they may carry with them a seeming show both of honour and profit, which cannot be permanent in the midst of so many distractions in the government'.[38]

Coote's forays into Connacht were the pay-off for Parliament's material and strategic investment in Ulster. The complementary plan to ship 2,000 troops from Ulster to Munster, though, had failed to come off,[39] and

---

[31] It is unclear whether Clanricard envisaged this as following a peace between Ormond and the confederates, though he had long preferred an Ormond–confederate alignment against the 'Scots': *Letter-book*, pp. 182–3.

[32] Coote later returned with a reinforcement: Hogan (ed.), *Letters and papers*, pp. 189–90.

[33] *Letter-book*, p. 187; Carte MS 15, fos 551, 560.

[34] Clanricard to Taaffe, 8 September, to Captain Richard Burke, 21 September 1645, *Letter-book*, pp. 186–7, 188–90.

[35] *Letter-book*, p. 173.

[36] Clanricard to Sir George Hamilton, 4 September 1645, *Letter-book*, pp. 185–6.

[37] Bagwell, *Ireland under the Stuarts*, ii, 96; see also O'Dowd, *Power, politics and land*, pp. 118–20, 126–7 for Luke Taaffe.

[38] Clanricard to Captain Richard Burke, 21 September 1645, *Letter-book*, p. 189.

[39] HMC *Egmont MSS*, i, 257.

Protestants in the southern province remained under grinding pressure across the summer of 1645 as Inchiquin saw his quarters dwindle under prolonged confederate assault.[40] On 1 July Parliament named a new committee 'to receive, prepare and consider of Propositions for the speedy relief of that Kingdom, and particularly for the Province of Munster'.[41] Broghill was present at its first session, and the Commons, too, held Munster in their view that summer as a series of letters from Inchiquin hammered home the prospect of the fall of Youghal and the dangers of mutiny and desertion.[42] For the first time since the outbreak of fighting in England, it was proposed that English soldiers be raised for service in Ireland, 2,500 being mandated for Munster, the cavalry under Sir William Jephson, Munster planter, MP for Stockbridge and veteran of the fighting in both kingdoms, the infantry under the Scottish colonel Robert Sterling.[43] Funds from the existing assessment for Ireland had been directed to pay for the supplies dispatched thence by John Davies, who continued to collect new contracts to provision the forces in Ireland, and who commanded a network of agents to collect what remained of the assessment across England and Wales.[44] A new assessment for Ireland was passed in September and its disposal, and the vitally important right to raise loans on the security of the assessment, was placed in the hands of the July 1645 committee (known, from its place of meeting, as the Star Chamber committee).[45] Moving far beyond its original advisory remit, the new committee rapidly accumulated executive functions over the raising of troops and money, and authority over the Ulster commissioners and the presidents of Munster and Connacht.[46] Over the ensuing years it would be a formidable instrument for the direction of resources into the Irish war.[47]

The smashing of the royalist field army at Naseby in June, and the ensuing run of victories, cleared a space for the re-direction of parliamentarian

[40] Lenihan, 'Confederate military strategy', pp. 163–5. Cf. Ó hAnnracháin, *Catholic Reformation*, pp. 35–6 for a discussion of accusations against Castlehaven, the confederate general, 'that he had deliberately allowed the campaign to peter out'.

[41] Firth and Rait (eds), *Acts and ordinances*, i, 722–3; *CJ*, iv, 195.

[42] *CJ*, iv, 216, 222; McNeill (ed.), *Tanner letters*, pp. 190–3; *CSPI, 1633–47*, pp. 405–6.

[43] *CJ*, iv, 203, 251–2; *CSPI, 1633–47*, pp. 407, 410, 413–14.

[44] *CSPI, 1633–47*, pp. 407, 412; *CJ*, iv, 251, 255, 276; Firth and Rait (eds), *Acts and ordinances*, i, 776–83; BL Harleian MS 166, fo. 258b.

[45] Firth and Rait (eds), *Acts and ordinances*, i, 746–9.

[46] *CJ*, iv, 270; *CSPI, 1633–47*, p. 414; BL Additional MS 4,769A, fo. 3a.

[47] In its accumulation of functions it resembled the March 1645 army committee (set up to handle the requirements of the New Model Army) as discussed by John Adamson, 'Of armies and architecture: the employments of Robert Scawen', in Ian Gentles, John Morrill and Blair Worden (eds), *Soldiers, writers and statesmen of the English revolution* (Cambridge, 1998), pp. 47–8, 50–2, though not (yet) its control by the parliamentary 'Independents'.

bellicosity towards Ireland. As leading royalists, though hardly Charles himself, pondered the prospects of capitulation, the Ulster commissioners finally set forth in October, bearing an official letter claiming that there was now 'good ground to hope' that the king would abandon wicked counsels for his 'most faithfull Counsell', Parliament.[48] Instead the commissioners were caught up in attempts to win the Ulster British, and Monro's army, back to royal service, undertaken by Ormond's agent Archdeacon Humphrey Galbraith. Ormond's 'remembrances' to Galbraith had sought to build upon the legitimist foundations of the 1642 Anglo–Scottish treaty, approved by the king, and thereby to heal relations between the Scottish commander-in-chief and his notional superior, the lord lieutenant. In practice it would mean extricating the Ulster British from Monro's command, though placing them under a commander-in-chief chosen by the lord lieutenant but acceptable to the Scots general. Neither the worship of the established church nor the alternative of the Covenant and the Presbyterian order would be imposed until, tellingly, the Church of England was settled by king and Parliament, to which settlement 'subiects heere will in all likelihood submitt'.[49] Galbraith sent some hopeful reports from the north, allowing himself, perhaps correctly, to be persuaded that the Ulster leaders 'dislyke the designe to ingadge them in the cause of the parliament', though reliant on Parliament for supplies, and that the Scottish army was growing increasingly wary of an Edinburgh–Westminster breach. Galbraith recorded of the commanders in east Ulster 'an earnest desire that this warr weare carryed on with your all allowance and concurrence'.[50] Clearly a return to war would be essential to any deal which the lord lieutenant might cut with Protestant Ulster. Within Ormond's own camp William Cadogan, commander at Trim, expressed his hope that Galbraith would heal the 'slight breach' with the Ulster Protestants, but so as to enable joint action against the Irish who 'have played the poltrons with a good King, that I believe hath suffered too much for their sake'.[51]

From the commissioners' perspective, Ormond's disillusionment with the confederates following recent events, notably in Connacht, had led him to seek 'power and opportunity to breake of [off] all Treaty and fall upon them, . . . the Brittish and Scotts Forces to joyne with him against the Rebells'.[52] Sir Robert King, 'bent wholy to make a party heere for the parliament', was believed to be 'very desirous to enterteyne the motion, and see what can be further effected'.[53]

[48] BL Additional MS 4,769A, fo. 3a; Smith, *Constitutional royalism*, pp. 125–7.
[49] Gilbert (ed.), *Contemporary history*, i, 670–1.
[50] Galbraith to Ormond, 14 November, 21 December 1645, Carte, *Ormonde*, vi, 327–8, 331–3.
[51] HMC *Ormonde MSS*, old series, i, 24–5.
[52] *Irish cabinet*, pp. 14–15.
[53] Carte, *Ormonde*, vi, 327–8.

The Ulster commissioners noted, correctly, that they could not move to a settlement without the participation of their Scottish co-commissioners.[54] But King, for one, was soon to reckon Ormond's initiative but 'a Plot to draw this Army' under Ormond's command.[55] He had a point. The opening of contacts with the Ulster commissioners may be an indication that Ormond perceived the need to begin building bridges to Parliament.[56] Perhaps Galbraith's mission was an indication that Ormond was angling for a local manifestation of a wider, hoped-for accommodation of king and Parliament. But it also fitted into his long-term sponsorship of painstaking efforts to recruit as much support for the king within Ireland as possible, pardon and some accommodation being won through service.[57]

Formal negotiations with the confederates, of course, rumbled on, and all the while the parliamentarian naval blockade of Dublin ever more effectively hindered communication between Ormond and the king. By November Ormond believed he had long since conceded repeal of what could be reasonably be construed as 'penal' legislation, while the confederates had retreated on some of the other contentious religious issues. Even so, the opinion of Ormond's high-powered legal team that the latest confederate terms precluded legal punishment for Catholic worship in pre-war Protestant churches was made the explicit basis for Ormond's rejection of those terms on 10 November.[58] Was he not aware of the raft of concessions which Glamorgan had already signed over? Historians have both denied that he could have known quite what Glamorgan was up to and denied that he could not have known, in general terms at least, given the closeness of his contacts with those working with Glamorgan.[59] Perhaps the answer lies in the gaps between what were considered 'public' and 'private' offers, and between a 'petition' and an agreement. Too many actors followed the king's ill example of two-tier negotiations: even in what he deemed his 'final' offer in November, Ormond had included 'private explanations and additions'

[54] They were empowered to act alone in January: Patrick Little, 'The marquess of Ormond and the English Parliament, 1645–1647', in Barnard and Fenlon (eds), *Dukes of Ormonde, 1610–1745*, p. 89.

[55] *Irish Cabinet*, p. 15.

[56] Little, 'Marquess of Ormond', pp. 87–9.

[57] Perhaps, after all, such objectives were not incompatible. Ormond seems to have avoided giving explicit undertakings to engage in renewed warfare, even with the Ulster forces absorbed into a unified military structure. Like the Connacht venture, Ormond was working to bring new and existing bodies of armed men back behind the royal banner. Those they would oppose would be persistent opponents of the crown, and that crown might well find itself willing to accommodate Catholic as well as Protestant support.

[58] Gilbert (ed.), *Irish confederation*, v, 169–70, 176–80.

[59] Kelly, 'John Barry', p. 153; Ó Siochrú, *Confederate Ireland*, p. 95; Ó hAnnracháin, *Catholic Reformation*, pp. 78–9.

to be appended only when the 'public' substance of the treaty had been agreed.[60] Glamorgan certainly did not go out of his way to give the lord lieutenant a clear view of his dealings, but presented them as generating a 'petition' for presentation to the king, alongside the terms agreed with Ormond.[61] Ormond, in turn, made a seemingly modest, but intensely important, modification to his previous stance that all aspects of a settlement should be tied up before moving to their legislative enactment in Parliament,[62] namely that if the confederates were not agreeable to the safeguards he had tried to stitch into the religious articles, he was happy to have all referred to the king directly, unprejudiced by previous concessions by either side.[63] If Ormond believed that Glamorgan had hatched a scheme whereby detailed demands in matters religious would be covertly delivered to the king, as a more or less humble petition of subjects proving their loyalty with an accompanying army, and that he, Ormond, could avoid granting public status to terms which struck at his own convictions and, he firmly believed, would undermine the king in Protestant Ireland and Britain, surely that would be an admirable solution. He would not need to know the details, nor the degree of commitment Glamorgan had made.

The 'Ormondist' line was that further concessions would have to be earned by military service to the king.[64] All the while the king, as he frantically insisted that an Irish peace be concluded, remained adamant that without 10,000 troops it would be worthless.[65] Ormond received these letters only on 13 January, by which time Dublin, and Kilkenny, had been thrown into turmoil by his arrest of Glamorgan (26 December) following the leak of his 'treaty'. To George, Lord Digby, the king's secretary of state, now fetched

[60] Ormond to Glamorgan, 22 November, Gilbert (ed.), *Irish confederation*, v, 199; Ormond to Muskerry, 21/22 November 1645, Clanricard to Glamorgan, 24 November, *Letter-book*, pp. 190–1, 191–4, 194–5. Ormond's 'additional' offers included the appointment of specified numbers of Catholic generals, privy councillors and judges, abolition of the court of wards (seen as threatening the faith of landed Catholics) and permission for Catholic schools and an Irish inn of court. As Clanricard noted these were 'religious' concessions making for Catholic security; certainly they countered the onward march towards a Protestant confessional state.

[61] Lowe, 'Glamorgan mission', pp. 170–1; Ó Siochrú, *Confederate Ireland*, pp. 94–5.

[62] Such a provision was of course intended to prevent the subversion of a future parliament to implement a more radical settlement. Fitzwilliam claimed that this insistence only hampered negotiations by making the confederates adamant that the most detailed of provisions be worked out now, and not deferred: *Lord George Digby's cabinet*, pp. 49–51.

[63] Gilbert (ed.), *Irish confederation*, v, 190. A similar provision was retained in the final treaty terms of the following year: Gilbert (ed.), *Irish confederation*, v, 286–311.

[64] Ormond to Muskerry, 15 December 1645, Carte, *Ormonde*, vi, 330–1; Clanricard to Glamorgan (24 November 1645), Leyburn (7 December 1645) and Muskerry (7 December 1645), *Letter-book*, pp. 194–5, 197–8, 198–9.

[65] Charles to Ormond, 1–2 December 1645, *Calendar of the Clarendon state papers*, i, 289; Carte, *Ormonde*, vi, 328–9.

up in Dublin, nothing less than the charges of treason lodged against Glamorgan could vindicate the king or allow any Irish treaty to proceed, from the royalist end.[66] No doubt he was right.[67] The king, in due course, moved to disavow Glamorgan's actions.[68] Though Glamorgan insisted that he had not committed the king to anything,[69] the language in which the articles were framed was perhaps the most startling revelation – rather than making a 'petition' for royal favour Glamorgan had applied his authority to 'treat and conclude' actually to 'grant, conclude and agree' terms on the king's behalf. The arrest was no doubt a face-saving exercise, though that does not preclude surprise, or even horror, within the royalist camp. More surprising perhaps was the release and re-employment of the earl, though in turn that does not imply a recognition that Glamorgan was following royal wishes in making such a grant (though perhaps he was doing so in offering to act as a conduit for such requests). Above all, as before, Glamorgan's value lay in his supposed logistical aptitudes, witnessed by his ability to raise forces for the crown in Wales in the early 1640s, and his capacity to act as go-between to where the Protestant state could not venture. Ormond relied on Glamorgan to move forward efforts to obtain an interim 3,000 soldiers ahead of completion of a settlement, and to do so by negotiating, among others, with the papal nuncio Rinuccini, who had reached Ireland in October 1645 and whom Ormond could not approach.[70] In the twilight before news reached Ireland of the king's repudiation of Glamorgan's treaty, he made headway in assembling an expeditionary force.[71] Like Clanricard, he appears to have continued to vest hope in royal generosity if only an army could be dispatched in time.[72]

Charles moved to reassure Glamorgan, though gently chiding him that he had 'given consent to conditions much beyond your instructions' and telling Ormond that, though the prosecution of Glamorgan was necessary 'for clearing of my honour', he considered 'misguided zeal, more than malice' to

---

[66] Digby to Nicholas, 4 January 1646, *The earl of Glamorgans negotiations*, pp. 12–16.

[67] For Dublin Protestant delight at the arrest, see Nicholas Loftus to Perceval, 22 December 1645, HMC *Egmont MSS*, i, 267.

[68] *CSPD, 1645–7*, p. 326; Gilbert (ed.), *Irish confederation*, v, 252–4; Carte, *Ormonde*, vi, 347–9, 349–50.

[69] Lowe, 'Glamorgan mission', p. 182.

[70] Gilbert (ed.), *Irish confederation*, v, 255–6, 260–1; *Letter-book*, pp. 201–2; Carte, *Ormonde*, vi, 352–3.

[71] Lowe, 'Glamorgan mission', pp. 188–92.

[72] If he did not quite keep clear of his resolve to avoid further entanglements, he could opt out somewhat in the belief that the queen was in process of negotiating a more secure settlement for Catholics: Glamorgan to Ormond, 8 February 1646, Gilbert (ed.), *Irish confederation*, v, 260–1; Glamorgan to Clanricard, 9 February 1646, *Letter-book*, pp. 205–6. For Clanricard's hopes of royal generosity in return for aid, and that Dublin could be bound to royal concessions, see *Letter-book*, pp. 206–8, 210–12.

be the cause of his lapse.[73] The king continued to try and juggle plans for armed intervention from Ireland with his efforts to seek out a 'personal treaty' with Westminster. In his personal casuistry, he believed that his latest offer to the Houses committed him to take Parliament's advice on Ireland but only *after* the arrival at an English peace and, implicitly, *after* he had been made aware of his engagements in Ireland. His reasoning was that by the time he needed to square things with Parliament the Irish peace would be made, as he hoped, or broken definitively.[74] His private offers in matters religious, with which he seemed peculiarly pleased, carry distant echoes of his stance towards Ireland. Still unconvinced that Scottish demands for the establishment of Presbyterianism in England were motivated by religious zeal, he made it a point of conscience to safeguard the 'church's patrimony' in England from Scottish rapacity, offering 'to stay their stomachs' with lands in Ireland instead, and to allow Presbyterians in England, like Catholics in Ireland, to erect their own churches rather than usurp those of the king's church.[75] As he later informed the queen, he would no more establish Presbyterianism in England than agree to Glamorgan's 'giving away the church lands in Ireland, and all my ecclesiastical power there'.[76] As chances for a settlement in England faded, still Ormond was urged ahead, and the lieutenant's estimate that perhaps 6,000 soldiers could be ready by 1 April, with more to follow, accepted as a basis for negotiation.[77]

As spring approached, Ormond clearly felt that the curtain was about to drop on an Irish settlement. If nothing less than the Glamorgan terms would satisfy, he noted, 'then is his Majestie noe longer kept in hope of the

---

[73] Charles also noted that Glamorgan was 'abused' in having 'your treaty . . . revealed to all the world': Lowe, 'Glamorgan mission', p. 194.

[74] King to queen, 8 February 1646, *Charles I in 1646*, pp. 17–18. To Parliament (15 January), he said he would 'endeavour to give them satisfaction' over Ireland, only to tell the queen (18 January) that by these very words 'it may be I give them leave to hope for more than I intended . . .': *LJ*, viii, 103; *CSPD, 1645–7*, p. 311; *Charles I in 1646*, p. 11.

[75] J. G. Fotheringham (ed.), *The diplomatic correspondence of Jean de Montereul and the brothers Bellievre, French ambassadors in England and Scotland, 1645–8*, Scottish History Society 29–30 (2 vols, Edinburgh, 1898–99) i, 105–7; king to queen, 8 January 1646, *Charles I in 1646*, pp. 4–5. The negotiations between the king and the Scots in May 1646 included the option of a civil settlement now and a deferred consideration of religious questions, a solution unattractive to the Scots: Fotheringham (ed.), *Correspondence of Montereul*, i, 207, 212.

[76] King to queen, 3 March 1646, *Charles I in 1646*, pp. 21–2. Even Ormond's insistence on a definite article on the return of churches found an echo, as late as 1647, in the king's response to the 'heads of the proposals', where he noted that 'though there was nothing done against the Church-government established, there was nothing done to assert it', implicitly rejecting Sir John Berkeley's argument that 'the law was security enough for the Church' (Smith, *Constitutional royalism*, p. 152), the line Clanricard had adopted in insisting that an Irish peace would see churches legally revert to the Protestants (*Letter-book*, pp. 163–5).

[77] Charles to Ormond, 17 February, Carte, *Ormonde*, vi, 353.

advantages he hath hitherto promised himself by a Peace here, and soe he will be at liberty to propose to himselfe and prosecute such other ways of preserveing himself as perhaps are not consisten with the Irish Peace.' The Irish would thus share the blame for their own 'extirpation' with 'the Parliament, that covet their land and thirst for their blood' since they would 'accept of noe conditions but such as for noe earthly considerations his Majestie can graunt, nor any honest Protestant Minister of his can be an instrument to convay unto them'.[78] With the terms of the eventual 'Ormond peace' relatively unchanged since the previous November, it took a prolonged period of soul-searching, some intense debate and not a little duplicity before the confederate negotiating team signed a deal with Ormond on 28 March 1646, to be kept secret for now.[79] A monument to failed hopes, outdated almost from the moment of its emergence, given the collapse of the king's cause in England, the treaty was nonetheless not without its merits, at least as compared with the fumbling attempts at settlement in England.[80]

Ormond had been pressing for a conclusion, insisting that further extensions of the cessation would bring 'inevitable ruine . . . upon all his Majestie's true servants heere, through want, and the consequences of muteny, disorder, and treachery that will certainly accompany it, and are alredy, upon the noyse of a barren Peace, beginning to appeare'. If the northern Protestant forces moved against Dublin it was in expectation of finding 'more frends than enemyes'.[81] He had a point, though it was moot whether he would improve his position within the Protestant zones by a peace. The winter of 1645–46 had seen Parliament's commissioners nestle into Ulster and strengthen their hold on parts of Connacht.[82] Sir Robert King, whose pre-war interests largely lay in the west, slipped into Connacht to test loyalties; if he failed to sponsor a successful coup in Athlone,[83] Roscommon was betrayed to a garrison of Coote's men by the ever-versatile Ranelagh, recently commended by Ormond for his fidelity.[84] As spring campaigns loomed, with lunges expected in Connacht and through counties Monaghan, Cavan, Westmeath and Longford, confederate sources suggested that 'Dundalke, the Newry, Drogheda, and the rest of the [Ormondist] English garrisons in those

---

[78] Gilbert (ed.), *Irish confederation*, v, 285–6 (undated memorandum, apparently for Ormond's own use).

[79] Ó Siochrú, *Confederate Ireland*, pp. 99–103, 105–6; Ó hAnnracháin, *Catholic Reformation*, pp. 134–6.

[80] For different assessments of the 'Ormond peace', see Ó Siochrú, *Confederate Ireland*, pp. 109–11; Armstrong, 'Ormond . . . and protestant royalism', pp. 129–30, 137.

[81] Ormond to Glamorgan, 14 March 1646, Gilbert (ed.), *Irish confederation*, v, 272–3.

[82] McNeill (ed.), *Tanner letters*, pp. 201–2, 203–6.

[83] Carte MS 16, fos 469, 495, 500, 510, 535, 533–4, 552.

[84] Ormond to Ranelagh, 5 and 23 January 1646, Carte MS 17, fos 498, 457; Ranelagh to Ormond, 25 February 1646, Carte MS 16, fo. 557.

partes will martch out with them, notwithstandinge of any Peace'.[85] Parliamentarian naval officers reported rumours of proposed defections from within Dublin itself, were a peace to be concluded.[86] With the articles about to be signed Dublin witnessed a 'desperate plot' in March as a corporal, 'being frantic', and seventeen men tried to seize the castle itself. If 'no man of quality was found to have a hand in it' great suspicion was generated.[87]

Ormond was being backed into a corner. He remained wary of confederate calls for military association ahead of a formal peace; for him it was essential that a settlement be framed as a restoration of allegiance, of the reception of the errant into pardon and favour, with military aid the proof of their resumed loyalty. While eager to conclude a deal, Ormond was against publication ahead of the dispatch of troops to England, validating the Irish peace. The confederate negotiating team had made a commitment to the papal nuncio, Rinuccini, to conclude nothing until additional religious articles, drawn either from separate papal negotiations with the queen or from the Glamorgan terms, could be published alongside the civil terms agreed with Ormond. By signing on 28 March the negotiators were in breach of this undertaking, a fact which provided them with a strong incentive to keep the deal secret.[88] Though the king was brought to admit (26 March) that the collapse of his military position in England meant that the landing of unsupported Irish infantry would only mean their ruin, and should be stopped, he then reversed the instruction in the space of one letter. The Irish peace must go ahead so as to be in place before any terms were made with Parliament.[89] What Ormond had sought all along was a settlement which could bring all 'loyal' Ireland back under its Protestant monarchy, isolating the recalcitrant, of whatever hue. Instead he faced the prospect of seeing his shrinking Protestant constituency absorbed into another 'rebel' camp, and perhaps of hitching himself to a settlement which reversals in England would render precarious. As far back as January he had sought instructions about how to respond to possible overtures from Parliament,[90] liable to become ever more appealing

---

[85] Richard Bellings to Ormond, 26 February 1646, Gilbert (ed.), *Irish confederation*, v, 261–3.
[86] *CSPI, 1633–47*, pp. 437–8.
[87] Ormond to Glamorgan, 24 March 1646, Carte MS 16, fo. 694; V. Savage to Perceval, 2 April 1646, HMC *Egmont MSS*, i, 284–5. John Borlace junior, the regimental commander of the men involved, seems to have fallen into odium, as his repeated letters seeking intercession with Ormond attest: Carte MS 17, fos 68, 231. Ormond wrangled £3,000 from the confederates, alleging the need to quell discontent in Dublin: Gilbert (ed.), *Irish confederation*, v, 327–32.
[88] Gilbert (ed.), *Irish confederation*, v, 266, 282–3, 312–13, 330–2, 332–3. Ó hAnnracháin, *Catholic Reformation*, pp. 134–7.
[89] Charles to Ormond, Charles to Digby, 26 March 1646, Carte, *Ormonde*, vi, 356–7, 357–8.
[90] Ormond to Nicholas, 19 January 1646, Carte, *Ormonde*, vi, 344–7. It was Nicholas who had alerted Ormond to the possibility of approaches from Parliament in his letter of 3 December 1646, Carte MS 16, fo. 286.

to the Dublin Protestant community.[91] The Ulster commissioners had renewed contact with Ormond in February, explaining that they now had the authority to treat with him, but though he offered to receive propositions, Ormond's response was non-committal.[92] When word came through from the king it appeared to brush off any contact between Ormond and Parliament, Secretary Nicholas suggesting no more was heard 'of the rebels purpose to treat with your lordship', with their nomination of Philip, Viscount Lisle, to the lord lieutenancy of Ireland.[93]

The brief and turbulent episode of Lisle's lieutenancy has rivalled Glamorgan's Irish career as a subject of focused research and discussion, enabling Parliament's Irish policy to be read against partisan developments within Parliament and shifts in Westminster–Edinburgh relations.[94] At least since the winter of 1644–45 significant factional realignments had been underway, resulting in an increasing awareness of the presence of antagonistic 'Independent' and 'Presbyterian' interests within parliamentarian ranks as the need to consider the shape of a post-war England, and notably its re-formed national church, became ever more pressing.[95] Along the way relations between the Scots and some of those to the fore in drawing them into the English war, and now deemed 'Independents', had turned decidedly frosty, as hostility to Scottish religious ambitions were compounded with scathing assessments of their military contribution. Meanwhile a 'Presbyterian Alliance' coalesced between the Scottish representatives in England and a relatively heterogeneous assortment of Westminster politicians, not least the friends and supporters of the earl of Essex, recently displaced from his position as Parliament's lord general, and those who saw a Presbyterian church settlement, even one along Scottish lines, as less threatening, socially or theologically, than the toleration of religious independents and sectaries.[96] Over the winter of 1645–46

[91] HMC *Egmont MSS*, i, 278.

[92] Annesley and Beale to Ormond, 16 February 1646, Ormond to Annesley and Beale, 2 March 1646, Carte MS 16, fos 525, 573.

[93] Nicholas to Ormond, 18 February 1646, Carte, *Ormonde*, vi, 354–5.

[94] The significance of the Lisle episode was made clear in John Adamson's vigorously argued and broad-ranging essay, 'Strafford's ghost: the British context of Viscount Lisle's lieutenancy of Ireland', in Ohlmeyer (ed.), *Ireland from independence to occupation*, pp. 128–59. See also the earlier discussion in Bottigheimer, *English money*, pp. 97–110 and Patrick Little's sophisticated and convincing reassessment, 'The "Irish Independents" and Viscount Lisle's lieutenancy of Ireland', *Historical Journal* 44 (2001), 941–61.

[95] In neither case, of course, was the 'party' in question neatly defined by its commitment to an Independent or Presbyterian mode of organization in church matters, such issues being but one component in the factional alignment, and never coinciding completely with allegiances on other issues. For a valuable treatment, see Scott, *Politics and war*, chapters 3–5.

[96] This interpretation (though refined by subsequent research) receives its classic statement in Mahony, 'Presbyterian party'.

Parliament produced its revised terms for settlement with the king, later known as the Newcastle propositions, which represented an erosion of Scottish influence within both England and Ireland from the heady days when Anglo–Scottish joint authority had been entrenched in the schemes of the Uxbridge propositions. That existing bilateral arrangements for Ireland were also now unilaterally dismantled, and Lisle installed as an English chief governor, has, not surprisingly, been taken as an 'Independent' triumph.

Parliament's reassessment of its Irish war was indeed related to the realignments within the Houses, though in such a manner as to bring out the continuing complexities surrounding the consolidation of partisan coalitions. A comparison with developments in the north of England is instructive. Genuine anger at the oppression of the Scottish army quartered in the region had been building for some time, resulting in a dialogue between disgruntled provincial opinion and anti-Scottish 'Independent' politicians at Westminster. As David Scott has convincingly shown, this served to strengthen the 'Independent' interest within Parliament, where reports could be exploited to further an anti-Scottish agenda, and regionally, making the north of England the party's 'principal regional power base'.[97] Many of the criticisms levelled against Scottish conduct in the north of England could be replicated for Ulster. Protests at the Scottish garrisoning of castles and towns in the north of England, even after their field army had departed, could be matched by complaints at continued Scottish occupation of Belfast.[98] Scottish exactions in northern England were considered not only oppressive, but indiscriminate as between friend and foe; the Ulster commissioners were mandated to investigate complaints of exactions in their fiefdom too. As northern grievances were harnessed more successfully to Westminster debates in the late summer and autumn of 1645, so the period saw the new (Star Chamber) Irish committee set to get to grips with Scottish malpractice, utilizing its men on the spot in Ulster.[99]

Sir John Clotworthy remained the obvious link-man between Ulster and Parliament, consolidating his position within the Westminster structures as by far and away the leading frequenter of meetings of the Star Chamber Irish committee.[100] Yet the committee as a whole retained a 'Presbyterian' complexion about its active membership,[101] and Clotworthy's political

[97] Scott, 'Northern Gentlemen', especially pp. 348–9, 356–9.

[98] *CSPD, 1645–7*, pp. 114–15, 194–5, 198, 226–7; David Stevenson, *Revolution and counter-revolution in Scotland 1644–1651* (London, 1977), pp. 18, 55–6; for Belfast see *CSPI, 1633–47*, p. 417; *CJ*, iv, 340–1; *LJ*, viii, 14; BL Additional MS 4,769A, fo. 4.

[99] BL Additional MS 4,769A, fos 3b, 6b–8a; Scott, 'Northern Gentlemen', pp. 355, 359.

[100] Clotworthy was present on 62 of 79 occasions between July 1645 and July 1646; Knightley (42) and Jephson (39) lagged far behind.

[101] I am grateful to Patrick Little for sharing the results of his unpublished investigations into the political alignments of the parliamentary Irish committees.

trajectory over the years 1645–47 was far removed from that of the 'Independent' 'northern gentlemen', with him landing up among the execrated 'Presbyterian' grandees. Clotworthy had, of course, long articulated a 'planters first' line towards Ulster, critical of the subordination of local forces to Scottish command and ready to press for support for local forces even while their allegiance could be construed as ambiguous. On into the spring of 1646 the committee continued to probe Scottish malpractices in Ulster, with every indication of zeal, and with the apparent support of such leading 'Presbyterians' as Denzil Holles and Sir Philip Stapleton, as well as such representatives of the long-established Irish interest as Clotworthy, Reynolds and Robert Goodwyn.[102] For now, in the autumn of 1645, it was the Star Chamber Irish committee which probed past Anglo–Scottish entanglements over Ireland for presentation ahead of the Commons' debate on the government of Ireland, set for 8 December. It is unlikely, to say the least, that Reynolds's report was intended to bolster the Scottish command.[103]

Parliament's ongoing revision of its terms for settlement with the king had already signalled a reduction in Scottish influence. Power over the militia in England and Ireland was now to be vested solely in the English Parliament, as was nomination to top Irish posts, from the lord lieutenant down.[104] A series of debates in the Commons, sitting as a committee of the whole House, would tease out the implications for current arrangements in Ireland. If the 8 December resolution that 'the Government of *Ireland* shall not be continued in any Person or Persons, longer than One whole Year' implied that agreement had not been reached, and that all sides wanted to guard against a major defeat, 'a Long debate' on 15 December clarified the position that it was for Parliament to resolve whether the government of Ireland should be committed to 'One or more' and that joint Anglo–Scottish arrangements should exist only during Parliament's pleasure.[105] Some MPs at least were thinking terms of a 'single person' to head the government of Ireland, Lord Lisle being named in the House, though one informed observer believed that the drift was towards management 'by committees for this season'.[106] The 20 December debate was reported as the moment when the House resolved to dismantle the machinery constructed in 1644, of a joint, Scottish,

---

[102] *CSPI, 1633–47*, p. 444; BL Additional MS 4,769A, fos 6b–8a. Clotworthy, Holles and the political 'Independent' Richard Knightley had been named to write to the Scottish Parliament protesting the retention of Belfast: *CJ*, iv, 340–1.

[103] *CSPI, 1633–47*, p. 422; *CJ*, iv, 367, 368–9; BL Additional MS 4,769A, fo. 4b.

[104] *CJ*, iv, 359; see Gardiner (ed.), *Constitutional documents*, pp. 293–6, 304 for the final version of the Newcastle propositions.

[105] *CJ*, iv, 368–9, 376; BL Additional MS 31,116, fos 247a, 248a; HMC *Portland MSS*, i, 326.

[106] Perceval to Waller, 22 December, HMC *Egmont MSS*, i, 268.

command and governance by committees of both kingdoms. The protests of the Scots commissioners, aired in the Lords if not the Commons, plaintively concluded 'that if these articles may bee infringed, wee knowe not what a Treaty is, nor what wee may trust unto hereafter'.[107] On 5 January, a tight vote (61:50) defeated the motion that the government of Ireland 'be committed to more persons than one', and on 21 January the Commons resolved that Lisle be 'Governor' of Ireland for the period of one year.[108] On 16 March the Commons moved to commission Lisle as lord lieutenant, with power to act as commander-in-chief, under the direction of Parliament. The solicitor-general was to draw up his commission, and the English members of the Committee of Both Kingdoms to prepare his instructions.[109] Despite a rearguard action by the Scots,[110] it had been easier to excise them from the command structure in Ireland than to create an agreed alternative.

Voices raised in support of the Scottish command came from a quarter with diminishing influence over the war in Ireland, the London adventurers, or at least a segment of them. From anticipatory ticket-holders to a post-war share-out of Irish property, many of the London adventures had mutated to present-day beneficiaries of the need to supply and sustain the war effort in Ireland by 1642–43.[111] By the mid-1640s, though, they had been increasingly squeezed out by John Davies, his Irish contacts and his London partners. Out-bid for contracts before both the Committee of Both Kingdoms (erstwhile supporters of the London adventurers against the criticisms of the Clotworthy–John Goodwyn–Reynolds committee) and the Star Chamber Irish committee, they were given a chance to re-establish themselves within the logistical loop with a request for an advance to sponsor the new expedition planned for 1645–46. Since the summer the adventurers had been pressing their own agenda, an amalgam of schemes to re-launch funding

---

[107] CJ, iv, 381, 384–5; HMC Portland MSS, i, 326; BL Additional MS 37,344, fo. 31a; LJ, viii, 61, 64–5; BL Additional MS 31,116, fos 249a, 250a; Perceval to Waller, 24 December, HMC Egmont MSS, i, 268.

[108] CJ, iv, 396–7, 413, 418; BL Additional MS 37,344, fos 33b, 36a; BL Additional MS 31,116, fo. 252a; HMC Portland MSS, i, 326–7. However, the Ulster commissioners were also voted to remain in place, acting without the necessary conjunction with their Scottish counterparts: CJ, iv, 408; CSPI, 1633–47, p. 429.

[109] The commission was returned from the Lords, and sent for issue under the Great Seal on 9 April: CJ, iv, 475, 504; BL Additional MS 31,116, fos 260a, 262b. The delay may be have due to the Great Seal being 'under a vacancy', which delayed the fresh commission to the Ulster commissioners: BL Additional MS 4,769A, fo. 6a.

[110] Perceval to Waller, 30 March, HMC Egmont MSS, i, 284.

[111] Armstrong, 'Protestant Ireland', chapter 4 and appendices 2–3. For the manner in which the 'Magazine' of the old Virginia Company had allowed mercantile profits to be made from provisioning while the colonial tasks for which the company existed stagnated, see E. S. Morgan, American slavery, American freedom: the ordeal of colonial Virginia (New York, 1975), pp. 97, 113.

upon adventure principles of money now for land later. The Irish committee had not been unsympathetic but the Commons proved uninterested, and the adventurers retaliated with an angry refusal to advance money to speed soldiers to Munster, topped with a denunciation of funding based upon assessments rather than confiscatory schemes.[112]

As the debates swirled within Parliament, the London adventurer leadership published its collection of papers and responses charting the sorry tale, but including its latest proposals opposing the appointment of a lord lieutenant, defending a system of provincial governance, the employment of commissioners and a continued Scottish command in Ulster.[113] The interests of a knot of prominent Londoners, members of the adventurers' committee at Grocers' Hall and of the Goldsmiths' Hall committee (with its sequestration duties and Scottish responsibilities), were bound up with the financial and logistical machinery, with the loans and supply contracts, put in place to sustain the Scottish armies in England and in Ireland.[114] Given the 'radical' and 'war party' complexion of the London adventurers' committee,[115] their stance is a reminder that allegiances and alignments were still in flux in the winter of 1645–46, that perhaps not all of the Scots' old win-the-war friends in London had deserted their interests.

Not that the London adventure community spoke with one voice. The rather tired agenda of extra adventure schemes had also been argued before the Star Chamber Irish committee by the leading London merchant, religious Independent and adventurer William Hawkins. Hawkins, though, came out in favour of the appointment of a new 'commander-in-chief' endowed with civil and military powers. He also gave a twist to the standard demand for a new urban adventure, based on the confiscation of property in Munster towns, asking that the re-granted towns have civil and martial 'immunities' akin to London, but ecclesiastical immunities as in New England.[116]

Hawkins's scheme gives some substance to the recurring allegations that some at least of his brethren foresaw the benefits of an Independent 'haven'

---

[112] Many of the votes, petitions and other documents are printed in *The state of the Irish affairs* (London, 1645) E314 (7), issued by the adventurers in late December 1645 or early January 1646; Thomason's copy is dated 2 January. Cf. Bottigheimer, *English money*, pp. 92–6.

[113] *State of the Irish affairs*, pp. 21–2.

[114] See above, chapter 4, note 48.

[115] Lindley, 'Irish adventurers', pp. 1–12.

[116] *CSPI, 1633–47*, p. 418. William Hawkins was not, as sometimes suggested, the William Hawkins of Iver, solicitor to Lisle's father, Leicester (HMC *De L'Isle MSS*, vi (London, 1966), 113, 117; Firth and Rait (eds), *Acts and ordinances*, i, 1150–1). For the merchant see Firth and Rait (eds), *Acts and ordinances*, i, 623, 970, 1087; *CSPI, adventurers 1642–59*, pp. 23, 81, 148, 171, 185, 194, 202, 214, 236, 240, 322, 342, 343, 355, 385; T. C. Barnard, 'Planters and policies in Cromwellian Ireland', *Past & Present* 61 (1973), p. 42; Murray Tolmie, *Triumph of the saints: the separate churches of London, 1616–1649* (Cambridge, 1977), p. 140.

in Ireland, should a rigid Presbyterian system be established in England.[117] Such rumours circulated around secret contacts with the king in the autumn of 1645,[118] at the very time when Independent strategy within the Westminster Assembly of divines was shifting from comprehension within the anticipated Presbyterian settlement to 'tolleration, not only to themselves, but to other Sects'.[119] It may not be entirely implausible to connect them to Cromwell's apparent interest in a Munster expedition – his 'spirit leads much that way', as his fellow New Model officer Hardress Waller was obviously pleased to report, though Waller's promotion of Cromwell as a possible head of an Irish campaign (and 'our Deputy') in late 1645 fizzled out.[120] (Hawkins at least kept the faith with his plan: by the 1650s, having gobbled up numerous other adventure lots and transplanted himself to Co. Cork, he was to the fore in schemes to attract New England independents to settle in Irish cities.[121])

The idea of a religious bolt-hole across the water hardly had much attraction for an 'Independent' grandee like the earl of Northumberland, as opposed to the enticing prospect of securing for his nephew, Lisle, the position of lord lieutenant.[122] Leading 'Presbyterians' like Holles and Clotworthy acted as tellers against committing Ireland to 'single person' government, opposite 'Independents' like Strickland and Evelyn.[123] In the months ahead the former

---

[117] An anonymous pamphlet in the Thomason collection, E1190 (4), lacking a title page, but dated to December 1644, argued for the deployment of religious Independents in the conquest and settlement of Ireland.

[118] Montreuil to Mazarin, 13/23 November, Fotheringham (ed.), *Correspondence of Montereul*, i, 59.

[119] Robert Baillie, *Letters and journals of Robert Baillie*, ed. David Laing (3 vols, Edinburgh, 1841–2), ii, 326, 341; Robert S. Paul, *The assembly of the Lord: politics and religion in the Westminster Assembly and the 'Grand Debate'* (Edinburgh, 1985), pp. 482–9.

[120] Waller to Perceval, 4 December 1645, Perceval to Waller, 22 December 1645, HMC *Egmont MSS*, i, 265, 268; on 31 January 1646, Nicholas reported to Ormond that Cromwell had turned down the command 'resolving first to see the Independents settled in their hoped for gouernment in England': Carte, *Ormonde*, vi, 351–2. The New Model had dispatched £1,000 in cash for the relief of Youghal, as well as supplies: Rushworth to Lord Fairfax, 3 December 1645, R. Bell (ed.), *Memorials of the civil war* (2 vols, London, 1849), i, 262; PRO SP 63, 261/9, fo. 96.

[121] T. C. Barnard, *Cromwellian Ireland: English government and reform in Ireland, 1649–1660* (Oxford, 1975), pp. 53, 56–7, 58 and note 43.

[122] His appointment as lord lieutenant may have been a manoeuvre to wrest advantage from more general calls for a new commander-in-chief or 'deputy'; see e.g. McNeill (ed.), *Tanner letters*, pp. 203–6 for such calls from the Ulster commissioners. Perceval (to Waller, 22 December) noted that the nomination of Lisle was 'contrary to the expectation of those who set that business first on foot, aiming at another, and conceiving the north the fittest place to begin the work': HMC *Egmont MSS*, i, 268.

[123] HMC *Portland MSS*, i, 326–7. Evelyn had first nominated Lisle: HMC *Egmont MSS*, i, 268. Perhaps avoiding a new lord lieutenant meant leaving the door open for approaches to Ormond. Nicholas's reports of possible approaches to Ormond come from this time, though the fact that Lisle was not yet directed to Munster perhaps leaves his appointment not incompatible with hopes of gaining Dublin, by negotiation or otherwise.

would develop an alternative model based on provincial commanders and committees, though with no restoration of a Scottish dimension. Lisle himself was undoubtedly a partisan candidate, and the divisive implications of his appointment would make themselves felt with force over the next year and more.[124] No doubt there was an 'Independent' agenda to reduce Scottish influence, but it operated alongside, and did not absorb, the longstanding efforts of the 'planter' lobby to strengthen ties between Parliament and the British of Ireland, and drew upon the sentiments of MPs in general, whose enthusiasm for Scottish confederal schemes had never been strong. Attitudes to the Scots, it might be suggested, were less a confrontation of opposite, partisan, opinions than a spectrum of views, ranging from a 'hard' anti-Scots stance, through a critical attitude tempered by a hope that co-operation could be continued,[125] to a friendlier disposition, but one aware of tensions which needed to be resolved if amicability was to be sustained.

The Lisle initiative also built upon the general mood of the Houses in pressing forward the Irish war. There is no need to embed Lisle within a new ideological agenda, as least as regards Ireland, but rather within the context of a new vigour exercised in pursuit of the long-set goals of military victory in Ireland, pushed forward by the 'Presbyterian' Star Chamber committee for some months past. The vote for 'a single person to be nominated by both houses' was accompanied by an insistence that 'all Treatyes with the Rebelles shall be nullyfyed'; a new lord lieutenant could also be a political guarantor of a core parliamentarian value.[126] But Lisle was also clearly intended to be a fighting lieutenant. His future bitter rival, Inchiquin, for the moment expressed the hope that the 'one man' named to govern Ireland would begin in Munster, 'the first province in the kingdom'. Inchiquin's report on conditions in Munster was incorporated into an extensive review drawn up by the Irish committee for presentation to Parliament in early February, covering forces in Ireland, reinforcements sought and past, present and future finances. This advocated an additional 500 cavalry and 3,500 infantry for Munster, 1,340 cavalry and 3,000 infantry for Ulster, forces not far short of the army sent in 1641–42, and computed costs for all forces at £48,961 per month, more than the original estimates for the pay of the New Model Army.[127] A third assessment ordinance

---

[124] Little, 'Irish "Independents" ', pp. 951–8.

[125] A stance attributed to the earl of Northumberland by Jason Peacey, 'The exploitation of captured royalist correspondence and Anglo–Scottish relations in the British civil wars, 1645–1646', *Scottish Historical Review* 79 (2000), 229–30.

[126] BL Additional MS 37,344, fo. 33b. In the light of the Glamorgan revelations, Reynolds was charged to bring in a bill to outlaw Catholicism in Ireland, read on 20 January: *CJ*, iv, 394–5, 411; BL Additional MS 31,116, fo. 252a.

[127] PRO SP/63, 261/9, pp. 90–9; *CSPI, 1633–47*, pp. 432–6; Ian Gentles, *The New Model Army in England, Ireland and Scotland, 1645–1653* (Oxford, 1992), p. 29.

for Ireland was already worming its way through the system, though not passed until March.[128] The September 1645 ordinance was still operational, but the reality had long been that expenditure on Ireland did not wait upon the slow process of collection, but operated from loans advanced upon future taxation. Ongoing collections were thus already committed, and on 30 March the ever well-informed Perceval lamented that 'Want of money is the chiefest stay', there being 'not yet any thorough course taken for the speedy raising of money designed for the Lord Lisle's despatch'.[129]

Despite ongoing efforts by the Irish committee, it was only in the months between April and June that Parliament finally got to grips with the February recommendations.[130] Mechanisms were put in place to provide further credit so as to enable the mass reinforcement sought in January to get underway. In the short term, Parliament even took the unusual step of diverting large sums of money for Ireland from other centralized funds.[131] John Davies, Clotworthy's crony, and his partners were 'in hand wholly to furnish him [Lisle] (the citizens and adventurers being backward)', with all to be ready by midsummer.[132] The Irish committee grappled with the logistics of the future expeditions, in particular the assembly of troops, largely drawn from the rolling disbandment of Parliament's provincial forces. Ex-soldiers were lured into service at the point of disbandment, while the committee also allowed officers to submit offers to recruit companies for Ireland.[133]

The counter-current, of Irish troops destined for England, though bandied about by Parliament as a threat, would clearly not now come to pass as the last of the ports and garrisons in royalist hands surrendered. With the peace not proclaimed, and its literal terms now broken by the failure to send troops, Ormond avoided an open break with the Protestants of the north.[134] On 9 April, he wrote to the Ulster commissioners, asking again for propositions, though in the meantime apparently lending countenance to shadowy attempt to capture them.[135] By the middle of April, the marquis of Argyll had landed in

---

[128] *LJ*, viii, 205.

[129] Perceval to Waller, 30 March 1646, HMC *Egmont MSS*, i, 284.

[130] *CJ*, iv, 465; *CSPI, 1633–47*, pp. 443–4.

[131] Firth and Rait (eds), *Acts and ordinances*, i, 848–52; *CJ*, iv, 520–1, 524.

[132] Perceval to Broghill, 7 April 1646, HMC *Egmont MSS*, i, 285–6, 288. Davies's co-operation had become all but indispensable by now, given his entanglement with credit arrangements and the collection of assessments.

[133] For examples, see *CJ*, iv, 537; *CSPI, 1633–47*, pp. 448–50. It hardly helped that the New Model Army had been engaged on a recruiting drive from January, in the south-western counties where the Munster units were to be raised: Gentles, *New Model Army*, pp. 33, 38.

[134] Ormond told Digby that the inclusion of the conditional military clause was vital in winning the council's support for the Peace: Carte, *Ormonde*, vi, 365–6.

[135] Carte MS 17, fo. 104. The plan to capture them centred on Major Galbraith, brother of Humphrey; a counter-plan existed to capture the latter: Carte MS 17, fos 38, 40, 143.

Ulster, along with fellow Scottish commissioners, to make a brief effort at an Ulster committee of both kingdoms even as Westminster was voting down the system. Just as in July he would work wonders for the Scottish position at Westminster, so now Argyll managed to win a last moment of Covenanter co-operation in Ireland. Together the English and Scottish commissioners apprised Ormond of what they wanted – nothing less than the discounting of a treaty with the Irish, the admission of their troops to Dublin and Ormond's submission to 'King and Parliament'.[136] Though the lieutenant did not throw out their surrender terms, but secured the council's approval for a meeting of delegates, his letter to Digby rings true in its assertion that he was only playing for time and safeguarding his quarters against attack, with contacts designed 'to satisfie some wavering mindes, and in full assurance to make aduantage of it; their insolence is such vpon their late successe.'[137]

On 3 April Charles wrote to Ormond of his intentions to depart Oxford and place himself in the hands of the Scottish Covenanting army. He intended Ormond to use the letter to woo Monro's Ulster forces to what he fondly hoped was a new collaboration with his erstwhile Scottish opponents. As passed on to Westminster by Sir Robert King, the king's letter had considerable potential to sour Parliament–Scots relations further, though the Houses preferred to blame the king for seeking to wreak division.[138] But Charles's communication also caused turmoil in Dublin. On 11 June Ormond warned him that instructions were urgently needed to prevent the 'dissolution of your governement heere'.[139] Charles's latest dispatch, also dated 11 June, added another twist. When he told Ormond 'to proceede noe further in treaty with the rebels, nor to engage vs uppon any conditions with them after sight thereof' he thought he had conveyed his intention that Ormond was 'only to stop treating there, after the receipt of it, but meddles nothing with what was done before.'[140] Instead, when the royal letter reached Dublin on 26 June, it effected a halt by the council of all proceedings relating to the treaty. Dublin was reduced to communicating with the king through Monro and the Ulster commissioners. In a series of letters the council attempted to re-orientate itself to the prospect of a Protestant war, though pressing for a temporary cessation given conditions in Dublin. In its plea for the persons, estates and consciences of its members and the other loyalists, it thought fit

---

[136] In return promises were made that Ormond would have personal security to a degree unparalleled in the late wars – Annesley saw this as opening 'a faire way for the flourishing estate of the protestants in this kingdome': Carte MS 17, fos 146, 157, 159; Stevenson, *Scottish Covenanters*, p. 219.

[137] Carte MS 17, fos 206, 214; Ormond to Digby, April 26, Carte, *Ormonde*, vi, 372.

[138] *CJ*, iv, 567, 570; BL Additional MS 31,116, fo. 273a.

[139] Carte, *Ormonde*, vi, 392–3.

[140] Carte, *Ormonde*, vi, 392; Charles to the queen, *Charles I in 1646*, pp. 47–8.

to include a vindication that it had acted as it thought best, and its language is that of commitment to Anglo–Scottish union, the flourishing of Protestantism and the conversion and suppression of its opponents.[141] The Dublin government was let off the hook of a new war with Digby's arrival back in the Irish capital and his ability to persuade them that Charles did indeed want a peace with the confederates.[142] But the language of the 29 June letters was not feigned; it expressed sentiments which jostled with a determined obedience to the royal will.

Oddly enough, as Parliament shifted up a notch in its war preparations, its position in Ireland was being undermined by a run of defeats. Westminster had dreamed of amphibious assaults on points west and south since 1642. In March 1646 such an operation finally came to pass, as 1,500 soldiers sailed up the Shannon and lodged themselves in the earl of Thomond's majestic but formidable stronghold, Bunratty castle. The earl had proved compliant; his defection came suspiciously close in time to that of his old associate, Ranelagh, for it to look like coincidence that parliamentary forces landed on his doorstep. Glamorgan, his son-in-law, berated him as 'a traytor to your king and country'.[143] Ormond offered Clanricard the authority to 'lead and make use of any forces you can get' to repel 'those that adhere to the parliament', but this was merely to repeat the unsuccessful formula of the 1645 Connacht campaign.[144] Parliament's admiral, Moulton, was buoyant at the prospects opened up by possession of Bunratty, though wary too of possible isolation. His pessimistic instincts were sounder. The confederates poured resources into the siege of Bunratty, including the troops wistfully assembled to aid Charles I in England; the castle fell on 14 July. Meanwhile the confederates' reinvigorated Leinster general, Thomas Preston, captured Roscommon, stamping further on Protestant hopes of a grand western design.[145] Demoralizing as such losses were, though, they paled besides the 'great defeat' at Benburb on 5 June, when the Scottish forces in Ulster were smashed by Owen Roe O'Neill's Ulster Catholic army.

Between the skirmish at Sligo and the mass battle at Benburb, Protestant Ireland faced not only the elations and despondencies of war but the enticements of closer participation in more coherent, if opposing, political formations. Ormond had kept channels of communication open, signalling

---

[141] Carte, *Ormonde*, vi, 400–14.

[142] Ó Siochrú, *Confederate Ireland*, p. 109.

[143] Hogan (ed.), *Letters and papers*, p. 189.

[144] Ormond to Clanricard, 22 April 1646, *Letter-book*, pp. 226–7.

[145] Bagwell, *Ireland under the Stuarts*, ii, 115–22; for Clanricard's concerns for the west in the spring, see *Letter-book*, pp. 220, 222–4.

a receptiveness to a return to allegiance by Protestant as well as Catholic 'rebels', possibly with increasing concern lest his royal master choose a political deal in Britain incompatible with the Irish peace. All the while he sprinkled inducements and rewards, a Protestant earldom, a Catholic viscountcy, promises of generals' rank in a new-minted army.[146] Parliament extended its political and military structures in and over Ireland, recycling the established offices of Irish government and adding its own committees and commissioners. What its regime might lack in legitimacy, it made up for in the motive power of soldiers, money, munitions and supplies. As peace broke out fitfully in England, politicos in London, Dublin, Edinburgh and Kilkenny scrambled to piece together some solid settlement, with royal blessing, which would ready their nations for peace, or for war.

---

[146] Ormond successfully recommended an earldom (of Donegall) for Chichester and viscountcies for Nicholas Barnewall (Viscount Barnewall of Kingsland) and his kinsman Sir Edward Butler (Viscount Galmoy): Carte MSS 16, fos 443, 482; 164, fos 61, 143; G. E. C., *Complete peerage*, i, 427–8; iv, 389; v, 609.

7

The failure of settlement
and the triumph of party, 1646–47

The summer of 1646 shimmered with prospects of peace. The king's lieutenant in Ireland made his way to a Kilkenny bedecked to celebrate a peacemaker. Within weeks the triumphal arches would be torn down, the Ormond treaty itself trampled and traduced. England's agony appeared to have ended as the last royal garrisons and armies surrendered or melted away and the monarch stole himself to the Scottish army. Yet if Charles could not win, he convinced himself he could not lose, no royal blessing was conferred on Parliament's proposed settlement, and discontent grew against oppressive taxes, vicious soldiery and Scots occupiers. The months between July 1646 and February 1647 witnessed attempts to reconstruct something lasting from the shards of shattered peace terms. Ormond fell back to the painstaking task of piecing together a loyalist coalition, to be connected in turn to the king's proven friends beyond Ireland. Parliament pursued its long-expressed intention to see the Irish war through to victory, now more willing to match words with armed men and money. But the divisions within the parliamentarian camp which hampered the implementation of a post-war settlement were to impinge on policy for Ireland too.

News of the disaster at Benburb reached the floor of the Commons on 15 June, and 'ye whole Afternoone of this day was spent in Considering how reliefe might be sent to ye Protestants there'. Clotworthy's report from the Irish committee secured a vote in favour of the raising of 5,000 infantry and 1,500 cavalry for Ulster, additional to the 5,000 infantry and 1,840 cavalry for Ireland approved in the spring.[1] The earlier recruiting drive was still in progress, funded by advances from various central funds; now a City loan of £50,000 would be drawn upon. Of all the tensions and strains which beset

---

[1] And, indeed, to the regiment commissioned for Munster in September 1645, which Colonel Robert Sterling was still recruiting. *CJ*, iv, 576–8, 582; BL Additional MS 31,116, fo. 274a; BL Additional MS 37,344, fo. 54b; *LJ*, viii, 377, 380, 384; Armstrong, 'Protestant Ireland', appendix 4, pp. 349–50.

the English body politic as it passed through a period of intense disorder to outright civil war in 1647–48 none was perhaps as all-encompassing as the financial crisis which would precipitate excise riots, mutinies, large-scale sales of royalist and ecclesiastical property and the perpetuation of well-hated money-gathering committees, local and national.[2] As Parliament maintained, intermittently, its elusive search for a single all-encompassing revenue system, Ireland was increasingly in competition with calls for money to sustain the New Model Army, or pay off the Scots in England, all seeking both access to ready cash through loans and the collateral of such solid foundations as confiscated property of English delinquents. As in 1641–42 such money as was forthcoming was swallowed up in recruitment, despite the pledges of successive assessment ordinances to sustain forces actually in Ireland.[3]

The post-Benburb measures extended to approval of an ordinance empowering Lisle to issue commissions for new regiments, a measure initiated as far back as April, on the back of a report delivered by his uncle, Northumberland.[4] If in this regard he matched the role placed by his father, Leicester, in 1641–42, in co-operation with committee or commission, his grip on the reins of power also signalled a tighter hold by those associated with the 'Independent' party. In May, Lisle was named to the Star-Chamber Irish committee alongside his family friend and ally Sir John Temple and four 'Independent' MPs, two of whom, Sir Gregory Norton and Thomas Challoner (both lacking any record of active service on earlier Irish committees), would join Lisle and Temple in being consistent in their attendance at the committee.[5] Potentially at least, the Irish committee could succumb to an 'Independent' hegemony, part of a pattern of the politicization of committees, with the 'Independent' grandees particularly adept at the capture of key committees for themselves, their allies and their followers.[6]

---

[2] Robert Ashton, *Counter-Revolution: the second civil war and its origins, 1646–8* (London, 1994), chapters 2–3.

[3] See e.g. the September 1646 report of the Star Chamber committee, PRO SP 63/262/9, pp. 114–18; cf. Armstrong, 'Protestant Ireland', appendix 2.

[4] *LJ*, viii, 288; *CJ*, iv, 530. Lisle already had powers to issue commissions for some regiments ahead of the ordinance, which encompassed all 7,840 recruits authorized by Parliament to date. Though passed by the Commons in May, it stalled in the Lords until June. Clotworthy's post-Benburb report included empowering Lisle to issue commissions for the additional troops then approved: *CJ*, iv, 555, 577, 580, 582.

[5] *CJ*, iv, 532; *CSPI, 1633–47*, pp. 466–532. Nathaniel Fiennes and Evelyn of Wiltshire, named alongside the other four, were less diligent in attendance.

[6] As discussed in the work of John Adamson. See, in particular, Adamson, 'Parliamentary management, men-of-business, and the House of Lords, 1640–49', in Clyve Jones (ed.), *A pillar of the constitution: the House of Lords in British politics, 1640–1789* (London, 1989), pp. 21–50; Adamson, 'Of armies and architecture'; Adamson, 'Triumph of oligarchy'.

Temple was of course one of the pro-war faction within the Irish Council in 1642–43. On 12 June the Irish committee considered a petition seeking arrears from the former lord justice Sir John Borlace, whom it would set to work on his old profession, examining the ordnance. Soon it had a petition from Arthur Shirley on behalf of his father, Sir George, still signing letters as a member of the Irish Council. By 18 June it had moved on to Sir William Parsons himself.[7] In the summer of 1646 Nicholas Loftus resumed the handling of the Irish revenue at Westminster. The New English elite was breaking for Parliament. Influential figures from within the Protestant community in Ireland gravitated into Lisle's orbit, drawn by the build-up to what promised to be a decisive intervention in the Irish war, and almost certainly repelled by the imminence of the Ormond peace. They would bring their zeal and expertise, but also their own factions and rivalries, into the oversight of the Irish war.[8]

The party politicization of the Irish war was a crucial part of the pattern of late 1646, but it is vital to distinguish the arenas in which it applied. Essentially it was a matter of power, not policy. The position of chief governor of Ireland had always held its place within the ranking order of English politics, but as the English war scaled down, it became apparent that Ireland would become a major reservoir of military power within the dominions of the crown of England, enhancing the potency of the post.[9] Safe hands were essential. Here too, the 'Independent' leadership had not only shown itself adept at recognizing, but almost ideologically fixated upon, the powers, and the patronage, that could be seized and held through securing such offices.[10] 'The New Model Army, which was largely their creation, was still their ally, but it was the principal cause of the continuingly heavy taxes, and a large reduction in its establishment . . . became a popular policy.'[11] As party conflict spilled over into treatment of the various other armies now in process of disbandment the powers held by Lisle and the Irish committee to re-recruit and appoint officers for the Irish service were no mean prerogative. Opinion from within Ireland had always sought 'recruits', that is, additional men to fill the ranks of existing regiments, often seriously depleted but usually boasting fairly full officer quotas.[12] It was Westminster which invariably

---

[7] *CSPI, 1633–47*, pp. 458, 459, 461, 463. Parsons and Loftus, prisoners since 1644, had refused to put themselves up for exchange, unlike Temple and Meredith, apparently preferring to remain in Dublin: Carte, *Ormonde*, vi, 343.

[8] See Little, 'Irish "Independents" ' for a much fuller discussion of these issues. As will be seen, the interpretation offered here differs in some details from Dr Little's important study.

[9] Adamson, 'Strafford's ghost', p. 137.

[10] For their success in this regard, see Scott, *Politics and war*, pp. 97–8.

[11] Woolrych, *Britain in revolution*, p. 341.

[12] See e.g. Holles's report on Munster in January 1646 of 3,698 infantry with 615 officers and 848 cavalry with 120 officers, *CJ*, iv, 432; *CSPI, 1633–47*, p. 432.

substituted new regimental formations, partly no doubt for ease of recruitment, though the patronage implications among serving officers can hardly be overlooked. More study of the complex regional patterns of disbandment would need to be undertaken to demonstrate any partisan connection. For the moment, it should be noted that it was the Commons, not the Irish committee, which put aside the idea of sending four New Model regiments to Ireland in July 1646 (moved by Stapleton, 'who never loved them'), defeating the proposition by one vote.[13] When the axe fell on Colonel Massey's cavalry brigade in the south-west, though, the allegedly 'Presbyterian' leanings of the mini-army surely affected the decision to cannibalize the force rather than send it as a formation, under its own officers, as it sought.[14]

Irish-based officers too would be drawn into the webs of patronage and division, with dangerous consequences. By early July, Inchiquin, and faithful allies like William Jephson, were aware of threatening reports concerning their reputation, embracing alleged military failings, financial misconduct and leniency towards, or even collusion with, the enemy. Over the summer, Inchiquin's concerns appear not to have focused on Broghill, his lieutenant-general, who may even have joined the Munster military leadership in signing a vindication of the lord president's past conduct, drawn up in August and subsequently published in London.[15] Yet whatever Broghill's attitude on leaving Ireland in that month, by mid-September Inchiquin detected 'pretences' behind Broghill's claims to friendship, and linked them to his gaining recruits for his Munster regiment at the expense of the president's, and to favouritism in the award of payments to Munster officers.[16] All along the commanders in Munster had been seeking recruits for the 'old' regiments in the province, as the remnants of the pre-rising elite looked to their commands as a last peg of support in Ireland. It was London which changed these into newly commissioned regiments. Only the well-connected among the Old Protestants were able to secure favour at Westminster and appointments alongside redundant parliamentarians, as part of the attempt to give Lisle an appropriate and independent military command. Broghill, with his ties to the 'Independent' peers,[17] not only received resources to stabilize his old cavalry regiment but was awarded command of a brigade of four new infantry regiments to serve under Lisle. Sir Arthur Loftus, Broghill's

[13] *CJ*, iv, 631–2; Thomas Juxon, *The journal of Thomas Juxon, 1644–1647* ed. Keith Lindley and David Scott, Camden Society, 5th series, 13 (Cambridge, 1999), p. 131.

[14] *CJ*, iv, 630; R. K. G. Temple, 'The Massey brigade in the west', *Somerset and Dorset Notes and Queries* 31 (1985), pp. 437–8.

[15] *A letter from a person of quality residing in Kinsale* . . . (London, 1646) E354 (6), p. 8 places Broghill's name at the head of the list.

[16] HMC *Egmont MSS*, i, 316.

[17] Little, 'Irish "Independents" ', p. 948.

brother-in-law, obtained command of one of the new regiments designed for Ireland, despite an indifferent military record, and Sir Hardress Waller received favourable consideration for a scheme to raise another four regiments, and won the rank of major-general for himself.[18] Broghill was given command of all new forces to be sent into the province until the arrival of Parliament's lord lieutenant, and freed from Inchiquin's authority.[19] On 5 September Lisle wrote to Inchiquin, in effect prohibiting any re-modelling of the Munster forces in advance of his arrival.[20] The Irish committee ruled that supplies then being sent to Munster were not to be issued but were to be held in reserve for the coming over of Lisle, who would carry with him funds assembled for his campaign.[21]

'Independent' power meant partisan patronage. Clotworthy, though, remained a fly in the ointment. On into the summer his attendance record at the Irish committee was bettered only by Lisle and Temple, and he continued to be appointed to subcommittees on important issues.[22] His persistence with the preparations for Lisle's long-awaited campaign, like that of his associate Davies, was a link back to the win-the-war lobbying of the mid-1640s and the anti-cessation movement in Ireland. Supporters of such efforts could all hop on the Lisle bandwagon, though hoping to steer it along slightly different paths to the same destination. Parliament remained committed to the same goals for Ireland – repudiation of all treaties and cessations with the confederates, war until Parliament declared it over and the restoration of a notionally Protestant Ireland to the crown of England – which it had espoused since 1642. The Newcastle propositions might ditch the Scottish elements in Parliament's position, as expressed at Uxbridge, but the fundamentals of policy were retained, and would continue to be retained in all Parliament's peace terms thereafter.[23]

---

[18] *CSPI, 1633–47*, pp. 470, 500, 501, 506, 509; HMC *Portland MSS*, i, 390–1.

[19] *CSPI, 1633–47*, pp. 506, 510, 520, 524; HMC *Egmont MSS*, i, 342; Little, 'Irish "Independents" ', p. 952.

[20] HMC *Egmont MSS*, i, 312. Inchiquin seems to have wanted to amalgamate undersized companies, which may have caused discontent. A similar reorganization was undertaken in 1647 by Michael Jones when he gained control of Ormond's forces after the surrender of Dublin.

[21] HMC *Egmont MSS*, i, 309; *Perfect Occurrences* 40, 26 August – 2 September 1646, E513 (13) – Clotworthy signed this order alongside Denbigh, Temple, Norton and Challoner, perhaps as a result of the ruling that all committeemen present must sign orders: Little, 'Irish "Independents" ', p. 952 for further examples.

[22] For example, he and Temple were nominated to press for funds on 14 July; on 1 August he was named to a five-strong sub-committee to determine which forces should be sent to Ireland, alongside Cromwell, with whom he clashed in the Commons over the payment of the Scottish army in England: *CSPI, 1633–47*, pp. 475, 485; John Harrington, *The diary of John Harrington MP*, ed. Margaret Stieg, Somerset Record Society 74 (1977), p. 32.

[23] Little, 'English Parliament', pp. 116–18.

Formally and publicly, the quest for an English settlement remained focused on the Newcastle propositions. They had, of course, caused contention and recrimination between Parliament and its Scottish allies. It was reported that Scots regained some goodwill at Westminster over the summer, with news of their defeat at Benburb, of their 'severe carriage towards the King' and, particularly, with the Scottish government's acceptance, despite their qualms, of the final Newcastle terms.[24] Their stock would rise more with the departure of their army from England, playing to the English assumption that amity was best served by mutual distance.[25] The key figure in all this was the marquis of Argyll.[26] He smoothed Parliament's feathers with his visit to Westminster in June, delivering the assent to the peace terms, and throughout the next several months acted to shore up good relations, not least by removing Leven's army from England.[27] Argyll was an advocate for the Scottish army in Ulster, having lately been an 'eye-witness to their sufferings', and their case was pressed alongside that of their fellows in England. Both armies were locked into contests for scarce resources with local forces, both still clung to 'cautionary towns' as they awaited satisfaction of their claims. As Argyll sought acceptable terms for a negotiated withdrawal from England, so, as the time for the departure from England drew near, the officers in Ulster proved not unwilling to bargain for a final settlement allowing them to leave with their money.[28] Argyll was not without his own motives for withdrawing troops from Ireland, as he endured the activities of the remnants of Antrim's Irish brigade in his territories in the Western Isles.[29]

Though animosities would be stoked up again in the autumn, so long as the agreed Newcastle propositions were being advanced by both sides even the king saw little chance of a split between the two nations.[30] French diplomatic efforts, at the heart of the drive for a settlement in the three

[24] Baillie, *Letters and journals*, ii, 376.

[25] Stevenson, 'Early Covenanters and the federal union', pp. 173–4.

[26] Argyll has been described as 'the foremost and most formidable Scottish politician of the 1640s', and as having 'personified' 'concentric British loyalties': Allan I. Macinnes, 'Covenanting ideology in seventeenth century Scotland', in Ohlmeyer (ed.), *Political thought*, pp. 192, 205. See also Edward J. Cowan, 'The political ideas of a covenanting leader: Archibald Campbell, marquis of Argyll, 1607–1661', in Roger A. Mason (ed.), *Scots and Britons* (Cambridge, 1994), pp. 241–62.

[27] See *The Lord Marques of Argyle's speech . . .* (London, 1646) E 341 (25), pp. 3–6 for his speech of 15 June, pp. 7–10 for the Scottish commissioners' acceptance of the Newcastle terms; Fotheringham (ed.), *Correspondence of Montereul*, i, 283–4.

[28] HMC *Portland MSS*, i, 386–7; *The Lord Marques of Argyle's speech*, pp. 10–12; *CSPI, 1633–47*, pp. 567–8; Stevenson, *Scottish Covenanters*, pp. 211–12, 244–5.

[29] Ohlmeyer, *Civil war and Restoration*, pp. 177–9, 186–8.

[30] *Charles I in 1646*, pp. 53–4.

kingdoms, presupposed religious concessions by Charles at least in the short term, to Presbyterianism in Britain (at least to buy off the Scots) and to Catholicism in Ireland.[31] In neither case could they find a willing concessionary in the king,[32] but he was at least wiser than those around him in so far as he saw an Irish accommodation as in itself blocking settlement with the English and Scots.[33] His response to the Newcastle terms on 1 August had been vague and non-committal, and was read in the Lords in conjunction with Scottish offers to withdraw their troops and to consult on the 'disposal' of the king.[34] With the allies remaining firm, Charles had long recognized that he would have to be able to present a fait accompli in terms of an Irish treaty, and sought the continuation of negotiations by means of the queen and prince of Wales, while resorting to ever more desperate attempts to win the support of European Catholic powers.[35] Despite efforts to sell the Ormond treaty as 'useful to all' in Ireland, Scots included,[36] the king soon recognized of the Scots that 'the Irish peace angers them much'. As he told the queen (31 August), the news of the Irish peace 'will take away the question whether the Presbyterian government shall be granted by me or not (for . . . that alone hinders all accommodations infallibly)'.[37] Defeat of the confederates remained a core value for Charles's British opponents, whatever their disagreements on other matters. French reports into the autumn suggested that Ireland remained one of the sticking points in negotiations, one report suggesting that those at Westminster 'best disposed' to the king remained 'obstinate' on winning Ireland.[38] Hints from the 'Independent' camp of softer terms on religion and on the fate of delinquents and to 'waue Ireland till the King and Parliament be agreed' look like an equivocation worthy of the monarch himself, deferring an agreement on paper while Lisle's forces battled to deliver a conquered Ireland.[39]

---

[31] Fotheringham (ed.), *Correspondence of Montereul*, i, 218, 228–30.

[32] Smith, *Constitutional royalism*, pp. 128–32, 149–50.

[33] Charles to Henrietta Maria, 19 and 31 August 1646, *Charles I in 1646*, pp. 60–1, 62.

[34] Parliament passed an ordinance against libellers of their brethren and began the financial talks which would settle a sum of £400,000 of arrears by the month's end: Gardiner, *Great civil war*, iii, 133–4, 137–8; Gardiner (ed.), *Constitutional documents*, pp. 306–8.

[35] *Charles I in 1646*, pp. 51–2, 54–6; Fotheringham (ed.), *Correspondence of Montereul*, i, 226–7; *Calendar of the Clarendon state papers*, i, 328.

[36] S. R. Gardiner (ed.), *The Hamilton papers*, Camden Society, new series, 27 (London, 1880), pp. 109–10.

[37] *Charles I in 1646*, pp. 62, 63–4.

[38] The other core issues were religion, the militia (i.e. the three Uxbridge terms), the disposal of places and the fate of royalists: Gardiner (ed.), *Hamilton papers*, pp. 113–14; Fotheringham (ed.), *Correspondence of Montereul*, i, 266–7, 283–4, though cf. Bellievre's views: Fotheringham (ed.), *Correspondence of Montereul*, i, 276–7.

[39] Gardiner (ed.), *Hamilton papers*, p. 115.

The Ormond peace had been proclaimed on 30 July, though it had taken personal assurances and commitments from Digby and Ormond to secure the Dublin council's acquiescence in the absence of an explicit command from the king.[40] Richard Bellings, of the confederate peace party, noted dangers, but expressed optimism that the treaty provided the basis for an Ireland which would not henceforth undergo 'revolutions' every forty years; Ormond himself professed the hope, to Hyde, of a 'foundation for a happy settlement in his majesties other kingdomes'.[41] From the royalist perspective, the treaty had merits as a model for a wider settlement. Unlike the terms placed before the king in England, it could be read in an ideologically appropriate manner; as the return of errant confederates to their allegiance, it contained few institutional trammels upon the king, and was more concerned with accessing military capability now than with worrying about the long-term location of the power of the sword. Yet its swift collapse belied even the hopes that it might provide the beginnings of a settlement in Ireland. At first Dublin had attempted to give universal application to the peace. Efforts in June–July to entice the Protestant north into compliance with the upcoming treaty having failed, the council now commanded its obedience to the new arrangements, and tentative efforts were made to have heralds proclaim the peace in Inchiquin's Munster holds.[42] Ormond maintained contact with the generals of both the confederates' Leinster and Ulster armies, Thomas Preston and Owen Roe O'Neill, bitter rivals as they were. Now in theory under his authority, by the terms of the treaty, he sought to resolve the formidable problems thrown up by competition between the two armies, and with his own forces, over quarters, and over allegations of oppression and plunder directed against the Ulster Catholic army, now lodged in Leinster.[43] Ormond won from the Protestant clergy in Dublin a remonstrance in favour of the peace, as the 'only meanes to continue these blessings of religion and loyaltye among vs, and to be the only hopefull way to reduce this kingdome wholly to his majesty's obedience',[44] but the Catholic synod that met at Waterford in early August was not so accommodating.

Clerical repudiation of the peace, deemed a violation of the confederate oath of allegiance, and the demand that the confederate government remain in being, despite the official dissolution of the Kilkenny regime under the terms of the treaty, with all authority offered up to Ormond, signalled the

---

[40] Gilbert (ed.), *Irish confederation*, vi, 55–60; Gardiner, *Great civil war*, iii, 155–6.

[41] Gilbert (ed.), *Irish confederation*, vi, 62–3; Carte, *Ormonde*, vi, 421–2.

[42] Carte MS 18, fo. 303; Gilbert (ed.), *Irish confederation*, vi, 114, 119.

[43] O'Neill sent Ormond a complete list of his forces, seeking inclusion in a 'settlement of meanes', Gilbert (ed.), *Contemporary history*, i, 690–7; HMC *Ormonde MSS*, old series, ii, 44–5; Gilbert (ed.), *Irish confederation*, vi, 61, 63, 65–7, 78–86.

[44] Carte, *Ormonde*, vi, 423–5.

impending implosion of the confederate cause. Internal negotiations were pursued within the Catholic camp in the hope of restraining internal division, alongside manoeuvres to gain factional ascendancy.[45] For Ormond, the condemnation of the peace prompted efforts to circumvent or overwhelm opposition. He persisted with efforts to secure O'Neill's adherence to the treaty into late August, offering a military command and custody of lands in Ulster taken from Protestant opponents of the peace, though by then it was clear that O'Neill had come out in favour of the clerical position.[46] Daniel O'Neill, still in contact with his uncle's army, reported that 'ther quarrell iss to all peaceable men', Protestant and Catholic, and pointed to support for the peace in Meath and Westmeath.[47] By 22 August Dublin was exploiting the stance taken by the Catholic clergy in its attempts to rally support from Protestant Ulster. Opponents of the peace were depicted as those dependent on the Pope and Spain, or bound to the Old Irish, unsatisfied in their ambitions or guilty of the blood shed in 1641, and with whom no Protestant, nor any 'considerable' Catholic could ally.[48]

Ormond was still resolved to hold the confederate leadership to the treaty, and marginalize opposition. He responded to pleas from the 'peace party' to journey to Kilkenny, where his appearance would epitomize the restoration of amity between the king and his Catholic subjects. Hints were exchanged of co-ordinated military action against opponents of the peace, principally Inchiquin's Protestant forces, a pay-off for Catholic support of the treaty.[49] Lodged in Kilkenny, at the heart of the Butler country, by 31 August, Ormond insisted that he stood above the quarrels between the confederate peace commissioners and the Catholic clergy. He was willing to countenance efforts to heal the breach so long as these were by means of private assurances, principally on matters of religion, 'severed from the articles of peace to which my Lord Lieutenant hath not power to add anything'.[50] Instead the clergy set their face against such flimsy guarantees, and hostility to the peace spread through confederate quarters, and intensified. As Ormond became aware that anti-treaty forces were being

[45] Ó hAnnracháin, *Catholic Reformation*, pp. 147–53; Ó Siochrú, *Confederate Ireland*, pp. 111–17.

[46] Gilbert (ed.), *Contemporary history*, i, 700.

[47] Daniel O'Neill to earl of Roscommon, 1 September 1646, Gilbert (ed.), *Contemporary history*, i, 701–2.

[48] Carte MS 18, fos 318, 325.

[49] Carte, *Ormonde*, vi, 85–6, 92–3, 94, 95; *Letter-book*, pp. 275–7. The 'peace party', in control at Kilkenny, insisted that it could not respond to the clergy's propositions ahead of Ormond's arrival in the capital, a move which only increased clerical suspicions: Ó hAnnracháin, *Catholic Reformation*, p. 156.

[50] Gardiner, *Great civil war*, iii, 158; Gilbert (ed.), *Contemporary history*, i, 704; Ó hAnnracháin, *Catholic Reformation*, pp. 158–9.

massed against him he fled Kilkenny, narrowly avoiding interception at Leighlin bridge.[51] The consequences of his discomfiture were profound, for he saw treachery at work which struck at the heart of all his political and personal presuppositions, as man of honour, as lord of Ormond and as king's lieutenant. Anger and disgust permeate his subsequent letters and declarations. To Jermyn in Paris he professed 'shame that soe little faith is found in a place where I haue soe much interest of blood and alyance, and . . . greefe that the perfidy heere should force mee to councells contrary to my former way of serveing his majestie and my own inclination'.[52]

Back in Dublin, Ormond and the council not only re-opened channels of communication with pro-war Protestant interests in Ireland, but resolved upon direct approaches to the Parliament of England. Clanricard, among others, counselled caution in throwing over Catholic support.[53] But efforts by the confederate 'peace party' to secure Catholic unity included an informal return to the Glamorgan articles, and Ormond categorically maintained that these 'are things I have nothing to doe with, nor will have'.[54] His root assumptions come out in his 27 October letter to Preston, blasting confederate disloyalty and asserting that the terms accepted by the commissioners should 'have been inviolably stuck to' in honour 'whether advantageous or prejudicial to those that trusted them'.[55] He told Clanricard that his appeal to Parliament was grounded upon 'the law of nature and selfe preseruation . . . yet soe as wee have yet don nor declared noething that may cause despair in any that shall resolutly indeavour the peace of the kingdome'.[56] Over the next several months Ormond was at the centre of a web stretching out to interests from all three Stuart kingdoms. His multiple entanglements, with Parliament, with the Scottish army in Ulster and with potential dissidents from the confederate ranks, defy easy unravelling, and are perhaps better envisaged as a series of layers of concern, already sketched out in the latter days of September.

At the core of Ormond's concerns lay the immediate problem of securing Dublin and his outer garrisons, mere prudence given the rapidity with which the anti-treaty confederates moved to launch an attack on the city.[57] To that end he was ready to take measures, such as the destruction of corn in the Pale counties, which he was warned could alienate local opinion.[58] He

---

[51] Ó hAnnracháin, *Catholic Reformation*, pp. 153–4; Ó Siochrú, *Confederate Ireland*, p. 115.

[52] Carte, *Ormonde*, vi, 436–7. See also Ormond to the king, 27 September 1646, and Lane's letter to Thomas Nugent, 25 September 1646, Carte, *Ormonde*, vi, 435–6, 433–4.

[53] *Letter-book*, pp. 283–5.

[54] Gilbert (ed.), *Irish confederation*, vi, 132–4, 137–9, 142–3, 147–8; Carte, *Ormonde*, vi, 433.

[55] *Letter-book*, pp. 305–6.

[56] *Letter-book*, pp. 287–8.

[57] Ó hAnnracháin, *Catholic Reformation*, pp. 158–60.

[58] Correspondence between Ormond and Digby, October 1646, Carte, *Ormonde*, vi, 441–6.

signalled that he was prepared to admit troops sent by Parliament, or by the
Scots, to his garrisons, in a spirit of Protestant co-operation, pledging his
honour that they would not be used against their sponsor's interest.[59] As will
be seen, it was a deal he was not willing to countenance with Catholic forces.
Yet beyond immediate safety, Ormond still retained a commitment to
safeguarding the truly loyal constituency at large. In his approaches to
Parliament, he was adamant that the rights of all Protestants 'and others'
who had supported him be safeguarded, and even ex-'rebels' encompassed
if now loyal. Attempts were made to distinguish between categories of
'rebels', setting limits to land confiscation, and the late peace was defended.[60]
Writing to Sir James Montgomery in east Ulster, Ormond presented his
efforts as designed to counter a 'second rebellion' aimed at detaching Ireland
from the crown of England. Ormond was in effect arguing the same case he
had put against the lords justices in 1641–43, of the need to rally as much of
loyal Ireland as possible against the truly subversive. All like-minded men
should oppose 'soe pernicious a plott . . . However, thorough the distemper
of the tyme, wee may have differed in our wayes, I hope this adress will
waken the people of the other two kingdomes, and be a meanes to procure a
happy reconcilement of all differances'.[61]

The outer layer to Ormond's schemes, as he hinted to Montgomery, was
the hope that he could tap into a reconciliation between the king and at least
some of his subjects in Great Britain, maybe even be a means to effecting
such a meeting of interests. He professed to believe in the prospects of 'a
breach betweext (at least) the best party of the Scots and the parliament; and
both will bid faire for vs'.[62] It was a false hope, at least while Argyll held
sway in Scotland. The king huffed that he had 'been excessively (indeed
unmannerly) pressed by . . . Argyle to persuade Ormond to submit to the
parliament, which I have absolutely refused.'[63] Within Ireland, there seems
no reason to doubt the truth of the Scots' claims that they were militarily
unable to aid Ormond as far south as Dublin.[64] But they bear out Carte's
summation of Ormond's expressed intentions 'to keep the old Irish, now

---

[59] Stevenson, *Scottish Covenanters*, pp. 240–2.

[60] Carte, *Ormonde*, iii, 269–71. But when he sought legal opinion on how to preserve
gentlemen worried about joining 'us' because formerly outlawed for treason his legal advisers
were unable to find a means whereby they might legally be put in a state of 'preservation':
Carte MS 19, fo. 146.

[61] Ormond to Sir James Montgomery, 18 September 1646, Carte, *Ormonde*, vi, 431.

[62] Ormond to Digby, 22 October 1646, Carte, *Ormonde*, vi, 446–7. On 12 October he had
said he believed that he was 'persuaded their [the Scots'] affections to the king are better then
is beleeved': Carte, *Ormonde*, vi, 440–1.

[63] Stevenson, *Revolution and counter-revolution*, pp. 77–9; *Charles I in 1646*, p. 70.

[64] Stevenson, *Scottish Covenanters*, p. 242.

possessed of the power of the confederates, from shaking off the government of the crown of England, and putting the nation under a foreign power; and the hopes that Dublin might be restored to his majesty without trouble when the Scots should assert his majesty's cause, or the English return to their duty', if not necessarily the need to take them entirely at face value.[65] The one hope, however slender, of a royally approved bi- or tri-kingdom settlement of course resided in the efforts of the French diplomatic corps, sponsors of the original Ormond peace, and it was surely no accident that Ormond's denunciation of 'foreign' powers invariably targeted a Spanish–papal alignment.[66]

As autumn passed preparations progressed for an assault on Dublin by the restored and realigned confederate organization. Ormond's approaches to Parliament became entangled with ongoing contacts with Catholic interests, coming to a head in mid-November. Clanricard busied himself spinning out terms to re-unite Ormond with the confederates as a body, while the option was explored of detaching Preston and his army for use against the clerical party and the bitterly detested Ulster 'Old Irish'.[67] The Clanricard concessions, if more cautious than the Glamorgan terms, still hinged upon 'undertakings' being delivered by a trusted go-between, Clanricard pledging 'the reputation and honour of a peere' and the 'faith of a Catholique' to his engagement. The principal terms were the revocation of all laws hindering the 'free exercise' of the Catholic faith, retention of church property ahead of the deliberations of a free Parliament and a free king, and incorporation of Catholic forces into the royal army with a Catholic lieutenant-general, room for existing Catholic general officers and the admission of Catholic troops to royalist garrisons.[68] Ormond was unenthusiastic. All that was required of him, Clanricard insisted, was an assurance to follow instructions from the queen and prince of Wales and disregard orders from a captive king which would harm Irish Catholics, pledges Ormond was willing to give.[69]

Instead by the middle of November, the confederate campaign had collapsed, and Ormond had entered into direct negotiations with Parliament's commissioners, backed with troops sent from England. Though Clanricard

[65] Carte, *Ormonde*, iii, 264.

[66] Fotheringham (ed.), *Correspondence of Montereul, passim*; Ó hAnnracháin, *Catholic Reformation*, pp. 140–6.

[67] Jerrold I. Casway, *Owen Roe O'Neill and the struggle for Catholic Ireland* (Philadelphia, 1984), pp. 157–9; *Letter-book*, pp. 288–9, 292–3, 294–5, 295–9.

[68] *Letter-book*, pp. 309–11; *The marques of Clanrickards engagement* (1646) Wing M707, pp. 1–3; *The Kings Majesties manifesto to the kingdom of Ireland undertaken and published by the marquesse of Clanrickard* (London, 1646) E371 (11).

[69] *Letter-book*, pp. 334, 335.

had failed with his overtures to the confederate Supreme Council, he even now coaxed out of Preston and his officers a submission to the Ormond peace coupled with Clanricard's supplementary terms.[70] Preston was prey to the 'application of personal and spiritual pressure' by Rinuccini,[71] to divided opinion within his own army, but also to pressing logistical dilemmas. The proposal that Catholic forces be admitted to Ormondist garrisons was absolutely non-negotiable for him, for reasons of sustenance as well as evidence of security. As Clanricard recognized, only with such concrete grounds of assurance could military alliance against O'Neill and the confederate irreconcilables be won: if it was unreasonable to insist on admission ahead of submission to Ormond and the onset of hostilities, it was also unreasonable to expect the Leinster army to move against former associates until secured through acceptance into the garrisons. Ormond, eventually, refused to admit Catholic forces to Dublin.[72] Suspicious of bad faith, or at least of Preston's resolution, he recognized that it was asking too much of his primary constituency, the Protestants of Dublin and Leinster, to admit to their remaining holds those who had threatened them militarily for the last several years. In Dublin the option of closing with Parliament had proved considerably more appealing.[73]

Was Parliament open to a deal with Ormond? Parliament had never entirely given up on Dublin. All through the cessation years, admirals and naval captains in the Irish Sea had cajoled Ormond towards a re-alignment with Parliament, facing repeated rebuffs.[74] The lord lieutenant, on his part, had old family and friendship ties to leading figures at Westminster.[75] It has been argued that Ormond stood a better chance of a satisfactory arrangement from the leading 'Presbyterians' than from the 'Independent' leadership and their allies from Ireland, who were determined to squeeze Ormond out in favour of Lisle, drew upon deep-grained antagonism at Westminster based

---

[70] *Letter-book*, pp. 313–14, 315–16, 316–17, 317–19, 321–2; Gilbert (ed.), *Irish confederation*, vi, 158–62; Ó Siochrú, *Confederate Ireland*, pp. 120–3.

[71] Ó hAnnracháin, *Catholic Reformation*, p. 162.

[72] Gilbert (ed.), *Irish confederation*, vi, 164–5; *Letter-book*, pp. 336–7.

[73] Ormond to Digby, 23 November 1646, Carte, *Ormonde*, vi, 468–9. The remnants of the Dublin Parliament reportedly favoured such a move: Savage to Perceval, HMC *Egmont MSS*, i, 334–5.

[74] Moulton to Ormond, 2 November 1645, Carte MS 16, fos 157–8.

[75] Little, 'Marquess of Ormond', pp. 85–7. Dr Little argues forcefully for closer ties between Ormond and the 'Presbyterians', particularly Holles and Essex (died August 1646), and a range of 'Presbyterian'-leaning 'old Protestants' though also noting that Sir Thomas Wharton, brother of the 'Independent' peer Philip, Lord Wharton, was an old associate and present 'well-wisher'. Dr Little's valuable essay provides the fullest account of Ormond's dealings with Parliament in the 1640s, though the present account differs from it in interpretation on some points.

on Ormond's actions over several years, and presented their case through anti-Ormond propaganda.[76] The Ormond–Parliament interface needs to be viewed from both directions, and account needs to be taken, too, of the different ways in which engagement was undertaken, from the formal to the subversive, from the personal to the rhetorical, features present in all of the principal arenas of negotiation within the three kingdoms. For all shades of Westminster opinion a deal with Dublin was a means to close the loop, to bring England, Scotland and Protestant Ireland within one agreed settlement, with the acquiescence of a hostile monarch. To this end Lisle and Holles were harnessed together to write to the king in July, calling on him to order Ormond to deliver Dublin and his other garrisons to the Parliament, without success.[77] But from Ormond's angle, it might be possible to work out from a Dublin arrangement to a wider realignment of forces favourable to the monarch, united against a common foe. The defence of Dublin might be squared with its role as a counter in a bigger game.[78] Contacts with Westminster could replicate, on a grander scale, Ormond's dealings with Parliament's men in Ulster, which had long since been characterized not only by their attempts to secure, if not his allegiance, then his territories, but also by his attempts to ingest Protestant Ulster with or without them. The New English or Old Protestants of Ireland were vital to the progress of negotiations, from either angle. Though the community had its own bitter internal rivalries, to be sure, it had generated densely woven, sturdy webs of kinship and old association, and would be characterized by a determination to restore Dublin and the Ormondist garrisons to their rightful place within the 'Protestant interest', with or without Ormond himself.

The arrival of agents from Dublin in October 1646 prompted most Parliamentarian newsletters to a spree of delight at the good news, 'such indeede as we cannot wish for better'. It was left to the pro-Scots and 'Presbyterian' *Scottish Dove* to wonder 'what security is in a revolting enemy I yet know not, but hope all is reall; but if hee doe deliver *Dublin* into the Parliaments hands, it will be good security'.[79] Such sentiments were indicative

---

[76] Little, 'Marquess of Ormond', pp. 85–7, 95–7; Little, 'Irish "Independents" ', pp. 946–7, 953–4; cf. Adamson, 'Strafford's ghost', pp. 131–2, 140–1, 146.

[77] *CJ*, iv, 599, 603, 618; *CSPI, 1633–47*; Carte, *Ormonde*, vi, 417–8.

[78] Little, 'Marquess of Ormond', p. 98 notes Ormond's efforts to use contacts with Clotworthy and King to advance a settlement in 'all' the king's dominions, as well as his better-known involvement in brokerage between the king and his parliamentarian opponents in 1647. The construction of a broad coalition in the king's interest was at the heart of Ormond's activities after his return to Ireland in 1648–49.

[79] *The Moderate Intelligencer* 83, 1–8 October 1646, E356 (8), p. 678; *Perfect Diurnall 67*, 5–12 October 1646, E13 (17), p. 1341; *The Scottish Dove* 154, 30 September – 8 October 1646, E356 (10), p. 44.

of the mixed messages transmitted about Ormond. If he seemed inclined to do good, then august personages could be found to speak well of him. When the Ormond terms were first delivered to Parliament they were accompanied by letters from Sir William Parsons and Sir Adam Loftus. Both men were found to 'speak very honourably' of Ormond and his intensions, despite his having had them confined in Dublin for the past several years, albeit not in over-harsh circumstances.[80] By contrast the 'moderate' Perceval (financially entangled with Ormond, but whose letters show little personal warmth) pondered whether 'all's but a plot of Orm[ond]'.[81] Timing was all-important in attitudes to the king's lieutenant. If his military successes in 1642 prompted his associates to celebrate (and implicitly to defend) him in England,[82] his perceived defection in pursuing and promoting the cessation and dispatch of troops to the king prompted denunciation from Clotworthy and moves to impeachment by the Essex supporter and future 'Presbyterian' grandee, Stapleton.

Ormond's moves to a formal treaty with the confederates could only further damage his reputation with Parliament. October 1646 saw the publication of *Ormond's Curtain drawn*, a vigorous denunciation of the lord lieutenant and all his works and a defence of the anti-cessation faction within the Irish Council in 1641–43.[83] Its author, Captain Adam Meredith, was the son of one such individual, the chancellor of the exchequer, Sir Robert Meredith. If the pamphlet can be seen as a propaganda piece, intended as a counter-blast to any possible generosity to Ormond, and especially to his employment under Parliament,[84] it could also stand duty as an argument for the re-employment of those within the Irish administration not stained with Ormondist misdeeds, and who were tumbling into Parliament's camp at just this time.[85] Sir John Temple, involved in the production of *Ormond's*

---

[80] *CJ*, iv, 684; *Kingdomes Weekly Intelligencer* 168, 29 September – 6 October 1646, E356 (4), p. 264; HMC *Egmont MSS*, i, 330, 331; Colum Kenny, *King's Inns and the kingdom of Ireland: the Irish 'inn of court' 1541–1800* (Dublin, 1992), p. 122.

[81] HMC *Egmont MSS*, i, 324. Perceval appears to have retained a high opinion of the countess of Ormond.

[82] Little, 'Marquess of Ormond', pp. 85–6.

[83] [Adam Meredith], *Ormond's Curtain drawn: in a short discourse concerning Ireland* (London, 1646) E513 (14). George Thomason dated his copy of the pamphlet 5 October. The published version, which breaks off in mid-sentence, is only the first half of the MSS found at BL Additional MS 4,763, fos 4–5 and BL Additional MS 4,819, fos 320–44, which ends with the date 'Sept. 1 1646'.

[84] Adamson, 'Strafford's ghost', pp. 140–2, also argues that it was advanced by the circle around Lisle.

[85] It did not stand alone in its criticisms of Ormond: for example, *Very sad newes from Ireland* (London, 25 October 1646) E358 (19), lamenting the fall of Protestant garrisons in Maryborough and Athlone, included swipes at Ormond for denuding them of troops during the cessation, and exposing them to greater danger through the treaty.

Curtain drawn,[86] had earlier voiced the Irish committee's call for power to negotiate the surrender of forts and towns and 'grant any terms to any upon service don for us', revealing some openness to a negotiated return of at least some errant Protestants.[87] The denunciation of chosen opponents was a necessary rhetorical strategy for all sides in the 1640s conflicts, and prescription of hardened malignants always played well on the floor of the Commons.[88] Yet the terms of settlement to be put to Ormond included the demand that he resign the lieutenancy, but with a generous redundancy package.[89] The danger of under-estimating the ties of kin and friendship among the interlocking elites of the Stuart kingdoms at the expense of the abstractions of ideological blocs has receded in light of modern research, but the danger perhaps runs in the other direction too. Aristocrats and 'grandees' could trade favours with old foes but they had to be aware of snarling backbenchers, provincial soldiers and oppressed supporters of their cause who needed hate figures to believe in and to blame.

Dublin's approaches to Parliament were reported to the Commons on 5 October. Early consideration was referred to the English members of the Committee of Both Kingdoms, reinforced by Lisle, Holles, Clotworthy and Temple.[90] On a report from the committee, the Commons resolved that Ormond resign the lieutenancy and a treaty commence, with the matter referred back to the committee, which, with further additions, can now be considered as having metamorphosed into the soon-to-be formidable Derby House Committee for Irish Affairs.[91] The whole basis both of an autonomous Irish regime, and of an internal Irish settlement constructed from the remaining shards of the Ormond peace, was even then being threatened with

---

[86] Adamson, 'Strafford's ghost', p. 140, note 45. It seems likely that Temple's alterations were largely motivated by his long-standing feud with Sir Philip Perceval.

[87] Such powers were to last three months: *CJ*, iv, 676. Other indications of calls for sweeping powers appear in *The Moderate Intelligencer* 82, 24 September – 1 October 1646, E355 (23), p. 665 describing the call for 'a Plenipotent for our Commissioners, there to take to mercy such as will come over from the Rebels and their party' and Harrington's report that he considered moving the restriction of terms to exclude 'murderers' and those who had acted 'against religion': Harrington, *Diary*, p. 39.

[88] The Newcastle, and Uxbridge, terms (or the later 'Four Bills' and Newport propositions), argued out on the floors of the Houses, were much harsher on individuals than the 'Heads of the proposals' sponsored by leading officers and their aristocratic allies, or indeed the private approaches made to the king: Smith, *Constitutional royalism*, pp. 201–6.

[89] The original offer, in October 1646, was of £5,000 down, plus a pension of £2,000 per annum for five years, or longer if the Irish war continued: *Severall papers of the treatie between . . . James marques of Ormond . . . and Sir Thomas Wharton . . .* (Dublin, 1646) E378 (4), p. 4.

[90] *CJ*, iv, 684, 690.

[91] The Commons also voted Fiennes, Lewis and Robert Goodwyn on to the committee on 14 October: *CJ*, iv, 684, 690, 693.

efforts to push many of the main elements of the Newcastle terms into legislation, in the absence of royal approval, among them the voidance of the cessation and all treaties not approved by Parliament,[92] authority to nominate to Irish as well as English offices and authority to vest forces in Ireland in Parliament's keeping.[93]

The opportunity presented by Ormond's terms prompted a diversion of forces assembling in England, Lisle being re-directed from Munster to the Irish capital, and additional funds were voted for Ireland.[94] The Derby House Committee, like the Star Chamber Irish committee, had an 'Independent' complexion, though also a heavyweight, and active, 'Presbyterian' membership.[95] The probability is that the terms produced for negotiations with Ormond, including relatively generous offers for him personally, were broadly acceptable to both the Derby House Committee and the Houses, and the treaty was entrusted to a team of five commissioners, all bar one with long-established Irish connections.[96] In addition to the financial offers to Ormond, the commissioners were instructed to receive all Protestants willing to submit to Parliament and its ordinances, with security for their Irish estates and the right to compound for property in England, to offer protection to all willing to pay contribution and to 'imploy such of the Officers now under . . . Ormond as you shall thinke fit'. Factional advantage might more readily be detected in the votes to award the position of governor of Dublin to Lisle's brother, Algernon Sidney, with that old Sidney associate George Monck as his deputy.[97]

The negotiations themselves commenced when the commissioners, with two infantry regiments in tow, arrived in Dublin bay on 15 November, and ran for a week.[98] The very news of their arrival prompted the beginning of the disintegration of the confederate drive on Dublin, no doubt in turn

[92] Passed into an ordinance on 14 December: Firth and Rait (eds), *Acts and ordinances*, i, 910.

[93] J. R. MacCormack, *Revolutionary politics in the Long Parliament* (Cambridge, Massachusetts, 1973), p. 145; *CJ*, iv, 691, 695; BL Additional MS 31,116, fo. 286a; Harrington, *Diary*, pp. 43–4; BL Additional MS 37,344, fo. 67a.

[94] *CJ*, iv, 697–8, 702, 710; Harrington, *Diary*, pp. 44–5; *CSPI, 1633–47*, pp. 529–30, *1647–60*, p. 726.

[95] See Little, 'Marquess of Ormond', pp. 91, 95 for the changing active membership of the committee between the October 1646 and March 1647 dealings with Ormond. The terms on offer remained broadly the same; if a more amenable attitude to Ormond did develop over 1646–47 it is quite possible this was in reaction to the failed Lisle initiative, rather than being a result of ingrained 'Presbyterian' attitudes coming to the fore.

[96] *Severall papers*, pp. 3–4, 8, 12–13. The commissioners were Wharton, King, Clotworthy, Meredith and, the odd man out, Richard Salwey, an 'Independent' MP and adventurer.

[97] *CSPI, 1647–60*, p. 726.

[98] *Severall papers* prints the various papers exchanged between Ormond and the commissioners. See also Little, 'Marquess of Ormond', pp. 92–3.

affecting the stance adopted by Ormond towards the commissioners.[99] Though Parliament believed it had chosen to address Ormond's 'second way of Overture', a set of offers which it believed to encompass his resignation, this was to prove the breaking point, for Ormond insisted that he had never intended to surrender his office without royal approval.[100] But the negotiations also throw interesting light upon other points of contention. If Ormond's stance represents his true intentions then he stood out for little less than the adoption of the present Dublin civil and military operation as a going concern by Parliament (with implied royal approval). The commissioners agreed to extend Parliament's protection even to those Protestants who consented to the cessation or peace and added, almost certainly with sincerity, and that they were not averse to the employment of those in post, though they could not give blanket assurances that none would be removed. Ormond held out for the application of parliamentary assurances to his flock of loyal Catholics. Again, this fell outside the remit held by the commissioners, and their assumptions that if 'any such be, it's probable the number is not considerable'[101] and so special provision was unnecessary were not reassuring. Finally, Ormond probed the extent of the obligation behind the demand that Dublin and its out-garrisons submit to ordinances of Parliament, and particularly those with implications for the shape of Protestantism in Ireland. He won an admission that 'We know of no Ordinance of Parliament, that requires the Covenant to be taken in the Kingdome of Ireland',[102] nor of any orders to suppress the Prayer Book or enforce the Directory of Worship, though he contrasted this with the realities of religious change in parliamentarian quarters, and professed concern for the future. Whether such demands would have constituted an insuperable obstacle in other circumstances or not, they are indicative of the tenor of Ormond's position, to maintain the distinctiveness of Irish arrangements even in the event of an alignment with the Parliament of England. Likewise they indicate the readiness of the commissioners to tackle obstacles to the restoration of the lost tribes of Protestant Ireland to the fellowship of their brethren.

---

[99] Lenihan, *Confederate Catholics at war*, pp. 97–8.

[100] Since Westminster had determined not to forward Ormond's letter to the king there was little that could be done by the time the commissioners reached Dublin: *CJ*, iv, 693. Ormond appears to have raised this directly only on 18 November, three days into what had been intended as a four-day debate, a move perhaps indicative of a toughening of his stance in light of confederate dispositions: *Severall papers*, pp. 15–16. *Some passages of the treaty between the marquesse of Ormond and the parliaments commissioners* (London, 1646) denounced the 'perfidiousnesse' of Ormond, 'playing fast and loose' with the commissioners, and claimed that he was in receipt of 'Letters from Newcastle', from the king, guiding his hand.

[101] *Severall papers*, p. 25.

[102] *Severall papers*, p. 27.

Ormond had juggled the Clanricard–Preston and Westminster negotiations, and ultimately found himself still in control in Dublin, with no intruded forces of either stamp.[103] The parliamentary commissioners sailed north, adding their troops, depleted by shipwreck, to the Ulster forces, and diverting the troops and supplies being assembled for Dublin north, or south to Munster.[104] Back at Westminster the Derby House Committee for Irish Affairs had taken to itself the principal role in shaping policy for Ireland, with the Star Chamber committee filling in the details and, crucially, dispersing the funds. Both had an 'Independent' profile over the winter of 1646–47, like so many of the parliamentary revenue committees, to be reflected in the enhancement of Lisle's position, as lieutenant in fact as well as name, and the generous treatment meted out to his allies.[105] On 10 December the Derby House Committee voted to present Parliament with a paper delivered by Lisle, alongside a vote that he should be hastened to Munster.[106] The 'paper' was almost certainly that drawn up by a batch of leading New English figures, Parsons, Sir Adam Loftus, Temple, Sir Hardress Waller and Annesley, urging Munster as the site for a revitalized war effort[107] and according a prime position therein to Parliament's lord lieutenant. Lisle should carry with him no fewer than seven newly raised regiments, £30,000 advanced by the assessment treasurers and further advances from the excise, though, given the small area held in the south of Ireland, a 'monthly provision' must also be provided. Ulster and Connacht, too, would require money and supplies, and Ulster should 'be reduced into one command subject to the Lord Lieutenant' rather than, as now, being 'distracted under different commands'. A unified strategy should be driven forward, with 'additional' forces, geared to 'destroy' the 'subsistence' of the Irish.[108] If the proposals reflected the reality that Dublin had drifted out of reach, and the sustained prognosis on the north that the devastation of the region was such that deployment of mass reinforcements, in the short term, was unwise, if not totally unfeasible,[109] they also signalled the extent to which the hopes of

---

[103] Ormond had made a closing bid to receive the commissioners' troops into his garrisons and under his command, pending a settlement, an offer, unsurprisingly, rejected: *Severall papers*, pp. 42–3.

[104] *CSPI, 1633–47*, pp. 547–9.

[105] Adamson, 'Strafford's ghost', p. 136; J. S. A. Adamson, 'The peerage in politics, 1645–49', PhD dissertation, University of Cambridge, 1986, chapter 1.

[106] *CSPI, 1647–60*, p. 727.

[107] Cf. Lenihan, 'Confederate military strategy', pp. 161–6, 174–5 for confederate strategic priorities.

[108] HMC *Portland MSS*, i, 399–401. The delivery of the report to the Commons prompted their resolution that Lisle duly depart for Munster: *CJ*, v, 25–7.

[109] Cf. McNeill (ed.), *Tanner letters*, pp. 204–5.

leading New English figures had become pinned to Lisle and his Munster expedition.[110]

Broghill departed for Munster in December, secure in the command he held 'independent from' Inchiquin and soon suspected, by the latter, of attempting 'to make the new colonels of his faction'.[111] Inchiquin continued to rally his supporters in London, and won an earnest of approval from John Booker, lieutenant-colonel of one of the new regiments, as one 'most reall in the Cause, of much gallantry and resolution . . . who most seasonably secured those Parts for the Parliament against the common Enemy'.[112] Efforts were being made to accord Lisle both prestige and power. In January the Derby House Committee pressed the Houses to confirm his 'instructions' (including the resolution to conform church government in Ireland to that of England), provide him with a sword of office ('an ensign of authority') and secure to him a privy council. It may have been as concerned to exclude the unreliable as to intrude its own choices, though it did nominate the English 'Independent' MPs Norton and Salwey as well as Annesley as among the select group to accompany Lisle to Ireland. As approved by the Commons, the Irish Council would comprise a slate of 'old Protestants', including Sir Adam Loftus, Temple, Parsons, Borlace, Valentia, Meredith, Shirley and, already in Ireland, Inchiquin and Sir Charles Coote, the hope being expressed that at least five of the seven then in London could be coaxed back to Ireland (with sweeteners of £300 apiece) 'if they could be able diverse of them being at this tyme sick, & Infirme'.[113] While soldiers in Ulster waited for promised shoes and stockings, the new councillors had more success in tapping into their pensions (£500 p.a.) and bonuses. Funds were channelled into reliable hands: Broghill had been entrusted with £6,000 for Munster, Sir Arthur Loftus with £5,000. Ahead of their participation in Lisle's expedition Sir Hardress Waller and Algernon Sidney each gained access to £2,000 of their arrears. While the Ulster 'British' won £1,400 and Monro's men £1,600, on 14 January it was ordered that the £30,000 advanced for Lisle's expedition be packed into chests to accompany him at his departure.[114]

---

[110] For this and the following paragraph see Little, 'Irish "Independents" ', pp. 955–6.

[111] HMC *Egmont MSS*, i, 328–9, 342, 349–50, 355–6.

[112] Printed sheet (untitled) by Booker, dated 25 November 1646 (Wing B 3723). Booker had arrived in Munster in September, but was dispatched back to London to seek supplies.

[113] BL Additional MS 31,116, fo. 296a. The Derby House Committee's plans appear to have intended that Temple and Loftus, plus the new councillors Annesley, Norton and Salwey, accompany Lisle, with only Parsons, Borlace, Meredith, Valentia, Inchiquin, Coote and King also retaining councillor status. The list delivered to the Commons instead encompassed the nine listed above: *CJ*, v, 40–1, 42; *CSPI, 1647–60*, pp. 727–9.

[114] *CSPI, 1633–47*, pp. 586, 595; *1647–60*, p. 728; *Calendar of the Proceedings of the Committee for Compounding*, i, 52–3, 800, 802; *Calendar of the proceedings of the Committee for the Advance of Money 1642–1656*, ed. M. A. E. Green (3 vols, London, 1888) i, 58, 60; *CSPD, addenda, 1625–49*, p. 705.

Events in Ulster would follow a very different course from that driven forward in Munster by a combination of regional feud, parliamentary factional interests and the strategic aspirations of a high-powered New English lobby at Westminster. Three of those lately charged to negotiate with Ormond – Clotworthy, King and Meredith – had succeeded as Parliament's commissioners for Ulster and landed on 30 November to face a bleak situation. Tension over quartering arrangements had long troubled a province recognized as providing but 'poor relief' for the forces there. The commissioners negotiated the relocation of Scottish and local forces to provide room for the newly landed regiments in Lecale (dubbed the 'marrybone' of Ulster by Monro). Pressure on limited resources agitated the old sore of Scottish retention of Belfast, and when, on 15 December, the commissioners dispatched Owen O'Connolly to the Scottish Parliament to urge surrender of the town, their plea for urgency lest their men perish, and the offer of money to Scottish troops evacuating the town, were not necessarily rhetorical ploys.[115] The commissioners' arguments extended to a defence of the Ulster Protestants and a rehabilitation of their erstwhile commander, Chichester. Though 'mistakes' may have been made, even 'reprehensible' actions by Chichester and his associates were now classified as less than rebellious or treasonable, insufficient to justify past expulsions and the seizure of quarters. The complexities of the situation in 1643–44 were emphasized, with Scottish hesitation over the cessation and British co-operation in the destruction of corn remembered, and not Chichester but his conveniently deceased lieutenant-colonel, Matthews, blamed for the proclamation against the Covenant. The commissioners suggested that even in 1645 the Scots had not really acted as if Chichester was in rebellion, and had defended actions undertaken under Ormond's authority while the latter was at war.[116]

If the planter population was reckoned 'rich in nothing . . . but of factions and divisions', the commissioners were set on healing and settling.[117] As well as jam tomorrow with the promise of regular supply from Parliament, the commissioners proved willing to act on their own account within the limits of their powers. Davies delivered some of the goods for which he had contracted, with allotment among the local forces recorded on 15 January.[118] The right to set out the limits of quarters was used in favour of some of those set back by the recent arrivals,[119] and, most notably, the granting of custodiums was liberally used in favour of a significant number of planter

---

[115] *CSPI, 1633–47*, pp. 561–2. O'Connolly was directed specifically to Argyll and Wariston.
[116] *CSPI, 1633–47*, pp. 558–60, 560–1.
[117] Wemyss to Perceval, 9 December 1646, HMC *Egmont MSS*, i, 341. See also Sir William Stewart to Perceval, 9 December 1646, HMC *Egmont MSS*, i, 341–2.
[118] *CSPI, 1633–47*, pp. 579, 580, 587.
[119] *CSPI, 1633–47*, pp. 581, 583, 586, 587, 588, 589, 595.

figures, drawing upon property of Catholic 'rebels', but with at least one grant from episcopal property, albeit that of the 'excepted' bishop of Derry.[120] In marked contrast with Munster in 1647 the new expedition to Ulster sought to overcome logistical difficulties without challenging the local power of the established elite. Robert Thornton, perennial mayor of Londonderry and long-time opponent of the Scottish clergy, was awarded additional powers over recently arrived troops in the city, and their money, and Coote, temporarily governor of the city, empowered to use martial law against any threats to the mayor.[121] And this at the same time as the accounts committee at Westminster was securing orders for Thornton to be arrested and sent back to London, having earlier absconded to Ireland when faced with charges of fraud and peculation.[122]

Nor were relations with the Scots characterized solely by confrontation. Crucial to any amicable arrangement was the question of whether the Scottish army in Ulster could secure a deal of a well-funded withdrawal akin to that won by their brethren stationed in England. In the short term, the Scottish army insisted upon fair pay and an equitable delineation of quarters, but pressed for a 'final settlement' which would allow it to depart, delivering up the towns in its hands. The reply to the commissioners signed by Crawford–Lindsay on behalf of the Scottish Parliament (31 December) denied Belfast, but offered to ensure that Monro's soldiers would be quartered 'closely' within the town, leaving 'convenient' room for the English, and sought a resolution based on the departure of the army with payment of arrears.[123] Plans to reinforce the Scottish army fizzled out in a mutiny in Peebles in February, but such an outcome was not entirely unwelcome either to the forces already in Ulster (loath to share any final pay-out with raw newcomers) or to Argyll, still plagued with threats to the Campbell homeland.[124]

By then the Derby House Committee had also spelt out the need to regain Belfast as a source of support for the new English regiments.[125] But Anglo–Scottish negotiations in Edinburgh still held out some hope of a mutually acceptable pay-off.[126] That the situation was fuelled by English dislike of having the army in Ireland is not to be doubted. The Commons, on 13 March, accepted the committee's recommendations that the war in Ireland now be carried without Scottish assistance and that the Scottish army be dismissed strictly according to the terms of the 1642 treaty (one month's notice and

---

[120] *CSPI, 1633–47*, pp. 579, 582, 585, 595–6, 597–8.
[121] *CSPI, 1633–47*, pp. 557, 562, 569, 599.
[122] *CJ*, v, 62; PRO SP 28/253B.
[123] *CSPI, 1633–47*, pp. 567–8, 571.
[124] Stevenson, *Scottish Covenanters*, pp. 245–6.
[125] McNeill (ed.), *Tanner letters*, pp. 231–2; *CSPI, 1647–60*, pp. 728, 729.
[126] Stevenson, *Scottish Covenanters*, p. 247.

two weeks' pay) with promises that the soldiers would subsequently be paid up to date. Of course, the suspicion would have been strong that once soldiers were dismissed arrears would be foregone.[127] The decision reflected not only the undoubted strains in Anglo–Scottish relations, or the influence of anti-Scottish 'Independent' sentiment, but the 'big picture', from Westminster's angle of vision. There rolling demilitarization in England was to be matched by re-deployment of English troops to Ireland, financial retrenchment was underway, and English soldiers had yet to show that they simply would not stand for the kind of deal now being proposed for the Scottish army in Ulster. Likewise controlling counsel in Scotland still sought to square equitable treatment with at least passable relations with Parliament. From Edinburgh, Montereul reported his belief that the Scots would deliver all Ireland rather than break with Parliament; in April he groused that they would cede Edinburgh castle if asked.[128]

By mid-January the commissioners had made ready to depart from Ulster, gloomily concluding that 'having nothing to give the soldiers they would but be derided by them that wish them ill, and scorned and abused by them they should depend on to be aiding and obedient unto them'.[129] John Davies was inclined to blame the new soldiery and declared he 'would rather . . . have to do with ten thousand of the old men than with five hundred of these new ones, who will have beef, butter, cheese, pease, and wheaten bread – things difficult to manage anywhere, and especially here'.[130] But the commissioners could take some pride in their efforts, for they left behind defined quarters and institutionalized councils of war for both old 'British' and the recently landed 'English' regiments,[131] had worked to smooth tensions and consolidate Parliament's hold upon the local forces, and had made contact across the leaky south Ulster frontier to troops nominally under Ormond's command. As early as mid-December Tichborne, in command at Drogheda, had offered his co-operation in the event of military activity.[132]

---

[127] *CSPI, 1647–60*, pp. 736–7; Stevenson, *Scottish Covenanters*, p. 248. *Moderate Intelligencer* 105, 11–18 March 1647, E 381 (3*), p. 971 felt a need to explain the decision on Ireland 'that this may not seem to any strange', reminding readers of the original agreement to return on a month's notice; *Perfect Occurrences* 11, 12 March 1647, E381 (7), p. 86 claimed that the army 'will be content to be dismist, if they may receive satisfaction of by-gones, as *Monro* intimated very lately in a letter to *Argile*'.

[128] Fotheringham (ed.), *Correspondence of Montereul*, ii, 41, 64, 93.

[129] Davies to Perceval, 13 January 1647, HMC *Egmont MSS*, i, 352–3; cf. *CSPI, 1633–47*, pp. 588–9.

[130] HMC *Egmont MSS*, i, 365–6, 366, 369–70.

[131] *CSPI, 1633–47*, pp. 600, 601.

[132] *CSPI, 1633–47*, pp. 558, 563.

Some contacts had been kept up with Ormond, though to little effect. By 13 January John Davies was prepared to declare Ormond 'a very knave', adding that 'all the old English are inclinable to adhere unto him and cometh in to him daily'.[133] He was witnessing another turn in Ormond's designs, still driven by the goal of securing room and resources for the king's party in Leinster, possibly allied to larger designs. Having sallied forth from Dublin on the assumption that Preston would join him to secure Leinster from O'Neill's Ulster army, Ormond was not sent scurrying back to the capital by the plan's failure.[134] Instead, with force and persuasion, he undertook a poaching of Preston's constituency, conciliatory Catholic Leinster gentry whose detestation of the alien 'Ultaghs' (Gaelic Ulstermen) and their depredations was deep-seated and intense. Richard Osborne sounded an Ormondist rejoicing in the Irish divisions. With support already secured from the Bourkes and Butlers (Clanricard's kin and his own), Ormond, 'if not diverted by some conceived neglect of the Parliament of England or seduced by some reginal letters, will be able with some helps and supplies from England to give a period to these base wars, or more properly rebellion . . .' since Leinster and Munster were now swinging against the Ulster Irish, who plundered them as they formerly did 'our nation', so that they now cursed those first fomenters of rebellion.[135] The Leinster regiments of Sir James Dillon and the earl of Westmeath, veterans of the 1645 Connacht campaign, were reported to have joined Ormond by the end of December as he moved towards Athlone.[136] He ranged over Co. Meath, receiving submissions in ex-Catholic quarters in return for 'protection', and Co. Westmeath, where the gentry were summoned to meet and arrange supply for his forces.[137]

Rinuccini and his supporters insisted that Ormond's actions showed he was no longer concerned with the treaty but was out to 'extirpate' the nation. The confederate General Assembly gathered in January to take the failed peace into consideration. Preston salved his conscience by referring thence the Clanricard-brokered arrangements he had recently repudiated.[138] Ormond insisted that he stood by Clanricard's efforts, but would never admit

---

[133] HMC *Egmont MSS*, i, 352–3.

[134] Casway, *Owen Roe O'Neill*, pp. 166–8; Savage to Perceval, 19 December 1646, HMC *Egmont MSS*, i, 348–9.

[135] Osborne to Perceval, 10 January, HMC *Egmont MSS*, i, 350.

[136] Savage to Perceval, 19 December, HMC *Egmont MSS*, i, 348–9.

[137] Ormond's report of submissions in ex-Catholic quarters in Co. Meath, Carte MS 19, fo. 639; circular letter of 23 December 1646 for a meeting of the gentry of Co. Westmeath to win supply for Ormond's army by consent, Carte MS 19, fos 676, 681; John Nugent to Sir James Dillon, 29 December 1646, announcing that the county had appointed delegates to meet with Ormond, Carte MS 19, fo. 780.

[138] *Letter-book*, pp. 340–1, 344–5; *CSPI, 1633–47*, pp. 552–3, 555–6. Cf. Clanricard's angry response, *Letter-book*, pp. 341–2.

a further treaty, and wanted his friends to know as much. The statement Ormond dispatched to Kilkenny on 25 January was little more than a denunciation of confederate perfidy from the time of the proclamation of the peace. The concession that Taaffe and Barry visit the city in response to an invitation for talks was hardly of great significance at the tail end of such a message.[139] Ormond's hard line pre-dated the assembly's formal rejection of the 1646 peace. Instead he empowered Taaffe and Barry to obtain a one-month cessation of hostilities in return for £1,000, he himself undertaking to withdraw from confederate quarters; extension for another month would cost another £1,000.[140] Despite limited successes in Westmeath and Longford,[141] Ormond had managed to fix quarters in the Pale counties for specified units, supported by local payments,[142] and this despite reports that the formerly flourishing area faced depopulation and an additional levy imposed by the confederates.[143]

Yet the pressures on his position were simply too great. Taaffe and Barry sent word of the ascendancy of opponents of the treaty at Kilkenny, but Ormond had already contacted the Ulster commissioners (28 January) seeking safe-conducts on a matter of importance.[144] Within the Pale his troops were under pressure from O'Neill's soldiers, suffering a 'sad disaster' in a clash at Kells, Co. Meath. O'Neill's men, in turn, defended their actions as a response to Tichborne's co-operation with the 'Scoich' in plundering forays.[145] Tichborne had maintained his contacts with the Ulster commissioners through the garrisons at Dundalk and Lisburn. By January he had notified Ormond that he planned to take part in raids in Monaghan and Cavan; he was not over-ruled.[146] As his subordinates declared their hand,

[139] *Letter-book*, pp. 348–53.

[140] Gilbert (ed.), *Irish confederation*, vi, 172–3.

[141] Ormond to Westmeath, 1 January 1647, Roscommon to Ormond, 2 January 1647, Clanricard to Ormond, 9 January 1647, Carte MS 20, fos 10, 18, 95; *Letter-book*, pp. 346–7.

[142] Ormond to Sir William Hull, etc., 26 January 1647, Ormond to Barnewall, 30 January 1647, Ormond to Armstrong, 30 January 1647, Carte MS 20, fos 196, 220, 222.

[143] Cadogan to Ormond, 29 January 1647, Carte MS 20, fo. 214. Ormond admitted that his troops might have taken supplies but promised restitution and urged full payment, but to Tichborne he suggested that some regions would not pay up until they had known more suffering: Ormond to Sir Thomas Nugent, 6 January 1647, Ormond to Tichborne, 7 January, Carte MS 20, fos 75, 68.

[144] Taaffe and Barry to Ormond, 30 January 1647, Carte MS 20, fo. 223; Ormond to Meredith, etc., 28 January 1647, Carte MS 20, fo. 205.

[145] Bagwell, *Ireland under the Stuarts*, ii, 137; Gilbert (ed.), *Contemporary history*, i, 138, 717, 718–19; HMC *Egmont MSS*, i, 360.

[146] *CSPI, 1633–47*, pp. 558, 563; Ward to Tichborne, 4 January 1647, Tichborne to Ormond, 5 January 1647, Ormond to Tichborne, 7 January 1647, Carte MS 20, fos 7, 44, 68. This is not to say that Tichborne did not harbour a fair amount of distrust for the northern parliamentarians.

the Old English counties failed to rally sufficiently, and Dublin grumbled over burdensome assessments and collapsing trade,[147] Ormond and his council formally resolved that they would appeal to Parliament, and that he would quit the government.[148]

While Ormond laboured, with little success, to fashion some sort of loyalist coalition which could sink its differences in light of a common allegiance, Parliament, and the Anglo–Scottish alliance, appeared to succumb to fissiparous tendencies. Modern research has uncovered the potency of partisan energies at Westminster, from the colonization and manipulation of bicameral committees to the cultivation and exploitation of regional allies and power-plays (and the reciprocal tapping of support at Westminster from within the communities of provincial England), developments pertinent to Parliament's engagement with Ireland too by the mid-1640s. Yet despite the nods to the truism that most MPs were not party stalwarts, who voted neither for a ticket nor for a platform, they are all too easily lost to view. The Newcastle propositions, ultimately rejected by the king, can bear the musty air of shelved blueprints, but rather than being considered either a 'Presbyterian' or an 'Independent' production, perhaps they are best regarded as a compromise that both 'juntoes' were forced to make with the predilections of the backbench MPs. At once limiting Scottish engagement in England – and Ireland – and upholding a Presbyterian church settlement, marking out for destruction ranks of individuals and categories of enemies, and entrenching Parliament, as an institution, in the future settlement of England, such an agenda bears comparison with the impersonal national and religious goals staked out in other representative bodies, confederate assemblies and Scottish parliaments, as against the offers of generosity and the grasping at personal advantage of the well-connected peers and aspiring statesmen who dabbled in backstairs negotiations with the king.

Outright victory in the Irish war, and the securing of a Protestant and English future for the island, sat foursquare in successive parliamentary productions, a common goal, a core value even. Yet if consensus at Westminster on the wisdom of securing the withdrawal of Scottish soldiers from England could span the range between the aspiration to see old friends depart for home with money in their pockets and the inclination to send off the New Model Army to chase out pestilent neighbours, so different paths would be mapped out towards the common destination of a safely secured Ireland. Alongside the consistent determination to win Ireland ran

[147] Carte MS 20, fos 146–7, 149. For the pressing crisis of resources affecting the confederates as well as Dublin in 1647 see Gillespie, 'Irish economy at war', pp. 176–7.
[148] Council Act, 5 February 1647, Carte MS 20, fos 247–9.

the development of alternative policies, not based on ideological divergence but inched forward in a multitude of little decisions, some the effect of choices made within English politics, others the product of entanglement in provincial disputes or patronage in Ireland. By the spring of 1647 perhaps the most consistent strategy for settlement to date – to demilitarize England, appease Scotland, conquer Ireland – would be derailed when Parliament's own armies rose up to challenge its faithfulness to the cause it proclaimed.

8

Armies in politics, 1647

On 28 July 1647 Ormond stepped aboard Captain Matthew Wood's warship and departed from Dublin, ceding the last redoubt of royalist Ireland to the representatives of the Parliament of England. Events had moved full circle since 1642: newly arrived English troops were gathering in the Irish capital, as restless and disgruntled at pay and conditions as their predecessors. Plans were afoot to tackle Dublin's encirclement by 'rebel' forces. Quashing insurrection in Ireland was at last to be undertaken vigorously, in turn as part of grander schemes for a post-war English settlement, with demilitarization, reduced taxation, a 'return to normalcy' in local governance and amicable, if distant, relations with Scotland.[1] In fact, as Ormond sailed away, for now, English politics was entering what Austin Woolrych has dubbed one of the 'climacterics' of the period, 'in which political crisis was particularly intense and decisions particularly momentous', conditioned by the political rise of the New Model Army.[2] The present chapter deals principally with three sets of events – the integration of Dublin into Parliament's Irish subsidiary, the fiasco of Viscount Lisle's Munster expedition and the Irish dimension to the New Model Army's plan of action – which demonstrate how far Protestant Ireland had become bound into parliamentarian politics, paralleling developments within England, yet with its own distinctive twists.

On 6 February 1647 Ormond signed off a whole batch of letters including, interestingly, one to Parsons in which he claimed he sought to retire, and in which he asked Parsons to help smooth the way for his recruitment of a force for the service of France. To Wharton and Salwey he declared that he was now satisfied with surrender on the terms offered in November 1646, and sought to yield his command as soon as possible, in the meantime holding

---

[1] The fullest account of the 1647 'Presbyterian' plans remains that of Kishlansky, *Rise of the New Model Army*.

[2] Woolrych, *Britain in revolution*, p. 155.

his possessions for the English crown and nation.[3] Though the confederates still sought to press for substantive talks, Ormond was clear that he was interested in no more than a simple truce.[4] Instead the Dublin council made contact with Inchiquin, recounting its actions and asking for a loan of ammunition.[5] In Dublin the remnant of the Irish Parliament swung behind the approach to Westminster, issuing a remonstrance which laid much of the blame for past sufferings on the failure to enforce the recusancy laws and urging that this be a non-negotiable requirement laid on future governors. One informed observer surmised that 'the Parliament here being engaged, no submission made by the rebels will hinder the receiving of such forces as shall be sent over . . .' by Westminster.[6]

Parliament did not delay in making its response. After hearing Ormond's papers read on 20 February the Commons ordered the Derby House Committee for Irish Affairs to assemble so as to report back that same morning. It hastily got to work to draft a letter to Ormond, and others to Lisle and the various regional commanders to undertake diversionary attacks; to produce instructions for the commissioners; and to pass votes of £3,000 for Ormond (with £10,877 14s 9d to follow, matching his exact requirements) and £12,000 to send forces. Parliament was approving both of the actions taken and of the speed of the response and approved the November negotiations as a basis for fresh talks. Four of the regiments destined for Lisle's expedition were still in England, and it was resolved that these be re-deployed for Dublin, while the regiments landed in Ulster in late 1646 should now march south to their then-intended quarters in Ormondist territory.[7] Rapid reaction was essential. As a first stage, Parliament authorized Lieutenant-Colonel Huetson and Major Astley to hasten to Dublin and ensure that Parliament's forces were admitted to the out-garrisons (at Drogheda, Dundalk, Newry, Carlingford and Greencastle) or, if Ormond agreed to

---

[3] A second letter, concerning his personal financial settlement, specified a hand-over by 10 March, through fear of holding out longer. Ormond also contacted the other three late commissioners, Clotworthy, Meredith and King, in Ulster, and his own agents of 1646 (Lowther, Willoughby and Sir Paul Davies): Carte MS 20, fos 252, 254, 256, 258–9, 260.

[4] Gilbert (ed.), *Irish confederation*, vi, 182–5. Ormond secured O'Neill's participation in the three-week cessation: Gilbert (ed.), *Contemporary history*, i, 719, 720–1.

[5] Carte MS 20, fo. 268.

[6] Carte MS 20, fo. 307; Sir William Usher to Perceval, 16 February 1647, HMC *Egmont MSS*, i, 361; *A remonstrance from the . . . Parliament at Dublin . . .* (Dublin, 1646) E 382 (3).

[7] *CJ*, v, 91, 92, 93–5; *CSPI, 1647–60*, pp. 729–31; *CSPD, 1645–7*, pp. 523–4; Derby House Committee for Irish Affairs to Ormond, 20 February 1647, Carte MS 20, fo. 336. A detailed financial schedule kept just within the £12,000 voted, though the Houses added another £10,000 in early March, encouraged by favourable reports: *CJ*, v, 100–2, McNeill (ed.), *Tanner letters*, pp. 232–4. The first of the new regiments from England, under Colonel Castle, reached Dublin on 6 March.

give hostages, to have the first units on the scene put under Ormond's command until further forces could arrive. The full treaty would be handled by the previous commissioners, plus Annesley, though only he, Meredith and King would go in the first instance.[8]

Ormond's approaches pre-dated the capture of the Derby House Committee for the 'Presbyterian' interest, or even the departure of Lisle for Munster, and his personal channels of communication ran to Wharton as well as Clotworthy. While the former commissioners as a body urged Ormond to 'open dealing', Wharton gave the assurances Ormond had requested about the future for his family, and Clotworthy claimed that Ormond would get his money, characteristically adding that he hoped the confederate miscreants would suffer for their treachery.[9] If some of those around Ormond would soon he hinting at the advantages of a factional alignment with the 'Presbyterians', the over-riding impression is one of continuity – it was Ormond, not his interlocutors, who shifted most in the offers made and accepted.[10] And the securing of Dublin was still a predominantly New English enterprise. In London, Ormond's agents, Lowther and Sir Paul Davies, secured testimonials from Parsons despite having been members of the Irish Council which had gaoled him. The Derby House Committee expressed 'confidence in their loyalty to the English nation and the Protestant religion'.[11] Ormond could perhaps count on less sympathy in some quarters – for all the gentle handling at Westminster in 1646–47 rumours seeping out of Dublin suggested that some believed he 'hath not deserved any favour himself, who hath so far hazarded God's cause, the safety of the poor Protestants there and his own preservation and interest upon nice punctilios', even that 'innocent people should perish rather than he should escape unpunished, grounded, as I conceive, upon that text that evil is not to be done that good may come thereof'.[12]

Ormond informed Digby that he must go through with the arrangement despite a recent confederate approach, dismissing their terms as unreasonable and indicating that he intended no more than to keep them talking.[13] Instead

---

[8] Clotworthy's omission is unlikely to have been caused by concerns about his political reliability since he was assigned to vet correspondence going to Ormond: *CSPI, 1647–60*, pp. 732–3, 733–4; *CSPD, 1645–7*, pp. 525–6. Ormond agreed to safe-conducts for Huetson and Astley on 9 March 1647: Carte MS 20, fos 410, 412.

[9] Carte MS 20, fos 367, 347, 343; Little, 'Marquess of Ormond', pp. 93–5.

[10] Little, 'Marquess of Ormond', pp. 95–6. Dr Little argues for more favourable treatment for Ormond from the 'Presbyterian' side.

[11] HMC *Portland MSS*, i, 407, 413; *CSPI, 1647–60*, p. 734.

[12] Edmund Smyth to Perceval, 25 February 1647, HMC *Egmont MSS*, i, 363–4. Smyth subscribed to the former, not the latter, sentiment.

[13] Carte MS 20, fo. 409; Gilbert (ed.), *Irish confederation*, vi, 185–7. Cf. Ó Siochrú, *Confederate Ireland*, pp. 136–8.

he won his cessation extension from them, from 13 March to 10 April.[14] His actions in March suggest he was readying himself for departure, that his decision to match with Parliament was irrevocable. On 15 March he began the process of admitting forces from Lecale to his garrisons;[15] the following day he wrote to vouch for his hostages, three trusted associates, Chichester, Roscommon and Ware, on 17 March adding his second son, Richard.[16] Then, on 17 March, he wrote to his king, denouncing Irish perfidy, with even the Clanricard–Preston terms now presented as an underhand means to capture Dublin, lamenting Kilkenny's failure to salvage its honour by submitting to the king and professing that surrender to Parliament was best for the sake of religion, the crown and the king's faithful servants.[17] On 22 March he formally broke off negotiations with Kilkenny.[18] Ormond's actions in the latter half of March suggest he was tidying up loose ends ahead of his departure. As he busied himself with allocations and arrangements for garrisons and quarters, he demanded that the new forces refrain from plunder, and that garrisons preserve the property of resident Catholics.[19] The earl of Roscommon was called upon to press the case of loyal Catholics in London,[20] and, along with Dudley Loftus, to promote Ormond's design of taking the nucleus of an army into French service.[21] The confederate Supreme Council, meanwhile, moved to secure the adherence of uncommitted Catholics, circulating warnings of dire plans laid by the Parliament.[22]

The rush for Dublin threatened to open a hornet's nest for Parliament. It was not really feasible to recruit, supply and transport the forces required with the speed deemed necessary, and while some units in process of formation could be used, the urgency of the task had prompted an approach to Sir Thomas Fairfax stating the need for two further regiments drawn from

---

[14] Gilbert (ed.), *Irish confederation*, vi, 189–90, 190–1. In standing by the truce, of course, he was unable to join the Ulster British in co-ordinated hostile actions: Carte MS 20, fo. 457.

[15] Carte MS 20, fos 441, 443, 447. Colonel Castle was called upon to garrison Dublin: Carte MS 20, fo. 451.

[16] Ormond to the Derby House Committee for Irish Affairs, to the Derby House Committee and commissioners, 16 March, 17 March 1647, Carte MS 20, fos 453, 487, 491.

[17] Carte MS 20, fos 478–9. It is not clear if he was aware of Rawdon's 5 March letter to Eustace, which suggested the likelihood of a settlement in England, including the king's agreement to prosecute the Irish war: Carte MS 20, fo. 396.

[18] Gilbert (ed.), *Irish confederation*, vi, 192.

[19] Ormond to Lecale officers, 24 March 1647, to Gibson, 26 March 1647, to Coote's regiment, 29 March 1647, Carte MS 20, fos 534, 547, 572; circular to garrison commanders, Carte MS 20, fo. 581.

[20] Ormond to Roscommon, 18 March 1647, Carte MS 20, fo. 469.

[21] Ormond to Roscommon, 16 March 1647, Carte MS 20, fo. 463; Ormond to Loftus, 26 March 1647, Carte MS 21, fo. 150; Ó hAnnracháin, *Catholic Reformation*, pp. 178–9.

[22] Letters to Sir Nicholas White, Sir Henry Talbott, Sir Andrew Aylmer (all 28 March 1647), Carte MS 20, fos 556, 558, 560; Gilbert (ed.), *Irish confederation*, vi, 192–3; *Letter-book*, p. 382.

the New Model Army under his command. Moves were made towards the departure of 2,000 men, under Colonel Robert Hammond, but the fact that Parliament deemed Hammond's terms unsatisfactory was a straw in the wind for the looming clash of army and Parliament sparked off by Irish service.[23] The countdown to the revolt of the New Model Army has been masterfully studied, but some of the points where Irish matters intruded into or extruded from the sequence of events needs to be addressed. As with the Lisle expedition, it is crucial to bear in mind that what was at stake was the engagement of factional manoeuvres with policies likely to have a broad appeal among Parliament's supporters, namely the scaling back of military commitments and financial obligations. The form this would take would owe much to the partisan dominance of the 'Presbyterians' in the Commons and, from April at least, in the Derby House Committee, their chosen executive instrument.[24] Where a partisan struggle would ensue was over the question of whether the reforms would mean the effective destruction (by disbandment or re-modelling) of the New Model Army, long a target of 'Presbyterian' anxieties, not least given its reputation for religious radicalism, or its retention, however slimmed down, as the sole remaining military support of the parliamentarian cause. In turn, all reform plans, following the logic of the Newcastle propositions, necessarily entwined the military establishments, with their panoply of commands, in Ireland and in England.

The Commons had mandated the Derby House Committee to supply a statement on the proposed size and support of forces for Ireland back in December. As delivered, by the hardline 'Independent' Armine, on 6 March, it merely specified numbers, 8,400 infantry, 3,000 cavalry and 1,200 dragoons, considerably more than were to be retained in England.[25] It was the Commons which resolved to draw upon the New Model Army and referred to the Derby House Committee the task of determining a single 'establishment' to pay all forces, in both countries, duly delivered, by Holles, now the leading 'Presbyterian' in the House, on 15 March, to a total of £1.2 million per annum.[26] Finance was a crucially debilitating dimension to the reform plan. Even aside from the Lords' stalling the new assessment, set at £60,000 per

---

[23] *CSPI, 1647–60*, p. 737; *CSPD, 1645–7*, pp. 525, 531, 534; *CJ*, v, 112; HMC Portland MSS, i, 414; *Moderate Intelligencer* 105, 11–18 March 1647, p. 970. As well as requesting the post of governor of Dublin, Hammond insisted on only a temporary (two-to three-month) transfer of the forces to Dublin.

[24] J. S. A. Adamson, 'Politics and the nobility in civil war England', *Historical Journal* 34 (1991) 253–4; Kishlansky, *Rise of the New Model Army*, pp. 164–5.

[25] England would retain 5,400 horse, 1,000 dragoons and some garrison forces: *CJ*, v, 26, 107; Austin Woolrych, *Soldiers and statesmen: the general council of the army and its debates, 1647–1648* (Oxford, 1987), p. 28.

[26] *CJ*, v, 112.

month for forces in England and Ireland, until June, and the failure of its collection in the country at large, it would not have met half the costs of even the Irish side of the equation, despite the overloading of all other revenue sources.[27] By April the Derby House Committee appears to have envisaged a rough equality of misery for troops in England or Ireland – arrears were to be respited in either country, in England upon the public faith, in Ireland upon confiscated lands, and while soldiers not going to Ireland were, notoriously, to receive a mere six weeks' back pay, those who volunteered received the less-than-princely reward of eight weeks' arrears and the usual month's advance.[28] Later assertions from the army insisted that neither disbandment nor Irish service was being challenged in principle but legitimate grievances needed to be addressed. Concern over how they would be funded once across the water in Ireland was apt indeed, in light not only of current woes but of the treatment of all who had preceded them to the Irish front. Questions of command also loomed, and had become dangerously entwined with the future government of Ireland.

There seems little doubt that the 'Presbyterian' leaders sought to re-mould what would remain of the New Model and place it under reliable commanders before dispatching most of it to Ireland. March saw a series of votes, limiting the number of senior officers, excluding MPs from commands and enforcing upon officers a conformity to the present church government, the Presbyterian system now mandated by parliamentary ordinance. On 29 March came the decisive vote to disband all infantry save those assigned to garrisons or to Ireland.[29] On 6 March it had been agreed in the Commons that the government of Ireland should be re-opened as a matter for discussion. But it was only on 27 March, the day on which Clotworthy, one of the delegation sent to the army to promote the Irish expedition, reported the officers' queries about pay and command, that the House voted 55:42 to debate the government of Ireland and the command of the forces there.[30] In debate on 1 April, the December 1645 vote to limit any government chosen to a period of one year was made the basis for change. Lisle's term of office would end on 15 April. The new dispensation progressed through four votes:

[27] Gentles, *New Model Army*, p. 30; Kishlansky, *Rise of the New Model Army*, pp. 152–3. The ordinance was the responsibility of Robert Reynolds and of the chairman of the old army committee, and client of Northumberland, Robert Scawen: *CJ*, v, 114.

[28] *CJ*, v, 138, 140, 155; *CSPI, 1647–60*, pp. 740, 741.

[29] Woolrych, *Soldiers and statesmen*, pp. 29–31. Some garrisons were being dismantled already and the troops used for Irish service: *CJ*, v, 101, 104.

[30] *CJ*, v, 107, 127. In two divisions the 'Independents' Hesilrig and Morley went down to the 'Presbyterians' Stapleton and William Waller and Stapleton and Lewis. See Woolrych, *Soldiers and statesmen*, pp. 31–3 for the mission to the army, which consisted of Salwey and Sir William Waller alongside Clotworthy.

to separate military and civil power in Ireland; to entrust the former to lords justices; to name commanders to existing and new forces under the control of parliamentary commissioners; and that the military commanders be Waller and Massey, their authority limited to three provinces, leaving Inchiquin secure in Munster. Only the last two resolutions led to divisions, but while the first succeeded 64:56, the 'Presbyterian' officers, designed for intrusion over forces drawn from the New Model, were voted down 99:76. The following day the veteran Skippon was successfully voted field marshal with Massey as lieutenant-general, though Waller failed even as major-general.[31]

The next two weeks saw political juggling as future military commands were voted on, and service in England or in Ireland, or disbandment, was apportioned to the various units of the army. That 'political considerations strongly affected the choice of regiments for retention or disbandment', it has been convincingly argued, 'is beyond reasonable doubt'.[32] This was the nub of the 'Presbyterian' counter-offensive. Military reorganization in both kingdoms would be combined with a reversal in the allocation of political and civil office as a means both to a diffusion of power and to the exclusion of opponents, and of perceived supporters of toleration and the sects. The Derby House Committee was the political dynamo, now with additional members and with powers to transport and disband forces and commission officers as approved by the Houses.[33]

The 'Presbyterian' plan appears to have encompassed the dismantling of what has been seen as an interlocking system of committees and army commands controlled by 'Independent' grandees and their allies.[34] If there was a logic to an aristocratic 'Independent' sponsorship of settlement terms which handed power over to coteries of office-holders and officers[35] (and perhaps a congruence between the rights of peers and of congregations to ease themselves out of a tightly uniform ecclesiastical system[36]) then there was a similar logic for 'Presbyterian' leaders, like Holles and Stapleton, increasingly able to command the Commons, to tap a preference for both diffused authority and the collegial power of national parliaments and

[31] *CJ*, v, 131, 133; BL Additional MS 31,116, fos 306b, 307a; Harrington, *Diary*, pp. 46–7; Juxon, *Journal*, p. 152. Harrington states that a vote against putting the question of giving Waller the command led to Waller himself suggesting Skippon.

[32] Woolrych, *Soldiers and statesmen*, pp. 40–3 (quotation at pp. 42–3).

[33] *CJ*, v, 134, 138; Kishlansky, *Rise of the New Model Army*, pp. 166–7.

[34] Scott, *Politics and war*, pp. 97–8; Adamson, 'Baronial context', pp. 118–19.

[35] Scott, *Politics and war*, p. 149.

[36] Adamson, 'The *Vindiciae veritatis* and the political creed of Viscount Saye and Sele', *Historical Research* 60 (1987), pp. 58–9; cf. Firth and Rait (eds), *Acts and ordinances*, i, 750, 793, 835.

ecclesiastical assemblies (whether this fitted their personal predilections or not). Towards Ireland, such an approach would fit with schemes to curtail the power of a Lisle-like figure and scatter authority, not merely among regional commanders, but commissioners too, such as had been used in Ulster, would be used in Dublin, were repeatedly sought for Munster, and had so regularly plodded after armies in the recent English conflict. Lisle's authority had been terminated in his absence. On 8 April, the day on which decisions were made on the futures of individual New Model regiments, the last vestiges of Sidney power were snuffed out when it was successfully moved that Michael Jones be made governor of Dublin, replacing Lisle's brother Algernon.[37]

Some reports out of London suggested the prospects of a partisan alignment for Ormond too. Sir John Gifford, writing on 15 April, noted that some there blamed him for spilling Protestant blood owing to his sending troops to Charles in 1643; others, and here he mentioned Holles and Stapleton, were more favourable. He even cited the nomination of lords justices, rather than a lord lieutenant, to replace Lisle, as calculated to please Ormond.[38] Ormond gave little evidence of inclining towards an exploitation of Westminster divisions. His word to Clanricard (1 May) was that 'Men have long fed themselves with hope of advantage to his majesty out of those differences. I for my part think their animosities but such a trick as the Dutchman who cheats all the world by bargaining when he is drunk'. Or, as he later claimed in response to attempts to persuade him to build hopes on English political reversals, 'all this stir in England is for the putting down of one rebellious faction for the setting up of another, without hope of advantage for the King or his party'.[39] His position was becoming increasingly perilous: within days of the ending of his cessation with the confederates Preston moved to capture Carlow, and Ormond appealed north, south and west for help by diversions and supplies. Even the dispatch of English troops, placed under his command, could increase his problems since their arrival was provocative towards the confederates, and increased pressure Ormond's supply problems.[40]

---

[37] Jones had been named deputy governor, in Sidney's absence, on 18 March, following a resolution at a Derby House Committee meeting with an 'Independent' majority – it was not the choice of Jones but the displacement of Sidney which carried factional connotations: *CJ*, v, 121, 136; *CSPI, 1647–60*, pp. 737; HMC *De L'Isle MSS*, vi, 565–6. Jones resembled Fairfax, not only in his military competence, but in standing apart from obvious factional alignments.

[38] Carte MS 20, fo. 613. The other matter reputedly held against Ormond was his participation in what was seen as Dillon's and Taaffe's dispossession of Protestants for rebels – Ormond's predictions about the fall-out of the Elphin incident had proved all too true.

[39] *Letter-book*, pp. 424, 458–9, 461–2, 462–3.

[40] Captain Wood to Lenthall, Carte MS 20, fo. 646.

In a proclamation of 3 April Ormond assured all Catholics within Protestant quarters that, despite the arrival of forces from England and the north, protection was to be maintained, and pillage punishable by death, until 10 June, and if it was not to be extended thereafter they would have notice and the right to depart with their goods.[41] Even so reports reaching London in May stated that 'most of the Irish that was worth anything has left this place [Dublin] and gone to Kilkenny or to the Irish quarter, themselves and goods'.[42] Ormond applied much of his time to negotiating their safe departure in return for the safe delivery of Protestants from such now-threatened outposts as Athlone.[43] All the while, dogged progress was made to secure to the parliamentary commissioners the powers and the cash needed for their mission.[44] Even when they had reached Chester, by the end of April, the commissioners were held up by adverse winds.[45] Yet Ormond continued to spurn confederate last-ditch offers, mediated now through the queen's agent, George Leyburn (alias 'Winter Grant').

The fall of Philip Sidney, Viscount Lisle, was not just a matter of shifting alignments and priorities at Westminster. His tenure of power was cut short within weeks of his arrival in Munster, yet the fall-out from the episode demonstrates how both far the regional politics of Protestant Ireland had been caught up into parliamentary high politics, where the stakes played for were crucial pieces in alternative patterns for the political future of England, and how parliamentary governance could see the replication of similar contentions in provincial England and Ireland. Within days of Lisle's arrival in Munster he and his critics had dispatched representatives to put their case in London.[46] With the non-renewal of Lisle's commission, Inchiquin celebrated the termination of the lieutenant's year of office on 9 April by assembling his forces and bundling Lisle and his supporters out of Munster.[47] The disputes then gained a further lease of life as several of the principals shuffled back to London by the beginning of May.[48]

The Munster dispute produced five main set of charges hurled by each side at the other: financial mismanagement; military incompetence; ill use of custodiums and 'protections'; factionalism; leniency to malignants, or

---

[41] On 7 April the order was extended to any beyond the quarters who would make an agreement to pay contribution: HMC *Ormonde MSS*, old series, ii, 56–7.

[42] Wemyss to Perceval, 12 May 1647, HMC *Egmont MSS*, i, 402.

[43] Carte MSS 20–1. He also authorized Dudley Loftus to continue negotiations for Ormond's departure with troops to France.

[44] *CJ*, v, 137, 143, 144, 148, 149; *CSPI, 1633–47*, p. 607; *CSPI, 1647–60*, pp. 734, 737, 738, 739.

[45] *CSPI, 1647–60*, pp. 746; HMC *Egmont MSS*, i, 403, 404.

[46] HMC *Egmont MSS*, i, 370–2, 376.

[47] Bottigheimer, *English money*, pp. 104–7.

[48] HMC *De L'Isle MSS*, vi, 566.

support for the subversive. Much of the resulting debate echoed accusations routinely tossed across the floor of the Houses whenever failures elsewhere stirred animosities and the defence of maligned champions. Lisle's supporters alleged rackets in Munster: musters where up to half of those recorded were missing, custodiums of 'rebel' lands granted to cronies and to the detriment of the general good, 'protections' leniently awarded in return for supplies. Inchiquin retorted in kind, but had a stronger card to play in the failure of the well-heeled new forces to accomplish any great tasks, and with claims that all the treasure was blown, largely on an inflated officer list. Inchiquin claimed that only £6,400 cash and £1,900 goods were left at Lisle's departure, which could barely stretch to five weeks' pay.[49] Favouritism rankled particularly with the lord president. Accusations that only the factional followers of Broghill and his friends were favoured appear to have had some justification: reports were passed on of old regiments pushed to the edges of territory, at Mallow, Tallow and Lismore; of established officers displaced from their garrison commands in favour of newcomers – Percy Smyth from Youghal, Brockett from Cork, losing also his regiment to George Monck and, apparently, receiving in return a martial law death sentence, albeit commuted to banishment.[50]

Inchiquin was placed on the defensive over his actions at the time of the cessation, admitting that he could not square 'all my then actions as consonant to the pleasure of the parliament, my sending men to England then and other actions declaring me then to be for the King's service . . .'.[51] His counter-charge was that he was side-lined for 'not adhering to the Independent party' and, more starkly, that 'the doctrine here preached by the Lord Lieutenant's chaplains is strong and direct Independency, and the [Presbyterian] government prescribed and pursued by the Parliament both inveighed against and decried publicly in the pulpit'.[52] Such claims have been seen, no doubt correctly, as a means to curry favour with the 'Presbyterian' leadership, though presumably also with a great many lesser MPs. But though Inchiquin admitted that he was hardly the sort of man to attract odium for the strength of his devotion to any religion,[53] and though Broghill and his allies, Inchiquin's principal foes, many have been no more perfervid sectarians than Lisle's uncle, the earl of Northumberland, there was enough truth in

---

[49] Lisle had apparently reorganized income from land so as to give more of the profit to the 'English' of Munster, in return for a fixed charge to the army, thus cutting down custodiums, but Inchiquin alleged to no great financial effect: HMC *Egmont MSS*, i, 381–2, 395; HMC *Portland MSS*, i, 418–9; *Perfect Occurrences* 14, 2–9 April 1647, E383 (25), pp. 109–10.

[50] HMC *Egmont MSS*, i, 389–90, 391.

[51] HMC *Egmont MSS*, i, 377.

[52] HMC *Egmont MSS*, i, 368, 374, 380.

[53] HMC *Egmont MSS*, i, 452.

Inchiquin's claims to make the case plausible.[54] Whether Lisle's new lieutenant-general, his brother Algernon Sidney, had embarked upon his future path of 'radicalism' or not as yet,[55] he was flanked by Major-General Hardress Waller, who within a year would publicly cast doubt upon a role for magistrates in matters of faith, and Commissary-General Thomas Harrison, who had long since earned his reputation as a 'preaching major'.[56] Waller had probably already adopted as his chaplain one Thomas Larkham (or Larkin), a man for whom the religious climate of New England had proved too strict, and there is just a hint in Larkham's claim that he was once 'chaplain to one of greatest honour in the nation, next unto a king' that he was Lisle's chaplain too.[57]

Inchiquin claimed that he was eager to pass controversial matters over to parliamentary commissioners, and had indeed petitioned for a body to handle finances and questions of rebel property since 1645 at least.[58] He sought 'such instructions as goes to other parts of the kingdom for taking of people under contribution and giving protections'.[59] Even so stony an officer as Coote recognized that in some cases protection would have to be granted to the unworthy as a means of sustaining the meritorious.[60] Inchiquin insisted he had acted 'merely for our own preservation, for that in case we had prosecuted with fire and sword, and proceeded so rigorously as they now condemn us to death for not doing, we had utterly perished'.[61] But he also asserted that his rivals were at least as ready as he to give protection 'even to the very rebels'; intriguingly, though, their condemnation of him as overly favourable to the ethnically Irish was countered with his complaint that they saw no great harm in an 'honest Papist'.[62] Inchiquin was certainly playing to

---

[54] Thomas Juxon's reading of these events was that 'the Independents, to support their own party, do not only court and do favours to the lord Northumberland's party – whom they know are not godly – but send upon that account such men for the conduct of the Irish business as they do pre-intend and know shall come to nothing . . . and all this for support of the faction' and to clear the ground for Cromwell later: Juxon, *Journal*, p. 147.

[55] Scott, *Algernon Sidney*, chapter 5.

[56] A. S. P. Woodhouse (ed.), *Puritanism and liberty* (London, 1938), pp. 136–7; C. H. Firth, *Cromwell's army* (London, 1902), p. 318.

[57] Anne Lawrence, *Parliamentary army chaplains, 1642–51* (London, 1990), pp. 145–6; 'Larkham, Thomas', *Dictionary of National Biography*, ed. L. Stephen and S. Lee (63 vols, London, 1885–1900).

[58] On 22 April his requests had included commissioners 'as went along with Sir Thos. Fairfax': HMC *Egmont MSS*, i, 367, 371, 399, 407, 419–20.

[59] HMC *Egmont MSS*, i, 395. Cf. his articles with 'the gentlemen, freeholders, and inhabitants of . . . Barrymore' for protection until 1 May 1648: HMC *Egmont MSS*, i, 396.

[60] HMC *Egmont MSS*, i, 413, 434–5.

[61] HMC *Egmont MSS*, i, 385.

[62] HMC *Egmont MSS*, i, 366–7, 368, 377, 380. Of course, for Protestants of Irish background it remained imperative that religion rather than nationality be advanced as the badge of reliability – see for instance the letters of Richard Fitzgerald, Old English Protestant, once the Irish Council's agent in England and currently employed collecting assessments in Wales, e.g. HMC *Egmont MSS*, i, p. 411.

his intended audience, whether sincerely or otherwise – probably their ambitions matched his own in terms of upholding the established order in his province. As an indication of changing times at the Derby House Committee, a vote was taken on 20 April to implement an old resolution from the previous November and grant Inchiquin £900 to recruit his cavalry, signed by a 'Presbyterian' phalanx of Suffolk, Willoughby, Holles, Stapleton and Clotworthy with Inchiquin's old comrade, Jephson.[63]

Whether he would fare so well in the maelstrom of the Commons was another matter. Though polite thanks were extended to Lisle, Sidney, Temple and Harrison upon their reappearance in the House, Temple lost no time in attacking Inchiquin for 'disservice to the state and desire he might be called to answer it', nor Jephson in pledging to 'ingage upon his life the Lord Insequin would approve himself faithful to the Parliament'.[64] Of Inchiquin's foes he had clearly made one, perhaps for the first time, of Sir Hardress Waller. Clearly Waller had decided his return to Ireland in 1647 was to be a lasting one, since he had stayed on after Lisle had gone and pleaded for a reduced role in the Munster army. But for Inchiquin he had stood on his seniority too long, and was dismissed from the service. On his return to England, his voice joined the chorus of complaint.[65] But he was a more dangerous foe, for he retained not only a New Model regiment, but the confidence of that army, including that of the agents or 'agitators' elected by the regiments to represent their grievances. In early May nine officer-agitators and fourteen soldier-agitators wrote to Fairfax asking that the troops drawn off for Irish service indeed be duly ordered into companies and regiments, 'unfaithful' officers removed and trustworthy ones placed in charge, and that overall command of all forces destined for Ireland be given to Sir Hardress Waller.[66]

Inchiquin's survival, indeed his resurrection to favour, was partly a story of Parliament backing a winner. Fortuitously or not, the Commons delayed their investigation. Then, on 19 May, they heard Inchiquin's latest reports of the capture of Cappoquin and of Dungarvan. It was as useful a turn of events as Inchiquin could hope for, and though it promised nothing in terms of supplies, or even his long-sought commissioners, he at least got a letter of thanks, and a resolution that the Derby House Committee consider his propositions.[67] The

---

[63] HMC *Egmont MSS*, i, 391. By 22 April Inchiquin had taken to addressing Holles, Stapleton, Clotworthy and Davies as a bloc: HMC *Egmont MSS*, i, 392.

[64] *CJ*, v, 166; *Perfect Occurrences* 19, 7 May, E 387 (5), p. 146; *Kingdomes Weekly Intelligencer* 208, 4–11 May, E 386 (13), p. 522; *Moderate Intelligencer* 113, 6–13 May 1647, E 386 (20), p. 1067; Harrington, *Diary*, p. 51.

[65] HMC *Egmont MSS*, i, 392, 393–4, 395, 405–6.

[66] Woolrych, *Soldiers and statesmen*, pp. 67–8.

[67] *CJ*, v, 175, 176; McNeill (ed.), *Tanner letters*, pp. 240–2; Harrington, *Diary*, p. 52.

Inchiquin dispute reveals just how far the politics of Protestant Ireland could parallel the common disputes of post-war England. Charges of financial impropriety were routinely tossed about, often with good cause, and often focused upon accusations of being soft on past or present enemies, a tendency as liable to entice 'Independent' grandees as provincial 'moderates'.[68] The 'Presbyterians' had the resource of a partisan committee of accounts at Westminster to vindicate or condemn, and Inchiquin would look to Fenton Parsons, a committee member with long-standing Irish links.[69] Provincial disputes throughout an England now under Parliament's sway would invariably embrace accusations of employing malignants or countenancing sectarians, though the likes of the disputatious Colonel King of Lincolnshire could hammer both on the basis of faithfulness to the Covenant. Not that there were any neat patterns: religious Independents and those with royalist associations in the north-west of England could make common cause from a common antipathy to the Scots.[70] Inchiquin's struggle could be presented as a battle to repel the forces of centralized, factional power, and radical religious and political sentiments, and as such could resonate at Westminster, but it also encompassed those dilemmas of wartime compromise between dabbling with dubious associates and intractable realities, and upholding the integrity of 'the cause', which would likewise baffle those in power in the counties and towns of England.

Inchiquin's position was also related to the fragility of the alliance built up around Lisle. The Munster element centred on Broghill, and such established associates as Temple, remained resolute against the lord president,[71] but grumbling from within the New English community had started early. Though he accompanied Lisle's expedition, Valentia was known to be favourable to Inchiquin even in February. By May Perceval reported him as a supporter of the lord president, alongside captains Parsons and Meredith (author of *Ormond's Curtain drawn*); indeed the elder Parsons and the younger Annesley could probably be relied on too. If Sir William Parsons was detaching himself from the Lisle camp, he was also being touted as a suitable lord justice once more, by April–May 1647.[72] John

---

[68] John Morrill, *Revolt in the provinces: the people of England and the tragedies of war 1630–1648* (2nd edition, Harlow, 1999), pp. 158–9; John Adamson, 'The English nobility and the projected settlement of 1647', *Historical Journal* 30 (1987), 584.

[69] Jason Peacey, 'Politics, accounts and propaganda in the Long Parliament', in Kyle and Peacey (eds), *Parliament at work*, pp. 67–8, 75.

[70] Ashton, *Counter-revolution*, pp. 216–22, 241–5; Clive Holmes, 'Colonel King and Lincolnshire politics, 1642–1646', *Historical Journal* 16 (1973), 451–84; David Scott, 'The Barwis affair: political allegiance and the Scots during the British civil wars', *English Historical Review* 115 (2000), 843–63.

[71] Little, 'Irish "Independents" ', pp. 957–8.

[72] HMC *Egmont MSS*, i, 358, 382, 384, 398, 401, 402, 404, 406.

Davies, who had also declared for Inchiquin, lauded the Annesleys and Sir Robert King, and sought to cultivate Ormond's erstwhile envoys Lowther and Sir Paul Davies (vouched for, it will be recalled, by Parsons).[73] The New English were re-grouping, those who had never backed Lisle restoring links to those alienated or exasperated by recent events.[74] Sir Robert King 'did not like the recalling of my Lord Lisle, and I like as little the accusing of my Lord of Inchiquin, . . . and indeed he will deceive me much if he do not vigorously prosecute the war this summer.'[75]

The fall-out from the Lisle–Inchiquin dispute forced unwelcome choices upon Protestants of Ireland who had old ties of co-operation and association. Coote, who had pursued his usual energetic and destructive course of action in the north-west, had worried over 'that torrent that carrieth all to Munster . . .', as had John Davies.[76] By early April Coote warned against the possibility that his officers would be replaced or units under his command dissolved. His ties to those in question were too close to countenance this. 'If I have exceeded my commission let me suffer', he remarked, but 'if I have advanced the service, I hope those who have engaged with me and myself shall not receive so great a mark of the Parliament's disfavour as this would be'. His reasoning is so close to Inchiquin's as to raise the question of whether Lisle would not have stirred as much trouble in Connacht. After all, the western men had hardly a clean record regarding co-operation with Ormond, and Coote had made his own use of contribution.[77] Coote also pondered the fate of 'reliable' Catholics. In June he noted a request that he be allowed to formally employ the Costello brothers, Thomas and Dudley, who though 'of an old English extraction' had served in his campaigns. 'It is true they are Papists which is all can be said to their prejudice'. Other officers backed his request. No decision seems to have been taken at Derby House, and Perceval's response that 'I do not think the time fit for doing much, but I observe the Commissioners at Dublin and the President of Munster protect and defend such men' did not offer hopeful models.[78]

The commissioners sent to negotiate with Ormond had send ahead offers

---

[73] HMC *Egmont MSS*, i, 328, 337, 339, 366, 371, 379.

[74] See Little, 'Marquess of Ormond', pp. 84–5 for an alternative view of New English alignments.

[75] HMC *Egmont MSS*, i, 404.

[76] HMC *Egmont MSS*, i, 379–80.

[77] HMC *Egmont MSS*, i, 386–7. See T. C. Barnard, 'The Protestant interest, 1640–1660', in Ohlmeyer (ed.), *Ireland from independence to occupation*, p. 231 for the 'affinity' which the Cootes built up, mainly in the west of Ireland, 'thanks to prowess on the battlefield' of the Charles Cootes, elder and younger.

[78] HMC *Portland MSS*, i, 426–7, 427; HMC *Egmont MSS*, i, 435.

of Parliament's protection to all 'without distinction of Religion'.[79] By 7 June they were in Dublin bay with 2,000 soldiers, and more on the way.[80] Even Digby, at that point, thought surrender inevitable, and like Ormond showed more concern over future destinations.[81] The articles were sent to the lieutenant on 15 June and rapidly concluded, allowing him residence in Dublin castle until 28 July.[82] Ormond accepted the November terms with only three quibbles. The first, on the handing over of artillery and stores, he himself 'waived', while the third concerned security for his own money. Yet it was he who tightened the wording of the clause on protections, adding to the commissioners' statement that those who paid contribution would be protected the phrase 'and will continue payment of contribution', while cutting the words 'or will come under contribution' lest it allow 'the most bloody rebels' to avail of protection. The commissioners protested that Parliament had made them 'dispensers of mercy to all indifferently' but they would concur so as to remove any advantage to those 'we never intended to admit . . . to protection whose horrid murders and outrages rendered them as well incapable as unworthy thereof'.[83] Only hints exist of a back channel, even at this late stage, whereby Ormond still hoped to link his actions in Dublin with the wider resolution of the problems besetting the multiple monarchy, but to no avail.[84]

The realities of the new order in Dublin soon bit. As early as 9 June reports were circulating that some of the new troops were 'plundering the mass-houses and divers Papists houses, and under colour of them many a Protestant

---

[79] Carte MS 21, fo. 109. Ormond's messenger, Lieutenant Leigh, argued that links between the king and the army would lead to liberty of conscience even for the Irish, though with the loss of part of their estates, but seems to have rested his hopes for Ormond on the friendship of Holles and his associates: Carte MS 21, fo. 119 (18 May 1647). As for 'Independent' friendliness to Ormond, there is a hint in Stephen Smith's letter of 6 June 1647, which praises Sir Thomas Wharton and Salwey as especially helpful to Ormond, albeit in personal matters: Carte MS 21, fo. 302.

[80] Commissioners to Ormond, Carte MS 21, fo. 188.

[81] Digby to Ormond, 9 and 11 June 1647, Carte MS 21, fos 198–9, 206–7; Ormond to Digby, 11 June 1647, Carte MS 21, fo. 204.

[82] Commissioners to Ormond, 15 June 1647, Carte MS 21, fo. 216.

[83] *CSPI, 1633–47*, pp. 677–8, 678–80.

[84] On 1 June Ormond wrote to Sir Robert King stating that he had hoped by now to have offered a proposal to settle the present disturbances, but because of delays he was now sending this via one Slingsby; if King approved, he should sent it on: Carte MS 21, fos 173–4. An undated paper exists which Slingsby presented to the Derby House Committee (though the committee's records mention him only in connection with Ormond's hopes to carry a contingent to France); its terms are somewhat unclear but hinged on a proposal to receive Prince Charles in Dublin as a means to a general settlement. Neither the commissioners, nor Northumberland, whom Slingsby approached in London, offered any encouragement for him to pursue the initiative: Carte MS 21, fo. 365.

did suffer the loss of all he had'.[85] The commissioners held the power to purge the army and garrisons of papists, to proceed against non-contributing 'neutrals' as 'rebels', to execute laws against 'rebel Papists' and convict rebels by law, 'if possible', and to prepare laws for the good of the 'Protestant cause', the king and kingdom.[86] It was not a completely unrelenting approach, and indeed carried through the distinctions hammered out with Ormond. The new government, speaking to a situation of exactions by the soldiers and apprehension by the populace, condemned unauthorized free quarter or sale of goods by the troops, and promised protection for one year 'without any distinction of offence or religion', including any from beyond English quarters who would offer to pay contribution within the next twenty-eight days. This was 'to take away all apprehension from the people of this kingdom, that the Parliament (as hath been insinuated by desperate persons) intend the extirpation of the Irish nation', as well as to encourage husbandry and tillage.[87] Their stance was reiterated in the instructions issued by the new governor, Michael Jones. In his orders to the garrison at Trim (3 September), he allowed continued protection to any 'formerly . . . of the Irish party' who still sought to avail of it, in return for a composition and weekly payments, and even allowed protection to those who had formerly abandoned the same, albeit with payment of arrears.[88] Protection, as Ormond had long since noted, was a far cry from acceptance, let alone alliance, but was, in Irish conditions, an economic necessity if armies were to be sustained.

As well as the continued economic needs of the garrison, the scale of the commissioners' problems with their own forces is striking. On 6 July the commissioners reported a serious mutiny in Dublin, mostly among Kinaston's men, 'accustomed to like practizes in North Wales', which led to several deaths. They could hardly avoid further such with less than £30,000 for pay – they were voted £10,000. Otherwise they reported their reorganization of the existing army, reducing eleven old regiments to seven, and holding musters.[89] No wonder Annesley and King reacted badly to the news that they were expected to stay on until 1 September, though their original task had been accomplished by 28 July, following Ormond's delivery of the sword of state and his departure from Dublin. They went so far as to advise the sending of a deputy commander to assist Jones rather than replacement

[85] HMC *Egmont MSS*, i, 413.
[86] *CSPI, 1633–47*, p. 762. They were empowered to order the war by land and sea, and to ensure that military officers held rank on the basis of merit and were well affected to religion and the cause.
[87] *CSPI, 1633–47*, pp. 668–9; cf. HMC *Egmont MSS*, i, 437–8.
[88] HMC *Ormonde MSS*, old series, ii, 63–4.
[89] HMC *Portland MSS*, i, 429–30; HMC *Egmont MSS*, i, 425; HMC *Ormonde MSS*, old series, ii, 61–2.

commissioners, 'a name odious to the soldiers'.[90] The commission had its internal problems, Meredith acting at odds with the others to add to the problems of unruly troops.[91] Sir John Gifford was not the only Protestant officer to lose his command through the re-modelling, and he protested both the loss of 'the bread his sword (the only estate now left him) might purchase him' (or at least his arrears) and the disgrace his being cashiered would bring when 'neither his faith, honesty, or courage have suffered blemish'. Though the commissioners protested only the necessity of reductions, and the fact that the articles had not promised security of command, and though they offered command of a cavalry troop as compensation, Gifford was convinced that 'the malice of some false friend' (he thought Meredith) had put him out.[92]

Meanwhile, the early summer saw things moving Inchiquin's way. By late June the Commons had earmarked £10,000 for recruits, provisions and money for the province; by early July he obtained, on paper, his long-sought commission, with three MPs named for the province. When the commissioners proved unwilling to go, the alternative was to vest control of the funds back with the president and the provincial council, though this could give some room to Inchiquin's opponents on the council.[93] 'Presbyterian' ascendancy may have helped sustain the beleaguered lord president, but he also held a strong hand in the backing of his own troops.[94] A council of war on 23 June produced a 'Remonstrance' which set out their position since the departure of Lisle and which, in its printed version, claimed the signatures of thirty-three officers, among them seven colonels and nine lieutenant-colonels.[95] While avoiding any condemnatory language, and insisting 'we looked back not to what we were' before Lisle's departure, they implicitly backed the assessment previously made by Inchiquin by drawing attention to the depletion of resources during Lisle's time in the province, and noted how desertions, resulting from shortages, had reduced their 10,606 soldiers to 9,000 'sick, and whole'. Lacking resources for a major engagement, the troops were stationed on the outer edge of the area under their control. They asked that 'some person, or persons of quality and trust' be sent to audit all local accounts and thus prove their assertions, and to give a 'certainty' to an unsettled revenue. The neutral tone was breached

---

[90] McNeill (ed.), *Tanner letters*, pp. 255–6.

[91] HMC *Egmont MSS*, i, 432–3, 438.

[92] HMC *Egmont MSS*, i, 423–4.

[93] *CSPI, 1647–60*, p. 760; *CJ*, v, 224, 247, 255, 256, 260; *CSPI, 1633–47*, pp. 703, 705, 736, 756, 758, 761; *CSPD, addenda, 1625–49*, p. 710; HMC *Egmont MSS*, i, 416, 435, 436, 442.

[94] Despite his laments over the conduct of the newly arrived troops: HMC *Egmont MSS*, i, 419–20.

[95] *A Copy of a Remonstrance setting forth The sad condition of the Army under . . . INCHEQUINE . . .* (London, 1647) E399 (33), pp. 1–5.

only in that it was hoped that the audit would show 'that those that faithfully desire, and second their desires with endeavours, may not suffer in their reputation under the severe censure of being careless in their actions for the publique, or cold in their performances'.

The three agents dispatched, by early July, to England with the Remonstrance were all 'new' officers, Lieutenant-Colonel Peter Stubber, Major John Choppyne and Major Christopher Elsyng.[96] An impression of unity behind Inchiquin could be created, especially given that the publication of the Remonstrance (24 July) was undertaken by the agents to counter a malicious pamphlet published under the name of Lieutenant-Colonel Knight. Consisting of two letters (22 June and 4 July), this attack on Inchiquin's generalship accused him of wasting the opportunities provided by the men, money and supplies left by Lisle. As troops starved, Inchiquin was able to 'play at bowls on the Fast day, to sit up whole nights a Feasting, with Dancing and Fidling'. More was at issue than incompetence, as the author's attacks on command by 'the natural *Irish*' show.[97] Denying Knight's authorship, the agents claimed the 'materiall objections' raised against Inchiquin were 'false, injurious and unworthy credit', and that 'the honor and reputation of the Army in generall' was impugned.[98]

Across England and Wales, as across Ireland, armies and assorted bodies of soldiers were taking their fate into their hands, their frustration and anger congealing into protest or mutiny, or mutating into political activism. Attempts to recruit for Ireland from among the New Model Army, which, by May, stood 'on the very brink of a revolt that was to give the whole course of political events a new direction',[99] had proved disastrous. By mid-May the Derby House Committee had drawn the contingent for Ireland away from the rest of the army, and gathered them into four regiments, though the numbers fell far short of the anticipated 8,400 recruits. Instead, by the month's end, they were losing recruits back to the main body of the army, which had united, emitting the pro-Ireland officers, and faced Parliament as a body. Efforts in early June to heal the breach between army and Parliament included some notable concessions, but trust had clearly broken down. Accusations were levelled at the 'Presbyterian' leadership of attempting to

<hr />

[96] HMC *Egmont MSS*, i, 422. Other 'new' officers included Needham, Roe, Sterling, Crispe, Marshall, Pinchon, probably Patterson and possibly Knight, Ryves or Daniel.

[97] *A Letter from Lieutenant Colonel Knight* . . . (London, 1647) E 399 (23). Regarding his unnamed colonel, Knight mentioned that his 'Recruit is Disbanded' recently, which would seem to point to Sir Arthur Loftus, whose new regiment was presently disintegrating in England. Perceval was unsure whether Knight had written to Loftus, but it seems likely that this was who was intended to use the information: HMC *Egmont MSS*, i, 401.

[98] *Copy of a Remonstrance*, p. 6.

[99] Woolrych, *Britain in revolution*, p. 361.

use the soldiers destined for Ireland as part of a counter-force, drawing upon disbanded officers and men from provincial forces ('reformadoes') and upon Presbyterian interests in London. The charge, as regards the forces for Ireland, appears unproven, and was certainly short-lived: by 20 June all such forces had been ordered to their embarkation zones.[100] Some continuity prevailed regarding Ireland over the turbulent summer of 1647, as the army levelled impeachment charges against eleven leading 'Presbyterian' MPs, the Houses were assaulted by a pro-Presbyterian London mob – leading numerous parliamentarians to seek succour with the army – and the army itself marched upon London to impose his demands in August. Though the army's supporters insisted that 'deserters' enlisted for Irish service be disbanded, moves were made to ensure that other troops gathering for Irish service were dispatched,[101] further efforts were made to secure promised funds for Ireland, including Ormond's pay-off,[102] and by August negotiations had re-opened on the prospects of sending New Model forces to the Irish front.[103]

Yet at another level the army's political campaign set the seal on the integration of Protestant Ireland into the internal political struggles of the Long Parliament, as well as stymieing the 'Presbyterian' scheme for English peace, Irish war and factional victory. The minor, but symptomatic, case of Sir Philip Perceval is telling. From commissary at Dublin, and an implicit supporter of the cessation on grounds of necessity, Perceval had tracked a course which had taken him through disillusionment in Oxford to a 'recruiter' seat in the Commons, for Newport in Cornwall, in May 1647.[104] His earlier actions now came back to haunt him: not merely his assent to the cessation, but allegations that he had dispatched information to Oxford to engineer the truce, that he advised the sending of soldiers to England, that he was a 'special confidante' of Ormond. As always, private vendettas had their part to play, in this case Perceval's old battles with Temple over control

[100] Most suspicion must attach to an order to gather the forces at Reading 'for conveniency of paying them' issued on 6 June, though this did not apply to O'Connolly's ex-New Model soldiers, nor to those drawn from non-New Model regiments: *CSPI 1647–60*, pp. 754, 755, 756; see *CJ*, v, 203 for the 8 June vote to send the regiments on to Worcester; and see Ashton, *Counter-revolution*, pp. 380–1.

[101] Notably those drawn from the Northern Association by Colonel John Ponsonby, a veteran of Drogheda: *CJ*, v, 248–9, 263; Gentles, *New Model Army*, p. 231; C. H. Firth and Godfrey Davies, *The regimental history of Cromwell's army* (2 vols, Oxford, 1940), ii, 604.

[102] *CJ*, v, 219, 224, 229, 235, 246, 250, 270, 281, 291; *CSPI, 1647–60*, pp. 758–60, 765.

[103] *CJ*, v, 254, 268, 281, 287, 298.

[104] HMC *Egmont MSS*, i, 430. See David Underdown, 'Party management in the recruiter elections, 1645–48', *English Historical Review* 83 (1968), 258–64 for a discussion of claims of electoral manipulation, in the 'Presbyterian' interest, in Wales (including Annesley's seat) and Cornwall (including Perceval's); Underdown finds it likely that many of the seats were won by normal patronage methods.

of profit-making bakeries in wartorn Dublin. In Perceval's account of events, it was Temple who prompted the MP laying the charge, Hoyle, who in turn admitted he did not even know Perceval's full name. Lisle and his brother Algernon Sidney soon joined in the attack, though Perceval strove to retain Waller's good opinion. Though Clotworthy's counter-charge of Temple's 'applying himself to the King' went nowhere, after a three-hour debate Perceval was not suspended but referred to an investigative committee.[105]

There seems little doubt the Perceval had been caught up in a campaign against 'unreliable' MPs pursued by the army and its friends and directed at securing the purgation not only of their eleven most wanted foes, but of up to thirty other MPs, largely on the basis of accusations of past dabbling with the king's party.[106] The detailed accusations against the eleven appeared on 9 July.[107] Ireland featured in more than just the alleged misuse of the New Model recruits. Clotworthy (one of 'the eleven') would have been included on the basis of his performance as a commissioner to the army in the spring of 1647 regardless of his Irish activities. In the event, peculation charges against him were re-hashed, with John Davies tagged on. It was claimed that Clotworthy, alone of the 1646 commissioners to Dublin, had 'held secret intelligence' with Ormond and Digby, well after the negotiation expired. He had indeed maintained contacts, though whether this fell outside the generally subscribed goal of securing Dublin for Parliament is another matter, and the accusation falls in with the broad attack on Holles's associates as soft on malignants.[108] The accusation of fraud was of course a smear uniformly administered to foes, and the specific charges levied at Clotworthy (as opposed to Davies) failed to add any significant examples of wrong-doing to the small, uncertain, cases bandied about in 1643–44.[109] By now Clotworthy could call on the considerable energy and not inconsiderable abilities of William Prynne, chairman of Parliament's accounts committee,

---

[105] BL Additional MS 31, 116, fo. 311a; Harrington, *Diary*, p. 51, 54; HMC *Egmont MSS*, i, 416, 417, 423, 425, 426–7, 430–1, 432; *CJ*, v, 195, 203, 233, 238, 245.

[106] David Underdown, *Pride's Purge: politics in the puritan revolution* (Oxford, 1971), pp. 81–2.

[107] *A particular charge of impeachment in the name of Sir Thomas Fairfax and the army under his command* (London, 1647) E397 (17). The first statement was delivered to parliamentary commissioners on 14 June: *A charge delivered in the name of Sir Thomas Fairfax and his army . . .* (London, 1647) E393 (5). See also Gentles, *New Model Army*, pp. 176–7.

[108] Clotworthy had made contact with Ormond, but the surviving letter shows no covert purpose. Davies had made contact with Eustace (as did Clotworthy) but professed himself dissatisfied. Perceval's letter to Lady Ormond recommended not only Clotworthy, but also Wharton and King: HMC *Egmont MSS*, i, 325, 336. Clotworthy was formally cleared by the Commons in 1648.

[109] The inclusion of John Davies is telling, not only because he may well have had more to answer for, but because he had lately been commissary to Lisle.

legal counsel for the accused MPs and pamphleteer in their interest to defend his reputation for probity. Prynne went a step further and launched counter-charges against Lisle and Waller.[110]

The army's impeachment charges even re-told the Munster imbroglio, alleging that the 'Presbyterian' leaders had prompted Lisle's recall and blocked the efforts of Broghill and Loftus to impeach Inchiquin 'for betraying the Parliaments Army to the enemy (as formerly he had done)'. Much was made of Inchiquin's claim that orders from London meant that 'no man that favoured the Independents . . . should have any trust or warrant therein' and of the expulsion of Sir Hardress Waller.[111] Waller thus became the link-man in the harnessing of Irish charges to the attack. Perceval, Inchiquin, Clotworthy and Davies had all been caught between the converging scissorblades of army animosity and desire to purge its foes, in the process becoming tarnished with all possible evidence of malignancy, and the importation of factionalism from Protestant Ireland. Both strategies were designed to exclude enemies from positions of control,[112] and in so doing could appeal to the more unremitting side of the parliamentarian sensibility, an urge to punish the guilty, even the guilty by association, which was less a product of partisan alignment than a sentiment which faction leaders could manipulate. June to October 1647 saw a comprehensive campaign for the exclusion of ex-royalists from Parliament, the franchise and local office.[113]

All the while Munster was edging towards its own army revolt. By 25 August the Munster officers had produced another 'Humble Remonstrance'.[114] On that date Inchiquin wrote to Fairfax and to Lenthall claiming that the Remonstrance was sparked by 'distractions and tumults' in and about London, and concerns among his officers for their arrears and the retention of their commands. He alleged that the 'happy and clear composure of all differences' in England had made him stay the document though, to avoid discontents, he had offered to voice his officers' worries over possible loss of their commands with 'the double disadvantage of dishonour and of not providing for their future subsistence by the settlement of any course for the payment of their arrears'. He insisted that his forces

---

[110] Peacey, 'Politics, accounts and propaganda' pp. 74–6; see [William Prynne], *The hypocrites unmasking* (London, 1647), pp. 7–8 for attacks on Waller and Lisle. [William Prynne], *A brief iustification of the XI accused members* (London, 1647) E398 (3), p. 6 insisted that one of Lisle's 'friends in the House hath really held correspondency with the Lord ORMOND'. See also [William Prynne], *A full vindication and answer of the XI accused members* (London, 1647) E398 (17), pp. 20–6.

[111] *A particular charge*, pp. 19–20.

[112] Kishlansky, *Rise of the New Model Army*, pp. 252–4.

[113] Ashton, *Counter-revolution*, pp. 216–17.

[114] HMC *Egmont MSS*, i, 456.

would stand for 'the State's interest' until Parliament's pleasure was clearly known, repudiated any claim that his intention was to 'stand upon my own terms and capitulate for my conditions of security', and neatly sought to align his army with the New Model, both being instruments of providence, both deserving of their arrears.[115]

The whole performance was a highly skilled, if hardly candid, attempt to extricate his army from a dangerously exposed position, reminiscent of Inchiquin's tortuous defence of the Covenant in 1644. It was left unclear exactly which 'tumults' the Munster army were condemning, though other commentators were less guarded. What was significant was the progression of grievances. Non-payment of arrears was a grievance common to all armies, and a desire to avoid being re-modelled quite natural for serving officers; these alone could ignite disturbances, even on an organized scale. But all too rapidly practical concerns could cede priority to talk of the vindication of army honour and integrity, particularly when faced with what was regarded as the prospect of unfair dismissal. With the New Model the quest for self-justification rapidly took shape, both in calling for public disavowal by Parliament of its attacks on them, and the insistence on indemnity arrangements.[116] But Munster, too, saw a similar progression.[117] The next or final step, 'politicization', in the sense of a pledging of support for a political, constitutional or religious platform, was of course most apparent among the New Model, though the wider aspirations, sincere or otherwise, of at least some of those caught up in the 'counter-revolutionary' moment in summertime London, drawing upon disbanded 'reformadoes' from English regional forces, should not be forgotten. One Munster observer alluded to the 'Presbyterian' generals co-opted in London when he claimed that all but a handful of the Munster officers stood by a set of demands 'which is most in substance with that of Massey's and Poyntz's'.[118]

Perhaps any attempt at a Presbyterian counter-revolt in southern Ireland was too much the brainchild of Major-General Sterling and Lieutenant-Colonel Thomas Marshall. Not only did they circulate the Remonstrance to leading Scots figures in and beyond Ireland, but they accompanied it with letters overtly condemning Fairfax's army and calling for a defence of

[115] HMC *Egmont MSS*, i, 456–8, 468–60. Earlier in August Inchiquin, already concerned at the army's adoption of censures on his conduct, purported to believe his days in command numbered, but not to mind this if only he could resign with suitable support thereafter for himself and family. Indeed he appears to have wanted Perceval and Jephson to devise suitable resignation terms: HMC *Egmont MSS*, i, 447–8, 452, 454–5.

[116] Kishlansky, *Rise of the New Model Army*, pp. 198–200; Morrill, *English revolution*, pp. 310–17.

[117] Cf. events in Wales, in 1647–48, Ashton, *Counter-revolution*, pp. 347–8, 416–22.

[118] HMC *Egmont MSS*, i, 461; Woolrych, *Soldiers and statesmen*, pp. 33–4; Ashton, *Counter-revolution*, pp. 390–6.

Presbyterianism.[119] The idea was not totally mistaken, for the force of popular Presbyterianism was to be harnessed in Ulster in 1648–49, but Sterling overshot his mark in 1647 in claiming that the Munster officers 'will never be subservient to them [the Independents], but will withdraw hence on the best terms they may and spend their lives and what is dearest to them in defending the Covenant'. More significant was his admission that 'they waive the inserting of any particular expressions against that faction, until they are assured what course will be taken for their future support or the satisfaction of their desires specified in the Remonstrance'.[120]

Inchiquin's friends in London suggested two courses of action – arrest Sterling and Marshall and win favour by military success.[121] The prescription was followed, Perceval's advice to show ruthlessness in destruction, to let his army 'do all they can with fire and sword, and leave off this way of capitulating', to 'burn and waste the enemies countries, . . . which is the surest way to gain your honour and to satisfy the Parliament of your clear intentions' being most notoriously demonstrated in Inchiquin's sack of Cashel.[122] Perhaps Inchiquin was honest in disclaiming an originating role for the Remonstrance and in stating that the officers willingly let it drop in view of the changes at Westminster, though it would not be beyond belief that he might even have encouraged Sterling to sound out his countrymen.[123] By 30 November a draft amnesty had appeared for all involved in the Remonstrance, now that it had been withdrawn and obedience rendered, though not for Sterling or those 'who have acted beyond the said general Engagement'.[124]

Inchiquin had long since disavowed 'being religious'. At best, at this stage of his peculiar spiritual odyssey he could be said to combine a heated anti-Catholicism with a solid Erastian profession. In August he noted that 'I

[119] HMC *Portland MSS*, i, 433–5; McNeill (ed.), *Tanner letters*, pp. 259–65. In all thirteen letters were sent, but probably very few arrived, for they were intercepted by Michael Jones at Dublin, probably with the assistance of Wemyss, one of those addressed.

[120] McNeill (ed.), *Tanner letters*, p. 260 (Sterling to Leven).

[121] Jephson and Perceval (23 September 1647) said that the disowning of the Remonstrance had succeeded until the arrival of the Sterling letters. If action was not taken it would be looked upon as a declaration of war by the Munster army: HMC *Egmont MSS*, i, 467–8.

[122] HMC *Egmont MSS*, i, 462, 466, 468, 472; McNeill (ed.), *Tanner letters*, pp. 265–7; J. A. Murphy, 'The sack of Cashel, 1647', *Journal of the Cork Historical and Archaeological Society* 70 (1965), 55–62.

[123] In October the province's officers asked Perceval to act in their defence. Inchiquin said that all they wanted was to be assured they were not odious to the Parliament and army, but would obey while employed and, if ousted, would seek only their arrears: HMC *Egmont MSS*, i, 470–1, 475.

[124] The accused claimed that all their letters were dispatched owing to the council of war's authorizing that to Leven. By 29 October Sterling and Marshall had been put aboard parliamentary ships bound for England: *CSPI, 1647–60*, pp. 765, 769; McNeill (ed.), *Tanner letters*, pp. 278–9; HMC *Egmont MSS*, i, 480, 481.

wished for a public form of [church] government, which I always thought
the Parliament competent judges to establish or alter as they see convenient',
a sentiment which chimed with the views of many English 'Presbyterians',
though hardly with those of Waller and his fellow New Model officers. There
are hints that Inchiquin had sought to keep in step with Parliament's earlier
pronouncements.[125] Dublin, by contrast, had become something of an
Anglican redoubt by the winter of 1646–47, as not a few bishops and other
eminences of the Church of Ireland, a number of them recently fled to
England, sought the shelter of the Irish capital, where the 'full and free
exercise of the true reformed Religion according to the Liturgy and Canons
so many years received in the Church' had been preserved.[126] On 24 June
1647 the parliamentary commissioners issued a proclamation forbidding the
use of the Book of Common Prayer and substituting the Westminster
Assembly's Directory of Worship.[127] Earlier negotiations had seen them urge
a minimalist form of worship, of prayer, psalms, Scripture and preaching,
but this was countered with a defence of the liturgy by resident clergy, largely
aimed at shielding established forms from charges of 'popery'.[128] The
proclamation was in turn met with a full response on 9 July, pointing out
that the order had 'debarred' the signatories from their churches. Only briefly
alluding to the intrinsic merits of the Prayer Book, the document built its
case on legal grounds, from the royal supremacy and Elizabethan legislation
to the role of ecclesiastical and civil authorities in ecclesiastical causes and
the status of the Church of Ireland as 'a free national Church independent of
Convocation of any other'.[129] On 21 July it was reported that the
commissioners 'have discontented the clergy, and the best officers . . . they
cashiered, which makes them jealous of their own shadows, inasmuch that
I think all our harvest will be spoiled, and then we shall want both horse and
man's meat this winter, if we live so long'.[130]

By October the same man was hoping for Michael Jones's long stay at the
helm in Dublin, as governor.[131] Parliament's authority, even in the
controversial and conscientious matter of religious change, could, it seems,

---

[125] HMC *Egmont MSS*, i, 452; Armstrong, 'Protestant churchmen'. See John A. Murphy,
'Inchiquin's change of religion', *Journal of the Cork Historical and Archaeological Society* 72
(1967), pp. 59–67 for his subsequent conversion to Catholicism.

[126] Bishops' remonstrance to Ormond, August 1646, Rushworth, *Historical collections*, vi, 414.

[127] McNeill (ed.), *Tanner letters*, p. 245.

[128] McNeill (ed.), *Tanner letters*, pp. 245–6, 246–7.

[129] McNeill (ed.), *Tanner letters*, pp. 247–50; Savage (7 July 1647) commented that the clergy
had indeed been silenced by the order and were ready to depart from the city. 'Those that were
never esteemed for any parts they had are preferred. This the Protestants here do much take to
heart': HMC *Egmont MSS*, i, 425.

[130] HMC *Egmont MSS*, i, 434.

[131] HMC *Egmont MSS*, i, 479.

be accepted if bound up with what counted most, success in arms against the Catholic enemy. Clotworthy's old design of an 'English' commander in the north was fulfilled that summer, though in two persons not one, with Monck named as regional commander in east Ulster, Coote in the west.[132] Both men established some sort of *modus vivendi* with the Scots-dominated presbytery in the province. The establishment had gone ahead of four regional armies in Ireland under commanders of Parliament's choice. If it was the fulfilment of anyone's plan, then it was a legacy of the 'Presbyterian' programme from the spring of 1647 and, with the exception of Inchiquin, it provided commanders Fairfax-like in their freedom from party involvement. It also provided four soldiers who could prove their worth in the field. Since the summer Inchiquin had touted the gains to be made from encouraging confederate divisions and defections. Alert to the threat to his position were he to dabble in such dealings, he had hoped this would be a task for the abortive parliamentary commission to Munster.[133] Instead the autumn saw precious little dallying with victory by stealth and a smashing victory over the Munster confederate army at Knocknanuss in November. It was preceded by, and bettered only by, Jones's destruction of the Leinster confederates at Dungan's Hill in August, possibly the greatest blood-letting of the entire war period.[134] By the latter end of 1647 the Protestants of Ireland had got the war most of them had long wanted.

In August 1647 English political life was shaken to its foundations as first the London mob, then the parliamentary army, threatened and overawed the latterly victorious Parliament of England. The tremors would be felt in Scotland and in Ireland months ahead. For the moment, as Parliament's cause seemed set to implode, events in Ireland had taken on a false clarity. The ground appeared to be being cleared for a straight fight between the English Parliament and the Catholic cause in Ireland. Colonel John Barry, Ormond's long-standing agent, wrote that he was resolved to abandon Ireland as 'equally averse to the Covenant as to the oath of association at Kilkenny', yet lamented that 'if I carry myself never so loyal to the King or so affectionate to the English interest, I must not hope to enjoy a foot of it, being a Papist, until the charge of the war and the undertakers be first satisfied'.[135] Protestant Ireland was bound into the political structures constructed by Parliament

---

[132] They were voted £7,000 and £8,000 respectively, while Leinster was to have £9,850: *CSPI, 1647–60*, pp. 758–9, 762; *CSPD, addenda, 1625–49*, p. 711.

[133] HMC *Egmont MSS*, i, 406, 413–14, 419, 422. See also Ó hAnnracháin, *Catholic Reformation*, pp. 185–9.

[134] See Lenihan, *Confederate Catholics at war*, pp. 209–12, 220 for the mass killing of the defeated confederate army after the battle.

[135] HMC *Egmont MSS*, i, 417.

and to the squabbles flowing into and out from Westminster; it also showed signs of emulating the political developments fermenting in the English provinces. Inchiquin's experiences in Munster fit both patterns, for the Lisle incident would be caught up into the highest of politics as conducted in the Houses and the army councils, while Inchiquin's command was set along a path which would see it stage its own revolt of a province. It was not the inevitable outcome for Munster nor the only option for Ireland. Dublin had permutated from Anglican-royalist hold to lynch-pin of the English interest in Ireland. Ormond's surrender was a declaration of the ultimate loyalties of the Protestant royalist, for the crown of England was deemed safer in the hands of the English than of those Irish who could, recidivist-like, turn back to rebellion, 'foreign' allegiance and 'foreign' religion. Ulster had been kept on board by the cultivation of the locally powerful though not at the expense of the broader religious and political goals of Parliament. Those who felt the squeeze were the officers and soldiers of the Scottish army in the province, a not altogether spent force, if a deflated one. Across the island, Protestant individuals and communities had accepted, with however much strain to conscience, the claim of the Parliament of England to be the upholder of the crown of England and the Protestant faith in Ireland and, implicitly, of their own lives and whatever liberties or properties they might aspire to enjoy. That claim could only be made good, or even plausible, in war. Protestant Ireland remained a war society, its structures as much as its prevailing ideologies, even its principal internal conflicts, moulded by the enduring sense of threat, peril or liberation by victory. Peace by agreement was hard to sell in such a society.

9

Conclusion: the Protestants of Ireland and the British crisis

On 15 August 1647 Owen Roe O'Neill wrote to the marquis of Clanricard, pressing him once again to side openly with the confederate cause, for 'your own great experience and wisdom will tell you, that there are left in Ireland but two parties, the one the malignant party of the Parliament that would destroy your religion, king and nation, and the other your own countrymen, kindred, alliance and dependents that fight for all three'.[1] He was not alone in depicting such a show-down, though it was not to be. In history there are no endings, only more beginnings. Even as Parliament appeared to have geared itself to decisive intervention in Ireland, and Protestants there to have rallied to its banner, Parliament itself began the downward spiral into confusion, division and conflict. The years 1647–49 have been dubbed 'the war of the engagement',[2] for they saw the pursuit of another round in the seemingly interminable conflicts of the three kingdoms, years which would see internal convulsions within each of the 'revolutionary' regimes centred on London, Kilkenny and Edinburgh with detached components re-forming in alternative allegiances and alignments. Protestant Ireland was hardly immune, but it would be too much to reckon that the ensuing years simply saw the hard-won allegiance to Parliament leach away until, by 1649, Westminster could count only on the isolated outposts of Dublin and Londonderry.

Inchiquin did apparently vindicate his foes and befuddle his friends in declaring for the king in April 1648, purging his army, and initialling a truce with the confederates. With the return of the king's man, Ormond, in September, the Protestant Munster enclave became his obvious base of operations from which to construct a royalist coalition built on a new treaty with the confederates, this one subsuming the confederate regime into one presided over by the lord lieutenant. Yet the course pursued by Inchiquin's army bore similarities to the provincial revolts among some of Parliament's

---

[1] *Letter-book*, p. 470.
[2] Scott, *Politics and war*, pp. 161–2.

regional forces, even elements of its fleet, in England and Wales. There was
the same combination of frustration at inadequate support and anger at the
failure to match with the king, indeed at his marginalization after the 'vote
of no addresses' in January 1648, declaring an end to overtures to or from
the monarch.[3] Inchiquin's army, even in its revolt from Parliament, bore the
marks of its parliamentary alignment. Officers who refused to follow
Inchiquin alleged that he justified his actions

> in order to the National Covenant, and to that particular branch thereof,
> which concerns the re-investing his Majesty in his Thron: he had with the
> advice of his officers taken a resolution to oppose the present pretended
> Parliament in *England*; who were forced by an Independent faction . . . he
> had correspondency with the King, with the *Scots*, and generally all the
> Presbyterian party that were agreed with the King: who resolved to
> endeavour to their utmost the re-inthroning the King, and restoring a free
> Parliament.[4]

Inchiquin's truce with the confederates in May 1648 caused ructions in
Kilkenny, precipitating the sequence of events whereby Rinuccini
excommunicated the adherents of the truce and 'a confederate civil war . . .
flared up . . . during the summer and autumn.' Yet the terms of the deal were
hardly more ominous than the ceasefires set in train by such staunch
parliamentmen as Jones, Coote and Monck, indeed seemingly less so by
being concluded not with the arch-rebel Owen Roe O'Neill with whom they
dealt, but with the softer 'peace party' of Muskerry, Taaffe and their like.[5]
From the moment when Ormond began the process of moving from truce to
treaty, rumblings of discontent were heard from within Protestant Munster.[6]
Inchiquin might be able to deploy his forces as part of Ormond's royalist
coalition but the hostility to combat with other English and Protestants was
strong. Behind his back his garrisons moved to conclude with Cromwell in
the autumn of 1649.[7]

---

[3] Ashton, *Counter-revolution*, chapter 11.

[4] *Papers presented to the Parliament, against the Lord Inchequin* . . . (London, 1648) E435
(33), pp. 3–4.

[5] Ó hAnnracháin, *Catholic Reformation*, pp. 200 (quoted), 201–2, which notes that
Rinuccini's objections were not directed at 'the merits of the truce itself' but at the truce as a
means to bring back a settlement based on the Ormond treaty.

[6] On his arrival, Ormond announced his intentions as being 'the settlement of the Protestant
religion according to the example of the best reformed churches . . . to defend the King in his
Prerogatives . . . to maintain the Priviledges and Freedome of Parliament' and to oppose
'those Rebells of this Kingdome who shall refuse their Obedience to his Majestie' as well as the
'Independent-Party': *A declaration of the Lord Lieutenant* . . . (Cork, 1648).

[7] Murphy, 'Politics of the Munster Protestants', pp. 16–19; Ó Siochrú, *Confederate
Ireland*, pp. 192–4.

A second story, the revolt of Ulster, has received less consideration, but is much more important in the long run. The 'national' and religious divisions within the Protestant zones of that province have been noted several times above. But so long as Westminster and Edinburgh could remain on amicable terms such tensions could be kept under control. The split came in two stages. The engagement concluded in December 1647 between some in Scotland and the king rent the Covenanting regime, and both sides appealed to their fellows in Ulster, the engagers winning the support of the bulk of the Scottish army in the province, or what was left of it, as well as of some of the Scots grandees. The collapse of the engagement was not the end of the story, for another turn of the screw set the triumphant 'kirk party' at odds with the now regicidal English regime by 1649. Both Scottish camps understood themselves in three-kingdom terms, and some in Ulster again heeded the call, banding together not as part of Ormond's new alliance but yet apart from the nascent English republic, as a Covenanted people. They would not so easily fall into line behind the conquering Cromwell. Instead the seeds of the Presbyterian revolution of the 1640s, blossoming in 1649, would turn rank in the 1650s as Scottish Ulster proved as indigestible to the Commonwealth as its motherland.[8]

A third story can be told, a quiet one, yet one redolent with future implications. The shallow commitment of Inchiquin royalism and the unsustainable 'fortress Ulster' of a Covenanted people-in-arms needs to be set alongside the retention of support by an ever more revolutionary English regime of the hub of Protestant Ireland, Dublin, and an array of leading figures from the English of Ireland in the years ahead. If, for many in England, the prospect of a further Scottish invasion over-powered any lingering disdain for the Westminster regime,[9] so in Ireland the old prospect of Catholic power, let alone the new one of a Scots-like mini-state in the north-east, kept many on side with Parliament despite their qualms. If the new republican regime was disinclined to look to those who were now the Old Protestants of Ireland for assistance, this was hardly their fault. Their climb back to prominence, then dominance, in Ireland is a central element of the island's story during the 1650s and 1660s.[10]

The reign of Charles I was a time of the shaking of the kingdoms. Sir John Clotworthy looked set to be one of its victims. The 'purge' of Parliament by the army in December 1648 saw him cast out the Commons and cast into 'Hell,' the insalubrious Westminster alehouse reserved for the army's least

---

[8] Stevenson, *Scottish Covenanters*, chapter 6; Armstrong, 'Viscount Ards and the presbytery'.
[9] Scott, *Politics and war*, pp. 193–5.
[10] Barnard, 'Planters and policies', pp. 31–69.

favoured foes. Prolonged detention would follow. Yet Sir John clambered out of the pit, if slowly. In little more than a decade he had secured for himself more than 11,000 additional acres of Co. Antrim, a guiding share in Ireland's transition back to monarchy in 1660 and, in due course, a viscountcy. He had not shed his commitment to the cause of godly reform, though he would indulge it with some discretion.[11] His long climb back to relative power mirrored the re-emergence of the community from which he sprang, the Old Protestants of Ireland, sidelined by the revolutionary English republic of the early 1650s, but the 'chief beneficiaries of Cromwellian rule'[12] in Ireland and of the Restoration settlement which elsewhere overturned it.

The 1640s bequeathed divergent legacies to each of the Stuart kingdoms, the products not only of their internal histories but of the interaction between them. For a decade deluged in conflict, it remains a matter of debate quite what manner of wars the participants believed themselves to be engaged in. '[T]he English experience in the Wars of the Three Kingdoms was an experience of civil war' first and foremost, it has been suggested, in that 'the English found themselves fighting each other over the nature of the English polity'.[13] Royalists and parliamentarians presented themselves as, and believed themselves to be, the true guardians of the political soul of the kingdom of England, but both were impelled to adopt more than merely English perspectives and commitments. They would have to grapple with the mundane complexities of multiple monarchy, but that very process fed back into the formation of conflicting English political creeds. 'Constitutional royalists' were characterized by a 'commitment to the English constitution, the English church and the rule of English law' and duly set on edge at the prospect of Scottish involvement in their native kingdom.[14] This was a political culture which could be transplanted to Ireland, where a similar fusion of English laws, church and parliamentary system could be upheld, at once in defence of the autonomy of the third kingdom and as an assertion of the Englishness of the kingdom of Ireland.

Yet Charles I knew full well the gains, if not always the perils, of being more than a king of England. Wartime Oxford buzzed with Scots and Irish, scheming alongside English in the king's, and their own, interest. If the king and his English supporters were to breach the uncritical acceptance of Parliament's interpretation of the Irish war as a singularly abhorrent rebellion to be relentlessly suppressed, they needed more than the tactical devices of

---

[11] Underdown, *Pride's Purge*, pp. 147–8, 195; Aidan Clarke, *Prelude to Restoration in Ireland: the end of the Commonwealth, 1659–1660* (Cambridge, 1999), p. 170 and *passim*.

[12] Barnard, 'Planters and policies', p. 34.

[13] J. G. A. Pocock, 'The Atlantic archipelago and the war of the three kingdoms', in Bradshaw and Morrill (eds), *The British problem*, pp. 184–5.

[14] Smith, *Constitutional royalism*, p. 67.

blaming Parliament for the failed war policy and alleging necessity for the promotion of truces and treaties. Instead they needed to relativize such awkward matters as rebellion, religion and nation against the over-riding importance of loyalty to the common monarch, a process which would give shape to royalism. The need to equate rebellion, wherever it might be found, could reach the heights of denouncing the English defection as 'a rebellion farre greater and more odious than either *Popish, Irish*, or any *Sect* or *Nation* of the world hath hitherto produced'.[15] The Scots could be depicted as an equal, or greater, 'foreign' threat to the integrity of the laws, liberty and faith, even the civility, of the English than Ireland, sponsors of an 'unjust Invasion' which 'all true *English* men must interpret as a Designe of Conquest'.[16]

Royalist propaganda strove to give form to these assumptions. The king could employ Catholic troops, from any of his kingdoms, since he 'looks not upon them as Papists, but as His Subjects, not upon their Religion, but their Allegiance'.[17] Ireland was not beyond mercy. 'Must the King of *England* receive all Petitions, and the King of *Ireland* refuse all?'[18] 'God forbid but the King of *Ireland* should receive His Subjects petitions, as well as the King of *Scotland*'.[19] There must be limits lest Parliament preside over 'eternal Warre', undertake the 'extirpating, at least of enslaving a whole ancient Nation who were planted there by the hand of providence from the beginning', or reckon 'the way to People *Ireland* with Protestants, is to cut the throats of the Papists'.[20] Ireland was an arena in which the king's sovereignty must be defended, his right to act by peace or by war, for 'he can no more give us away, and exclude us from His Protection, . . . then we can put off our subjection, & say He shall be Our King no longer'.[21] Ireland was more than a reservoir of possible troops for the English war. For all that Charles was prepared to let it fall to salvage his English kingdom, Ireland could fit into, indeed model, the kind of political settlement which would prove more acceptable than those generally on offer in England and Scotland. The 1646

---

[15] Griffith Williams, *The discovery of mysteries: or, plots and practices of a prevalent faction in the present parliament* (1643), p. 2.

[16] *A letter from the lords at Oxford . . . to the lords of the privy-councell . . . of Scotland* (Oxford, 1643 [1644]), p. 3.

[17] [James Howell], *Mercurius Hibernicus, or a discourse of the late insurrection in Ireland* (Bristol, 1644), p. 12.

[18] *A letter from a Protestant in Ireland . . . upon occasion of the treaty in that kingdom* (1643), p. 7. George Thomason considered this 'letter' to be 'pretended' as sent from Dublin 'but made at Oxon and printed at London'. The tone of the argument presented, including the denunciation of Scottish intervention in England, bears him out.

[19] [Howell], *Mercurius Hibernicus*, p. 9.

[20] *Letter from a Protestant*, pp. 3, 6; [Howell], *Mercurius Hibernicus*, p. 9.

[21] *Letter from a Protestant*, p. 6.

Ormond peace did not overthrow an established church, replete with bishops and royal supremacy, even if it did allow room for others outside its bounds; it supplemented royal office-holders and armies with the services of recusant candidates and ex-rebel forces rather than demanding the ceding of royal control over armies and government posts; it pardoned those who repented and exonerated the king's friends. If it failed to secure peace in Ireland, it represented, from a royalist perspective, an acceptable means whereby royal concessions could be meshed with 'rebel' demands.

Parliament, even more than the king, needed to burnish its national credentials. It dug deep into an 'almost mystical' identification with 'the nation itself' and proclaimed 'traditional roles as the guardian of English "liberties" and the upholder of the Protestant religion' to promote the identification of parliamentarianism and 'patriotism'.[22] For Parliament, participation in the Solemn League and Covenant was more than a temporary dalliance with Scottish 'federal' or 'confederal' schemes; it was a lifting of the cause on to the higher plane of international Reformation or, more mundanely, a revamped version of the age-old war on popery. Ireland had long seemed an inlet through which the European wars of religion threatened to seep into the other Stuart kingdoms. The breadth and intensity of connections between Catholic, and specifically confederate, Ireland and Catholic continental Europe which have been uncovered have expanded the horizons of historians, but should make the fears of English parliamentarians seem rather less than paranoid. While the 'avowed purpose' of the Rinuccini nunciature was 'the complete restoration of the damaged structures of the Irish church, beyond that again existed the glittering prospect that a regenerated Ireland might serve as a springboard for an even greater confessional advance, namely the recapture of England for the Catholic fold'.[23] Ireland kept anti-popery bubbling away as part of the parliamentarian brew. Perhaps, even, the rising enabled the Westminster leadership 'to connect their reforming agenda with popular anti-Catholicism, . . . creating a union of interests between the centre and the localities'.[24] War in Ireland meant more than deflecting the popish menace from English shores; it meant upholding the rights of the crown of England. Ireland epitomized the notion that Charles's real crime was less tyranny than a failure to exercise his obligation to defend his people, his kingdom and his crown.[25] Even some

---

[22] Mark Stoyle, 'English "nationalism", Celtic particularism, and the English civil war', *Historical Journal* 43 (2000), 1,116–17.

[23] Ó hAnnracháin, *Catholic Reformation in Ireland*, p. 7.

[24] Jason Peacey, 'The outbreak of the civil wars in the three kingdoms', in Barry Coward (ed.), *A companion to Stuart Britain* (Oxford, 2003), p. 303.

[25] Morrill, *English revolution*, pp. 297–8.

royalists were prepared to admit, if only to condemn, Parliament's standing as 'those Trustees' to whom the king had devolved the Irish war.[26] For Parliament 'Charles's voluntary assignation of his prerogative powers to make war and peace in Ireland' was an article of faith,[27] but also a prefiguring of acceptable arrangements for England.

Ireland and Scotland were not equal and opposite forces, or threats, from the Parliamentarian point of view. Even in 1648–49 when the revolutionary regime worried over both kingdoms as threatening royal-sponsored 'foreign' domination,[28] Scotland remained detachable in a way Ireland was not. War in Ireland was a core value for the parliamentarian cause, if often more obviously on the rhetorical plane. It allowed Parliament to pose as defender of the English nation (against Spain, Rome and the native Irish), of the crown (against bloody rebellion) and of Protestantism (against aggressive popery) and as inheritor of the English mission to deliver civility and true religion in Ireland as part of a programme of rolling plantation. Even as Parliament pulled apart into bitterly divided factions and 'interests', the reconquest of Ireland remained a common bond, however much 'Presbyterian' and 'Independent' might wrestle over who would implement that policy, how they would do so, and who would reap the credit.

The three-kingdom dimension of the Solemn League and Covenant might complicate Parliament's entanglements in Ireland, but it gave a spur to Covenanting Scotland's engagement with its western neighbour.[29] In the short term, Scottish involvement was vital in securing Ulster, for a crucial time the only bridgehead in Ireland for the Covenanting coalition, and not only through the presence on Irish soil of a Scottish army. Edinburgh represented a legitimate political regime to which bemused Protestant Ulster could appeal; the Covenant in turn legitimized enhanced Scottish intervention in an English kingdom (as the Scots readily accepted Ireland to be), shaping the attitudes as much as supplementing the military muscle of the planter population. In the long term the Scottish alliance, and not just the Scottish army, acted as protective cover for the permanent establishment of Presbyterianism in the province. Alongside an aggressive defence of home shores and migrant kin, Edinburgh oversaw the export of the Scottish ideology of Covenanting with its potent combination of local mobilization for global transformation.

---

[26] [Howell], *Mercurius Hibernicus*, p. 9.

[27] Little, 'English Parliament', pp. 120–1.

[28] John Adamson, 'The frightened junto: perceptions of Ireland, and the last attempts at a settlement with Charles I', and David Scott, 'Motives for king-killing', both in Jason Peacey (ed.), *The regicides and the execution of Charles I* (Houndmills, Basingstoke, 2001), pp. 36–70, 138–60.

[29] Macinnes, 'Covenanting ideology', pp. 191–220.

Covenanting brought to the fore the opportunity, indeed necessity, for participation, beyond the ranks of the elite, even in defiance of them, of a Covenanted people, a stance transposed into a 'Presbyterian revolution' calling out and calling forth congregations and elders, this in pursuit of a godly reformation not impeded by national boundaries. However they differed in their interpretations of their obligations, Scottish parties and factions, engagers or 'kirk party', remained committed to supra-national goals. Even in 1649 the latter voiced their claims to speak for 'the Lord's people in *England* and *Ireland*, who adhere to the cause and Covenant'.[30] It was not only Catholic Ireland which clung to a European vision. Ulster was a site for the working out of Scottish internationalism, where the emergent presbytery called its fast days for the churches of Ireland and of Britain, of Germany and of Bohemia.[31] It was not an imperialism of armies and churches which the Scots sent to Ireland so much as a colony of the mind.

The parliamentarian regime was one indelibly marked as a war institution, ideologically as much as institutionally. Parliamentarianism needed to place its enemies in sharp relief, those whose malignancy threatened to subvert their own nation, England, or whose alien nature threatened to overwhelm it.[32] It did not need Sir John Temple to convince it that the Irish insurgents were devilish barbarians. The priority for parliamentary discourse was the articulation of the claims that Parliament was the rightful and adequate body to respond to such a threat, and that the proper response was unrelenting war. Even in 1646–47, the most sustained plans for demilitarization in England involved massive military intervention in Ireland, prefiguring Ireland's future role as the location for the principal concentration of armed force within the Stuart multiple monarchy.[33] Parliament's aggrandisement towards Ireland, from the Uxbridge blueprint onwards, pinpointed control of military resources in Ireland alongside two other crucial areas, the control of appointments to office in Ireland and legislation to harmonize the reformed Irish and English churches. If it involved the acceptance of the previously contentious notion of the right to legislate for Ireland, in large part such

---

[30] 'A seasonable and necessary warning and declaration' issued by the General Assembly, 27 July 1649, in *A true copy of the whole printed Acts of the Generall Assemblies* (Edinburgh, 1682), p. 465.

[31] Adair, *True narrative*, p. 94.

[32] Cf. confederate allegations that pro-Parliament forces, in turn, intended 'the utter extirpation of the Irish Nation, the totall suppression of the Catholike Romane Religion, Subversion of Monarchicall government, and introduction of confused Anarchy' through 'inhumane and unparalleld Massacres': *The whole triall of Connor lord Macguire . . .* (London, 1645) E271 (10), p. 7.

[33] Alan J. Guy, 'The Irish military establishment, 1660–1760', in Bartlett and Jeffrey (eds), *Military history*, pp. 211–30. Of course Ireland before 1640 had also sustained a standing army but rarely one which posed much threat beyond Irish shores.

plans can be seen as a reaction to the threat of the enemy within the 'English' state system, a kind of Poynings's law solution for the seventeenth century, to block an Ormondist executive which (like a Straffordian one) could use Irish government and Irish arms to endanger the English empire as a whole.[34] If Ireland were to be an English kingdom it must be furnished with an English church regardless of opinion in Dublin. Such moves necessitated not the destruction of the kingdom of Ireland, but the insistence that it keep in step with the transformation of the English crown.

In the meantime Parliament's war-winning apparatus needed modification to extend to Ireland. The very strength of Parliament as representative of the whole nation of England could be a weakness here in so far as it envisaged the nation geographically rather than ethnically. Ireland lacked the web of connections which bound the English regions to Westminster, from the constituency MPs to county committees or regional associations, set up by drawing upon local knowledge to tap into trusted or hoped-for support in provincial England. Instead Parliament demonstrated its enviable adaptability and capacity to engineer operational systems of power without ever quite attaining a neat uniformity, let alone fully subsuming Ireland within common institutional arrangements. Informal networks were constructed in and around the Commons chamber and the committee rooms. Parliament tapped the old Irish state system where it could, co-operating with Dublin when possible, taking upon itself the filling up of key posts, like the provincial presidencies, but supplemented such moves with committees, commissioners and commanders to give on-the-spot control and direction and, for the most part, slotting established Old Protestants into such positions. While the king strained to sustain a shadow government, in church as in state, naming judges, bishops, governors and administrators,[35] Parliament targeted the offices of war, showing less shyness in dispensing military power than civil authority.

As often as not it was the resident Protestant establishment which absorbed new armed might into its political and military control, even if that control had been mandated by king or Parliament. The deployments of English troops by Ormond, Inchiquin, Jones or Coote were political triumphs compared with efforts to subordinate local forces to such outsiders as Monro, Lisle or, later, George Monck. The Protestants of Ireland, in turn, would need to continue to play the game in and around the Parliament in Westminster,

---

[34] Such ideas of course followed the logic of Scottish appeals to the Parliament of England to block military threats from Ireland against Scotland, appeals which were nonetheless to be buttressed by legislation of the Irish Parliament: Perceval-Maxwell, 'Ireland and the monarchy', p. 289.

[35] *CSPI, 1633–47*, pp. 379ff.

first learnt in the 1640s, as means to survival.[36] Their incorporation into the parliamentarian system went beyond the merely institutional. Despite their reluctance to become embroiled in the quarrels of England, by the later 1640s their politics rang with the sounds of English disputes, from the factional struggles within the Houses up to the awkward relations between the Covenanter partners, down to the strife at local and regional level arising from uneasy accommodations between the demands of war and the realities of provincial power. The Protestants of Ireland were drawn into the exploding print culture of London, not merely as newsworthy subjects or objects of compassion, but as participants, setting their own goals, even fighting their own wars of words.[37]

Roger Boyle, Viscount Broghill, now earl of Orrery, provided a safe reading of the 1640s for Protestant Ireland: Irish Catholics were 'seemingly good subjects, but to become more dangerous rebels. But the Protestants of Ireland, if seemingly rebels, were such, but to become more useful subjects'.[38] The perceived threat and the bloody realities of the insurrection had collapsed the categories of crown, Protestantism, the 'English interest' and the actual Protestant and 'British' inhabitants of the island into one endangered order, in the political discourse of England, whether royalist or parliamentarian, and of Scotland. If a culmination of old-established trends, it made of the Protestant inhabitants a living embodiment of regal, national and religious imperatives, one which all combatants in Great Britain vowed to uphold and sustain, whether under the category 'loyal', 'Protestant', 'British' or 'English'. These people were not merely an awkward encumbrance to broader designs. Given the determination of all players to secure Ireland within their schemes, they represented a bridgehead, whether to embark on the rebuilding of Ireland, on Ormondist lines, or to launch a new conquest. Such depictions of them in turn helped shape and form a 'Protestant interest' being pulled together by common participation in events not always of their own making. Among the geographically scattered, nationally divided and politically alienated clumps of Protestants, the experience of threat in 1641 was arguably more of a common bond than any

---

[36] T. C. Barnard, 'Protestant interest', pp. 221–2, 224, 233; Barnard, 'Conclusion. Settling and unsettling Ireland: the Cromwellian and Williamite revolutions', in Ohlmeyer (ed.), *Ireland from independence to occupation*, p. 286.

[37] Alongside the well-known Inchiquin controversies, lesser spats were being engaged in, notably that between the irascible Sir Frederick Hamilton and Sir William Cole, over events in south Ulster and north Connacht. See *Another extract of severall letters from Ireland* (London, 1643) E65 (34); *The humble remonstrance of Sir Frederick Hammilton; The answere and vindication of Sir William Cole* (London, 1645) E274 (30).

[38] Roger Boyle, earl of Orrery, *A collection of the state letters of . . . Orrery* (2 vols, Dublin, 1743), ii, 398.

experienced hitherto.[39] At first, 'the state' proved empowering in response to such threats, endowing Protestant militancy with a validation always implicit in the Protestant state which, however, now offered the prospects of overcoming the divisions of the 1630s, and of a common front with the English and Scottish regimes. As the decade proceeded, 'the state', like the king, came to be regarded by increasing numbers as having ceded its obligation of protection. The Ormond treaty, as much as the Protestant war, was presented as a means to secure not only the lives and liberties of the 'loyal' but the kingdom of Ireland of which they were the leading edge, but such a presentation proved unconvincing.

The years 1641–47 both strengthened Protestant unity and set up long-term divisions within that community. A Protestant mainstream, into which had flowed the scattered interests of pre-rising Protestant Ireland, absorbed the New Protestants of the 1650s into the 'Protestant interest' which faced into the Restoration.[40] If, as Aidan Clarke has remarked, the political climate of Restoration Ireland did not encourage 'group action' and the 'cohesive strength' of the Protestant community in 1659–60 did not long survive,[41] it could be re-formed in moments of crisis. Yet it was cut across by other perceptions, of solidarity or of division. Toby Barnard has identified the survival of the notion of an 'English interest' beyond 1660, with some capacity to span religious barriers, at once the inheritor of Ormond's schemes of the 1640s and one given form once more by Ormond himself as Restoration viceroy.[42] The residual Presbyterian interest, denied its aspiration to transform Ireland in the 'Presbyterian moment' of the 1640s and increasingly dominated by its Ulster, and Scottish, dimension, was as deliberately shunted outside the Protestant establishment by the Restoration regime as by the early English republic. Both these variants had their social dimensions. Ormond's efforts at establishing a royalist centre ground had been implicitly premised upon a harnessing of aristocratic support, a hope not without fulfilment, but inadequate for his needs. Social solidarity among the landed could help underpin some efforts towards building an 'English' interest after 1660. The Presbyterian tradition had already, in the 1640s, given its critics grounds for their complaints that it harkened too much to 'the people' or at least the 'sober, godly part' of them. Landed support for dissent was leached away over coming generations.[43] Yet a matrix, or an 'embryonic

---

[39] 'Because it appeared to them that the entire Catholic community had risen against them, those who endured were conscious that what happened in Ireland was entirely different from contemporary disturbances in England and Scotland': Canny, *Making Ireland British*, p. 549.

[40] Clarke, *Prelude to Restoration*, pp. 4, 16, 19, 230–1.

[41] Clarke, *Prelude to Restoration*, p. 320.

[42] Barnard, 'Protestant interest', pp. 219–20, 228–9, 240.

[43] Toby Barnard, *A new anatomy of Ireland: the Irish Protestants 1649–1770* (New Haven, 2003), p. 17.

free state'[44] of Presbyterian Ulster, was created into which to introduce subsequent, substantial, waves of Scottish migrants.[45]

What bound together a mainstream Protestant interest was a wariness lest '41 come again, a sentiment liable to ebb and flow, and with it the degree of Protestant solidarity and the ability to regain the support of Protestants squeezed out by religious or national distinctiveness. Even in the lulls between crises such concerns demanded a Protestant grip on the triad of land, state and the sword. The Protestant agents dispatched to the king in 1644 had stood out for confiscation and plantation, for a 'Protestant army' and Protestant garrisons, and for a safely Protestant parliament.[46] In 1659–60 it 'was essential that the land settlement should survive, . . . not merely because individuals had profited, but because it was the basis of a reconfiguration of power which excluded Catholic competition in a new colonial Ireland. The condition of Protestant survival was that the community should be made invulnerable to the forces that had almost destroyed it in the 1640s. . . . the interests of the group must be sacrosanct'.[47] Rather than being trodden on by the march of the modern state with its armies and bureaucracies, Protestant Ireland captured one largely, if not exclusively, for its own use.[48] The 1640s had speeded the incorporation of the Protestant population, not just its elite, into the Protestant state, not so much institutionally as practically, by service of arms. The commitment to an armed Protestant nation survived and revived. The militia would remain a focus of local reassurance alongside, even above, the standing army stationed in Ireland in decades to come.[49] Eighteenth-century Protestant Ireland saw both 'the glorification of the armed citizen and the denigration of standing armies' and 'attempts of plebeian Protestants to reassert their exclusive right to bear arms, interpreted as a badge of full citizenship'.[50] Lack of Protestant numbers in Restoration Ireland could be compensated for with social and military power, with 'far more Soldiers and Soldierlike-men'.[51]

The political progress of Protestant Ireland, as of Scotland or England, is a matter not of the unambiguous lines of descent of neatly packaged political 'ideologies', nor of mere unprincipled pragmatism, but of the accumulation

---

[44] Barnard, *New anatomy of Ireland*, p. 19.

[45] Connolly, *Religion, law and power*, pp. 161–2, 167–71.

[46] Curtis and McDowell (eds), *Irish historical documents*, pp. 156–8.

[47] Clarke, *Prelude to Restoration*, p. 317.

[48] In Toby Barnard's words, 'Irish Protestants could not aspire to form an independent state. Instead they settled for colonizing the state which England had established and preserved for them': Barnard, 'Settling and unsettling Ireland', p. 289.

[49] Barnard, 'Protestant interest', pp. 233–6; Barnard, 'Settling and unsettling Ireland', pp. 278–81.

[50] S. J. Connolly, 'Introduction: varieties of Irish political thought', in Connolly (ed.), *Political ideas in eighteenth-century Ireland* (Dublin, 2000), pp. 19–20.

[51] Sir William Petty (1672), quoted in S. J. Connolly, 'The defence of Protestant Ireland, 1660–1760', in Bartlett and Jeffrey (eds), *Military history*, p. 236.

of intellectual resources alongside the mounting pressure of immediate choices to build up a political culture. As Sean Connolly has suggested of later 'patriot' thinking in Protestant Ireland, the adaptation of ideological traditions, and their deployment at convenient moments or for selfish ends, qualifies such traditions but does not render nugatory the respective arguments.[52] That royalist-Anglican Dublin could stand firm on the rights of the Irish Parliament and the autonomy of the free, national Church of Ireland was of course an attempt to fend off unwelcome developments in England, but it was nonetheless resonant with commitments made and laid down in earlier decades. Commitment to the 'imperial' crown of England with implicit acceptance of Parliament's claims to be its executive agent, a short cut to decisive victory over hated foes in Ireland, also picked up understood ideas and deeper ambitions for the promotion of the 'English interest' in Ireland by confiscation and plantation and the spread of law and civility. Promotion of union schemes under the protectorate, even of a Cromwellian kingship, could mesh with promotion of the economic welfare of Ireland and with the entrenchment of a 'Protestant interest' wary of the radical face of the English Commonwealth.[53]

Protestant Ireland was as capable of holding both the notion of the kingdom of Ireland and the 'Englishness' of the Irish polity as any confederate. In 1660 the assertion of the rights of Irish parliaments by the Protestant Irish Convention was framed in language declaring that 'the Welfare and Interest of England and Ireland are so inseparably interwoven as the good or evil of either, must necessarily become common to both.'[54] Rather than looking for an 'imperial' or even 'unionist' tradition in conflict with a 'constitutionalist', autonomist or 'patriot' tradition, for Protestant Ireland a common stock of ideas and attitudes had become increasingly available to be drawn down in response to the needs of a 'Protestant interest' more aware of its common concerns,[55] whose experience of the 1640s was that as a 'sense of identity as a separate community grew, there was no decline in their feeling of Englishness'.[56] An Irish Parliament was not incompatible with an 'imperial' English crown to shield it from

---

[52] Connolly notes 'the danger that this necessary work of dismantling a simplistic myth of ideological continuity will be carried too far . . . If a patriot stance frequently cloaked self-interest, the arguments and imagery that sustained that stance had nevertheless to come from somewhere': Connolly, 'Precedent and principle: the patriots and their critics', in Connolly (ed.), *Political ideas*, pp. 131–3.

[53] Patrick Little, 'The first unionists? Irish Protestant attitudes to union with England, 1653–9', *Irish Historical Studies* 32 (2000–01), pp. 44–58.

[54] Quoted in Clarke, *Prelude to Restoration*, p. 250.

[55] See Clarke, *Prelude to Restoration*, pp. 302–6 for the readiness of the Irish Convention in 1660 to operate through 'alternative channels' in England or in Ireland, to safeguard a common Protestant interest.

[56] Little, 'The first unionists?', p. 45.

'foreign' danger; commitment to proscription of Catholicism and promotion of plantation did not demand a 'unionist' agenda. The rump Irish Parliament of the 1640s might condemn the Solemn League and Covenant but it retained a powerful anti-popery up to its demise. Protestant delegates to court had blended their demands for the destruction of Catholic power with the maintenance of the Parliament of Ireland, but also of Poynings's law to prevent 'dangerous consequences'. The 1660 convention defended recourse to English institutions in conditions where the crown might lose Ireland through rebel capture of the appropriate institutions in Ireland,[57] a danger all too readily apparent in 1641–42. An avoidance of being 'wedded and glued to forms of government' was a recognition that such structures were second-order priorities when the ends of widely shared English, even British, goals in Ireland were at issue.[58] The informal checks and balances sought, and sometimes exercised, in pre-rising Ireland were not discarded but re-worked, nor were constitutional safeguards erected into non-negotiable principles any more than then. But the 'loyal and dutiful people of this land of Ireland' being safeguarded were now more neatly identified with the Protestant inhabitants of the island.

Protestant Ireland in the 1640s had endured the 'English civil war', as participants in the struggle to determine the form and substance of the English polity. They had received the 'Scottish revolution'. They were unavoidably caught up into the war, or wars, of, among or between the three kingdoms, and in all the forms proposed by historians, including the distinctly Irish ones of 'war of empire' and 'war of secession'.[59] They were also combatants in an Irish 'civil war', albeit one fought in all its brutal reality of grime and blood over a 'virtual' kingdom. For those involved in the Irish conflict the 'kingdom of Ireland' had never merely existed, but was a means to the achievement of a greater goal. For Ormondists or royalists, that might mean no more than the embodiment of majesty and the support of the social order, accomplished by restoring and strengthening an English (and hence, necessarily, Protestant and common law) kingdom. For confederates it might mean the future achievement of the 'Catholic kingdom' of a once and future Ireland, or, more modestly, the filling up of the pattern sketched before 1641 of a 'constitutional' and legal kingdom, a full partner in the Stuart imperium,

---

[57] Clarke, *Prelude to Restoration*, pp. 318–9.

[58] Cf. Little, 'Irish "Independents" ', p. 959 for a different interpretation of the relations within Protestant thinking between 'the Old English constitutionalist line' and an 'alternative, radical tradition . . . based on conquest, resettlement and penal legislation' which 'included a vision of integration between England and Ireland'.

[59] Pocock, 'Atlantic archipelago', pp. 188–90; John Morrill, 'Three kingdoms and one commonwealth? The enigma of mid-seventeenth century Britain and Ireland', in Grant and Stringer (eds), *Uniting the kingdom?*, pp. 188–90.

where due process was observed and professions of loyalty accepted.[60] For many Protestants, though, the kingdom of Ireland could never be realized until the forces of sedition were finally and fully quashed. Only then could the island kingdom rest snug within the English 'empire' and Protestant Christendom, and their own lives, liberties and properties be safeguarded. If the 1640s taught anything it was that survival, let alone security, much less domination, needed to be fought for, and not only with musket and sword, but with resources of a less material kind, the capacity to seize and secure its own variant of the 'kingdom of Ireland'. Whatever else Protestant Ireland would become in the aftermath of that decade, it would remain a society never shy of belligerence.

[60] Cunningham, 'Representations of king, parliament and the Irish people', and Ó hAnnracháin, 'Though Hereticks and Politicians should misrepresent their good zeale', both in Ohlmeyer (ed.), *Political thought*.

Bibliography

PRIMARY SOURCES

Manuscripts

British Library, London
Additional MS 4,769A, letter book of the 1645 Irish committee
Additional MS 4,771, minute book of the joint-adventurers' committee, 1643–45
Additional MS 4,782, minute book of the MP-adventurers' committee, 1642–43
Additional MSS 4,763, 4,819, MS version of 'Ormond's curtain drawn'
Additional MSS 14,827–14,828, diary of Sir Framlingham Gawdy
Additional MS 31,116, diary of Lawrence Whitacre
Additional MSS 37,343–37,344, Bulstrode Whitelocke's annals
Egerton MS 80, papers relating to the earl of Cork, 1642–43
Harleian MSS 163–166, diary of Sir Simonds D'Ewes

Bodleian Library, Oxford
Carte MSS 1–22, 63, Ormond Papers

National Library of Ireland, Dublin
MS 14,305, minute book of the Commission for Irish Affairs

Public Record Office, London
SO 3, signet office Irish letter-book, 1636–42
SP 17/H/7, schedules and musters, 1642–43
SP 17/H/10, John Davies's accounts for shipments to Ireland, 1644–45
SP 28/1A, 1B, 1C, 1D, warrants and contracts, 1641–42
SP 28/139, miscellaneous accounts for Ireland 1641–47
SP 28/253B, depositions taken by the Committee of Accounts, mostly relating to
     Clotworthy and Davies, 1644–46
SP 28/302, warrants issued by the Ulster commissioners, 1646
SP 63/260, 261, 262, state papers, Ireland, 1642–46

Public Record Office of Northern Ireland, Belfast
T525/4, transcript of National Library of Scotland Wodrow MSS, fol. lxv, no. 84

Trinity College, Dublin
MSS 838, 840, depositions relating to 1641 rising

Pamphlets

Another extract of severall letters from Ireland (London, 1643) E65 (34)
The answere and vindication of Sir William Cole (London, 1645) E274 (30)
Bernard, Nicholas, *The whole proceedings of the siege of Drogheda in Ireland* (Dublin, 1736)
A charge delivered in the name of Sir Thomas Fairfax and his army . . . (London, 1647) E393 (5)
Cole, Robert, *A full and true relation of the late victory . . .* (London, 1643) E96 (6)
—, *The true coppies of two letters* (London, 1643) E94 (20)
A copy of a letter from the speakers of both houses . . . together with the answer of the Lords Justices and Counsell (Oxford, 1643) E78 (25)
A Copy of a Remonstrance setting forth The sad condition of the Army under . . . INCHEQUINE . . . (London, 1647) E399 (33)
A declaration of the Lords of His Majesties Privie-Councell in Scotland . . . (London, 1643) E56 (9)
A Declaration of parliament concerning the miserable condition of Ireland . . . (London, 1643) E55 (1)
A declaration of . . . Parliament shewing the present designe . . . for a cessation . . . (London, 1643) E69 (16)
A Declaration of parliament . . . whereunto are added the propositions made by the committees . . . (London, 1643) E55 (20)
A Declaration of the Commons . . . concerning the rise and progresse of the grand rebellion in Ireland . . . (London, 1643) E61 (23)
A declaration of the Lord Lieutenant . . . (Cork, 1648)
The earl of Glamorgans negotiations (London, 1645 [1646]) E328 (9)
The grovnds and motives inducing his Maiesty to agree to a cessation . . . (Oxford, 1643) E71 (20)
G. T., *Truth from Ireland* (London, 1643) E99 (12)
Howell, James, *Mercurius Hibernicus, or a discourse of the late insurrection in Ireland* (Bristol, 1644)
The humble remonstrance of Sir Frederick Hammilton [sic] (London, 1643) Wing H477B
Ireland's excise (London, 1643) E62 (16)
The Irish Cabinet, or his majesties secret papers . . . (London, 1646) E316 (29)
The King's Cabinet opened (London, 1645) E292 (27)
The Kings Majesties manifesto to the kingdom of Ireland undertaken and published by the marquesse of Clanrickard (London, 1646) E371 (11)
A letter from a person of quality residing in Kinsale . . . (London, 1646) E354 (6)

A letter from a Protestant in Ireland . . . upon occasion of the treaty in that kingdom (1643)

A letter from Lieutenant Colonel Knight . . . (London, 1647) E399 (23)

A letter from the lords at Oxford . . . to the lords of the privy-councell . . . of Scotland (Oxford, 1643 [1644])

A letter from the right honourable the Lord Inchiquin . . . to his Majestie . . . (London, 1644) E8 (37)

The Lord George Digby's cabinet . . . (London, 1646) E319 (15)

The Lord Marques of Argyle's speech . . . (London, 1646) E341 (25)

A manifestation directed to the honourable house of parliament . . . from the Lord Inchiquin . . . (London, 1644) E6 (1)

The marques of Clanrickards engagement (1646) Wing M707

[Meredith, Adam], *Ormond's Curtain drawn: in a short discourse concerning Ireland* (London, 1646) E513 (14)

Papers presented to the Parliament, against the Lord Inchequin . . . (London, 1648) E435 (33)

A particular charge of impeachment in the name of Sir Thomas Fairfax and the army under his command (London, 1647) E397 (17)

The petition of the committees for Ireland to His Majestie: with his Majesties Answer thereunto (Oxford, 1642)

Propositions made to the Lords and Commons . . . and the votes thereupon . . . (London, 1641 [1642]) E136 (9)

[Prynne, William], *A brief iustification of the XI accused members* (London, 1647) E398 (3)

—, *A full vindication and answer of the XI accused members* (London, 1647) E398 (17)

—, *The hypocrites unmasking* (London, 1647)

A remonstrance from the . . . Parliament at Dublin . . . (Dublin, 1646) E382 (3)

[Reynolds, Robert, and Robert Goodwyn], *The true state and condition of the kingdom of Ireland* (London, 1642 [1643]) E246 (31)

Severall papers of the treatie between . . . James marques of Ormond . . . and Sir Thomas Wharton . . . (Dublin, 1646) E378 (4)

[Sidney, Robert, earl of Leicester], *A letter from the Lord of Lecester* (London, 1642) E118 (48)

[Skout, J.], *Exceeding certain and true newes . . .* (London, 1643) E84 (26)

Some passages of the treaty between the marquesse of Ormond and the parliaments commissioners (London, 1646)

The state of the Irish affairs (London, 1645) E314 (7)

Tichborne, Sir Henry, *A letter of Sir Henry Tichborne to his lady, of the siege of Tredagh . . .* (Dublin, 1734)

A true and exact relation of the most sad condition of Ireland since the cessation . . . (London, 1643) E76 (4)

The True and Original Copy of the First Petition which was delivered by Sir David Watkins (London, 1642) E130 (26)

A true copie of two letters brought by Mr. Peters . . . from my L. Forbes . . . (London, 1642) E121 (44)

A true copy of a letter sent from Doe castle . . . (London, 1643) E84 (46)

The true state and condition of the Kingdom of Ireland . . . (London, 1642 [1643]) E246 (31)

Very sad newes from Ireland (London, 1646) E358 (19)

[Whitelocke, Bulstrode], *The speech of Bulstrode Whitelocke* . . . (London, 1642) E200 (30)

The whole triall of Connor lord Macguire . . . (London, 1645) E271 (10)

Williams, Griffith, *The discovery of mysteries: or, plots and practices of a prevalent faction in the present parliament* (1643)

Newsletters

Specific issues of the following newsletters are cited in the footnotes

Certain Informations
A Continuation of Certain Speciall and Remarkable Passages
England's Memorable Accidents
The Kingdomes Weekly Intelligencer
Mercurius Aulicus
Mercurius Civicus
The Moderate Intelligencer
A Perfect Diurnall
Perfect Occurrences
A Perfect Relation
The Scottish Dove
Speciall Passages
The Weekly Account

Printed sources

17th report of the deputy keeper of the public records of Ireland (Dublin, 1885)

The Acts of the Parliament of Scotland, ed. T. Thomson (12 vols in 13, London, 1814–75)

Adair, Patrick, *A true narrative of the rise and progress of the Presbyterian church in Ireland*, ed. W. D. Killen (Belfast, 1866)

Baillie, Robert, *Letters and journals of Robert Baillie*, ed. David Laing (3 vols, Edinburgh, 1841–42)

Bell, R., ed., *Memorials of the civil war* (2 vols, London, 1849)

Blencowe, R. W. (ed.), *Sydney papers* (London, 1825)

Bolton, Richard, *The statutes of Ireland* (Dublin, 1621)

Boyle, Roger, earl of Orrery, *A collection of the state letters of* . . . *Orrery* (2 vols, Dublin, 1743)

Calendar of the Clarendon state papers, ed. O. Ogle et al. (5 vols, Oxford, 1869–1970)

Calendar of the proceedings of the Committee for Compounding 1643–1660, ed. M. A. E. Green (5 vols, London, 1889–92)

Calendar of the proceedings of the Committee for the Advance of Money 1642–1656, ed. M. A. E. Green (3 vols, London, 1888)

Calendar of state papers, domestic series, of the reign of Charles I, addenda,
  1625–49, ed. John Bruce, W. D. Hamilton and S. C. Lucas (23 vols, London,
  1858–97)

Calendar of state papers and manuscripts relating to English affairs, existing in the
  archives and collections of Venice, ed. Rawdon Brown et al. (38 vols in 40, London,
  1864–1940)

Calendar of state papers relating to Ireland, of the reign of Charles I, ed. R. P. Mahaffy
  (4 vols, London, 1900–03)

Caulfield, Richard (ed.), *The council book of the corporation of Youghal* (Guildford,
  1878)

— (ed.), *The council book of the corporation of Kinsale* (Guildford, 1879)

Charles I in 1646: letters of King Charles the First to Queen Henrietta Maria, ed.
  John Bruce, Camden Society 63 (London, 1856)

Clarendon: see Hyde, Edward

Coates, W. H., Anne Steele Young and V. F. Snow (eds) *The private journals of the*
  Long Parliament (3 vols, New Haven, 1982–92)

Cox, Richard, *Hibernia Anglicana: or the history of Ireland from the conquest thereof*
  by the English to the present time (2 vols, London, 1689–90)

Croker, Thomas Crofton (ed.), *Narratives illustrative of the contests in Ireland in*
  1641 and 1690, Camden Society 14 (London, 1841)

Curtis, Edmund, and R. B. McDowell (eds), *Irish historical documents 1172–1922*
  (London, 1943)

Patrick, Darcy, An argument', ed. C. E. J. Caldicott, *Camden Miscellany XXXI,*
  Camden Society, 4th series, 44 (London, 1992)

D'Ewes, Simonds, *The journal of Sir Simonds D'Ewes from the first recess of the*
  Long Parliament to the withdrawal of King Charles from London, ed. W. H. Coates
  (New Haven, 1942)

Firth, C. H., and R. S. Rait (eds) *Acts and ordinances of the interregnum 1642–1660*
  (3 vols, London, 1911)

Fotheringham, J. G. (ed.). *The diplomatic correspondence of Jean de Montereul and*
  the brothers Bellievre, French ambassadors in England and Scotland, 1645–8,
  Scottish History Society 29–30 (2 vols, Edinburgh, 1898–99)

Gardiner, Bertha Meriton (ed.), 'A secret negociation with Charles I', *Camden*
  Miscellany viii, Camden Society, new series 31 (London, 1883)

Gardiner, S. R. (ed.), *The Hamilton papers,* Camden Society, new series, 27
  (London, 1880)

— (ed.), *The Constitutional documents of the Puritan revolution* (reprint of 3rd
  edition, Oxford, 1979)

Gilbert, J. T. (ed.), *A contemporary history of affairs in Ireland, from AD 1641 to*
  1652 (3 vols, Dublin, 1879)

— (ed.), *History of the Irish confederation and war in Ireland, 1641–53* (7 vols, Dublin,
  1882–91)

Harrington, John, *The diary of John Harrington MP.,* ed. Margaret Stieg, Somerset
  Record Society 74 (1977)

Harris, Walter (ed.), *Hibernica* (2 vols, Dublin, 1747–50)

Henrietta Maria, *Letters of Queen Henrietta Maria*, ed. M. A. E. Green (London, 1857)

Hill, George (ed.), *The Montgomery manuscripts* (Belfast, 1869)

Historical Manuscripts Commission:

    4th report (London, 1874)

    6th report (London, 1877)

    7th report (London, 1879)

    10th report, appendix 4 (London, 1885)

    Buccleuch MSS, i (London, 1899)

    Cowper MSS, ii (London, 1888)

    De L'Isle MSS, vi (London, 1966)

    Eglinton MSS (London, 1885)

    Egmont MSS, i (London, 1905)

    Hamilton MSS, supplementary report (London, 1932)

    Montagu MSS (London, 1900)

    Ormonde MSS, new series, i–ii (London, 1902–3)

    Ormonde MSS, old series, i–ii (London, 1895–1909)

    Portland MSS, i (London, 1891)

Hogan, James (ed.), *Letters and papers relating to the Irish rebellion between 1642–46* (IMC, Dublin, 1936)

Husbands, Edward, *An exact collection of remonstrances* (London, 1643)

Hyde, Edward, earl of Clarendon, *The history of the rebellion and civil wars in England*, ed. W. D. Macray (6 vols, Oxford, 1888)

—, *State papers collected by Edward, earl of Clarendon*, ed. R. Scrope and T. Monkhouse (3 vols, Oxford, 1757)

Journals of the House of Commons (London, 1742–)

Journals of the House of Commons of the Kingdom of Ireland (19 vols in 21, Dublin, 1796–1800)

Journals of the House of Lords (London, 1767–)

Journals of the House of Lords of the Kingdom of Ireland (8 vols, Dublin, 1779–1800)

Juxon, Thomas, *The journal of Thomas Juxon, 1644–1647*, ed. Keith Lindley and David Scott, Camden Society, 5th series, 13 (Cambridge, 1999)

Lowe, John (ed.), *Letter-book of the earl of Clanricarde 1643–1647* (IMC, Dublin, 1983)

Luke, Samuel, *Journal of Sir Samuel Luke*, ed. I. G. Philip, Oxfordshire Record Society (3 vols, Oxford, 1950–53)

McNeill, Charles (ed.), *The Tanner letters* (IMC, Dublin, 1943)

Moody, T. W., and J. G. Simms (eds), *The bishopric of Derry and the Irish society of London, 1602–1705* (2 vols, IMC, Dublin, 1968–83)

Murphy, W. P. D. (ed.), *The earl of Hertford's lieutenancy papers, 1603–1612*, Wiltshire Record Society 23 (1969 for 1967)

'Rawlinson manuscripts, class A.110', *Analecta Hibernica*, iv (1932)

Register of the privy council of Scotland, 2nd series, ed. David Masson and P. Hume Brown (8 vols, Edinburgh, 1899–1906)

Rushworth, John, *Historical collections of private passages of state . . .* (8 vols, London, 1721)

Simington, R. C., and John MacLellan (eds), 'Oireachtas library list of outlaws, 1641–1647', *Analecta Hibernica* 23 (1966)

Statues of the realm, ed. A. Luders et al. (11 vols in 12, London, 1810–28)

Steele, Robert (ed.), *Bibliotheca Lindesiana: a bibliography of royal proclamations of the Tudor and Stuart sovereigns*, ii, part 1 (Ireland) (Oxford, 1910)

Temple, Sir John, *The Irish rebellion* (6th edition, Dublin, 1724)

A true copy of the whole printed Acts of the Generall Assemblies (Edinburgh, 1682)

Verney, Ralph, *Verney papers: notes of proceedings in the Long Parliament*, ed. John Bruce, Camden Society 31 (London, 1845)

Whitelocke, Bulstrode, *Memorials of English affairs* (4 vols, Oxford, 1853)

Woodhouse, A. S. P. (ed.), *Puritanism and liberty* (London, 1938)

Yonge, Walter, *Walter Yonge's diary of proceedings in the House of Commons 1642–1645*, ed. Christopher Thompson (Wivenhoe, 1986), i, *18 Sept. 1642–7 March, 1643*

Young, Robert M. (ed.), *The town book of the corporation of Belfast 1613–1816* (Belfast, 1892)

SECONDARY SOURCES

Published

Adamson, John, 'The English nobility and the projected settlement of 1647', *Historical Journal* 30 (1987)

—, 'The *Vindiciae veritatis* and the political creed of Viscount Saye and Sele', *Historical Research* 60 (1987)

—, 'Parliamentary management, men-of-business, and the House of Lords, 1640–49', in Clyve Jones (ed.), *A pillar of the constitution: the House of Lords in British politics, 1640–1789* (London, 1989)

—, 'The baronial context of the English civil war', *Transactions of the Royal Historical Society*, 5th series, 60 (1990)

—, 'Politics and the nobility in civil war England', *Historical Journal* 34 (1991)

—, 'Strafford's ghost: the British context of Viscount Lisle's lieutenancy of Ireland', in Ohlmeyer (ed.), *Ireland from independence to occupation*

—, 'Of armies and architecture: the employments of Robert Scawen', in Ian Gentles, John Morrill and Blair Worden (eds), *Soldiers, writers and statesmen of the English revolution* (Cambridge, 1998)

—, 'The frightened junto: perceptions of Ireland, and the last attempts at a settlement with Charles I', in Peacey (ed.), *Regicides*

—, 'The triumph of oligarchy: the management of the war and the Committee of Both Kingdoms, 1644–1645', in Kyle and Peacey (eds), *Parliament at work*

Armstrong, Robert, 'Ormond, the confederate peace talks, and Protestant royalism', in Ó Siochrú (ed.), *Kingdoms in crisis*

—, 'Ireland at Westminster: the Long Parliament's Irish committees, 1641–1647', in Kyle and Peacey (eds), *Parliament at work*

—, 'Viscount Ards and the presbytery: the politics of the Scots of Ulster in the 1640s', in John R. Young (ed.), *Scotland and Ulster* (Dublin, forthcoming)

—, 'The Long Parliament goes to war: the Irish campaigns, 1641–3' (*Historical Rescarch*, forthcoming)

—, 'Protestant churchmen and the confederate wars', in Ciaran Brady and Jane Ohlmeyer (eds), *British interventions in early modern Ireland* (Cambridge, 2005)

Ashton, Robert, *The English civil war: conservatism and revolution, 1603–1649* (London, 1978)

—, *Counter-revolution: the second civil war and its origins, 1646–8* (London, 1994)

Aylmer, G. E., 'Collective mentalities in mid-seventeenth century England, II: royalist attitudes', *Transactions of the Royal Historical Society*, 5th series, 37 (1987)

Bagwell, Richard, *Ireland under the Stuarts and during the interregnum* (3 vols, London, 1909–16)

Barnard, Toby, 'Planters and policies in Cromwellian Ireland', *Past & Present* 61 (1973)

—, *Cromwellian Ireland: English government and reform in Ireland, 1649–1660* (Oxford, 1975)

—, 'Conclusion. Settling and unsettling Ireland: the Cromwellian and Williamite revolutions', in Ohlmeyer (ed.), *Ireland from independence to occupation*

—, 'The Protestant interest, 1641–1660', in Ohlmeyer (ed.), *Ireland from independence to occupation*

—, 'Introduction: the dukes of Ormonde', in Barnard and Fenlon (eds), *Dukes of Ormonde*

—, *A new anatomy of Ireland: the Irish Protestants 1649–1770* (New Haven, 2003)

—, and Jane Fenlon (eds), *The dukes of Ormonde, 1610–1745* (Woodbridge, 2000)

Bartlett, Thomas, and Keith Jeffrey (eds), *A military history of Ireland* (Cambridge, 1996)

Baumber, M. L., 'The navy and the civil war in Ireland, 1643–1646', *Mariner's Mirror* 75 (1989)

Bottigheimer, Karl S., *English money and Irish land: the 'adventurers' in the Cromwellian settlement of Ireland* (Oxford, 1971)

Boynton, Lindsay, 'The Tudor provost-marshal', *English Historical Review* 77 (1962)

—, 'Martial law and the Petition of Right', *English Historical Review* 79 (1964)

Braddick, Michael J., *State formation in early modern England c.1550–1700* (Cambridge, 2000)

Bradshaw, Brendan, and John Morrill (eds), *The British problem c.1534–1707* (Houndmills, Basingstoke, 1996)

Brady, Ciaran, 'The decline of the Irish kingdom', in Mark Greengrass (ed.), *Conquest and coalescence: the shaping of the state in early modern Europe* (London, 1990)

—, 'The captains' games: army and society in Elizabethan Ireland', in Bartlett and Jeffrey (eds), *Military history*

—, 'England's defence and Ireland's reform: the dilemma of the Irish viceroys, 1541–1641', in Bradshaw and Morrill (eds), *The British problem*

—, and Raymond Gillespie (eds), *Natives and newcomers: essays on the making of Irish colonial society, 1534–1641* (Dublin, 1986)

Brenner, Robert, *Merchants and revolution: commercial change, political conflict and London's overseas traders, 1550–1653* (Princeton, 1993)

Burgess, Glenn, *The politics of the ancient constitution* (University Park, Pennsylvania, 1992)

Canny, Nicholas, 'Irish, Scottish and Welsh responses to centralisation, c.1530–1640: a comparative perspective', in Grant and Stringer (eds), *Uniting the kingdom?*

—, 'The attempted Anglicisation of Ireland in the seventeenth century: an exemplar of "British History" ', in Merritt (ed.) *Thomas Wentworth*

—, 'The origins of empire: an introduction', in Canny (ed.), *The Oxford history of the British empire*, i, *The origins of empire* (Oxford, 1998)

—, *Making Ireland British 1580–1650* (Oxford, 2001)

Carte, Thomas, *History of the life of James, first duke of Ormonde* (2nd edition, 6 vols, Oxford, 1851)

Casway, Jerrold I., *Owen Roe O'Neill and the struggle for Catholic Ireland* (Philadelphia, 1984)

Clarke, Aidan, 'The army and politics in Ireland, 1625–30', *Studia Hibernica* 4 (1964)

—, *The Old English in Ireland, 1625–42* (London, 1966)

—, 'Colonial identity in early seventeenth-century Ireland', in T. W. Moody (ed.), *Nationality and the pursuit of national independence* (Belfast, 1978)

—, 'The genesis of the Ulster rising of 1641', in Peter Roebuck (ed.), *Plantation to partition* (Belfast, 1981)

—, 'The 1641 depositions', in Peter Fox (ed.), *Treasures of the library: Trinity College Dublin* (Dublin, 1986)

—, 'Colonial constitutional attitudes in Ireland, 1640–60', *Proceedings of the Royal Irish Academy* 90C (1990)

—, 'The 1641 rebellion and anti-popery in Ireland', in Mac Cuarta (ed.), *Ulster 1641*

—, *Prelude to Restoration in Ireland: the end of the Commonwealth, 1659–1660* (Cambridge, 1999)

—, 'Patrick Darcy and the constitutional relationship between Ireland and Britain', in Ohlmeyer (ed.), *Political thought*

Cogswell, Thomas, *Home divisions: aristocracy, the state and provincial conflict* (Manchester, 1998)

Connolly, S. J., *Religion, law and power: the making of Protestant Ireland 1660–1760* (Oxford, 1992)

—, 'The defence of Protestant Ireland, 1660–1760', in Bartlett and Jeffrey (eds), *Military history*

—, 'Introduction: varieties of Irish political thought', in Connolly (ed.), *Political ideas*

—, 'Precedent and principle: the patriots and their critics', in Connolly (ed.), *Political ideas*

— (ed.), *Political ideas in eighteenth-century Ireland* (Dublin, 2000)

Cope, Joseph, 'Fashioning victims: Dr Henry Jones and the plight of Irish Protestants, 1642', *Historical Research* 74 (2001)

Cowan, Edward J., 'The political ideas of a covenanting leader: Archibald Campbell, marquis of Argyll, 1607–1661', in Roger A. Mason (ed.), *Scots and Britons* (Cambridge, 1994)

Cregan, Donal F., ' "An Irish cavalier": Daniel O'Neill in the civil wars 1642–51', *Studia Hibernica* 4 (1964)

Cunningham, Bernadette, 'Representations of king, parliament and the Irish people in Geoffrey Keating's *Foras Feasa ar Éirinn* and John Lynch's *Cambrensis Eversus* (1662)', in Ohlmeyer (ed.), *Political thought*

Donald, P. H., *An uncounselled king: Charles I and the Scottish troubles, 1637–1641* (Cambridge, 1990)

Edwards, David, 'Beyond reform: martial law and the Tudor reconquest of Ireland', *History Ireland* 5 (1997)

—, 'Ideology and experience: Spencer's *View* and martial law in Ireland', in Hiram Morgan (ed.), *Political ideology in Ireland, 1541–1641* (Dublin, 1999)

—, 'The poisoned chalice: the Ormond inheritance, sectarian division and the emergence of James Butler, 1614–1642', in Barnard and Fenlon (eds), *Dukes of Ormonde*

Edwards, Peter, *Dealing in death: the arms trade and the British civil wars, 1638–52* (Stroud, 2000)

Ellis, Steven G., 'The Tudors and the origins of the modern Irish state: a standing army', in Bartlett and Jeffrey (eds), *Military history*

Firth, C. H., *Cromwell's army* (London, 1902)

—, and Godfrey Davies, *The regimental history of Cromwell's army* (2 vols, Oxford, 1940)

Fissel, Mark Charles, *English warfare 1511–1642* (London, 2001)

Fletcher, Anthony, 'Concern for renewal in the root and branch debates of 1641', *Studies in Church History* 14 (1977)

—, *The outbreak of the English civil war* (London, 1981)

Ford, Alan, 'The origins of Irish dissent', in Kevin Herlihy (ed.), *The religion of Irish dissent 1650–1800* (Dublin, 1995)

Furgol, Edward M., 'The military and ministers as agents of Presbyterian imperialism in England and Ireland, 1640–1648', in John Dwyer et al. (eds), *New perspectives on the politics and culture of early modern Scotland* (Edinburgh, 1982)

Gardiner, S. R., 'Charles I and the earl of Glamorgan', *English Historical Review* 2 (1887)

—, *History of the great civil war* (4 vols, London, 1893)

G. E. C[okayne], *The complete peerage*, ed. V. Gibbs et al. (new edition, 14 vols, London, 1910–59)

Gentles, Ian, *The New Model Army in England, Ireland and Scotland, 1645–1653* (Oxford, 1992)

Gillespie, Raymond, *Colonial Ulster: the settlement of east Ulster, 1600–1641* (Cork, 1985)

—, 'Mayo and the rising of 1641', *Cathair na Mart: Journal of the Westport Historical Society* 5 (1985)

—, 'The end of an era: Ulster and the outbreak of the 1641 rising', in Brady and Gillespie (eds), *Natives and newcomers*

—, 'Destabilizing Ulster, 1641–2', in Mac Cuarta (ed.), *Ulster 1641*

—, 'An army sent from God: Scots at war in Ireland, 1642–9', in Norman Macdougall (ed.), *Scotland and war A.D. 79–1918* (Edinburgh, 1991)

—, 'The Irish economy at war, 1641–1652', in Ohlmeyer (ed.), *Ireland from independence to occupation*

—, 'The religion of the first duke of Ormond', in Barnard and Fenlon (eds), *Dukes of Ormonde*

Glow, Lotte, 'The Committee of Safety', *English Historical Review* 80 (1965)

Grant, Alexander, and Keith Stringer (eds), *Uniting the kingdom? The making of British history* (London, 1995)

Grell, Ole Peter, 'Godly charity or political aid? Irish Protestants and international Calvinism, 1641–1645', *Historical Journal* 39 (1996)

Guy, Alan J., 'The Irish military establishment, 1660–1760', in Bartlett and Jeffrey (eds), *Military history*

Hardiman, James, *The history of the town and county of the town of Galway* (Dublin, 1820, reprint, Galway, 1975)

Hexter, J. H., *The reign of King Pym* (Cambridge, Massachusetts, 1941)

Hill, George, *An historical account of the plantation in Ulster* (Belfast, 1877)

Holmes, Clive, 'Colonel King and Lincolnshire politics, 1642–1646', *Historical Journal* 16 (1973)

Hopper, Andrew James, ' "Fitted for Desperation": honour and treachery in Parliament's Yorkshire command, 1642–1643', *History* 86 (2001)

Hutton, Ronald, *The royalist war effort 1642–1646* (London, 1982)

Kaplan, Lawrence, *Politics and religion during the English revolution: the Scots and the Long Parliament 1643–1645* (New York, 1976)

Kelly, William, 'John Barry: an Irish Catholic royalist in the 1640s', in Ó Siochrú (ed.), *Kingdoms in crisis*

Kenny, Colum, *King's inns and the kingdom of Ireland: the Irish 'inn of court' 1541–1800* (Dublin, 1992)

Kishlansky, Mark A., *The rise of the New Model Army* (Cambridge, 1979)

Kyle, Chris R., and Jason Peacey (eds), *Parliament at work: parliamentary committees, political power and public access in early modern England* (Woodbridge, 2002)

Lake, Peter, 'Retrospective: Wentworth's political world in revisionist and post-revisionist perspective', in Merritt (ed.), *Thomas Wentworth*

Lawrence, Anne, *Parliamentary army chaplains, 1642–51* (London, 1990)

Lenihan, Pádraig, *Confederate Catholics at war, 1641–49* (Cork, 2001)

—, 'Confederate military strategy, 1643–7', in Ó Siochrú, *Kingdoms in crisis*

Lindley, Keith, 'The impact of the 1641 rebellion upon England and Wales, 1641–5', *Irish Historical Studies* 18 (1972–73)

—, 'Irish adventurers and godly militants in the 1640s', *Irish Historical Studies* 29 (1994–95)

—, *Popular politics and religion in civil war London* (Aldershot, 1997)

Little, Patrick, ' "Blood and friendship": the earl of Essex's efforts to protect the earl of Clanricard's interests, 1641–6', *English Historical Review* 112 (1997)

—, 'The marquess of Ormond and the English Parliament, 1645–1647', in Barnard and Fenlon (eds), *Dukes of Ormonde, 1610–1745*

—, 'The first unionists? Irish Protestant attitudes to union with England, 1653–9', *Irish Historical Studies* 32 (2000–1)

—, 'The English Parliament and the Irish constitution, 1641–9', in Ó Siochrú (ed.), *Kingdoms in crisis*

—, 'The Irish "Independents" and Viscount Lisle's lieutenancy of Ireland', *Historical Journal* 44 (2001)

Lowe, John, 'The campaign of the Irish royalist army in Cheshire, November 1643–January 1644', *Transactions of the Historic Society of Lancashire and Cheshire* 111 (1960)

—, 'The Glamorgan mission to Ireland, 1645–6', *Studia Hibernica* 4 (1964)

McCafferty, John, 'When reformations collide', in Allan I. Macinnes and Jane H. Ohlmeyer (eds), *The Stuart kingdoms in the seventeenth century: awkward neighbours* (Dublin, 2002)

McCavitt, John, *Sir Arthur Chichester, lord deputy of Ireland 1605–16* (Belfast, 1998)

MacCormack, J. R., 'The Irish adventurers and the English civil war', *Irish Historical Studies* 10 (1956–57)

—, *Revolutionary politics in the Long Parliament* (Cambridge, Massachusetts, 1973)

Mac Cuarta, Brian (ed.), *Ulster 1641: aspects of the rising* (Belfast, 1993)

McGrath, Br'd, 'County Meath from the depositions', *Ríocht na Midhe* 9 (1994–98)

McGurk, John, *The Elizabethan conquest of Ireland* (Manchester, 1997)

Macinnes, Allan I., 'Covenanting ideology in seventeenth century Scotland', in Ohlmeyer (ed.), *Political thought*

Macnamara, G. U., 'Bunratty, Co. Clare', *Journal of the North Munster Archaeological Society* 3 (1913–15)

M'Skimin, Samuel, *The history and antiquities of the county of the town of Carrickfergus* (new edition, Belfast, 1909)

Malcolm, Joyce Lee, 'All the king's men: the impact of the crown's Irish forces on the English civil war', *Irish Historical Studies* 21 (1978–79)

Manning, Roger B., *Village revolts: social protest and popular disturbances in England, 1509–1640* (Oxford, 1988)

Merritt, J. F. (ed.), *The political world of Thomas Wentworth, earl of Strafford, 1621–1641* (Cambridge, 1996)

Miller, David, *Queen's rebels: Ulster loyalism in historical perspective* (Dublin, 1978)

Milton, Anthony, 'Thomas Wentworth and the political thought of the personal rule', in Merritt (ed.), *Thomas Wentworth*

Moody, T. W., et al. (eds), *A new history of Ireland, iii, Early modern Ireland* (Oxford, 1976)

Morgan, E. S., *American slavery, American freedom: the ordeal of colonial Virginia* (New York, 1975)

Morrill, John, *The nature of the English revolution* (London, 1993)

—, 'Three kingdoms and one commonwealth? The enigma of mid-seventeenth century Britain and Ireland', in Grant and Stringer (eds), *Uniting the kingdom?*

—, *Revolt in the provinces: the people of England and the tragedies of war 1630–1648* (2nd edition, Harlow, 1999)

Morrissey, Thomas, 'The strange letters of Matthew O'Hartegan SJ', *Irish Theological Quarterly* 37 (1970)

Mullin, T. H., *Coleraine in by-gone centuries* (Belfast, 1976)

Murphy, John A., 'The expulsion of the Irish from Cork in 1644', *Journal of the Cork Historical and Archaeological Society* 69 (1964)

—, 'The sack of Cashel, 1647', *Journal of the Cork Historical and Archaeological Society* 70 (1965)

—, 'Inchiquin's change of religion', *Journal of the Cork Historical and Archaeological Society* 72 (1967)

—, 'The politics of the Munster Protestants, 1641–1649', *Journal of the Cork Historical and Archaeological Society* 76 (1971)

Newman, P. R., 'Catholic royalists of northern England, 1642–1645' *Northern History* 15 (1979)

—, *Royalist officers in England and Wales, 1642–1660* (London, 1981)

Notestein, Wallace, 'The establishment of the Committee of Both Kingdoms', *American Historical Review* 17 (1911–12)

O'Dowd, Mary, *Power, politics and land: early modern Sligo, 1568–1688* (Belfast, 1991)

Ó hAnnracháin, Tadhg, 'Rebels and confederates: the stance of the Irish clergy in the 1640s', in John R. Young (ed.), *Celtic dimensions of the British civil wars* (Edinburgh, 1997)

—, ' "Though Hereticks and Politicians should misrepresent their good zeale": political ideology and Catholicism in early modern Ireland', in Ohlmeyer (ed.), *Political thought*

—, *Catholic Reformation in Ireland: the mission of Rinuccini 1645–1649* (Oxford, 2002)

—, 'A typical anomaly? The success of the Irish Counter-Reformation', in Judith Devlin and Howard B. Clarke (eds), *European encounters: essays in memory of Albert Lovett* (Dublin, 2003)

Ohlmeyer, Jane H., *Civil war and Restoration in the three Stuart kingdoms; the career of Randal MacDonnell, marquis of Antrim, 1609–1683* (Cambridge, 1993)

—, 'Strafford, the "Londonderry business" and the "New British history" ', in Merritt (ed.), *Thomas Wentworth*

—, 'The civil wars in Ireland', in John Kenyon and Jane Ohlmeyer (eds), *The civil wars* (Oxford, 1998)

— (ed.), *Ireland from independence to occupation, 1641–1660* (Cambridge, 1995)

— (ed.), *Political thought in seventeenth-century Ireland: kingdom or colony* (Cambridge, 2000)

Orr, D. Alan, 'Sovereignty, supremacy and the origins of the English civil war', *History* 87 (2002)

—, *Treason and the state: law, politics and ideology in the English civil war* (Cambridge, 2002)

Ó Siochrú, Micheál, *Confederate Ireland 1642–1649: a constitutional and political analysis* (Dublin, 1999)

— (ed.), *Kingdoms in crisis: Ireland in the 1640s* (Dublin, 2001)

O'Sullivan, Harold, *John Bellew, a seventeenth-century man of many parts* (Dublin, 2000)

O'Sullivan, M. D., *Old Galway* (Cambridge, 1942)

Paul, Robert S., *The assembly of the Lord: politics and religion in the Westminster Assembly and the 'Grand Debate'* (Edinburgh, 1985)

Pawlisch, Hans S., *Sir John Davies and the conquest of Ireland* (Cambridge, 1985)

Peacey, Jason, 'Seasonable treatises: a godly project of the 1630s', *English Historical Review* 113 (1998)

—, 'The exploitation of captured royalist correspondence and Anglo–Scottish relations in the British civil wars, 1645–1646', *Scottish Historical Review* 79 (2000)

—, 'Politics, accounts and propaganda in the Long Parliament', in Kyle and Peacey (eds), *Parliament at work*

—, 'The outbreak of the civil wars in the three kingdoms', in Barry Coward (ed.), *A companion to Stuart Britain* (Oxford, 2003)

— (ed.), *The regicides and the execution of Charles I* (Houndmills, Basingstoke, 2001)

Pearl, Valerie, 'Oliver St John and the "middle group" in the Long Parliament, August 1643–May 1644', *English Historical Review* 81 (1966)

Perceval-Maxwell, Michael, 'Strafford, the Ulster-Scots and the Covenanters', *Irish Historical Studies* 18 (1972–73)

—, *The Scottish migration to Ulster in the reign of James I* (1973; Belfast, 1990)

—, 'The Ulster rising of 1641 and the depositions', *Irish Historical Studies* 21 (1978–79)

—, 'Ireland and Scotland 1638 to 1648', in John Morrill (ed.), *The Scottish national Covenant in its British context, 1638–1651* (Edinburgh, 1990)

—, 'Ireland and the monarchy in the early Stuart multiple kingdom', *Historical Journal* 34 (1991)

—, *The outbreak of the Irish rebellion of 1641* (Dublin, 1994)

—, 'Sir Robert Southwell and the duke of Ormond's reflections on the 1640s', in Ó Siochrú (ed.), *Kingdoms in crisis*

Perry, Nicholas, 'The infantry of the confederate Leinster army, 1642–1647', *Irish Sword* 15 (1982–83)

Phillips, W. A. (ed.), *History of the Church of Ireland* (3 vols, Oxford, 1933–34)

Pocock, J. G. A., 'The Atlantic archipelago and the war of the three kingdoms', in Bradshaw and Morrill (eds), *The British problem*

Reid, J. S., *History of the Presbyterian church in Ireland* (3 vols, Belfast, 1867)

Robinson, Philip S., *The plantation of Ulster* (Dublin, 1984)

Russell, Conrad, *The causes of the English civil war* (Oxford, 1990)

—, *The fall of the British monarchies, 1637–1642* (Oxford, 1991)

Scally, John, 'Constitutional revolution, party and faction in the Scottish parliaments of Charles I', *Parliamentary History* 15 (1996)

Scott, David, 'The "Northern Gentlemen", the parliamentary Independents, and Anglo–Scottish relations in the Long Parliament', *Historical Journal* 42 (1999)

—, 'The Barwis affair: political allegiance and the Scots during the British civil wars', *English Historical Review* 115 (2000)

—, 'Motives for king-killing', in Peacey (ed.), *Regicides*

—, *Politics and war in the three Stuart kingdoms, 1637–49* (Houndmills, Basingstoke, 2004)

Scott, Jonathan, *Algernon Sidney and the English republic, 1623–1677* (Cambridge, 1988)

Seymour, St John D., 'The church under persecution', in Phillips (ed.), *History of the Church of Ireland*, iii, *The modern church*

Shagan, Ethan Howard, 'Constructing discord: ideology, propaganda and English responses to the Irish rebellion of 1641', *Journal of British Studies* 36 (1997)

Sheehan, Anthony, 'Irish towns in a period of change, 1558–1625', in Brady and Gillespie (eds), *Natives and newcomers*

Simms, Hilary, 'Violence in County Armagh, 1641', in Mac Cuarta (ed.), *Ulster 1641*

Skinner, Quentin, 'The state', in Terence Ball, James Farr and Russell L. Hanson (eds), *Political innovation and conceptual change* (Cambridge, 1989)

Smith, Charles, *The ancient and present state of the county of Cork*, ed. Robert Day and W. A. Copinger (2 vols, Cork, 1893–94)

Smith, David L., *Constitutional royalism and the search for settlement, c.1640–1649* (Cambridge, 1994)

Stater, Victor, *Noble government: the Stuart lord lieutenancy and the transformation of English politics* (Athens, Georgia, 1993)

Stevenson, David, *The Scottish revolution, 1637–44: the triumph of the Covenanters* (Newton Abbot, 1973)

—, *Revolution and counter-revolution in Scotland 1644–1651* (London, 1977)

—, *Scottish Covenanters and Irish confederates: Scottish–Irish relations in the mid-seventeenth century* (Belfast, 1981)

—, 'The early Covenanters and the federal union of Britain', in Roger A. Mason (ed.), *Scotland and England 1286–1815* (Edinburgh, 1987)

—, 'Copies of the Solemn League and Covenant', *Records of the Scottish Church History Society* 25 (1995)

Stoyle, Mark, 'English "nationalism", Celtic particularism, and the English civil war', *Historical Journal* 43 (2000)

Temple, R. K. G., 'The Massey brigade in the west', *Somerset and Dorset Notes and Queries* 31 (1985)

Tolmie, Murray, *Triumph of the saints: the separate churches of London, 1616–1649* (Cambridge, 1977)

Treadwell, Victor, *Buckingham and Ireland 1616–1628: a study in Anglo–Irish politics* (Dublin, 1998)

Tuck, Richard, ' "The Ancient Law of Freedom": John Selden and the civil war', in John Morrill (ed.), *Reactions to the English civil war, 1642–1649* (London, 1982)

Underdown, David, 'Party management in the recruiter elections, 1645–48', *English Historical Review* 83 (1968)

—, *Pride's Purge: politics in the puritan revolution* (Oxford, 1971)

Vallance, Edward, 'Protestation, Vow, Covenant and Engagement: swearing allegiance in the English civil war', *Historical Research* 75 (2002)

Wanklyn, M. D. G., 'Royalist strategy in the south of England 1642–1644', *Southern History* 3 (1984)

Westerkamp, Marilyn J., *The triumph of the laity: Scots–Irish piety and the Great Awakening 1625–1760* (Oxford, 1988)

Wheeler, James Scott, *The making of a world power: war and the military revolution in seventeenth century England* (Stroud, 1999)

Wiggins, Kenneth, *Anatomy of a siege: King John's castle, Limerick, 1642* (Bray, 2000)

Woolrych, Austin, *Soldiers and statesmen: the general council of the army and its debates, 1647–1648* (Oxford, 1987)

—, *Britain in revolution, 1625–1660* (Oxford, 2002)

Wootton, David, 'From rebellion to revolution: the crisis of the winter of 1642/3 and the origins of civil war radicalism', *English Historical Review* 105 (1990)

Wormald, B. H. G., *Clarendon: politics, history and religion 1640–1660* (Cambridge, 1951)

Young, John R., *The Scottish Parliament, 1639–1661: a political and constitutional analysis* (Edinburgh, 1996)

Unpublished

Adamson, J. S. A., 'The peerage in politics, 1645–49', PhD dissertation, University of Cambridge, 1986

Armstrong, Robert, 'Protestant Ireland and the English Parliament, 1641–1647', PhD dissertation, University of Dublin, 1995

Bottigheimer, Karl S., 'The English interest in southern Ireland, 1641–1650', PhD dissertation, University of California, Berkeley, 1965

Hazlett, Hugh, 'A history of the military forces operating in Ireland, 1641–1649' (2 vols), PhD dissertation, Queen's University of Belfast, 1938

McGrath, Br'd, 'A biographical dictionary of the membership of the Irish House of Commons 1640–1641', PhD dissertation, University of Dublin, 1997

Mahony, M. P., 'The Presbyterian party in the Long Parliament, 2 July 1644–3 June 1647', DPhil dissertation, University of Oxford, 1973

Index